アジア立憲主義の展望

# アジア立憲主義の展望

アジア・オセアニア立憲主義シンポジウム

全国憲法研究会 編
編集代表　大須賀 明

信 山 社

# Perspectives of Constitutionalism in Asia

International Symposium on Constitutionalism in Asia and Oceania

edited by
Japan Association for Studies of Constitutional Law
Akira Osuka

©2003 by Authers & editor All rights reserved. Printed in Japan.
ISBN 4-7972-3133-5 C3332
Shinzansha International
6-2-9-102, Hongo, Bunkyo-ku, Tokyo 113-0033, Japan

# はじめに

大須賀　明

　1980年前後からNIESをはじめとするアジア諸国の経済発展は目覚ましいものがあり，アジアの活力と能力を示すものであって大変喜ばしいことであった。

　そして他方で，その延長線上に民主化という課題が浮上してきた。しかもそれは政治的事柄であって，経済分野の事柄である経済発展が一定の程度に達したときに必然的にそれに随伴して生じてくるものではない。民主化は，制度の民主化や国民の意識の民主化などもその対象であるが，何よりもその中核をなすのは政治的権力の民主化であり，権力を担う者の意識の民主的改革である。そしてこれは，権力者がそれまでの開発独裁で獲得した私的な利益と結びついている場合には，いっそうむずかしい課題となるのである。

　その時，そこに立憲主義が大きく関与している。というのも，立憲主義は，直接的に物質的豊かさを提供するものではないが，言論・出版の自由や自由選挙システムなどの民主的政治参加システムを確立することによって，人々が自らの苦境を公に主張し，政府に対してそれに効果的に対処する責任を課す。立憲主義を実現しないままに現在の開発体制を維持しつづけるならば，資源の枯渇や食糧不足，環境破壊が悪化の一途をたどり，また他方で従来から「開発独裁」として批判の対象とされてきたように，開発の名の下での人権蹂躙・人権侵害が，ますます人々を苦しめるであろう。

　したがって，各国の憲法研究者が一同に会し，そこでアジアにおける立憲主義の適用，ならびに創造的展開ないしは発展を理論的に検討することは，そこに参加した学者を媒介にして，アジア諸国における立憲主義の展開と発展の実現に向けて大きく貢献するという大きな意味があるといえよう。

　もっとも，アジア諸国における民主化の課題は，これまでの過去の植民地当時の遺制，あるいは民主化に対する国民の現代的な要求，あるいは国際社会からの影響などに関わる複雑な性質を有しており，従ってそれぞれの国ごとにその課題のあり方は異なっている。そういった各国ごとの事情については，本書の各論者に委ねるとして，私たちはそれらを参考にしながら，経済発展を可能とした開発体制と民主

化の課題との関係の中での立憲主義のあり方について，概括的に検討する作業など
を今後も続けていきたいと思う。

　本書は，日本の代表的な憲法学会である全国憲法研究会が，1999年にアジア・オ
セアニアの諸国の憲法学者を招いて，東京で開催した憲法シンポジウムの成果であ
る。日本の公法学界には，まず公法学会がある。憲法と行政法の専門家の学術団体
であって，会員数は約1200名である。さらに憲法学者によって構成されている全国
憲法研究会は，約500名の会員から成っている。平和主義と民主主義を維持しようと
する立場に立って，現行の日本国憲法を改正しようとする動きに反対する理論的な
活動を，積極的に行なっている。日本の憲法学者の大多数を会員とする重要な学会
であるが，私は1997年から2年間，この学会の代表をつとめた。本書は，その時期
における全国憲法研究会の理論的な活動と成果を基礎にして作られたものである。
従って本書は，全国憲法研究会の会員の献身的な活動に支えられたものであること
は言うまでもないが，本書の作成に当たっては，明治大学法学部助教授の清野幾久
子氏の大きな協力を得た。感謝の意を表しておきたい。

## 刊行によせて

樋 口 陽 一

　日本の学界で外国憲法の研究は大いにさかんであり，研究対象となっている国・地域との二国間交流も，だんだんに密度を高めてきている。その割りには，しかし，多国間の学問上の交流の場が十分に開かれてきたとはいえなかった。世界規模でいうならば，国際憲法学会 (Internation Association of Constitutional Law, Association Internationale de Droit Constitutionnel) が創設されるためには，1981年を待たなければならなかった。80年代以降「立憲主義」シンボルが「西」「東」「北」「南」の諸領域をまたぐ形で普遍化してくる傾向を背景にして，幸いなことに，同学会はすでに5回の世界大会を重ねて実績を積み上げてきている。アジアについても，同学会日本支部が「アジア憲法シンポジウム」を——小規模なものではあったが——，1989年横浜で開催し，相応の成果をあげることができた。そうした中で，1995年に東京で催された国際憲法学会第4回世界大会では，それまで参加者がヨーロッパに偏っていたきらいがあったのに対して，国外からの参加者総数208人のうちアジア・オセアニア地域から79人の出席を得ることができた。

　そのような流れをうけて，全国憲法研究会が1999年に東京で催した，アジア・オセアニアの研究者を一堂に集めたシンポジウムの記録が，出版されることとなった。この成果を手にして，私は，あらためてつぎのことを強調したいと思う。

　それは，要約していえば，①1999年という時点で，②全国憲法研究会が，③アジア・オセアニアの研究者を招いて，④立憲主義の現状と課題を論じ合う，ということの意義にほかならない。

　　① 20世紀をしめくくろうというこの時点は，その前半，すなわち1894-95年に始まる日本の軍事国家のあゆみと，その後半，すなわち1945年以降の国是となったはずの非軍事化の理念と現実をふりかえるにふさわしい時点であること。

　　② 20世紀後半のはじめに当って日本国民が「全力をあげてこの崇高な理想と目的を達成することを誓ふ」(憲法前文)としたはずのその日本国憲法を研究対象とし，同時にその基本理念を擁護する立場に立つ研究者の集団である全国憲法研究会の主催にかかるということ。

③ 20世紀の前半期に「軍事大国」としてアジアに深刻な損害を与え，後半期には「経済大国」をめざしてそこに進出したその広い地域から参集した研究者との，率直な対話の場を目ざしたということ。

　④ そして，最後に，そういう対話の場からの発信が，より広く，地球規模で当面している難問に立ちむかおうとする人びとへの，メッセージとなるべきはずだということ。この点については，少しくわしい説明が必要であろう。

　1989年の，ベルリンの壁の開放という出来事に象徴される大きな変動は，西欧起源という歴史的限定性を持つ立憲主義が普遍的なものでありうることへの信頼を，高めたかに見えた。しかし，そのような健康な信念を裏切る逆流もまた強く，いま世界を混迷にひきずりこもうとしている。「民主主義」や「人権」の名において市場の万能をまるごと正統化しようとする，市場原理主義とでもいうべき考え方が，アングロサクソン世界を中心に広まっている。一方では，社会主義という対抗理念を失った座標の混乱がもたらす自己過信があり，他方では，それと裏腹に，自己規律能力減退の意識がひきおこす他者への恐怖がある。こうした背景のもとで，立憲主義先進国の中には，その内側でも，また，とりわけ第三・第四世界に向き合う国際政治の場面でも，立憲主義の核心をなすべきはずの寛容という「徳」が磨滅してゆく傾向がある。この文章を書いている段階で，先進立憲主義諸国群のなかから，これまで数世紀にわたって構築されてきた国際的法秩序に対し，圧倒的な兵器の破壊力によって挑戦する行動が起こされた。西欧起源の立憲主義を継受したと同時に，さらにそれを超える可能性を提示する憲法9条を持つ日本，にもかかわらずその可能性を開拓することができていない日本。そういう日本と，アジア・オセアニアとの対話の芽を本書が含んでいるとしたら，これらの地域をこえたより広い議論の場にとって本書が何ほどかの貢献をしうるはずだと考えるのは，わたしの過大な期待ではないであろう。

## 目　次

はじめに …………………………………………大須賀　　明　v
刊行によせて ……………………………………樋　口　陽　一　vii

### 第Ⅰ部　アジア立憲主義の新たな模索

中国憲法と「一国ニ制度」原則 …………………甘　　超　英　3
　──「香港特別行政区」を中心として── 　　〔訳：土屋英雄〕

インドネシアにおける経済危機と ………………スリ・スマントリ　33
新たな立憲政府　　　　　　　　　　　　　　　〔訳：稲　正樹〕

第Ⅰ部　ま　と　め ……………………………吉　田　善　明　41

### 第Ⅱ部　アジアの人権保障

タイにおける人権及び立憲主義 …………………ウィサヌ・ワランヨウ　47
　　　　　　　　　　　　　　　　　　　　　　〔訳：今泉慎也〕

インドにおける公益訴訟による人権の保障 ……パーマナンド・シン　55
　　　　　　　　　　　　　　　　　　　　　　〔訳：孝忠延夫〕

台湾の民主化における司法創造的立憲主義 ……黄　　昭　元　79
　──大法官会議の役割と個人の権利の保障──　〔訳：安西文雄〕

第Ⅱ部　ま　と　め ……………………………石　村　　修　93

### 第Ⅲ部　日本国憲法とアジア

日本の憲法改正問題 ……………………………岩　間　昭　道　99
　──戦後日本における憲法改正論議と立憲主義──

日本国憲法9条と国際法 ………………………龔　　刃　韌　109
　　　　　　　　　　　　　　　　　　　　　　〔訳：中村睦男〕

日本国憲法と周辺事態法 ………………………鄭　　萬　喜　123
　──日本国憲法の平和主義に対する評価を中心に──〔訳：清野幾久子〕

日本国憲法の意義と全国憲法研究会 …………植野 妙実子 141

第Ⅲ部 ま と め ……………………………………大須賀　明 157

### 第Ⅳ部　アジア立憲主義の統括

アジア，オセアニアと立憲主義 ……………シェリル・ソンダーズ 161
　　　　　　　　　　　　　　　　　　　　　〔訳：阪口正二郎〕

アジアの立憲主義と日本……………………………杉原 泰雄 183

第Ⅳ部 ま と め ……………………………………樋口 陽一 191


あとがき・閉会の挨拶 ………………………………山下 健次 193

**資料：シンポジウム　プログラム**（195）

## Contents

Preface ················································Akira Osuka  199
Foreword ················································Youichi Higuchi  201

### Part I  Searching for Constitutionalism in Asia

Hong Kong Model under the Basic Law
　　——Practice of the "One Country, Two Systems" Principle in
　China ················································Gan Chaoying  207
The Economic Crisis in Indonesia and the New Constitutional
　　Goverment ················Sri Soemantri Martosoewignjo  251
The 1992 Constitution and the Institutional Reform in
　　Vietnam ················································Dao Tri Uc  259

### Part II  Protection of Human Rights in Asia

Why a Philippine Human Rights Commission? Its Place in a
　　Constitutional Order
　　——An Inquiry into the Power and Limits of Liberal
　Constitutionalism ················Raul C. Pangalangan  285
Human Rights and Constitutionalism in Thailand
　················································Vishnu Varunyou  301
Protection of Human Rights through Public Interest Litigation
　　in INDIA ················································Parmanand Singh  309
Judge-Made Constitutionalism in Democratizing Taiwan
　　——The Role of the Council of Grand Justices and Protection
　　of Individual Rights ················Hwang Jau-Yuan  333

## Part III  The Constitution of Japan and Asia

Problems of amending the Japanese Constitution
　——The controversy over constitutional amendment and
　constitutionalism in postwar Japan ·····················Akimichi Iwama　349
Japan's Constitution and International Law
　: Focus on The Peace Article —Outline— ···············Gong Renren　361
An Assessment on the Pacifism in the Japanese Constitutional
　Law····················································································Jeong Man Hee　367
The significance of the Constitution of Japan and
　Japan Association for Studies of Constitutional Law
　·································································································Mamiko Ueno　385

## Part IV  General Reports

Asia, Oceania and Constitutionalism ···············Cheryl Saunders　405
Asian Constitutionalism and Japan ···················Yasuo Sugihara　425

Afterword : Closing Adress ·····························Kenji Yamashita　433

## 執筆者・訳者紹介(掲載順)

| | | |
|---|---|---|
| 大須賀 明 (おおすか あきら) | (Osuka Akira) | 早稲田大学教授 |
| 樋口 陽一 (ひぐち よういち) | (Higuchi Youichi) | 上智大学教授 |
| 甘 超英 | (Gan Chaoying) | 北京大学法律学系準教授 |
| 土屋 英雄 (つちや ひでお) | (Tuchiya Hideo) | 神戸大学大学院教授 |
| スリ・スマントリ | (Sri Soemantri Martosoewignjo) | 1945年8月17日大学学長 |
| 稲 正樹 (いな まさき) | (Ina Masaki) | 亜細亜大学教授 |
| ダオ・チ・ウック | (Dao Tri Uc) | 国家と法研究所長 |
| 吉田 善明 (よしだ よしあき) | (Yoshida Yoshiaki) | 明治大学教授 |
| ラウル・C・パガランガン | (Raul C. Pangalangan) | フィリピン大学準教授 |
| ウィサヌ・ワランヨウ | (Vishnu Varunyou) | タマサート大学法学部準教授 |
| 今泉 慎也 (いまいずみ しんや) | (Imaizumi Shinya) | アジア経済研究所研究員 |
| パーマナンド・シン | (Parmanand Singh) | デリー大学法学部教授 |
| 孝忠 延夫 (こうちゅう のぶお) | (Kouchu Nobuo) | 関西大学教授 |
| 黄 昭元 | (Hwang Jau-Yuan) | 台湾大学法律学科副教授 |
| 安西 文雄 (やすにし ふみお) | (Yasunishi Fumio) | 立教大学助教授 |
| 石村 修 (いしむら おさむ) | (Ishimura Osamu) | 専修大学教授 |
| 岩間 昭道 (いわま あきみち) | (Iwama Akimichi) | 千葉大学教授 |
| 龔 刃靭 | (Gong Renren) | 北京大学法律学系準教授 |
| 中村 睦男 (なかむら むつお) | (Nakamura Mutuo) | 北海道大学教授 |
| 鄭 萬喜 | (Jeong Man Hee) | 東亜大学校法科大学教授 |
| 清野 幾久子 (せいの きくこ) | (Seino Kikuko) | 明治大学助教授 |
| 植野 妙実子 (うえの まみこ) | (Ueno Mamiko) | 中央大学教授 |
| シェリル・ソンダーズ | (Cheryl Saunders) | メルボルン大学比較憲法研究所長 |
| 阪口 正二郎 (さかぐち しょうじろう) | (Sakaguchi Shoujirou) | 一橋大学助教授 |
| 杉原 泰雄 (すぎはら やすお) | (Sugihara Yasuo) | 駿河台大学教授 |
| 山下 健次 (やました けんじ) | (Yamashita Kenji) | 立命館大学教授 |

所属・肩書は99年9月現在

## Authers

| | |
|---|---|
| **Akira Osuka** | Professor of Law, Waseda University |
| **Youichi Higuchi** | Professor of Law, Sophia University |
| **Gan Chaoying** | Associate Professor of Law, Peking Law School, Beijing, China |
| **Sri Soemantri Martosoewignjo** | President, The 17 Augustus 1945 University, Indonesia |
| **Dao Tri Uc** | Director, Institute of State and Law, Vietnam |
| **Raul C. Pangalangan** | Professor of Law, University of the Philippines, Philippine |
| **Vishnu Varunyou** | Associate Professor, Thammasat University, Faculty of Law, Thailand |
| **Parmanand Singh** | Professor of Law, University of Deli, India |
| **Hwang Jau-Yuan** | Associate Professor of Law, National Taiwan University, Taiwan |
| **Akimichi Iwama** | Professor of Law, Chiba University |
| **Gong Renren** | Professor of Law, Peking Law School, Beijing, China |
| **Jeong Man Hee** | Professor of Law, Dong-A University College of Law, Korea |
| **Mamiko Ueno** | Professor of Law, Chuo University |
| **Cheryl Saunders** | Professor and Director, Institute for Comparative and Inaternational Law, The University of Melbourne, Australia |
| **Yasuo Sugihara** | Professor of Law, Surugadai University |
| **Kenji Yamashita** | Professor of Law, Ritsumeikan University |

Profession as of 30th September 1999

第Ⅰ部
アジア立憲主義の新たな摸索

# 中国憲法と「一国二制度」原則
——「香港特別行政区」を中心として——

甘　　超　英

土　屋　英　雄　訳

## 一　「一国二制度」政策の登場

### 1　「一国二制度」政策のルーツと基本的意味

　「一国二制度（1つの国家，2つの制度）」の政策は，国家の統一問題を処理するための中国政府の基本原則である。この政策は，1976年の秋にいわゆる「四人組」を粉砕した後に出されてきた他の新しい政策と同じく，もともとは鄧小平によって提示されたものである。彼は1984年，「一国二制度」は「中華人民共和国内において，10億の人口の大陸は社会主義制度を実行し，香港・台湾は資本主義制度を実行する」ことであると述べた[1]。

　鄧小平によって出されたこの政策の意味は，香港・マカオまたは台湾のような区域に，もし必要ならば，特別行政区が中央政府によって設立されることになるということである。このような区域は，中央政府の下で，外交・防衛事項を除いて，行政・立法・司法の各面で高度の自治権を享受することが認められる。また，特別行政区では，既存の資本主義制度と生活様式は50年間，変えられずにおかれる。換言すれば，社会主義の制度と政策は少なくとも50年間はその区域に持ち込まれないということである[2]。

　「一国二制度」の政策ないし原則をより正確に理解するには，さらに次の解説を加えておく必要がある[3]。

　①　この原則は何よりも，国家統一と国家主権を堅持するという信念を意味する。複雑な歴史的原因によって，中国政府は，長らく，香港，マカオおよび台湾に対する管轄権を喪失してきた。だが，このことは，中国がこれらの土地に対する主権的権利を喪失していたことを意味しない。よって，それらの土地の中国への回帰は，中国が新たにそれらを獲得したと理解することはできず，中国がそれらに対して管轄権を行使する権利を回復したと理解すべきである。

② 国家は，特別行政区が高度の自治権を享有することを認める。国家主権に関わる権力および中央政府によって処理されるべき事項に対する権力を除いて，高度の自治権には，行政権，立法権，独立の司法権と終審権が含まれる。これらの自治権の自治の程度の高さと範囲の広さは中国大陸内の民族区域自治地区の政府が享有できる自治権をはるかに超えている。

③ 特別行政区でのそれまでの資本主義制度と生活様式は少なくとも50年間は変えられずに保持される。これらの不変の部分は主として社会制度，経済制度および生活様式を含む。このいわゆる「不変」は3つの点で説明を必要とする。第1に，中央政府は，主動的にそれまでの制度を改変する措置をとることはできないということである。他方では，これらの制度を香港人民自身によって変えることができないということを意味しない。いかなる制度も，自身の法則に従って，時の推移に合わせて発展，変化するものである。これは，人類の自然的発展過程であり，基本的には人の意思によっては動かせない。第2は，香港自身の変化の方向に関係する。つまり，香港が大陸と対立する方向で変化するのは許容され得ず，他方で，たとえ香港側からの強い願望ないし要求があっても，少なくとも50年間は社会主義の方向へ変化することはできないということである。後者については，香港基本法にそのことが明記されている。第3は，回帰以前の変化の可能性に関係する。つまり，1997年7月1日以前に何らかの変化が発生しても，それらは中英共同声明および中英間の他の協定に影響を与えることはできないということである。

④ 香港の法律制度は基本的には不変のままである。基本法第81条2項は，「それまで香港で実行されていた司法体制は，香港特別行政区終審裁判所の設立にともなう変化を除いては，保持される」と規定しているが，この変化は必要な例外である。香港に適用されるものとして基本法の付属文書Ⅲに掲出されている大陸の法律は，国家主権を維持するために必須のものである。香港法のなかの，それまでのイギリス統治に関連する文言は変更されなければならない。

⑤ 行政機関と立法機関は香港の地元の住民によって組織される。これが，いわゆる「香港人による香港統治」である。これは，中央政府の自己抑制でもある。地元の住民は香港の中国人とその他の国籍の香港住民を含む。このうち，中国人住民が法律上と事実上において，決定的で重要な地位を占める。

## 2 1950年代以後の統一問題に対する中国指導部の姿勢

 1949年,中国人民解放軍が旧体制を一掃したとき,軍は香港とマカオに入らなかった。1950年代でもそれ以前でも,人民を解放するために深圳河を越えるべきだという考えは確かに存在した。しかし,毛沢東や周恩来のような指導者は,新政府の樹立以前にすでに香港問題に対する政策の枠組をつくっていた。

 毛沢東は1949年1月にこう述べた[4]。

 「大陸の問題は比較的に処理しやすく,我々がそこでの問題を解決するために軍を派遣することは簡単である。だが,島嶼の問題を処理することはより難しい。暫定的な平和協定の手段をとるなど,別の柔軟な方法が必要である。長期的観点から処理すべきである。このような状況下で,香港・マカオ問題を焦って解決しようとするのはよくない。むしろ,大陸の輸出入を発展させたり海外との関係を進展させたりするために,それら(特に香港)の地位を活用することがより賢明であろう。全般的には,我々は条件の許す範囲内で決定をなすべきである」。

 この言説は,事実上,香港・マカオ問題に関する中国共産党の重要な決定であった。その年の12月19日,香港の華僑日報は第1面で,毛沢東は香港の平和を誓い,イギリスは中国の新政府を承認することを約束した,と報じた。その時から,中国政府は香港問題に対する粘り強い姿勢をとってきた。つまり,香港は中国の領土であり,中国は過去1世紀の間に帝国主義列強によって押しつけられてきた不平等条約をいっさい認めないが,中国はその問題を適切な時期に,交渉によって解決することを求め,現在の状況は協定が獲得されるまで維持されるべきだ,ということである。1960年,中国の外の一部の人が香港・マカオ問題に対する中国の姿勢に疑問を呈したときに,中国政府はこの政策を世界に公表した。

 この政策にはいくつかの側面があった。第1に,それは政治の必要によるものであった。1949年9月,毛沢東は,中国人民政治協商会議全国委員会の第1回会議で,中国政府は歴史的諸問題を平和的手段で解決すると言明した。この約束を守り,そのことを香港・マカオの人々に理解させるためには,平和的な政策が必要であった。第2に,中国は,アメリカを先頭とする中国封じ込めを打破するために平和的な国際環境を必要とした。香港はその中国封じ込めの隙間であったし,イギリス政府も香港への権益を維持することを望んでいた。そこで,周恩来首相は,中国とイギリスの関係を進展させ,イギリスとの平和と協力を保とうとする政策を提示した。この政策が最も重要な意義をもっていたのは経済問題に関してであった。中国が1950

年代と60年代にアメリカとソ連からの強大な圧力に堪えていたとき，香港は世界への中国の唯一で最大の通路であった。中国は，それが必要とした外貨，技術，情報，資本および人材のほとんどすべてを，香港を通して得ていた。香港の地位は当時，他の都市では取って代われないものであった。

　したがって，1970年代以前，中国指導層の間では意見の相違もあったけれども，その時期の支配的な考えは，諸問題を平和的方法で解決するということであった。中国大陸における資本主義的工商業の社会主義化を完成させた後，周恩来首相は大陸と香港の間の関係についての演説のなかで，こう約束した。中国と香港の根本的な相違に鑑みて，大陸での政策と異なった政策を香港に適用し，香港の資本主義モデルを社会主義制度に変えることは中国と香港の両方に利益がなく，そうすることはあり得ない。経済発展の観点から，中国は，将来どのような変化が起きようとも，香港の資本家や実業家との協力を続ける[5]。

　このように，対外開放政策が出される以前，中国指導層の間では平和的政策の選択が統一への最初のアプローチであった。しかし，その道筋には障害があった。伝統的なレーニン主義によれば，社会主義が資本主義を負かすか，または資本主義が社会主義を負かすかのどちらかであった。このディレンマは当時，理論においては解決できなかった。第一世代の指導層にとって，それは彼らの射程外の任務であった。彼らは，香港・マカオの本土への回帰の方法を設計しなかったし，たぶんできもしなかったであろう。彼らがしたのは，香港・マカオは交渉によって中国の主権下に戻されなければならないという原則を立てることであった。この状況下では，国家の統一への道筋上の困難を克服するには，待つこと以外に良い方法がなかったように思われる。

### 3　「一国二制度」原則の登場

　夜明けは，「四人組」の粉砕と新しい思想解放運動の開始とともにやってきた。この思想解放運動は，1978年12月に開催された中国共産党第一三期中央委員会第3回総会後，鄧小平によって唱導された。この第3回総会は，理論的教義がどうであれ真理は実践を通して検証されるという原則を確認した。このことは，多年にわたって人々の頭脳を支配してきた諸理論（これらは誤りの場合もあれば正しい場合もあり，空虚である場合もあれば実際的である場合もあった）を再考させるのに広大な空間を切り開いた。

「実践は真理を検証する唯一の手段」という原則は，人々が望ましい生活をつくあげる新しい道具であるだけでなく，中国指導部が対内的・対外的な政策を点検したり形成したりする際の要点でもある。「一国二制度」政策の最初の閃光は，1981年，葉剣英元帥の国慶節演説のなかで出された。そこで，彼は，台湾が高度の自治権を享受して，その軍隊を保持し，社会構造と生活様式を変えないことが認められる特別行政区となる，という平和的方法によって統一する可能性について語った[6]。この演説には「一国二制度」という明確な表現はなかったけれども，それは実際上，その政策の内容を含んでいた。これは国家の平和的統一の土台となった。

　1982年9月，鄧小平は，イギリスのサッチャー首相と会見しており，香港問題の解決を目的として，「一国二制度」原則を公式に初めて提示した。彼はサッチャー首相に，主権の問題は交渉の余地はなく，中国への香港の回帰は時間の問題にすぎないと語り，さらに彼は，中国の主権下でイギリスに引き続き香港を管理させるという提案を拒否した。しかし，彼は，香港がその制度を変更なく維持し，イギリスの利益も保持されることに同意した[7]。

　この政治的立場に基づいて，1982年12月に公布された中華人民共和国憲法の第31条に次の文言が置かれた。「国家は必要ある場合，特別行政区を設けることができる。特別行政区内で実行する制度は，具体的状況に照らして全国人民代表大会が法律で定める」。この規定は，香港に対して，それが大陸での地方政府に類似のものにならないという憲法的保障を与えた。

　1984年5月5日，国務院は，全国人民代表大会（以下，全人代と略称）での政府活動報告のなかで，「一国二制度」原則を正式に提出した。この政府活動報告を全人代が承認したことによって，「一国二制度」原則は法的に香港に対する国家の基本政策となっただけでなく，その原則は中央政府が統一問題全体に対処するための基石となった。

## 二　香港特別行政区基本法と中国法制度内でのその地位

### 1　香港基本法の誕生

　1984年12月19日，中国とイギリスは，香港問題に関する共同声明に調印した。この共同声明によれば，中国は1997年7月1日から香港に対する主権的権利を取り戻すことになる。1985年4月10日，全人代の特別決議によって，香港に関する基本法

を起草する委員会が設立され，そうして1990年4月4日，第七期全人代第3回会議は「中華人民共和国香港特別行政区基本法」（以下，基本法と略称）を採択した。

基本法は前文，9章，160条で構成され，および法的効力をもつ付属文書が付されている。その構成と内容からして，基本法は本質的に香港に関する基本的な法的文書である。このため，それは「小憲法」または「香港憲法」とも呼称されている。

にもかかわらず，基本法は，香港住民の主権的行為の結果としての真の香港憲法ではない。それは形式的意味での憲法の必要条件が欠けている。それは中国の中央政府によって香港に与えられたものであった。中国憲法と基本法の関係は母法と子法のそれである[8]。基本法はその誕生のときに中国憲法と衝突することはできず，中国憲法の指導に従わなければならない。実際，基本法の法的効力の根源は授権関係上，中央の権力にある。この関係は連邦国家内の憲法間の関係とは異なる。連邦国家では，州憲法は連邦憲法と衝突することができないにしても，連邦憲法に由来するものではない。さらに，基本法が香港での最高の法的文書であると考えることは誤っている。最高の法的文書という地位を占めるのは，名称と法的段階構造からして，中国の憲法である。もしそうでないならば，香港に対する中国の主権は疑わしくなる。換言すれば，香港の特殊性は制度の具体的な設計の分野にあるのであって，1つの国家の問題にあるのではない。憲法が包含することができないような地方政府が中央政府の下で存在することはできない。

基本法を土台として，新しい関係が生まれたが，これは統一体としての人民による（連邦国家での）州憲法の下での関係でなく，中央による法律の下での関係である。そして，この法律は香港だけでなく中央にも義務を与える。このような結果は，基本法が中国とイギリスとの間の妥協の産物であることから来ているが，その際，中国サイドは香港に住んでいる中国人の利益を徹底的に考慮した。この妥協は，地方権力と中央権力の平等な地位を意味しているのでなく，平和的な統一へと導く相互利益を意味していた。

## 2　香港基本法の法的根源

**A**　基本法は中国の主権下で制定された。これは，基本法がその合法性を中国憲法から獲得しなければならないことを意味している。

既述のように，憲法第31条は，国家は必要ある場合に特別行政区を設けると規定している。これは，香港のケースにおいては少なくとも四つのことを含意していた。

第1に，特別行政区を設けることができるということであり，これはその必要性に応じて特別なものであって，既存の民族自治区とも特別経済区とも異なる。特別な法律への特別な要求は，中国大陸の他の地方と異なり，場合によっては対立さえしている。第2に，中国大陸の制度と対立する特別な社会的，政治的制度が香港において認められることができるということである。両者の相異は，本質的な隔絶であるかのようにみえるが，ひっきょう香港は中国本土と比べて極小にすぎない。第3に，特別な制度は国家の法律によって固定されなければならないということであり，それは中央政府の許容範囲内のものである。第4に，このような法律を制定する権限は全人代に与えられるべきものであるということである。これは基本法の合法性の最終的必要条件である[9]。

　憲法第31条とは別に，第62条は全人代の職権を列挙し，全人代に「特別行政区を設置し，およびその制度を決定する」権限を認めている。この設置権限は本質上，最高の立法権力であり，これを中国憲法は「最高国家権力」（第57条）と呼称している。憲法下では，全国人民代表大会は立法権，設置権，任命権，決定権等を有する最高国家権力機関である。

　全人代の設置権との関係では，憲法第62条12号は全国人民代表大会に「省，自治区，直轄市の設置を承認する」権限を認めているが，同条13号は上述のように，「特別行政区を設置し，およびその制度を決定する」権限を認めている。このことからして，特別行政区の設置は，中国大陸での地方政府の設置とは異なるものであると考えることができる。それは，中国大陸の外の区域における異なった政治制度が憲法によって容認されるということを示唆している。

　憲法の条文は，「一国二制度」原則の基本的な要求を反映している。1982年11月，憲法改正草案の報告のなかで彭真（憲法改正委員会副主任，後に全人代常務委員会委員長）は，もし主権，統一および国家保全の原則を維持することができれば，台湾はその社会構造のほとんどあらゆる分野で変わらないままであることでき，これは「我々が同種の問題に対処する際の基本的な立場である」と述べた。「同種の問題」とはもちろん香港とマカオの例を指している。


　**B**　香港基本法は中国憲法下の最高位の法律である。
　憲法の下で，全人代およびその常務委員会のみが国家の立法権を行使する。全人代が制定するのは「基本的法律」と呼ばれ，刑事，民事，国家機構およびその他の

基本事項に関わるものを規定する。他方，常務委員会は，全人代が制定すべき事項を除くその他の事項に関して規定し，「法律」と呼ばれる。このことは，厳格には，基本的法律が常務委員会の法律より効力において高次のものであることを意味している。にもかかわらず，常務委員会は，全人代の閉会中，全人代の基本的法律を改正，補充する権限を有している。ただし，この改正，補充は全人代が制定する法律の基本原則に抵触してはならない（憲法第58条，第62条3号，第67条2号，3号）。

香港基本法は，その制定過程からして，通常，基本的法律の範疇に属すると考えられている。だが，基本法は，全人代制定の他の基本的法律より少し高次のものである。基本法のこの地位は基本法そのものから得ている。香港基本法第159条1項は，「本法の改正権は全国人民代表大会に属する」と規定している。これは，香港基本法の改正権が全人代に把握されていることを意味する。常務委員会は改正権を有しない。このことによって，基本法はその他の基本的法律より高次の地位を有し，前者の改正は後者のそれより一層注意深くなされなければならないことになる。香港の権利は，この処置で，より慎重に保障されることになるが，このことは重要な意義を有している。

C 中英共同声明は「一国二制度」原則が香港基本法のなかに規定されることを保証した。

中国憲法は特別行政区としての香港の地位を確認し，香港が原則的に中国大陸とは異なる社会的，政治的制度を維持することを確保したけれども，その詳細を憲法で規定することは不可能である。そこで，別の法的文書つまり1984年12月の中英共同声明が，詳細な内容に関して重要な役割を果たすことになる。共同声明は次のような内容を含んでいた。(1)中国政府は，1997年7月1日に香港に対する主権行使を回復し，イギリスの支配は終結する。(2)中国政府の基本政策は，香港に特別行政区を設置することである。(3)中央人民政府は，香港特別行政区に対して立法権，行政管理権および独立した司法権を含む高度の自治権を認める。(4)中央人民政府は現地住民による統治を保証する。(5)香港特別行政区は人権と慣習的権利を保障する。(6)中央人民政府は香港特別行政区の財政的独立を保持させる。(7)中央人民政府は香港特別行政区政府に社会治安を維持させる。(8)香港特別行政区はイギリスその他の諸国の経済的利益に配慮する[10]。

共同声明の内容はすべて基本法に規定された。これらの内容は中国政府の責務を

構成する。というのも、共同声明は国際法上での中国とイギリスの間の一種の条約であるが、基本法は香港の法的権利を確保するために中国政府の責務を規定しているのである。

**D　香港基本法第8条。**

基本法第8条はこう規定している。「香港のそれまでの法律すなわちコモン・ロー、衡平法、条例、付属立法および慣習法は、本法に抵触するもの又は香港特別行政区の立法機関によって改正されたものを除いて、そのまま保持される」。

これは、基本法のなかに、イギリス法、伝統的中国法および慣習を法源とする多くの規定があることを予定していた。これらの条項は主に、社会的、経済的および司法的な制度に関わるものである。全体としての司法制度、司法的な原則と手続きは、小さな必要的調整はあるにしても、もとのコモン・ローの伝統の諸原則に基づいて変えられないままである。香港をコモン・ローの伝統の支配下に置くことは、「それまでの制度」を変えずに保持することにとって重要な意義を有する。というのも、香港は長らく法治社会であったからである。しかしながら、回帰前は法的効力をもっていたが、回帰後に必然的に法的基礎を喪失したものもある。例えば、イギリスの香港統治権のための基本的法的文書である「開封勅許状」および植民地時期の組織法である「皇室訓令」は、回帰後の香港で有効な法的文書から排除された。

ここで明確にしておく必要のある問題がある。つまり、中国憲法は「小憲法」をもつ香港において実行されるべきかどうか、ということである。あるいは、中国憲法は香港において最高位の法であるかどうか、ということである。答えは、イエスである。第1に、基本法を通して設立された香港特別行政区は「一国二制度」原則の結果である。「一国」は特別行政区の存在の前提条件であり、もしこれが否定されるならば、いかなる特別行政区も存在しない。よって、もし「一国」という前提条件が承認されるならば、中国の憲法はその国のいかなる部分によっても遵守されなければならない。第2に、基本法は中国憲法に合致するように作られた。このことは、もし最高位の規範が香港に対して無効となるならば基本法はその存在根拠を失う、ということを意味する。いかなる下位規範もその法的効力を自身の規定のみによって獲得することはできない。第3に、憲法と基本法の間に不可分の関係がある。基本法の条項が正しく理解されるには、その中核的意味は憲法のなかから見いだされなければならない。例えば、基本法のなかの多くの条文にある「中央人民政府」

や基本法第5条の「社会主義の制度と政策」は何を意味するのであろうか。それらの本来的意味は中国憲法に沿って説明されるべきであろう。

にもかかわらず，中国憲法は香港において絶対的かつ全面的に実行され得るわけではない。香港での中国憲法の実行の基本線は，所与の問題が主権に関わるものであるかどうかである。

### 3 香港の権利

香港と中央政府の関係において，香港は当然，中央に服する。だが，中央権力の下で，香港は基本法によって与えられた自己の権利を有する。

香港の権利を考える前に，中央がいかなる権力を香港に対して行使できるのかをみてみよう。それらは以下の五点に出ている。(1)基本的な諸制度は，たとえその構造と原則が不変のままであろうとも，基本法を通して中央によって決定される。(2)香港は主権国家としての全面的権力を付与されているわけではない。例えば，外交・防衛事項に関わる権力は中央によって行使される。(3)基本法の最終的解釈権は全人代常務委員会に属し，基本法の改正権は全人代自体が有している。(4)中央は，香港が反共産主義勢力の活動基地とならないように要求する権利を有する。(5)中央は監督権を保持しておくことができる。その他，中央は香港の防衛に対する責務をもち，香港に軍隊を駐留させることができる。駐留軍の存在は国家主権のシンボルである[11]。

共同声明およびそれに関する中央政府の詳細な説明によれば，香港は以下のような権利を有する。

(1)社会主義の制度と政策は香港において実行されない。立法機関は普通選挙で選出され，行政機関は立法機関に責任を負う。政府各部門および裁判所は中国語とは別に英語を使用することができ，香港特別行政区の区旗・区章を国旗・国章と並んで掲げることができる。(2)立法機関は基本法の規定と法的手続きに基づいて法律を制定することができ，また記録のためそれを全人代常務委員会に報告する。(3)最終的判断を除いて，司法の独立のような司法制度と原則は，裁判官の任命・解任権とともに，保持される。(4)公務員の制度と規定は，高級職の地位を除いてもとのままである。(5)財政収入は中央に上納されない。予算と決算は記録のため中央に報告される。(6)自由貿易政策は継続される。(7)通貨および金融制度は保持される。香港ドルはその独立が維持される。(8)それまでの海運管理体制は保持される。外国の軍用

船舶が香港特別行政区に入る場合のみ，中央の特別許可を受けなければならない。(9)香港は国際および地域航空センターとして提供される。(10)教育制度は維持される。(11)「中国香港」の名称は，香港が世界の各国・地域と様々な関係を発展させるときに使用される。香港は自己に関係する外交事項について半独立の地位をもつ。(12)中央政府によって派遣された駐留軍は香港地区の問題に干渉しない。駐留軍費用は中央政府によって負担される。(13)「市民的，政治的権利に関する国際規約」と「経済的，社会的，文化的権利に関する国際規約」のなかで香港に適用される関連規定は，香港特別行政区の法律によって施行される。(14)香港政府はパスポートとビザのような問題を決定する権限を有する。

　もちろん，基本法の内容は上記以外のものも含んでいる。しかし，以上の14点は基本法によってだけでなく，国際的性格を有する法的文書たる共同声明によっても保障されている。これが，我々が以上を香港の「権利」と呼ぶ理由である。

## 三　香港基本法によって規定された政治構造

　基本法が提示するものは「香港モデル」と称することができる。それは「行政の優越」の原則と表現され得よう。香港の政治構造はすべて，この原則を実行するために構想されている。

### 1　行政長官

　基本法は，香港での最高位の政治的地位に，香港総督に代えて行政長官を当てた。「行政長官」(the Chief Executive) は香港の首長であり香港を代表する。香港総督と異なって，中央と世界に対して，香港における中央の最高位の代理人でなく香港人民の最高位の代理人である。こうした構想は香港人民によって統治されるという香港の信念を具現，象徴しており，それは特別行政区を樹立する原則的目標である。

　しかしながら，このような位置づけによって，中央にとって，行政長官が中央の期待しないことを行ったり，中国全体ないし中央から離れるようなことを行ったりする危険性が出てくることになる。だが，香港は高度の自治権を有するにもかかわらず，結局のところ中国の領土の一部であり，基本法には，中国の主権を維持するための３つの防壁が存在する。第１は，基本法の付属文書Ⅰである。これによれば，行政長官は少なくとも2007年以前は，普通選挙でなく選挙団によって選出されるこ

とになっている。選挙団は香港各界人士の代表で構成され，そのメンバーは，立法機関の構成員，各区域組織の代表，各種職能別代表(工商，金融，専業人士，労働，社会サービスおよび宗教などの各層を含む)等である。この選挙団の構成は中央政府の権利とコントロールが侵されないことを保証している。というのも，メンバーの多くは統一への信念をもっている中央政府支持者であるからである。彼らは自分たちの考えに近い者を行政長官の地位に就かせるであろう。第2の防壁は，基本法自体のなかにある。その第44条は，行政長官は香港に通常20年以上引き続き居住する香港特別行政区永住民で，いかなる外国の居住権も有しない者でなければならない，と規定している。この条文が基本法に書き込まれたということは，香港の5万の家族にイギリス居住権を与えるというC．パッテン卿（最後の香港総督）の方針に対する中国政府の反撃を反映していた。香港首長の「二重忠誠」の危険を避けようとするこの第44条の対抗策は，中国政府への行政長官の法的忠誠を保証するものである。第3に，基本法第45条は，地元で選挙または協議を通じて選出された行政長官は，中央人民政府の任命の後にはじめて就任できると定めている。

　行政長官は香港の首長であると同時に香港政府の首長でもある。基本法第48条はその職権を次のように規定している。
(1) 香港特別行政区政府を指導する。
(2) 本法ならびに本法に基づいて香港特別行政区に適用されるその他の法律の執行に責任を負う。
(3) 立法会議の採択した法案に署名し，法律を公布する。立法会議の可決した財政予算，決算案に署名し，それらを中央人民政府に報告して記録にとどめる。
(4) 政府の政策を決定し，行政命令を発布する。
(5) 次の主要公務員の任命のための指名を行い，中央人民政府に報告する。各司司長，副司長，各局局長，廉政専員，会計検査署署長，警務処処長，入管事務処処長，税関関長。上述の公務員の解任について中央人民政府に提案する。
(6) 法的手続きに基づいて各級裁判所の裁判官を任免する。
(7) 法的手続きに基づいて公務員を任免する。
(8) 中央人民政府が本法に規定された関連事項について出す指令を執行する。
(9) 香港特別行政区政府を代表して，中央当局が権限を授与した対外事務とその他の事務を処理する。

(10) 財政の収入または支出に関する動議を立法会議に提出することを承認する。
(11) 安全と公共の利益に照らして，政府要員またはその他の政府の公務に責任を負う要員が立法会議で証言するかどうか，または証拠を提供するかどうかを決定する。
(12) 刑事犯罪者を赦免し，あるいは彼らの刑罰を軽減する。
(13) 住民の請願，苦情を処理する。

これらの規定は，行政長官の職権がアメリカ大統領，イギリス首相，さらにはフランス大統領の権限を混合させたようなものであることを示している。行政長官は立法会議に再審議のため法案を差し戻すことができる。立法会議はこの拒否権を全構成員の3分の2以上の多数で覆すことができる。そうした場合，行政長官はその法案に署名し公布しなければならない。行政長官が立法会議の可決した法案への署名を再び拒否したり，または立法会議が政府の提出した財政予算法案あるいはその他の重要法案の可決を拒否し，協議を重ねても合意に至らない場合，行政長官は立法会議を解散してもよい。しかし，行政長官はその5年の任期中に1回しか立法会議を解散できず，また解散する前，行政会議の意見を求めなければならない。現職の行政長官の董建華は1997年以来この職権を行使していない[12]。前の香港総督と比較して，行政長官の権限は削減されている。行政長官は，総督のようには，自己の意思のみで立法機関を解散したり法案を拒否したりすることはできない。行政長官と立法会議の間の関係のこのような変化のために，一種のチェック・アンド・バランスの観念が香港で出てきている。

行政長官の政策決定過程でたいへん重要な役割を果たす機関は行政会議である。これは，ほとんど同じ機能を果たしていたイギリス時代の行政会議を引き継ぐものである。行政会議は諮問機関であり，その構成員は，行政機関の主要公務員，立法会議メンバーと社会人士のなかから行政長官自身によって任免される。その任期は，彼らを任命した行政長官の任期を超えてはならない。このことは，彼らが行政長官によって信任されたものであることを意味している。行政会議は通常，15人の構成員からなる。行政長官は，重要政策の決定，立法会議への法案提出，付属法規の制定，ならびに立法会議の解散などを行う前に，行政会議の意見を求めなければならない。以前の総督と行政会議の間の関係と異なって，もし行政長官が行政会議の多数意見を受け入れない場合には，その具体的理由を記録にとどめなければならない。このような仕組みは，行政長官に対するある種のコントロールを及ぼす力を行政会

議に与えている。

## 2 行政機関

　行政長官は香港の政府つまり行政機関を指導する。行政機関には3つの最高位の部門がある。政務司，財政司，律政司であり，それらの下に各局，処，署が設けられている。政務司司長は，行政長官が短期間職務を遂行できない場合の行政機関の事実上の長であり，行政第1副長官である。これはフランス首相に類似しているが，政務司司長の地位は立法会議に依存しない。

　香港政府は以下の職権を行使する。

(1) 政策を制定，執行する。
(2) 行政事務を管理する。
(3) 基本法の下で中央人民政府が授権した対外事務を処理する。
(4) 財政予算，決算を作成し提出する。
(5) 法案，議案，付属法規を立案し提出する。
(6) 立法会議に要員を派遣・出席させ，政府を代表して発言させる。

　香港の政治制度の1つの特徴は，イギリスの植民地時代と同様に，外国籍の者が政府のなかの一定の下級の職務に就くことが認められていることである。香港で生活している外国籍の公務員は多い。新政府には，外国籍の者の技術と経験を使用する合理的理由がある。ただし，各司司長・副司長，各局局長，廉政専員，会計検査署署長，警務処処長，入管事務処処長，税関関長は香港の永住民のなかの中国公民でなければならない。これらは，政府の構成方法に関して世界でもユニークなものである。

　香港政府の公務員は立法会議の質疑に答える義務をもつけれども，公務員の任免は立法機関に依存しない。彼らは，犯罪または法律違反を除いて，政治的理由で解職されない。基本法のこうした構想は，政府の安定を保ち，経済的効率性を維持するためのものである。

## 3 立法機関

　香港の立法機関つまり「立法会議」（「立法会：the Legislative Council」）は，職能団体，選挙団，直接選挙によって，それぞれから選出された60人のメンバーから構成される。基本法の付属文書Ⅱによると，各部分の比率は，1998年の30人―10人―20

人から2000年の30人―6人―24人へと変わる。そして，第三期には，選挙団からのメンバー分はすべて直接選挙へ吸収され，職能団体による選出30人，直接選挙による選出30人となる予定である。2007年以後，もし付属文書IIの規定を改正する必要があれば，この改正は立法会議の全メンバーの3分の2以上の多数の承認と行政長官の同意でもってなされなければならない。さらに，これは記録のため全人代常務委員会に報告される。これらは，香港総督下の恣意的管理から香港人民による民主的秩序へとスムーズに移行させる措置である。これはまた，統治権の転換に香港人民を適応させるためのものである。1998年の最初の立法会議議員選挙以来，直接選挙のプロセスを促進させようとする声がいっそう強まってきている。

　立法会議の職権と機能は以下を含む。
(1)　法律を制定，改正，廃止する。
(2)　政府の提案した財政予算を審査し承認する。
(3)　徴税と公共支出を承認する。
(4)　行政長官の施政報告を聴取し検討する。
(5)　政府の活動について質疑する。
(6)　公共の利益に関わるいかなる問題も検討する。
(7)　終審裁判所裁判官と高等裁判所首席裁判官の任免を承認する。
(8)　香港住民の訴願を受理し処理する。
(9)　行政長官を弾劾する。
(10)　上述のそれぞれの職権と機能を果たすときに必要な場合，証言または証拠提出のために関係者を喚問する。

　行政の優越の下で，香港の立法機関は行政機関と協調する役割をもつ機関として構想されている。議会制においては，立法機関と内閣の関係は相互依存関係であり，政府は議会での多数派に依存している。これが，議会が政府を支持する主たる理由である。しかしながら，香港ではこの種の依存関係はない。行政長官も行政機関も，それらの地位と権限を立法会議を通して獲得してはいない。例外的な場合においてのみ，行政長官は立法会議の弾劾手続きに付される。もちろん，政府要員は立法機関のメンバーの出す質疑に答えなければならない。行政の効率を維持するために，基本法は立法機関に中枢的地位を与えていない。このため，基本法は，議員は公共支出，政治体制または政府の運営に関係しない法案を提出できるが，政府の政策に関係する法案は，それが立法会議に提出される前に，行政長官の書面の同意を得な

ければならない，と規定している。こうした行政の優越の下では，立法府は政府にコントロールされた「おしゃべりの館」の様相を呈している。

　行政機関の最も重要な権限は弾劾という武器である。これには4つの段階がある。第1に，立法会議の全メンバーの4分の1すなわち15人以上によって共同提起された動議によって，行政長官が重大な法律違反または汚職行為の疑いで指弾されたとき，行政長官が自ら辞職しなければ，第2の手続きが始まる。立法機関は調査のための動議を可決し，終審裁判所首席裁判官を主席とする独立した調査委員会を設置することができる。この調査委員会は調査を遂行し，その結果を立法会議に報告する。もし調査委員会の報告が行政長官の容疑を支えるのに十分な証拠を示していれば，手続きの最終段階に移る。立法会議はその全メンバーの3分の2の多数で弾劾案を可決し，それを中央人民政府に報告することができる。終局的に，行政長官が解職されるか否かは中央人民政府によって決定される。

### 4　司法機関

　香港の司法機関は終審裁判所，高等裁判所（これには上訴裁判所と第一法廷がある），地区裁判所，裁判署法廷とその他の特別法廷から構成されている。

　中国本土への回帰以前，香港はコモン・ローの伝統下にあり，その法制度，司法制度は本土とは大きく異なっていた。1997年7月1日以後，主権の回帰に合わせるために，司法制度は主に3つの点で変えられた。

　第一の変化は，最終裁判の権限が，イギリス枢密院司法委員会から香港の「終審裁判所（最終控訴裁判所）」（「終審法院：the Court of Final Appeal」）へ移されたことである。公的権力機関のなかで，司法機関のみが独立の地位を全面的に保持することができるといわれている。だが，「最終」という用語には1つの誤解がある。基本法のコンテキストでの「最終控訴」は，終審裁判所による判決ないし判断に対する更なる上訴が認められず，終審裁判所の上にいかなる裁判所も存在しないということを意味している。しかし，終審裁判所の判決ないし判断の究極的な法的基礎は別のところにある。基本法の第158条が規定しているように，基本法の解釈権は全人代常務委員会に属し，香港の裁判所の解釈権は全人代常務委員会の授権によるものである。もし香港の裁判所が事件の裁決において，外交，国防のような中央の管理に属する事項に関わる基本法の条項または中央と香港の間の関係に関わる条項を解釈する必要がある場合，また，もしこの解釈がさらに上訴できない判決に影響を与え

る場合，終局的判決を下す前に，終審裁判所を通して，全人代常務委員会による関連条項の解釈を求めることになっている。香港の裁判所はその判決に際して，全人代常務委員会の解釈に従わなければならない。この意味で，香港の司法は全面的，絶対的に最終のものというわけでなく，また中央から全面的，絶対的に独立しているというわけでもない。

　第2の変化は，裁判官の構成の分野である。イギリス統治下では，多くの裁判官はイギリス人またはイギリスの前植民地出身の他国籍の者であった。現在は，基本法によって，終審裁判所の首席裁判官および高等裁判所の首席裁判官は，外国の居住権をもたない香港永住民たる中国公民でなければならない。その他の裁判官は，コモン・ローが適用される別の地区から招請された外国籍の者であっても，また外国の居住権をもつ中国公民であってもかまわない。また，終審裁判所は，常勤裁判官とは別に，臨時的にコモン・ロー諸国の裁判官を招聘して事件の審理に加えることができる。外国籍の者や外国居住権をもつ中国人を裁判官として香港の裁判所に加える理由は2つある。1つは，中国の裁判官は，コモン・ローについての訓練の短さや経験不足のゆえにコモン・ローの先例にあまり習熟していない，ということである。もう1つは，裁判官は本質的に「法律の公務員」であって「政治の公務員」ではない，ということである。司法が追求するのは法の下の平等であるので，資格に厳格な制約を課す必要性はない。外国籍の裁判官に対する唯一の制約は，どこでも資格ある裁判官に同様に要求されている法の支配の追求ということである。香港の裁判官は基本法に忠誠を誓約した後にその職に就く。

　第3の変化は，香港の法律の適用に関わるものである。1997年7月1日以前，香港の法律より高次の効力を有するイギリスの制定法と判例法は，香港の裁判所においても適用され得た。現在は，基本法および付属文書Ⅲ（「香港特別行政区において実施される全国性の法律」）に掲出の中国の法律が適用される。裁判所が従わなければならないのも，これらの法律である。その他，基本法第18条によれば，全人代常務委員会は，戦争状態の宣布を決定し，あるいは国家の統一ないし安全に危害を及ぼし，香港政府による統制がきかない動乱が香港に起きた場合に香港が緊急状態に入ったことを決定するが，その際，中央人民政府は付属文書Ⅲのリスト以外の中国の全国性の法律を適用する命令を発することができる。もちろん，これは，通常はあり得ない例外的必要性である。

　最後に，正式の法源とは別に，香港の裁判所は，他のコモン・ロー適用地区の司

法判例を参考にすることができるが、これは裁判所に対して拘束力がない。もし裁判所が外国の裁判所の判例でもって判決理由を作成しても、それは上級の裁判所によって覆され得る。だが、もし外国判例による判決理由作成を上級の裁判所が行えば、それはどのように矯正され得るのであろうか。これはいまだ回答がない問題である。コモン・ローの伝統の下では、あらゆるコモン・ロー上の判例は他の諸国のコモン・ロー裁判所によって引用されることができる。全国人民代表大会であっても、香港の裁判官が外国の判例に含まれる諸原則を香港判例法の諸原則に変えることを抑えることができない可能性がないことはない。

## 四　香港モデルの成功と問題

基本法は2年以上にわたって香港で実行されてきた。いくつかの問題が生じているけれども、全体的には成功であったように思われる。「一国二制度」、基本法および特別行政区はすべて、中国にとっても香港にとっても新しい政治現象である。ここで我々は、基本法の下での香港の地位の強化、民主的発展、香港の現在の問題、基本法自体の展望について考えてみよう。

### 1　金融危機のなかでの香港の地位の強化

中国への香港の回帰は、主権の移行の成功した事例である。それは1840年のアヘン戦争以来の中国の屈辱の歴史を部分的に終わらせた。香港住民を含む中国人民にとって、香港の回帰は中国の国家的統一の新しい始まりを象徴している。回帰の実現は力の行使でなく、いくつかの原則下での交渉によるものであった。その結果が香港基本法であり、これは香港と中国政府の両方を拘束するものである。植民地下の条件では、香港はこのような法的地位をもつことができなかった。

香港の成功はその住民の努力によるものであったと同時に、その周囲環境にもよっていた。回帰後、香港はその発展への支えをもつことになった。東アジアの金融危機の間、香港はその金融制度と中央政府の財政援助によって安定を保った。まさに香港政府の始まりのときに、金融危機が香港に押し寄せた。香港の財政司司長は中央の支援を求めて北京へ赴き、中央は香港の対策を承認した。実際、香港は、金融危機の影響がマイルドであった国の1つである。それはいくつかの点で、中央の強力な財政的支援によるものであった。政治的、経済的に香港の安定性を確保す

ることは中央の義務である。基本法のコンテキストは中央と香港のこのような関係を前提としている。

## 2　香港の民主的発展

1997年7月1日以前は，香港はイギリス支配下の中国の領土の一部であった。イギリスは植民地主義的方法で香港を管理した。よく知られた理由で，植民地主義的統治はいかなる形態の民主主義も必要としない。香港は自由な社会であったが，決して民主的な社会ではなかった。植民地主義的支配がさらに継続されるものであったならば，香港の民主主義はイギリスにとって無意味で不都合なものであった。100年以上にわたって，香港でいかなる種類の民主的選挙も行われなかったのは，こうした理由による。香港での彼らの支配が終わるであろうとイギリスが確認したときにはじめて，彼らは1985年，香港での選挙をためらいがちに導入した。これが香港の民主的発展の始まりである。1985年から1997年まで，香港で4回の総選挙が行われた。1991年の選挙において，直接選挙制度が初めて香港に導入され，立法会議の議席の3分の2がこの直接選挙枠に割り当てられた。

回帰後の最初の立法会議議員選挙は1998年5月24日に行われた。1995年の選挙での投票率は35.8％であったが，今回は53.29％であった。これは，選挙当日が土砂降りの雨という悪天候であったにもかかわらず獲得された。この事実は，香港住民は植民地政府によって導入された民主主義にはあまり関心を払わなかったが，自分自身の社会の民主的発展にはたいへん熱心であることを示していた[13]。香港特別行政区の設置の主要な目標は，「一国二制度」，「住民自身が統治する香港」，「高度の自治」に関する中央の基本政策を現実化・具体化することである。香港住民自身が香港を治めるということは当然，寡頭政治またはエリート政治を意味しない。香港住民が望んでいるのは多数による統治である。このことが，1995年選挙の投票率が選挙前の予想よりずっと高かった理由である。

## 3　香港における人権の保護

既述のように，香港特別行政区の設立以前，最後の香港総督のパッテン卿は，特別行政区にとって障害ないし問題となるいくつかの措置をとった。人権法案の採択，5万の香港家族に対するイギリス居住権の付与，政治改革案の提示等である。

人民の人権を擁護することは，基本法を起草する際の一貫した中国の見地である。

あらゆる角度から考慮した後に，基本法草案に香港住民の権利に関する多くの条項が含まれた。だが，この草案が全国人民代表大会で可決される直前，イギリスは1990年3月，「市民的および政治的権利に関する国際規約」(自由権規約)を香港の法律とする香港権利宣言案を提出した。そして，1991年6月5日，この宣言案を香港立法会議は「香港人権法案」として採択した。

中国政府はイギリスのこうした措置を，「人権法案」のゆえでなく，その行動の姿勢と方法のゆえに抗議した。その抗議の理由は，来たるべく香港香港特別行政区において「人権法案」の執行力を否定するのに十分なものである。第一に，「人権法案」は基本法の実施に影響する可能性がある。というのも，「人権法案」と基本法の両者において類似の条項があり，両者の間での解釈の相違の問題が出てくる余地があるからである。第2に，「人権法案」の採択は香港のスムーズな移行のための措置に関する中英の了解事項を侵害していた。この了解事項によれば，香港に関する措置を有効にするためには中英の交渉が必要とされていた。

「人権法案」の重要なポイントは，「人権法案」がそれに基本法より高次の法的地位をあたえるような条項を含んでいたことである。「人権法案条例」の第3条2項は，「この条例と一致した解釈をする余地のない既存の法律はすべて，その不一致の範囲内で廃棄される」と定めている。さらに，同条例の第4条は，この条例以後に制定されるすべての法律は，そうすることが認められる範囲内で，香港に適用される「市民的および政治的権利に関する国際規約」と一致するように解釈されるべきである，と規定している。これら2つの条項は，その効力が香港での他の法律より高い「超越条項」と呼ばれている[14]。このことによって，住民の権利に関する事件において香港の裁判所が基本法を迂回する可能性が出てくる。

「人権法案」のこの種の条項は必然的に中国政府によって否定された。中英政府共同声明の付属文書IIの第2条と基本法第8条はともに，香港でそれまで効力のある法律は，基本法に抵触するか，あるいは香港特別行政区の立法機関が改正したものを除いて，そのまま保持されると規定している。これらの規範に基づいて，全人代常務委員会は，1997年7月1日以前の香港の諸法律の法的効力に関する決議を採択した。その決議は，「人権法案」の3つの条項は[15]，香港回帰の日に無効となると宣言した。

実のところ，香港人権法案の問題は単にその法的効力の問題ではなかった。その背景には，香港をめぐる政治闘争が存在していた。人権の保護は長い間，香港社会

の基本的価値観であった。中央政府も基本法を通して，特別行政区政府は香港住民の所与の権利を保護することを厳粛に約束した。だが，最後の香港総督は，中国政府と闘争する，もしくは権力の移行に障害をつくる政治的道具ないし武器として，「人権法案」を利用することを望んだ。中国政府による反撃は驚きではない。両国の対立は実際に香港に対して悪影響を及ぼしたし，及ぼしている。中央政府は，重要なことでも些細なことでも香港で起きることに過敏となり，このことは香港の自治にとって好ましいことではない。

### 4　司法審査の問題

イギリス統治下の香港の裁判所は，イギリスの議会優位の原則に基づいて，立法機関の制定法を審査する権限をもたなかった。だが，香港が特別行政区のための「成文憲法」（基本法）を有しているいま，依然として香港の裁判所は，立法会議の制定法に無条件に従わなければならないのであろうか。あるいは，立法会議はイギリスでの司法部に対する議会の優越のような地位をもっているのであろうか。

基本法の下では，立法会議の法的地位は優越的でない。香港の裁判所は，基本法が特定の事例でどのような意味をもつかに注意を払う義務を有しており，このことから論理的に，裁判所は，立法会議の制定法の用語と意味を審査する権限をもつことになる。そして，立法会議の制定法と基本法の間に矛盾があることを裁判所が見い出した場合，基本法が優越させられる。よって，香港の立法会議はイギリスの議会のような地位を享受することはできない。

しかし，このことは，「成文憲法」が香港の司法審査を通して守られなければならないことを意味しない。基本法，香港の裁判所，制定法より優越した地位をもっているのは全国人民代表大会である。全人代の権力は中国の領域では最高のものである。全人代のこの地位が，それに対して，あらゆる法律，法的文書の合憲的実施を監督する権限を与えている。よって，基本法が侵害されないように守る最高の権力を有しているのは全人代であるといえる。

全人代の権力の至高性と香港裁判所の審査権の間に，すでに複雑な矛盾が出ている。1999年1月29日，香港終審裁判所は，呉嘉玲（Ng Ka Ling）・呉丹丹（Ng Tan Tan）対入管事務処処長の事件に判決を下した[16]。そこにおいて，終審裁判所は，上訴人は永住民として香港での居住権をもつとした上で，こう述べた。

「論議のある問題は，特別行政区の裁判所は全国人民代表大会またはその常務委

員会の立法行為（以下,「行為」と略称）が基本法に合致しているかどうかを審査する司法管轄権を有しているのかどうか，およびもし基本法との抵触を見い出したときに裁判所はそれらの行為を無効と宣布する司法管轄権を有しているのかどうか，ということである。我々の見解では，裁判所は確かにこの司法管轄権を有しており，かつ抵触を見い出したときには無効を宣布する責任を有している。これに関して，我々はこの機会に，些かの曖昧さも残さずに明言すべきと考える」。

　この見解に基づくと，こういうことになる。香港の「成文憲法」としての基本法は，裁判官が従わなければならない香港の最高規範である。基本法は全人代によって制定された基本的法律であるので，その法的効力は全人代の制定法を除く他の法律より高い。基本法を解釈するのは裁判所の義務であり職責である。もし裁判所が，香港の立法機関の制定法にしても全人代常務委員会の制定法にしても，それらを基本法に違反していると判断すれば，裁判所は基本法に従って，それらの法を明確に無効とすべきである。

　中国大陸の一部の学者達は，中央政府の側に立って，上の見解を出した終審裁判所をこう批判した。全国人民代表大会は，基本法第158条が規定するように，基本法を解釈する最高機関である。国家権力の最高機関として，全人代およびその常務委員会の行為は，誰もがまたどの機関も従わなければならない主権の最高命令である。終審裁判所の今回の判決は受け入れがたい。裁判所はその誤りを正す明確な行動をとるべきである。

　結局，終審裁判所は，1999年2月26日，次のような補充的判断を出した。

　「1999年1月29日の当裁判所の判決は，特別行政区の裁判所が従うべき基本法第158条の下での全人代常務委員会の解釈権を疑問視してはいなかった。当裁判所は全人代常務委員会のその権限を疑問視できないということを承認する。当裁判所の判決は，全人代およびその常務委員会が基本法の規定およびその手続きに沿っていかなる行為をもなす権限を疑問視していなかったし，また疑問視できないということを当裁判所は承認する」。

　終審裁判所はこの判断において，全人代およびその常務委員会の行為の圧倒的な力にチャレンジする権利を裁判所がもっているかどうかを述べていないけれども，中央政府は，香港の自治的な事柄に深入りする意図はないということを示すために，裁判所の判断に沈黙を保った。しかし，1月29日の判決は，中国本土の100万人以上が香港に移住する法的資格をもつという途方もない結果をもたらした。これは香港

にとって重い負担であり，受け入れ能力を越えていた。この状況下で，香港政府は，移住の数を抑制しようとして，香港への移住の条件および香港住民の定義に関する基本法第22条4項と第24条2項の解釈を全人代常務委員会に求めた。常務委員会はこれに応え，こうした事例では最初の解釈を6月26日に発した。この解釈は，香港永住民の意味と範囲を明確にし，香港への移住資格を制限している。さらに，当解釈は，終審裁判所の1月29日の判断を否定し，香港の裁判所の権限に優越する全人代およびその常務委員会の権限を再確認している[17]。

ところで，1999年3月の憲法改正案の採択の前，江沢民主席はこう述べた。「我々は，社会全体において憲法の権威を樹立し，憲法の実施を保障する強力な監督システムを建立しなければならない。最も重要なのは，法規範によって国家機関の権力を制約し，国家権力が厳格に憲法規定に従って行使されることを確保することである。……違憲は最も重大な違法である。憲法と法律に違反するあらゆる行為は必ず追及されなければならない」。全人代とその常務委員会は当然，憲法およびそれらが自ら制定した法律に従う義務をもつ国家機関である。よって，全人代とその常務委員会は，憲法および基本法を含む法律を遵守しなければならない。もし将来，基本法第159条の改正手続きに従わずに，基本法の本質的部分の改正がなされれば，その改正は基本法と憲法に違反するものと宣示される場合もあろう。また，終審裁判所は中国本土の分野での法律の実施を審査する権限をもたないけれども，その裁判所は，地元の終審の独立した司法機関として，香港の領域内での，憲法を除く法律の実施を審査する権限を有する。だが，この権限も，基本法第19条3項（香港裁判所は国防，外交等の国家行為に対する管轄権をもたないことを規定）によって制約が課せられている。

他方，全人代とその常務委員会の権力は，憲法の権威より上でないのはもちろんそれと同等でさえない。法の支配下の国家では，あらゆる権力は憲法に由来し，憲法によって統制される。したがって，全人代とその常務委員会は憲法の精神によって否定される越権行為を行うことができないし，またそれらが可決した法律の外に自らを置くこともできない。

## 5 香港基本法の展望

我々は基本法の解釈の問題を論じてきた。ここで，基本法の将来の展望を考えてみよう。それは基本法の改正の可能性と関連する。

基本法第159条は事実上，全人代常務委員会による基本法改正権を制限ないし禁止している。基本法は，民事法，刑事法，訴訟法のような全人代によって起草される他の基本的法律（これらの改正権は全人代常務委員会にもある）よりも，地位的にいくらか高い。よって，基本法は中国の法制度のなかで，少なくとも特殊な位置を占めているといえよう。このことを通して，香港住民の権利と自由はより確かに保障されることができる。

　香港に関する基本的な法律として，基本法の安定性は香港の繁栄にとって重要である。それは頻繁に改正されるべきでない。必要な場合にのみ，それは厳格な手続きと広範囲な同意を通して改正されることができる。しかし，基本法の現行条項のいくつかは将来の改正をすでに予定している。基本法第45条2項は，次の可能性を示している。つまり，行政長官の地位は，最終的目標として，「広い範囲を代表する指名委員会が民主的手続きに基づいて指名した後に普通選挙で選出される」のである。このことは，基本法の付属文書IIに基づいて，2007年以後，行政長官が直接選挙の方法によって選出される可能性を意味している。同様に，基本法第68条2項は，立法会議の議席の最終的目標は「普通選挙による全議員の選出」であると規定している。この可能性もまた2007年以後であろう。立法会議の全議席が直接選挙で占められるとき，強力な議会多数派政党ないし政党連合が立法機関に出現してくるにちがいない。このことは，行政の優越の原則にも影響を及ぼすであろう。もし立法機関が政府の政策に対して絶えず異なった見解を出すならば，行政権力はどうするであろうか，何をすることができるだろうか。これは香港社会全体にどのような影響を及ぼすであろうか。基本法は，これらの問いに答え，そうした政治状況下での要求に自らを合わせなければならなくなるであろう。

　これらの問いへのあり得る回答を少し考えてみよう。行政長官と立法会議の直接選挙は，香港で権力の2つのセンターを生み出すかもしれない。こうした状況でそれまでの行政の優越を維持するには，2つの方法がある。1つは，イギリスの議会政府のモデルに従って，立法府の多数派を行政の優越へと向けることである。これには香港の政治制度を徹底的に変えることが必要である。別の方法は，行政権力と立法権力を分離するアメリカの権力分立のモデルから学ぶことである。この場合，行政長官による立法会議の解散権がなくなる。あるいは，問題を解決するには行政の優越の原則そのものが徹底的に再考されなければならないのかもしれない。いずれにしても，政党の影響が大きくなるであろう。ともあれ，政治制度を有効に運営

するには，基本法の改正が必須となるであろう。

## 五　香港モデルの意義

　香港モデルとは，簡単にいえば，「一国二制度」の原則に基づいて，一国の中央政府が，憲法に沿って，その国の領域内に，社会的，経済的，法的および政治的制度がその国の他の部分と異なるのが許された特別行政区を設置する，ということである。香港は中国内での最初の特別行政区であり，世界でも最初の事例であろう。よって，特別行政区の設置は，中国にとっても世界にとっても，深遠な歴史的意義をもっている。

### 1　香港モデルはマカオと台湾の問題を解決するためのもの

　歴史的背景がそれぞれ異なっているけれども，香港モデルは一般的には，マカオと台湾にも適用できる。香港モデルを念頭において，中国とポルトガルの両政府は，1987年4月13日，マカオの中国支配下への平和的移行のための共同声明に調印した。1993年3月31日，「中華人民共和国マカオ特別行政区基本法」が第八期全人代第1回会議で採択された（マカオの中国回帰は1999年12月20日）。これは，中国内の領土問題を解決する「一国二制度」原則の2番目の成功例である。

　中国の統一で残る問題は台湾である。この問題は，中国政府の1950年代からの主たる関心対象であるが，最終的には解決されるであろう。実際のところ，「一国二制度」原則の考え方は，1980年代初期，台湾当局に統一について中国本土と交渉を開始するよう促すために出てきたものである[18]。台湾問題が難しいのは，時には台湾独立騒ぎがあるにしても，中国を合法的に代表する資格を両岸の中国人が主張していることによる。我々は，台湾の独立ないし分離の主張に反対する一方で，「一国二制度」原則の下での平和的統一という選択を台湾指導者に提示している。この選択以外には，武力解放の方法しかなくなる。この平和的プランによって，台湾は香港が中国政府から得た以上のものを獲得することもあり得る。というのも，台湾の状況は，結局のところ，香港・マカオと比べてきわめて特殊であるからである。例えば，中国本土と台湾の交渉は，より対等な方法でなされることになろう。また，台湾の軍隊は，鄧小平が述べたように，現状のまま維持されるであろう。

## 2 香港モデルを通してのマルクス主義の発展

　かつて，カール・マルクスは，最初のプロレタリア政権たるパリ・コミューンの失敗の経験から，プロレタリア独裁は新しい人民の権力を強固にするために古い国家機構を打ち壊さなければならない，と結論づけた。その後，レーニンは，プロレタリア階級は他の階級と国家権力を共有できないと述べた。毛沢東はプロレタリア政権の階級連合を大きく拡大したけれども，彼および同志達は国家の人民的性格を固守した。

　より広い，実際的な視野から中国の現在の状態と位置を認識できたのは，総設計師たる鄧小平である。彼は，中国が全体として社会主義的であれば，中国内で大陸と異なった生活様式をとる特別な部分を認めることができ，このことは中国がプロレタリア独裁の原則と性質を放棄して，資本主義の国家に変わることを意味しない，と教示した。いずれにして，中国の人民にとって望ましい生活（この基準は人民自身によって証される）をさせることが共産党による統治の究極の目標である。よって，もし台湾の人民がそれまでの方式で生活することを望むならば，「純粋な理論」の正しさを示すために，そうした生活をかき乱すことがどうして必要であろうか。理論の正しさは，人民に危険を及ぼすことによってでなく，彼らの共同の幸福に有益であることによって立証されなければならない。中国政府と共産党が維持しなければならないことは，国家の全体としての社会主義的性質と中華民族の統一である。この2つの原則以外は基本的なものではない。このような理念的前提から，「一国二制度」の政治原則が形成された。

　「一国二制度」原則は，実践的，理論的にマルクス主義の国家理論の発展である。マルクス主義そのものが19世紀の労働者に必要とされて出現し発展してきたのと同じように，「一国二制度」原則の国家原理は現実の必要に応じて設定されたものである。中国的特質をもつこの種のマルクス主義は，中国政府が他の諸国と平和的な関係を取り結ぶ中核的基準の1つである。

## 3 香港モデルの影響による中国の憲法理論の発展

　国家原理の理論的解決によって，中国の憲法理論が発展する広大な空間が切り開かれた。基本法の実施と香港特別行政区の設置は憲法理論の研究に大きな刺激を与えた。

　香港が社会主義国家内の資本主義社会であるという現実は，中国の国家構造を複

雑にした。中国を単一国家とみなすには注意が必要である。というのも，1つの伝統的な国家のなかに，2つの法制度，2つの政治制度，2つの通貨制度，1つの国籍下での2つの居住資格制度等が存在しているのである。もしマカオ，さらには台湾を視野に入れるならば，中国は連邦のような多様な外観を呈することになる。だが，中国を連邦国家とみなすのは誤っている。中国は1つの憲法のみを有し，香港を含む区域のあらゆる権力はそこから由来する。ここでの問題は，中国が単一国家であることを理論的にいかに説明するかである。

　この問題に対しては，我々は，何が国家構造の形態の性質を決定する重要な要素であるかを見い出すことによって，答えるべきである。香港基本法第12条は，香港特別行政区は中国の高度の自治権を享有する地方行政区域であり，中央人民政府の直轄とする，と規定している。この規定から，我々は2つの要素を想定できる。1つは，下級の政府の権限ないし権力の性質と根源であり，もう1つは，中央政府と地方政府の関係である。これらによって，連邦に属するかそれとも単一体に属するかという国家構造の形態が決定される。香港政府の権限は基本法を通しての中央政府の授与に由来するものであり，換言すれば，香港は自分固有の権限をもたないのである。このことは，香港人民の権力は中央権力の存在以前に享有され得るものではないということを意味する。その上，香港人民は自分達独自に憲法と政府を創造することはできない。対照的に，連邦国家では，その構成部分の権限と権力は内在的で固有のものであり，連邦政府は権限を構成部分に授与することも，それから剥奪することもできない。連邦の内部において，その構成部分の人民は，自分自身の政府を形成するために自ら憲法を制定する自然権を有している。中央政府と下級政府の関係の問題については，香港政府は中央政府の従属的単位であることが分かる。香港は中国から独立した部分ではなかったし，現在もそうでない。既述のように，行政長官はその就任前に中央政府によって任命されなければならない。立法会議で採択された法律は記録のため全人代常務委員会へ報告されなければならない。終審裁判所と高等裁判所の首席裁判官の任命も同様に記録のために報告されなければならない。しかし，連邦国家では，その構成部分は中央政府へのこうした責務をもたない。これらはすべて，中国が単一国家，すなわち「1つの国家」であることを示している。

　他方で，香港人民は基本法の下で，連邦国家の構成部分の人民より多くの権利を享受している。例えば，紛争の最終的司法管轄権は香港に属するが，連邦国家では

連邦の最高裁判所へ上訴することができる。これは，中国が「2つの制度」を推進していることを表している。

　我々はいま，1つの国家のなかに全く異なった2つの制度をもっている。中国の現代史において，この状態は，かつて，中央政府と共産主義支配部分との間で存在していた。だが，2つの政府が革命時代に並んで存続したということは政治的現実であり，その具体相は，人民の支持と力のバランスの変化とともに頻繁に変わった。ところが，今日の中国での2つの制度は，全体としての人民の共同の意思に基づく法的ないし憲法的結果である。

　基本法は中国の学者の視野を拡大した。彼らはいま，憲法解釈，立法権力，法の性質と根源，法の機能，司法制度等のような，より細部のテーマを研究している。既述のように，基本法の条項に関する全人代常務委員会の解釈は，1949年以後の中国の法制史上，正式の立法府解釈の最初の事例であった。これは，全人代常務委員会の解釈権を行使するための立法府の手続きの完全化へと導いて行くにちがいない。特別行政区の法律の研究は，中国法学の新しい分野を形成しつつある。

## 4　香港モデルの国際法への影響

　本論文の最初で，我々は，「一国二制度」原則は，国際的紛争とりわけ歴史的に残されてきた問題を平和的交渉の方法で解決するためのルールとして使用され得ることを指摘した。この原則は，活力に満ち融通性をもつ基準である。関係諸国は，その基準を具体的必要に応じて，多くの状況に適用することができよう。

　例えば，日本の小渕恵三首相は，1998年，北方4島の主権問題をロシアと交渉する際に参照できるモデルとして，香港の例を引用した。同様に，韓国大統領も2つの朝鮮の問題を解決するために，香港モデルに言及した。

　だが，我々は，中英関係と日ロ関係その他との間の類似点と相違点についても知っておくべきである。外国権力による領土の占領という事実は類似点であり，これは領土と主権の返還の要求へと導く。別の類似点は，その問題を解決する方法は平和的交渉を通してであろうということである。その場合，原則が必要となる。その原則に関して両国の同意が得られたとき，問題は半ば解決したようなものである。政治問題の解決後に法律問題の交渉という段階が来る。「一国二制度」原則は，国家がその主権を維持して関連の領土問題を解決する際の最良の選択肢である。

(1) 鄧小平「一個国家，両種制度」『鄧小平文選』第3巻（人民出版社，1993年）58頁。
(2) 1990年3月の第七期全国人民代表大会第3回会議上の姫鵬飛（香港特別行政区基本法起草委員会主任委員，全人代副委員長）「関於『中華人民共和国香港特別行政区基本法（草案）』及其有関文件的説明」『基本法的誕生』（香港文匯出版社，1990年）187―199頁参照。
(3) 蕭蔚雲『香港基本法講座』（中国広播電視出版社，1996年）2―5頁参照。
(4) 李月蘭「党的三代領導人関心香港回帰」『中国共産党文献』第3巻（1997年）。
(5) 国務院港澳弁公室香港社会文化司編著『香港問題読本』（中共中央党校出版社，1997年）25頁。
(6) 『人民日報』1981年10月1日。
(7) 鄧小平「我們対香港問題的基本立場」前掲『鄧小平文選』第3巻，12―15頁。
(8) 蕭蔚雲，前掲『香港基本法講座』73―74頁。
(9) 蕭蔚雲主編『一国両制與香港基本法法律制度』（北京大学出版社，1990年）86頁。
(10) 『中華人民共和国和大不列顛及北愛爾聯合王国政府関於香港問題的聯合声明』（北京外文出版社，1984年）3―5頁。
(11) 蕭蔚雲，前掲『香港基本法講座』86―88頁
(12) この理由については，蔡子強『香港選挙制度透視』（香港明報出版社，1998年）4―6頁参照。
(13) 韋舜基「豈因小小記念咭」香港『大公報』1998年5月25日。
(14) これについては，宋小庄『香港基本法與後過渡争拗』（香港文化教育出版社）1988年，117―118頁参照。
(15) 「人権法案」の解釈と適用に関する第2条3項，それ以前の制定法に対する「人権法案」の効果に関する第3条，将来の制定法の解釈に関する第4条。「全国人民代表大会常務委員会関於根拠『中華人民共和国香港特別行政区基本法』第一百六十条処理香港原有法律的決定」『人民日報』1997年2月24日。
(16) FACV14/1998, Hong Kong. これは，香港人が中国本土で生んだ子女の香港居住権に関する事件である。
(17) 『人民日報』1999年6月27日。
(18) いわゆる「葉剣英の9個条」である（『人民日報』1980年12月31日参照）。

〔訳者付記〕
英語原文は相当に長文であるが，紙数の制約上，シンポジウムの主催責任者とも協議の上，いくらか簡潔に訳出（特に注の部分）ないし意訳している。また，本報告は主に香港での立憲主義に関わるものであるが，中国大陸の立憲主義については，全国憲法研究会の学会誌『憲法問題』第11号（2000年5月）掲載の土屋英雄「中国の立憲主義」を参照されたい。

# インドネシアにおける経済危機と新たな立憲政府

スリ・スマントリ

稲　正樹訳

### はじめに

　インドネシア憲法は，インドネシア独立準備委員会という名称をもつ委員会によって起草され，公布された。この委員会によって1945年8月18日に公布された1945年憲法は，次の2つの期間，すなわち第1期は1945年8月18日から1949年12月27日まで，第2期は1959年7月5日から今日に至るまで効力をもった。
　1949年12月27日から1959年7月4日までは，インドネシア連邦共和国暫定憲法（Constitution of the United Republic of Indonesia: R.I.S.）と1950年インドネシア共和国暫定憲法（Provisional Constitution of 1950: UDD-Sementara）が，相次いで効力をもっていた。
　1950年の暫定憲法が制定された時期には，1955年に行われた総選挙を通じて憲法制定会議（Konstituante）という名前の会議体が組織された。憲法制定会議には，1950年の暫定憲法に代えて新憲法を起草する仕事が委託された。憲法制定会議は立法機関として1956～1959年の間開会して，憲法の実質的な内容を規定する数多くの条文を起草することに成功したが，国家の基本思想または基本原則を定式化することには失敗した。したがって，政府は，1950年暫定憲法に代えて，1945年憲法を恒久憲法として宣言することを憲法制定会議に提案した。
　憲法制定会議のすべての党派（集団）は，政府の要求に従って，1945年憲法を恒久憲法として宣言することに同意したが，イスラムの党派は，「唯一の神」の言葉の後に，「イスラムのシャリーアを信者のために実施する義務」を加えることを主張した。
　このいくつかの単語を付加することについての提案は，投票によって決定されるべきものだった。しかしながら，出席していた憲法制定会議の少なくとも3分の2の議員の多数の支持をえることができず，この提案は失敗に終った。以上のような

次第で，憲法制定会議はふたたび，インドネシア共和国のために恒久憲法を宣言することに失敗したのである。

## 経済危機と大統領の没落

1998年3月に予定されていた国民協議会（Majeris Permusyawaratan Rakyat: MPR）の総会（Sidang Umum: SU）より少し前の1997年の半ばに，インドネシアは経済・財政危機を経験した。それは実際，今日まで続いている。この危機は当初，いくつかの他の東南アジア諸国にも打撃を与えた。対アメリカ・ドルに対するルピアの交換価値は，15ルピアにまで急激に下落した（US＄1＝Rp. 15）。ルピアの平価切下げの衝撃は，特に9つの主要食料品の価格上昇に示されたように，壊滅的なものであった。それはまた，ドル・レートの増大によって輸入原材料の価格が急上昇したために，製造業や貿易にも影響を与えた。

そのため，製造業は原材料を輸入することができなくなり，その結果多くの事業所は閉鎖されて，労働者の一時解雇も不可避となった。これらの出来事は，インドネシアの人民に苦痛を与えるものとなった。しかしながら，権力の座にいる者が堅い統制を維持したために，インドネシアの人民は無力だった。政府に反対する十分な勇気を示した唯一のグループは，インドネシア全土の大学生たちだった。国民協議会の総会は，治安部隊によって厳重に防御された。最終的に総会は，（いつもどおりに）全員一致で，スハルト（Soeharto）（退役）将軍を連続7期目の任期5年の大統領に選出した。しかしながらスハルトを大統領に選出したことによって，政治情勢は緊張を高めることになった。経済的・財政的雰囲気も同様な傾向を示した。それに加えて，学生活動家たちの誘拐事件も起こった。

ジャカルタ学生会議コミュニケーション・フォーラム（Forum Komunikasi Senat Mahasiswa Jakarta）に結集する75人の学生が，1998年5月18日に国会と国民協議会の建物を占領したときに，政治的雰囲気は耐え難い状態になった。

翌5月19日と20日には，建物を占領した学生の数は莫大なものになった。数多くの野党もまた，学生に加わった。最終的に著名な政治家に支援された学生たちは，スハルトの解任を各政党と国会議長に要求した。当初の5月20日には，国家記念碑の周りに100万人の人々を集める努力がなされた。しかしながら，治安部隊の厳重な防御のために，この計画を実現することはできなかった。

このような驚くべき状況のなかで，スハルト大統領は，改革委員会の設置と改革内閣の組閣を準備することによって解決策の提案を試みた。この提案は，スハルトが前の副大統領のスダルモノ (Sudharmono) と5月20日の夜遅く議論したときになされた。

会合の直後に，スダルモノは急いで部屋を出て，副大統領のハビビ (B.J. Habibie) と会い，1つのファイルを抱えて出てきた。そのファイルには，数多くの大臣が辞表を提出したという声明が入っていた。以上に紹介した事実が，なにゆえスハルト大統領が辞職し，1945年憲法第8条に基づいて，大統領に代わって副大統領のハビビが大統領の後継者になったのかという事情を，実際に説明するものである。

## ハビビ大統領のリーダーシップと改革の時代

スハルト大統領の辞任に関しては諸説があるが，現在まで依然として，ハビビが「インドネシア共和国」の第3代大統領である。1945年憲法第8条は以下のように規定している。

「大統領が任期中に死去，辞任し又は職責を遂行することができなくなった場合には，大統領は，任期の満了まで副大統領によって後継されなければならない」

就任の宣誓をしてハビビ副大統領が第3代大統領になった後の初仕事は，国務大臣の任命であった。これは1945年憲法第17条に規定されていた。すなわち，

(1) 大統領は国務大臣によって補佐される。
(2) 国務大臣は大統領によって任免される。
(3) 国務大臣は政府の各省庁の長となる。

新たに任命された国務大臣には，統一開発党 (Partai Persatuan Pembangunan: PPP) とインドネシア民主党 (PDI) の出身者も任命された。そのほかには，前の閣僚も何人か含まれていた。

ハビビ政府を新たな立憲政府として宣言できるかどうかについては，問題が残っている。

新内閣の組閣後，「インドネシア共和国」第3代大統領は，政治・経済・法律の領域で，自らの政策を開始した。

政治の領域では，大統領と国民協議会議長は，国民協議会の特別会合を開くことに同意した。この会合は，1998年11月10日から3日間開かれた。この会合から結果

として生じた諸決定は，国民協議会令として宣言された。すなわち，以下の事項に関する国民協議会令である。
 1．国会議長と国民協議会議長の分離
 2．国民投票に関する国民協議会令の失効
 3．改革と開発の原則
 4．腐敗した身内びいきの政府機構から自由で，清潔な〔人々の〕任命
 5．大統領すなわち統治権保持者に与えられている，特別課題と特別権限の配分に関する国民協議会令の撤回
 6．大統領・副大統領の任期の制限
 7．人民票決（総選挙）に関する国民協議会令の条項の改正と付加
 8．統一国家の範囲内における，中央政府と諸地域間の均衡のとれた財政と地方自治の規定
 9．経済民主主義を増大させる枠組における経済政策
10．人権

　上記の国民協議会の諸決定は，新しい立憲政府を創造しようという試みのなかでだされたものであった。とりわけ非常に重要なものと考えられた決定は，1945年憲法第7条が規定する大統領・副大統領の再選制限に関するものであった。その規定は，以下の通りである。

　　「大統領及び副大統領は5年の任期の間職に就き，その後再選のため選出されることができる」

　この条文は，大統領と副大統領を何回再選できるのかを，明白に述べていない。
　実際に，1968年3月に暫定国民協議会によって最初に大統領に選出されたスハルト将軍は，ひき続き7期，大統領となった。このようなことが起きることを防ぐために，国民協議会は，特別会合の間の1998年11月13日に，以下のことを宣言した。

　　「大統領と副大統領は5年の任期の間職に就き，その後1度だけ同一の期間をもって選出されることができる」

　大統領と副大統領の任期の再選制限に加えて，特別会合はまた総選挙のことにも言及した。以前の総選挙は3党のみが参加するものであったが，国民協議会の新たな決定によると，総選挙は多数の政党が参加するものでなければならず，また総選挙は，直接的，一般的で自由かつ秘密の投票によって，民主的で公平かつ公正に実施されなければならないことになった。

他方で，自治地域の設立および中央政府・各州（諸地域）間の均衡のとれた財政に関する国民協議会の決定に従って，中央政府と地方政府に関する規則と，中央政府と地域間の均衡のとれた財政に関する規則が出された。この規則において地域の首長は，公正で比例配分に応じた財源の分配を含めて広範な自治を与えられる。
　以上の2つの規則に加えて，立法者はまた政党，総選挙，国民協議会の構造と位置，国会と地方議会にそれぞれ関連するその他の規則を制定した。
　上記の規則に基づいて，100以上の政党が出現することになった。しかしながら調査と選抜を受けた後に，1999年6月7日の総選挙には，48の政党が適法に参加することになった。この総選挙は，国会議員と地方議会議員を選出するために行われた。
　国会議員500名の内訳は，462名が総選挙を通じて選出され，残りの38名は大統領によって任命されるインドネシア国軍と警察の出身者である。1945年憲法第2条第1項によって制定された規則に従うと，

　　　国民協議会は，国会（Dewan Perwakilan Rakyat: DPR）議員と，法律によって規定された規則に従って選出される，地域と集団の代議員によって構成される。

　国民協議会，国会，地方議会の構造と地位に関する法律の規定によると，国民協議会の総議員は以下のものから構成される：
　1）500名の国会議員。
　2）27の州から選出される135名の議員。
　3）職能集団から指名される65名の議員。
　州から選出されるそれぞれ5名の議員は，地方議会によって選出される。65名の職能集団の代表議員は，それぞれの職能集団によって指名される。

## 大統領・副大統領の選挙と憲法改正問題

　a）1945年憲法第6条第2項は，大統領・副大統領の選挙を次のように規定している。すなわち，

　　　「大統領及び副大統領は，国民協議会の過半数の投票によって選挙される」

　過半数の投票とは，少なくとも国民協議会の議員総数の半分以上を意味する。国民協議会には700名の議員がいるため，少なくとも国民協議会の351名の議員によって支持される人が大統領・副大統領として選出される。
　1999年6月7日の総選挙からは，いかなる政党も，国会の251の議席を占めていな

いことが明らかになった。

　このことから，少なくとも351議席をもつ政党は生まれないということが，理解できる。このことは，11月に予定されている国民協議会の総会における大統領と副大統領の選出に問題を引き起こすであろう。直近の総選挙で明確になったことは，5大政党の出現であった。すなわち，インドネシア闘争民主党 (PDI Perjuangan)，ゴルカル (Partai Golongan Karya: Golkar)，統一開発党 (PPP)，民族覚醒党 (PKB)，国民信託党 (Partai Amanat Nasional: PAN) が，その5大政党である。

　もしも総選挙で勝利した5大政党のうち少なくとも3つの政党によって支持されるならば，または国民協議会の少なくとも351名の議員を集めうる強さを発揮できる1つの政党があるときには，候補者は大統領に選出されることになる。副大統領の選出の場合も，また同様である。したがって，2つの異なった政党から大統領と副大統領が選ばれる場合もでてくる。

　b）憲法改正問題

　インドネシアで現在広がっている憶測は，1945年憲法の改正の可能性である。国民協議会の決定がだされ国民投票法が廃止された後に，多くのグループによってこの問題が議論されるようになってきた。

　1945年憲法の改正については，国民協議会が唯一の権利をもっている。これは，憲法第37条の規定するところである。すなわち，

　　(1)　憲法を改正するためには，国民協議会の総議員の少なくとも3分の2が出席しなければならない。
　　(2)　決議は，出席した全議員の少なくとも3分の2の同意を得て，採択されなければならない。

　1945年憲法を改正する場合の基本的な課題は，憲法上大統領に与えられている支配的な地位と権限の見直しである。憲法改正の気運はまた，インドネシアの人民と国家のすべての生活領域において改革が着手されていることによって，高まっている。

　提案されている憲法改正の内容は，以下の通りである。

　1．大統領・副大統領の再選出の場合の任期の制限
　2．立法・執行・司法権の間の抑制と均衡をもたらすための，国会と最高裁判所の地位の強化
　3．国民協議会の地位と権限の強化

それに加えて，多党制の普及のために，国民協議会において政党間の妥協がなければ，大統領と副大統領の選出は困難になるであろう。したがって，大統領と副大統領をインドネシア人民が直接選出することが望ましいという見解も，生じているところである。

## 第 I 部　ま　と　め

吉　田　善　明

　第1セクションは、「アジア立憲主義の新たな摸索（Searching for Constitutionalism in Asia）というテーマです。
　このセクションで取りあげたのは、中国（香港）、インドネシア、ベトナムのアジアにおける代表的な3つの国の立憲主義体制の現況と21世紀にむけた課題でした。
　第1報告は、甘超英（Chaoying Gan）氏による「中国憲法と人権」です。報告内容は、中国における1国2制度の1つの制度である香港の政治制度の紹介が中心でした。すなわち、中国は、1997年に香港の中国返還によって、1国2制度の政治体制をつくりあげました。中国の1国2制度とは、中国は、社会主義国家としての政治体制に1998年に返還された香港の政治体制をそのまま香港特別行政区として中国に組入れ維持しようとするものです。この香港特別区は、権力分立を基礎とし裁判所に終審管轄権を認める強い自治制度です。この制度のねらいは、中央政府からの監督をできるだけ排除することに特徴があります。中国共産党の指導が及んでいないと説明されていました。香港の政治体制のもとで違憲審査の導入が可能となるのか、台湾も香港同様、将来において1国2制度のような採用が可能となるのか。さらには、中国政府が政策として進めている「経済開放」、そして将来予想される「政治解放」が進めば香港はもとより中国の立憲化、民主化は一層推進していくのではないかなどが討論がされました。
　第2報告は、スリ・スマントリ（Sri Soemantri）氏によるインドネシアの「経済危機と新たな体制」（The Economic Crisis in Indonesia and the New Constitutional Government）でした。インドネシアでは、1998年にハビビ政権が登場しました。いままで続いてきたスハルト大統領の開発主義政策、人権政策が見直されています。新憲法の制定が検討されていますが、開発主義、人権問題がどのように扱われるのか興味あるところです。現在、治安は悪化し、軍事力が強化されています。しかし、ハビビ政権の下で特徴的なのは、プレスの自由、政党結成の自由など政治

的表現の自由が拡大されてきていることです。このことは立憲化への方向がみられることと解されます。討論では、弱者の人権が厳しく制限されているのは、開発主義の優先主義の結果によるものではないかとの質問、連邦と州との関係、とくに州自治権への連邦の抑制などについてどのような対処がなされているのか、また、東テモールの「独立」をどのように考えているかなどの質問がありました。報告者は東テモールについて、「独立」を問う住民投票をまたなければなりませんが、その結果に従うべきだとのべているのが印象的でした。

※　東テモールでは、99年8月30日「独立」を問う住民投票が行われ、独立に賛成する者(78.8％)が反対を上回りました。99年10月20日インドネシア国民協議会は9月4日の投票の結果を受け入れ、国連は、国連テモール暫定統治機構（UNTAET）を設置し、暫定統治をしていましたが、2002年5月20日正式に独立しました。

第3報告は、ダオ・チ・ウック（DAO Tri Uc）氏による「ドイモイ体制と憲法（DoiMoi policy and the Constitutional Freedom for Economic Development）の報告、つづいてドン氏による補助発言がありました。ベトナムは、ベトナム戦争によって、主権、民主主義が脅かされましたが、1975年のサイゴン陥落、南北統一への志向が急テンポではじまりました。80年12月18日に統一ベトナム憲法が制定された。80年憲法では、ベトナム国家をプロレタリア独裁国家として規定しました（第1条）。その後、国内法（刑法、刑訴法、民法、民訴法、労働法など）の法整備が行われ、従来の社会主義化路線が修正され、ドイモイ（刷新）路線が展開されています。そして92年には「1992年ベトナム社会主義共和国憲法」を制定しました。この憲法は、80年憲法にみられた「プロレタリアート独裁」「集団的」「社会主義的」という文言が削除され「人民の人民による人民のための国家」という国家の性格規定がなされています。また、論議では、司法の役割、経済の自由化による腐敗、汚職が増大してきているとの紹介があり、とくに後者を中心に論議がなされました。司法については、刑事、民事、経済裁判所のほかに行政管理裁判所が確立され、人権保障の担い手として重視されてきているとの意見がのべられていました。憲法裁判所または憲法委員会の必要性が論議されました。また、腐敗、汚職がおこる原因は、経済的、政治的、伝統的理由にもとづくものです。これらは、経済改革、行政改革を進めることによって解決されなければならないし、また社会全般の改革、報道の自由の改革等についても論議がなされました。

このように3国だけを対象にして、アジア立憲主義の傾向、今後の動きを判断す

ることは困難ですが、1つの流れを促えることができます。いままで紹介してきた中国は、香港の返還によって1国2制度といった政治体制をとらざるを得なかったのは、香港が宗主国（イギリス）法の影響を受けたこともあって民主主義、立憲主義の具体化としての制度に少なからず成熟していたからです。今後、香港を取り込んだ中国は、この影響を受け、また経済の自由化の推進によって立憲化、民主化がはかられるでしょう。このことは社会主義政治体制を採用しているベトナムについてもいえます。ドイモイ路線は、まさしく市場メカニズムの導入であり、「私的所有」の部分的導入とはいえ、これによって人権保障、立憲主義の方向が益々重視されることでしょう。インドネシアも開発主義、権威主義からの政治姿勢の転換が迫まられ、人権尊重をより重視した憲法改正が大きな課題となっています。いずれの国家も独立後、50年の歴史の中で政治、経済のあり様をめぐる葛藤を得ながら立憲主義的傾向に動き出していることは確かです。21世紀に向けて、これらの諸国は、人権保障の番人としての立憲制がより高められていくことになるでしょう。

# 第II部
アジアの人権保障

# タイにおける人権及び立憲主義

ウィサヌ・ワランヨウ

今 泉 慎 也 訳

## 序

　憲法が，一方で政治機関相互の関係を規定し，他方で国家とその市民との間の関係を規定する法的枠組みであるとするならば，タイ立憲主義は，1997年10月11日憲法の公布までは，タイ市民の権利及び自由を犠牲にして，専ら政治構造に関心を集めてきたことを認めざるを得ない。しかしながら，このような状況は，現行憲法の登場に伴いかなり急激に変化してきた。1996年の憲法の起草過程への大規模な民衆参加は，権利及び自由を大いに強調し，それゆえタイの人権状況の改善に大きな期待をもたらした。本稿においては，過去の憲法状況に起因するいくつかの人権問題にふれ，それから人権の伸張及び保護のための新たな憲法上の仕組みについて概観したい。

## 1997年憲法の登場以前のタイにおける人権に関する諸問題

　タイの人権も他国と同様に常に政治的争点であり，この国の立憲主義と結びついていた。それゆえ，立憲主義に問題がある場合には，そうした問題は人民の権利及び自由に不可避的に影響を与えた。

### 憲法の不連続性と人権の不安定性

　人権の憲法化は，抽象的原則を啓蒙的でかつ具体的事件への実施が容易な実定的権利へと変える利点がある。しかしながら，このことは憲章の変化が頻繁に起きすぎない国にのみあてはまる。憲法の不連続性を主たる政治的特色とする国では，同様に人権もその確固たる存在のための基礎を持たない。フランスのように人権が憲法以外の淵源，すなわち1789年の人と市民の権利宣言（*Declaration des Droits de l' Homme et du Citoyen de 1789*）を持つような国においてはこのことは問題とならな

い。

シャム（タイ）の政治レジームを絶対王政から立憲民主政へと変身させた6月革命後の1932年から，この国は9つの恒久憲法とそれと交互にあらわれる他の8つの暫定憲法を経験した。

たいてい暫定憲法は恒久憲法よりも長生きであった。一般にこれらの憲法の起草は，軍事クーデタという手段によって権力の奪取に成功した者の信頼を受けた少数の者の問題であった。ほとんどの場合，これらの憲法の規定は，クーデタ後も引き続き権力を掌握する軍の寡頭制の権力を永続させることを意図していた。人民の権利及び自由は，彼らの主たる関心事ではなかった。

**憲法起草の技術的問題**

意図的であるのかないのか，諸憲法によって承認されかつ保証された権利及び自由は限定されていた。これは，憲法起草者は憲法によって承認されかつ保証される権利及び自由のリストを確立するにあたって列挙的方法を用いたことによる。人権に関する憲法規定の列挙的で，従って，限定的な性格は，憲法に制限的解釈方法を適用する一般傾向によってさらに強められている。このことが意味するのは，実際には憲法に明記されていないのであるが，憲法によって承認されずかつ保証されないということである。

興味深いことに，18世紀の有名な憲法的文書に異なる技術を見いだすことができる。たとえば，合衆国憲法の第9修正は次のように定める。

「この憲法に特定の憲法を列挙したことは，人民の保有するその他の諸権利を否定し，または，軽視するものとして解釈してはならない。」訳注[1]

同様の記述は，フランスの有名な1789年の人と市民の権利宣言にも見られる。その冒頭において，次のように明確に宣言している。

「人権の不知・忘却又は蔑視が公共の不幸と政府の腐敗の諸原因にほかならないことにかんがみて，一の厳粛な宣言の中で，人の譲渡不能かつ神聖な自然権を展示することを決意したが…」（訳注――強調部筆者）訳注[2]

**権利及び自由は，法律的性格である**

人権の法律的性格は，憲法規定において明らかであった。と言うのも，それらの条項は人民の権利及び自由を実際に実施するためには法律の制定が必要であると定

めていたからである。これは権利及び自由に関する規定を即時的適用のない単なる一般原則へと自動的に変えた。従って，ほとんどの権利及び自由は，それらの規定を実施する法案が制定されない限り，死文と化し，いかなる機関に対して，裁判所においてさえも，援用し得なかった。

人権の法律的性格は別の興味深い問題も提起した。

法律は，権利及び自由の実施の不可欠の条件であるだけでなく，権利及び自由の行使の限界も定めたのである。このことは，いくつかの立法，たとえば出版法が，いったい出版の自由が存在するのであろうかと疑問に思うほどに，出版の自由に制限的であることの理由である。

**権利及び自由の実現のためのメカニズムの欠如**

かつては権利及び自由は一般原則として憲法に列挙されたにすぎなかった。憲法起草者が何ら実現のメカニズムをデザインしなかったため，権利及び自由の侵害は何の制裁も生じさせなかった。これは極めて嘆かわしい状況である。と言うのも，いくつかの事件は明らかに憲法規定に反していたからである。

## 1997年憲法における改革

現行憲法はそれ全体が，古い権威主義的な権力関係に代わってより民主的なシステムを確立するための試みである。それは，広範な権利及び自由を個人だけではなく，集団及びコミュニティに対しても保証する。かかる権利及び自由は参加型民主主義における実定的権利と見られる。憲法と政治的社会的改革への道を見るならば，タイ政治の民主勢力は非常に大きな一歩をなしたことが分かるであろう。紙の上では，国家権力の分権化，会計検査機関，並びに政治的，社会文化的及び経済的決定並びにこれら分野における公共政策形成への参加の拡大は，民主的変革のための推進力としてデザインされたのである。

**広範な権利及び自由の承認**

タイ人の権利及び自由を列挙するという技術を用いることによって，憲法起草者が時には細部に立ち入ろうとしたことは認めざるを得ないが，従来の憲法はそれらを本質的に限定的なものとした。法律家，特に裁判所は，単に憲法に明示されていないというだけで環境保全に対するコミュニティの権利のような権利を承認するこ

とを拒絶してきた。

　新憲法は，人民の権利及び自由に関する憲法規定の解釈及び適用を規律する一般原則条項を定めることによって，この憲法起草上の技術に対する全く新しい態度を明確に採用した。

　この問題に関して，以下の4つの条項は特に重要である。訳注[3]

(1)　第26条「国家機関による権力の行使は，この憲法の規定に従って，人の尊厳，権利及び自由を考慮しなければならない。」

(2)　第27条「この憲法によって明示的に，黙示的に又は憲法裁判所の判決によって承認された権利及び自由は保護を受けるものとし，また国会，内閣，裁判所及び他の国家機関を法律の制定，適用及び解釈において直接に拘束する。」

(3)　第28条「人は，他の者の権利及び自由を侵害せず，又は憲法若しくは人民の良俗に反しない限りにおいて，人の尊厳を援用し，又は自己の権利及び自由を行使することができる。

　②憲法によって承認された自己の権利及び自由を侵害された者は，裁判所に訴訟を提起し，又は裁判所において自己の抗弁として憲法規定を援用することができる。」

(4)　第29条「憲法によって承認された権利及び自由の制限は，この憲法が定めた目的のために特に制定された法律の規定に依拠し，かつ必要な限度においてのみ，行うができ，またかかる権利及び自由の本質的内容に影響を与えてはならない。

　②前項の法律は一般的に適用されるものでなければならず，特定の事件又は特定の人に適用されることを意図するものであってはならない。また，かかる立法を授権する憲法規定が明示されなければならない。

　③第1項及び前項の規定は，法律の規定に依拠して制定された規則及び実施規則に準用する。」

## 人権に関する憲法規定の実現のためのメカニズム及び措置

　すでに論じたように，人民の権利及び自由に関するほとんどの憲法規定は，法律的性格を有したのであり，従って，それらを実施するためには法的措置を事前に立法化することが条件とされた。政府及び国会が制定法によってそれらを実施することに消極的であったため，これらの権利及び自由が死文化することは頻繁であった。

　憲法は，人民の権利及び自由に関する規定の実現を支援するための3つの興味深い措置を定めている。

(1)　憲法規定は，拘束力を有しかつ直接に執行可能である。第28条は，憲法によって承認された自己の権利及び自由を侵害された者は，訴訟を提起し又は裁判所において自己の抗弁として憲法規定を援用することができる。

(2) 権利及び自由に関する規定を実施するために法案が必要な場合において，人民はかかる法案の制定を発議することができる。このことは第170条に明確に定められている。
　「5万人を下回らない有権者は，国会議長に対して，憲法第3章（タイ人の権利及び自由）及び第5章（国家基本政策の指針的原則）に定める法律の審議を求める請求を提出する権利を有する。
②前項の請求には法案が付されなければならない。」（訳注――（　）内は筆者）
(3) 国会に対する所信表明において，内閣は国家基本政策の指針的原則に従った国政の運営のため行われる活動について明確に陳述しなければならず，また，直面する問題及び障碍を含む実施成果の年次報告書を作成し，国会に提出しなければならない。訳注[4]

## 人権の保護及び伸張を任務とする諸機関

新憲法により人民の権利及び自由の伸張及び保護を任務とする3つの憲法上の機関が設置される。

## 国家人権委員会

国家人権委員会は，人民の権利及び自由の保護において顕著な知識と経験を有する者の中から，人権分野の民間団体の代表の参加についても考慮して，上院の助言に基づき国王が任命する委員長及び他の10人の委員によって構成される。

国家人権委員会の権限及び職務は憲法第200条に定められている。それは次のように定める。

(1) 人権を侵害し，又はタイが当事国となる人権に関する国際条約上の義務に反する行為又は不作為について審査し及び報告し，並びにかかる行為を行い又は行為を怠った私人又は機関に対して，とるべき適切な是正措置を提案すること。提案された行動がとられていないことが明らかである場合には，委員会はさらなる手続のため国会に報告する。
(2) 国会及び内閣に対して人権の伸張及び保護のため法律，規則又は施行規則の改定に関する政策及び勧告を提案すること。
(3) 人権に関する教育，研究及び知識普及を促進すること。
(4) 人権分野における政府機関，民間団体及び他の団体の間の協力及び調整を促進すること。
(5) 国内の人権分野の状況を評価するため年次報告書を作成し，国会に提出すること。
(6) 法律の定める他の権限及び職務

国家人権委員会は，法律の定めに従って，いずれかの者に関連する文書若しくは証拠の提出を求め，又は事実について証言させるためいずれかの者を召喚する権限，並びに職務遂行のための他の権限を有する。

### オンブズマン

人民が，その権利及び自由を考慮させるため，政府による誤った不当な行政又は過失に関する申立を提出することのできる制度としてのオンブズマンの創設は，きわめて長い間議論されてきた。この制度に関する公の議論は，1970年代にさかのぼることができる。オンブズマンが1997年に憲法上の機関の一つとしてその地位を得るまでに約30年がかかった。

新憲法の第196条は，オンブズマンは3人を超えず，人民から認められかつ尊敬され，国政，経営，人民の共通利益の活動において知識及び経験を有し，並びに明白な誠実性を有する者の中から，上院の助言に基づき国王が任命すると定める。

オンブズマンは，次に掲げる権利及び職務を有する。

(1) 次に掲げる場合について，申立に基づき事実認定のため審査及び調査を行うこと。
　　a）政府機関，国家機関，国営企業又は地方自治体の公務員，職員又は被用者の法律の不遵守又は法律が定める権限及び職務を逸脱する行為
　　b）政府機関，国家機関，国営企業又は地方自治体の公務員，職員又は被用者の職務の遂行又は職務の懈怠で，当該行為が違法であるか否かに関わらず，申立人又は公衆に不当に損害を生じさせるもの。
　　c）法律に定める他の場合
(2) 報告書を作成し国会に対して提出すること。

オンブズマンは，法律，規則若しくは施行規則の規定，又はいずれかの者の行為に合憲性の問題が有ると認めるときは，当該事案を意見と共に憲法裁判所又は行政裁判所に提出し，その意見を求めなければならない。場合に応じて，憲法裁判所手続又は行政裁判所手続法による。

### 憲法裁判所

ドイツ・モデルに由来する裁判権は，最も重要である。憲法裁判所は，次に掲げる者の中から上院の助言に基づき国王が任命した長官及び14人の裁判官によって構

成される。
- (1) 最高裁判所裁判官の職を下回らない最高裁判所の裁判官で，最高裁判所裁判官会議において秘密投票で選出された者5人
- (2) 最高行政裁判所裁判官会議において秘密投票によって選出された最高行政裁判所の裁判官2人
- (3) 選出委員会によって選出された法律学の有識者5人
- (4) 選出委員会によって選出された政治学の有識者3人

立法の憲法適合性の統制という役割とは別に，憲法裁判所は人権分野においてとても重要な規範的権能を有している。憲法裁判所は，その決定によって，憲法に書かれていない権利及び自由を創設し，すべての憲法上の機関を拘束する実定的権利とすることができる。憲法第27条は，「憲法によって明示的に，黙示的に，又は憲法裁判所の判決によって認められた権利及び自由は保護され，また国会，内閣，裁判所及び他の国家機関を法律の制定，適用及び解釈において拘束する」（訳注――傍点筆者）と定める。

**人権伸張のための行動計画**

ここで言及すべきタイの人権伸張の問題におけるもう一つの最近の発展は，行動計画の策定である。これは，政府と国会にとって公共政策形成の一種の参考書（*vademecum*）となるであろう。行動計画の策定は，実際に政府機関から民衆ベースの諸団体で働く者まで，すべての関係者に広く参加を求めている段階である。

## 結　論

現行憲法を適用して2年間で，新たな立憲主義の下での人権が成功したか失敗したか結論を下すことはまだ早すぎるかもしれない。数多くの措置が実施される必要がある。しかしながら，憲法による参加型民主主義は，人々が自らの権利及び自由を保護するため，自らの役割及び能力により一層関心を持ちつつあることの良い積極的な証拠を示している。唯一の心配は，まさにこの憲法が長生きしてくれるかどうかである！

訳注
[1] アメリカ合衆国憲法修正第9の訳語については，塚本重頼・長内了『註解アメリカ憲法』（全訂新版）（酒井書店，1983年）を参照した。

［2］　フランス人権宣言の訳語は，高木八尺・末延三次・宮澤俊義編『人権宣言集』（岩波文庫，1957年）を参照した。
［3］　憲法条文の引用部分についても原則として筆者の英語訳から翻訳し，必要な範囲でタイ語原文を参照した。
［4］　第88条

# インドにおける公益訴訟による人権の保障

パーマナンド・シン

孝 忠 延 夫 訳

## 1 はじめに

　1980年代初頭から，インド最高裁は，公益心をもった市民あるいは社会活動家が抑圧された階層に代わり司法的救済を求めることを可能とする手続きをつくりあげてきた。裁判へのアクセスを民主化する手段は，『公益訴訟（Public Interest Litigation）』（以下，PILと略記する）と呼ばれる。このPILは，インド国内で発展してきたものであり，インド独自の社会的，歴史的及び政治的背景の所産であって，アメリカ合衆国の公益訴訟と共通性をもつものではない。インドで最も著名な法学者の一人であるウーペンドラ・バクシ（Upendra Baxi）教授は，この新しい法的動きを「社会活動訴訟」と呼ぶことを好んだ。彼は，この訴訟を社会変革の手段であり，犠牲を強いられ抑圧された人々の事例を扱うものとみなしていた。バクシによれば，アメリカ合衆国の公益訴訟は，国による抑圧や政府の違法行為，あるいは農村の貧困問題に焦点を当てたものというよりは，『政策決定への市民参加』，消費者保護運動，又は環境問題に焦点を当てたものである[1]。バクシは，用語法を変えることによって，この新しい法的手段があらゆる公益問題になし崩し的に用いられることを避けようとしたのである。彼の懸念通り，幾年も経つ間にPILは，団体の利益，政治的あるいは個人的な利益のために用いられるようになった。現在では，環境，消費主義，政府の説明責任あるいは政治手法の問題がとりあげられることが圧倒的に多いのである。すなわち，PILは，もはや貧しく抑圧された人々の問題に限定されてはいない。

　この報告では，市民参加の問題にかんする事例を除き，PILが扱った人権の核心的な問題に焦点を当てる。政府の不法行為一般の問題，並びに拘禁中の暴力行為，レイプ，死亡事故，奴隷的労働及び児童労働という個別的な問題に対する裁判所の対応を批判的に検討する。あわせて，連邦人権委員会の人権保護のための活動についても検討する。

## 2 公益訴訟の生成

　イギリスの統治は，インドに植民地法体系の遺産をのこした。アングロ・サクソン型の裁判形態は，原告適格や当事者主義などの訴訟手続きの遵守を求めた。この結果，裁判所は，裕福で実力のある人々しかアクセスできないものとなった。疎外され，抑圧されたグループは，搾取されつづけ，基本的人権も認められないままであった。非常事態期間中 (1975—1977) には，インドの法律制度の植民地的性格が一層明らかとなった。この期間中，国による抑圧あるいは政府による違法行為はさらに広がった。反体制派を含む数千人の無実の人々が獄につながれ，そこでは市民的・政治的権利が完全に剥奪されていた。非常事態終了後，貧しい人々が裁判（正義）へアクセス出来るよう，アングロ・サクソン型の手続き的障害を公然と乗り越える機会を最高裁判事は与えられた。最高裁判事たちは，非常事態宣言下において，抑圧的な体制を暗黙のうちに支持する判決[2]を出したことで傷ついた最高裁のイメージを回復することも望んでいたのである。とりわけ，V.R. クリシュナ・アイヤール判事とP.N. バーグワティ判事は，原告適格の原則を緩和することによって，貧しく抑圧された人々が裁判を受ける道が開かれると考えた。非常事態終了後，政治状況は変わり，調査に熱心なジャーナリストたちが政府の無法性，弾圧，拘禁中の暴行などをあばき，法律家，判事，及び社会活動家たちの注目を集めた。PILは，活動的な判事，ジャーナリスト及び社会活動家たちの自然なネットワークによって生まれたのである。

　はじめてPILが提起されたのは1979年だといわれており，そこでは刑務所及び未決拘禁者の非人間的な処遇が扱われた。この*Hussainara Khatoon v. State of Bihar*事件[3]は，ビハール州内の幾つかの拘置所で数千人もの未決拘禁者が長期間にわたり収監されている窮状を扱ったニュース報道をもとに，ある弁護士が訴訟を提起したものである。この訴訟は，刑事裁判制度の欠陥を明らかにし，結果的には40,000人以上の未決拘禁者の釈放へとつながった。これらの未決拘禁者に保障されていなかった，迅速な裁判を受ける権利が基本的人権として認められるようになった。同時に，この訴訟は，刑務所改革についての公の論議をまき起こし，インドにおける刑務所運営の問題点に目を向けさせることになった。

　1981年の*Anil Yadav v. State of Bihar*事件[4]は，身の毛もよだつ野蛮さと警察

の横暴を明らかにした。報道によれば，33名の容疑者がビハール州内の警察によって，劇薬で目を焼かれ，盲目にされたというものであった。PILの提起に対応し，最高裁は登録官をバガルプールに派遣し，事実関係を調査させた。仮処分命令により，裁判所は盲目にされた容疑者の公判を無効とし，警察の残虐行為を非難し，州政府には被害者をデリーに連れていき，治療を受けさせるよう命じた。また，犯罪行為をおこなった警察官を速やかに起訴することも命じた。さらには，すべての刑事被告人は法律扶助を受ける基本的権利があることを示し，全国のセッション判事がこのことを刑事被告人に告げるよう命じた。

　Anil Yadav事件を皮切りに，社会的積極主義と調査的訴訟の増加が始まった。この事件の成果が広く伝えられることによって，刑務所の状況についてのPILが急速に増加していった。ある社会活動家は，4人の少数部族青年に代わり，彼らが未決のまま10年以上も収監されていることを最高裁に訴え，かれらの釈放を勝ちとった[5]。刑務所に関する事件は，多くの新たな権利を生みだした。Citizen for Democracy v. State of Assam事件[6]で，最高裁は，囚人が刑務所内にいる場合，刑務所間の移動，及び刑務所と裁判所との移動に際して手錠その他の強制具を強制してはならない，と判示した。この事件は，あるジャーナリストが，最高裁判事に対し，アッサム州ガウハティの病院においてTADA（テロリズム及び破壊活動防止法）に基づく拘留者が，錠をかけ，外には武装警官が警備する部屋でベッドに手錠で縛りつけられ，長いロープで結ばれて行動を制約されていることを手紙で知らせたものである。

　収監された児童たち，児童及び奴隷的労働，収監中の性的暴力，偽りの掃討作戦による死亡事件などについての報道や雑誌記事が，初期PILの基礎となった。1981年，P.N. バーグワティ判事は，S.P. Gupta v. Union of India事件[7]でPILの理念について，次のように述べた。

「ある個人若しくは特定の人々に対して，憲法上若しくは法律上の権利が侵害されることにより，又は，法律上若しくは憲法上の規定に反して若しくは法律の規定に基づかずに負担を課されることにより，違法行為，権利侵害を受け，あるいは違法な負担を課された場合に，これらの人々が貧困，疎外，無能力，社会的・経済的抑圧を理由として裁判所に救済を申し立てることができないならば，何人も第226条に基づき高裁に適切な指令，命令又は保護令状を請求することができ，これらの人々の基本的権利が侵害されている場合には，第32条に基づき最高裁に違法行為や権利

侵害について司法的救済を求めることができる。」

## 3　PILの特徴

　上述したように，PILは，基本的には貧しく疎外され，そして抑圧された人々で資力も知識もないために法的救済を求めることのできない人々の人権を保護するために発達してきた。これは，インドの司法手続きの中でも大きな変革であり，他の国に例を見ないものである。PILを通じて裁判所は，以下のような形で人権を保障しようとしている。

　(1)　平等，生命及び人身の自由という基本権の意味を拡大することで，新たな人権の諸相をつくり上げた。この過程の中で，迅速な裁判を受ける権利，無料法律扶助の権利，尊厳を保つ権利，健康への権利，教育を受ける権利，居住の権利，医療を受ける権利，並びに拷問，セクシュアル・ハラスメント，独房監禁，奴隷的苦役及び搾取などに対する権利が人権と認められてきた。新たに理念化されたこれらの権利は，裁判所がPILを通じて活動するにあたり，その法的拠りどころとなった。

　(2)　裁判へのアクセスの民主化。これは，原告適格という伝統的な原則を緩和することによってなされた。公共心を持つ市民，あるいは社会活動団体であれば誰でも，抑圧された人々に代わり裁判所に訴えることができる。裁判所は，書簡や電報による訴えであっても受理できる。これは，書簡による裁判権といわれる。

　(3)　裁判所の令状請求訴訟手続きの中で，新たな救済方法を生み出している。例えば，裁判所は，政府による違法行為の犠牲者に対して，暫定的補償を命じることができる。この手続きは，アングロ・サクソン型の裁判手続きとは大きく異なる。アングロ・サクソン型の手続きでは，仮処分手続きは，現状を維持し最終判断を引き延ばすものに限定されているからである。PILにおいて，賠償とは，損害を理由として民事訴訟を提起したものに限定されてはいない。PILでは，裁判所は，被害者に対していかなる形の救済をも行うことが出来るのである。

　(4)　拘置所，女性保護施設，少年院及び精神障害者保護施設など国の施設を裁判所が監視する。この司法的監視により，裁判所はこれら施設の管理運営の改善を求める。これは，人権保護のために裁判所がこれらの施設の運営を監督するという，潜在的管轄権と特徴づけることができよう。

　(5)　事実認定のための新たな工夫。多くの事件において，裁判所は独自の社会法

学的調査委員会を任命したり，その職員を調査にあたらせてきた。場合によっては，連邦人権委員会（NHRC）や中央調査局（CBI），あるいは人権侵害問題の専門家の支援を受けることもある。これらは，調査的訴訟と呼ばれている。

## 4　政府の無法性及び弾圧

### 1　拘禁中の暴行

　1981年，2人の法律学教授が最高裁に対し，アーグラー女性保護施設に収容されている人々の悲惨な状況についての書簡を送った。この訴訟は，最終的には当初の障害を乗り越え，収容者の人間的な状況を取り戻すことに成功した[8]。ラーンチーとデリーにある精神障害者保護施設の恐るべき状況について提起されたのが，*R.C. Narain v. State of Bihar*事件[9]及び*B.R. Kapoor v. Union of India*事件[10]である。PILの結果，これらの施設の運営は，地方自治体の手を離れることとなり，精神障害者保護施設の運営改善のためのガイドラインが発せられた。これらすべての事件において，調査委員会が任命され，調査の実行と改善プロセスを最高裁判事が監督した。精神障害者の人権保護は，他のPILにおいてもなされている。これは，ビハールの拘置所から精神障害者の患者を釈放するというもので，彼らの多くは責任能力があるとされ，20年から30年にわたって拘留されていたのである[11]。

　最高裁は，一つの歴史的な判決によって，すべての傷病者は迅速に治療を受ける権利を有しており，病院はかかる事件において治療を拒否してはならないと判示した[12]。ボンベイ市拘置所で5人の女性囚人が拘留中暴行の被害にあった。最高裁は，マハーラーシュトラ州全域に適用されるガイドラインを発し，女性被疑者又は女性囚人の警護又は取調べは，女性警官のみに限られるとしたのである[13]。

　非政府機関（NGOs）や社会活動団体（SAGs）の驚異的な増加とあいまって，宗派間抗争，警察の発砲，警察の過剰攻撃，掃討作戦による死亡，軍の過剰攻撃，テロリズムあるいは暴動にかんする報道の増加によりPILの件数も大きく増加した。警察の過剰攻撃についての裁判所の対応は，複雑であった。1984年に起きたインディラ・ガンディー首相暗殺直後，デリーをはじめ国内の複数の地域で宗派間抗争が発生し，多くのシク教徒が生命を奪われた。人権団体は，調査委員会を任命することと，抗争において警察の果たした役割について調査するよう中央調査局に命ずることの2点をデリー高裁に求める動きをおこした。これに対して，デリー高裁は，か

かる事例についてPILの先例がなく，PILで発する命令は，それが実効性をもつ場合に限るとして，訴えを斥けた。高裁によれば，警察も政治家も人権については関心を払っているのであり，彼らを信用できないとみなす必要はない[14]。高裁のこのような対応には驚かざるを得ない。このような事件でPILの先例がないというのは，誤りである。最高裁に提起された別の事件でも，そこでの司法の対応には不満が残る。この事件は，1982年，ウッタル・プラデーシュ州において，警察が強盗団の掃討作戦を行った際に多くの無実の人々が殺害されたというものである。無実の人々の殺害事件としては，ナクサライトの活動家とみなされた人々を排除するために，タミル・ナードゥ州で1980年から1981年にかけて実施された掃討作戦におけるものがある。これらの申立ては，*Chaitanya Kalbagh v. State of U.P.*事件[15]で扱われた。最高裁は，1989年に発した命令において，かかる事項は州政府の管轄下にあり，したがって，まず第一に，当該州政府に申立てを行うべきであるとした。

　警察の行為に対する上述の消極的な対応と対照的に，グジャラート州ナディアードで起きた司法官僚に対する警察の暴行行為を申立てたPILにおいて，最高裁は，「警察の専横」に対して非常に批判的な姿勢を明らかにした。この事件では，ナディアードの主任治安判事が複数の警察官により路上で手錠をかけられ，残虐な暴行を受けたという事件を知らせる電報が，デリー司法官協会から最高裁へ送られた。最高裁は，警察の残虐行為を強い姿勢で批判し，裁判所侮辱権の行使により彼らの処罰を命じた[16]。また，ある人権団体は，貧しい人々を強制的に警察署へ連れていき，無報酬で働かすという，警察の非道行為について最高裁に申立てを行った。この事件では，警察官による殴打で一人が死亡している。裁判所は，遺族に50,000ルピーを暫定的補償として支払うこと，その額は殴打した警察官が補塡すること，を命じた[17]。9歳の子どもが警察官の殴打により死亡した事件では，PILの結果，その母親に暫定的補償として75,000ルピーが支払われた[18]。21歳の若者が違法に拘禁された事例では，不服申立てを受けたデリー警察コミッショナーは，何ら対応をしなかった。裁判所が調査を命じた結果，その若者の身体からは51ヶ所もの傷が見つかり，この傷がもとで警察における拘禁中に死亡したことが判明した。デリー高裁は，遺族に対して5,50,000ルピーの刑事補償を行うことを命じた[19]。

　拘禁中の暴行についての訴訟数は多くはないが，この場合に人権を保護する唯一の方法は，刑事補償を行うことである。刑事補償についての判例理論は，1993年の*Nilabati Behera v. State of Orissa*事件最高裁判決[20]で最も明確に示された。この

事件は，22歳の青年が警察での拘禁中に死亡したことに対するPILである。裁判所は，人権侵害に対する補償についての公法理論を発展させた。この理論によれば，人権侵害に対して州の責任は絶対的であり，免責特権のような例外は認められない。この事件では，青年の母親に拘禁中の死亡に対する補償として1,50,000ルピーが支払われた。歴史的な，1997年の*D.K. Basu v. State of West Bengal*事件判決[21]において，最高裁は，市民を逮捕するとき及び逮捕者に対する最低限の処遇についての，インド全土に適用すべき詳細な警察手続きを指示した。このPILは，1986年7月から8月にかけてカルカッタで起きた，警察の留置場における死亡事故に端を発している。西ベンガル法律扶助協会会長は，最高裁に宛てた書簡の中で，拘禁中の死亡事件は西ベンガルに限られたものではなく，インド全土で起こっていることだと指摘した。また，その書簡は，全インドから拘禁中の暴行についての報告書を提出させることを最高裁に求め，さらに，拘禁死亡事件の被害者への補償金支払いのための基金を設けること，手続き的保障を裁判所が命ずることを提言した。

　拘禁中の暴行に対する補償理論は，PILの成果であるが，刑事補償の実施は裁量的であり，むしろ恩恵的なものと思える。犯罪を実行した警察官が，実際に処罰されたという事件はほとんどない。これらの事件で訴追された場合でも，審理手続きへの司法的監督が欠如しているゆえに，何年にもわたり審理がストップしているのが実情である。

## 2　テロリズム及び暴動

　補償による救済は，すべての種類の人権侵害に対する，司法による一般的な手法となった。パンジャーブのある弁護士が，その妻及び2歳の子どもとともに拉致され，弁護士は殺害された。パンジャーブ及びハリヤナ高等裁判所弁護士会は，PILを提起した。調査の結果，パンジャーブ警察の警察官が拉致及び殺害に関与していたことが分かり，最高裁は，1994年と1995年にパンジャーブ州政府に対し，死亡した弁護士の両親に1,00,000ルピーの補償金の支払いを命じた[22]。パンジャーブでは，弁護士の誘拐又は殺害は日常的な出来事になっていた。別のPILにおいて，最高裁は，中央調査局に弁護士の誘拐事件を調査するよう命じ，州政府には武装組織に反対する弁護士の家族の安全を保障するよう命じている[23]。

　1995年，最高裁判事の一人に電報が届いた。この電報は，Shiromani Akali Dal党の人権局事務局長Jaswant Singh Khalraが，パンジャーブ警察によって誘拐され

たことを知らせるものであった。Khalraの妻も，最高裁へ夫は警察署長の指示によって誘拐されたとして告発した。申立てによれば，この警察署長は，Khalraに対して，警察の過剰攻撃，拘禁中の死亡事件，身元不明遺体の大規模な埋葬などについての令状請求訴訟を取り下げなければ，不幸な災厄がおこるだろうとの脅迫を行っていたというのである。この*Paramjit Kaur v. State of Punjab*事件[24]において，最高裁が中央調査局に調査報告を命じたところ，妻の申立てが真実であることが明らかとなった。大規模な身元不明遺体の埋葬について，最高裁は次のように述べた。「わが国ではこのような事態が発生しないことを保障するものとして，民主主義や法の支配を尊重している。しかし，報道された今回の申立ては恐ろしいものであり，徹底的な調査を必要とするものであった[25]。」最高裁は，パンジャーブ州政府に犯罪を行った警察官を起訴するよう命じ，同時に，Paramjit Kaurへの補償金として1,00,000ルピーの支払いを命じた。1996年12月13日，裁判所は，中央調査局の提出した報告書を取り上げた。この報告書は，身元不明として埋葬された遺体のうち，585以上もの身元が判明したことを確認している。裁判所は，身元が判明した者の遺族は，連邦人権委員会が決定した補償金を受けとる資格があると判断した[26]。しかし，後になって，事件から一年という申立て期間を過ぎてからの人権委員会の調査権に関する技術的な問題が生じた[27]。*Paramjit Kaur v. State of Punjab*事件[28]において，最高裁は，憲法第32条に基づく権限の行使にあたっては，インド国内のいかなる機関にも第144条に基づきその行動を補完するために協力を要請することが出来ると判示した。したがって，最高裁は連邦人権委員会に，いかなる問題を扱うことをも命ずることができる。すなわち，この場合，人権委員会は，1993年人権保護法に基づいてではなく，最高裁の命令に基づいて行動することになるのである。別のPILで最高裁は，パンジャーブ警察の共同謀議の結果殺害された者の両親に対し2,00,000ルピーの補償金を支払うよう命じている[29]。

ジャンムー・カシュミール州における人権問題は，深刻な状態が続いている。この州はインドの他のどの地域におけるよりもテロリズムや武装ゲリラの状況が厳しい。ジャンムー・カシュミール州における人権侵害の事件が裁判所に申し立てられることはなかった。PILとして唯一とりあげることが出来るのが，ハズラットバルの事件である。スリナガルにあるハズラットバル寺院を武装ゲリラが包囲し，無実の人々が人質とされた。人質21人のうち2人は重態であった。PILに応え，最高裁は高裁判決を支持し，州政府に対して人質への食料や水の供給を止める装置をとらない

よう求めた。裁判所の発したさまざまの命令により，関係機関は，食料パックを準備し，寺院のフェンス越しに人質たちに手渡すことを要請された[30]。

　軍隊の過剰攻撃にかんする事件は，多くない。マディヤ・プラデーシュ州の軍射撃訓練場で81人の指定部族住民が死亡した事件では，PILの提起が射撃訓練場の閉鎖につながった[31]。また，あるPILによって最高裁は，ナガランド州において警備隊が無差別射撃を行い，複数の住民が死亡したという報告を受けた。裁判所は，その事件を調査するよう命じている[32]。

　1955年アッサム特別地域法及び1958年軍（特別権限）法により，軍には広範囲にわたる権限が付与され，軍の過剰攻撃についての裁判所の介入を難しくしている。連邦人権委員会でさえ，軍に対する不服申立てを受理する権限を与えられてはいないのである。

### 3　女性に対する暴行

　女性運動の活性化及び調査的ジャーナリズムが，ダウリ，レイプ，セクシュアル・ハラスメント及び差別的なハラスメントの事実を明らかにすることによって，女性問題が最高裁に持ち込まれる事件が増えてきた。女性に対する犯罪の調査は不十分であり，裁判官でさえも性差による偏見を示すことがあると言われている。したがって，下級審のみならず，上級審でも判決が出るまでに時間がかかりすぎるとの不満が出されてきた。ここでは，女性問題についてのPILを概観したい。

　*Delhi Domestic Working Women's Forum v. Union of India*事件[33]は，ラーンチーからデリーに向かう列車の中で，6人の家事手伝女性が7人の軍人に理不尽な性的暴行を受けたという事件に対するPILである。最高裁は，レイプ被害者を支援するという観点から，各種の広範なガイドラインを定めた。このガイドラインは，被害者への法的支援，匿名性の保持，補償及び社会復帰などを含むものであった。また，連邦女性委員会に対し，これらの被害者への適切な保護を与えうる計画を作るように命じている。その他の重要な意見としては，*Vishaka v. State of Rajasthan*事件[34]において示されたものがある。この判決の中で最高裁は，職場での女性へのセクシュアル・ハラスメントは，基本的権利であるところのジェンダーの平等と人間の尊厳への権利とを侵害するものであると判示した。インドの現行民事・刑事法体系では，職場でのセクシュアル・ハラスメントに対して十分な保護をなしえない，という事実を踏まえた上で，裁判所は，セクシュアル・ハラスメント防止のために

すべての雇用主が遵守すべき12のガイドラインを設定した。最も重要なこととして，インドのすべての裁判所が基本的権利の内容を解釈するにあたり，国際条約の内容が基本的権利と抵触しない限りにおいて，当該条約に基づき解釈を行わなければならない，としたことが挙げられよう。

　この節の結論を述べる前に，刑事裁判制度でレイプ事件を扱うにあたっての制度上の欠陥を明らかにした事件を概観しておかなければならない。グジャラート州において1人の女性が複数の警察官にレイプされた。彼女は，公衆の面前で裸にされ，トラックの荷台で複数の警官によりレイプされたのである。1人の弁護士がPILを提起した。この事件は，1986年に起きた。最高裁が調査を命じ，504人の証人からの証言が集められた。また，中央調査局は，長期間にわたる調査を実施した。この間，審理は何度も中断した。中央調査局の報告書は，最高裁により任命された調査委員会の報告書にもかかわらず，州政府が犯罪を行った警察官に対して何の処分も行っていなかったことを明らかにした。この事件の審理は，1986年から1993年にかけて行われ，2つの調査委員会が任命された。州政府による調査が先送りにされたことを受けて，1993年，最高裁は，被害者に対して50,000ルピーの補償金の支払を命じた[35]。また，トリプラ州西部のある地域において，アッサム・ライフル連隊の兵士が25人もの少数部族女性をレイプしたことが報じられた。PILに基づいてなされた調査により，これら数人の女性がレイプされていたことが判明した。アッサム・ライフル連隊と州政府は，この犯罪の解明に全力を尽くしたが，州政府の対応が後手にまわったことにより，この事件は長期にわたることとなった[36]。

　女性に対する不正義への司法的対応は，十分でない。裁判所が調査を命じた場合でさえ，長い年月がかかっている。拘禁中のレイプに関する多くの事件では，PILに持ち込んでも成果は上がっていない。最高裁が発した，レイプ裁判やセクシュアル・ハラスメントについての主要なガイドラインは，いまだに学問的な関心のみを持たれているにすぎないのが実情である。

### 4　奴隷的労働

　インドにおいては，人間的隷属の最も悪質な形態としての奴隷的労働制度が今なお存続している。かかる制度の下で，労働者たちは，その主人に対し，主人又はその先祖から受けた債務に基づいて仕え続けるのである。隷属状態には，世代を越えたもの，子どもの隷属，忠義による隷属又は土地割当を通じてのものなどがある。

以前の調査によれば，10の州のみで，26,17,000人もの奴隷的労働者が存在した[37]。これらの労働者のほとんどは，社会の中でも最下層のもの，すなわち不可触民，少数民族（adivasis）又は農業労働者で占められていた。インド政府がこの問題に関して連邦法を制定したのは1976年のことであり，これが1976年奴隷的労働制度（廃止）法である。この法律制定により，少なくとも理論上は，奴隷的労働制度は廃止され，奴隷的労働を行わせることは処罰の対象となった。

奴隷的労働に関するPILの多くは，上記の法律の実施を求めるものである。この問題に関する重要なPILの最初のものが，*Bandhua Mukti Morcha v. Union of India*事件[38]であり，1981年に訴訟が提起され，1983年12月16日に判決が出された。この訴訟は，ハリヤナ州内の砕石場で働いていた数百人もの奴隷的労働者の認定，解放及び社会復帰のために起こされたものである。P.N.バーグワティ判事の法廷意見は，奴隷的労働を経済的困難により強制的に働かされているもの，と定義しており，これは，法律上の定義をさらに拡げたものとなっている。裁判所は，この事件でハリヤナ州に対して21の命令を出している。審理期間中，裁判所は，その命令の実施状況について監督し，いくつもの調査委員会を任命した。残念なことに，多くの命令が実行に移されないまま，何年も放置された。裁判所は，社会復帰に関する計画の実施を獲得するには，その能力に限界のあることを認めざるを得なかった。1992年，裁判所が事件のこれまでの経過を検討したところ，砕石場の労働環境には何ら改善が見られなかったことに衝撃を受けた[39]。この訴訟は，裁判所の命令を実施に移すよう，政府に再度警告することで終結してしまった。

*Neeraja Chaudhary v. State of M.P.*事件[40]は，*Bandhua Mukti Morcha*事件で解放された奴隷的労働者たちが解放後自宅に戻ってから6ヶ月が経過しても社会復帰計画が遂行されていないことを知らせる書簡が最高裁に届いたことに始まる。最高裁は，これら極貧にあえぐ人々の社会復帰にかんする監視委員会を任命するよう命じた。このように当初の*Bandhua Mukti Morcha*事件では，PILの実効性に疑問が持たれたのにもかかわらず，奴隷的労働者の解放をめざして，マディア・プラデーシュ[41]，タミル・トードゥ[42]，ビハール[43]などの諸州で，PILは提起されている。

奴隷的労働者の窮状に焦点をあてた公益訴訟は，奴隷的労働廃止法の実施をある程度は促進したと思われる。しかし，この法律の執行は，奴隷的労働者の認定，解放及び社会復帰に重点を置いている。つまり，これら奴隷的労働者の雇用主を処罰するための試みはなされていないのである。奴隷的労働者の解放は，彼らを単に生

活基盤から切り離すだけでなく，むしろ彼らが労働しているところで十分に働けるような状況にすることによって達成されるものである。政府は，彼らが正当な報酬とより良い生活条件とを享受しうることを保障しなければならない。

## 5　児　童

　児童に関する公益訴訟は，児童に対しての憲法上又は法令上の義務を実施させることを求めたものである[44]。この問題に関する初期のPILは，刑務所に収容されている児童に焦点をあてたものであった。1981年，最高裁は，カンプール拘置所に収容中の児童が性的に虐待されているという情報に注目した[45]。裁判所は，カンプール県判事に拘置所を訪問して報告するよう命じた。報告により，児童を強制的に同性愛の相手とする犯罪行為が行われていることが確認された。裁判所は，児童たちを拘置所から児童施設へ移送することを命じたものの，拘置所の管理者には何ら処分を行わなかった。別のPILでは，デリーのティハール拘置所の非人間的な環境が明らかとなった[46]。また，オリッサの拘置所での児童たちへの性的虐待もPILの対象となった[47]。

　拘置所内の児童にかんするPILで重要なものは，1985年，あるジャーナリストによって提起されたものである。この訴訟は，16歳未満の児童の釈放と，このような境遇にある児童がどれだけ存在するかという情報の開示とを求めるものであった。また，裁判所は，少年裁判所，児童施設，学校などの適切な施設の整備を保障すること，県判事が拘置所を訪れることなどを命ずることをも求めるものであった。しかし，1985年以降多くの命令が発せられたにもかかわらず，それらは長い間実施されることはなかった[48]。1986年，少年裁判法の成立を受け，裁判所はこの法律の実施へと姿勢を変化させた。ところが，度重なる休廷と裁判所の命令の不遵守とに失望した訴訟提起者は，訴訟に消極的となり，取り下げようとした[49]。そこで，最高裁法律扶助委員会がこの訴訟を引き継いだのである。最終命令は1989年に出され，その中で最高裁は，少年裁判所，児童施設及び学校を設置する必要性を強調した。少年裁判法の実効性を高めるための計画案をまとめるために，弁護士により構成される委員会が任命された。この事件におけるPILは，現在，未成年の収監者が全く存在しないという成果を残したのである[50]。

　児童労働の問題についても概観してみたい。1980年代，タミル・ナードゥ州シヴァカーシの花火工場とマッチ工場及びウッタル・プラデーシュ州ミルザプールのカー

ペット産業における，児童への搾取の状況が多数報道されたことにより，児童労働にかんするPILが提起されはじめた。このような調査報道は，PILと相まって，1986年児童労働（禁止及び制限）法への制定とつながった。この法律は，危険な産業での児童の雇用を禁じるものである。

　PILの提起に基づき，最高裁は，ウッタル・プラデーシュ州におけるカーペット産業での児童労働に関する調査委員会を任命した。その報告書は，児童が労働する場では事故が起こる確率の高いことを明らかにした。そこで，地方自治体の手をかり，これらの児童の解放がなされたのである[51]。1986年，有名なPILが最高裁に対して起こされた。この訴訟は，タミル・ナードゥ州シヴァカーシのマッチ工場で数千人の児童が働かされているということについてのものであった[52]。これらの児童は，マッチ及び花火の製造過程において頻繁に起こる致命的な事故の危険に日々さらされていたのである。裁判所は，州政府に対し，工場法の適用及び児童が就業時間中に利用できる娯楽，医療及び食事施設並びに教育施設の設置を命じた。また，裁判所は，成人・児童を問わず，危険な産業に従事している者に対して強制保険事業を設けるという意見をも採用した。この事業は，すべての被用者に対して50,000ルピーの保険金支払いを保証するものである。これらの命令の実施状況を監督するための委員会が任命された。しかし，驚くべきことに，1986年児童労働（禁止及び規制）法がマッチ製造業における児童の雇用を禁止しているにもかかわらず，裁判所は，「若年労働者の柔軟な手先は，この業務を行うのに適している」との理由から，包装作業に児童が従事することを認めたのである。この事件で裁判所は，マッチの製造と包装とは不可分の作業であるということを認識していなかった。この意味で，裁判所の児童労働に関する対応は，表面的なものでしかなかった。

　1996年に出された最も新しい判決で，最高裁は，マッチ工場で違法に児童を雇用していた者に対し，20,000ルピーを支払わせ，これを児童労働者社会復帰及び福祉基金に委託した[53]。違法に雇用された児童は，雇用主の負担で教育を受けられるようになった。これは，幸福な改善点といえよう。

　上述の通り，刑務所（拘置所）に係わるPILについては，目ざましい成果を挙げてきたことが分かる。しかし，児童労働に関するPILについては，不満の残る結果となっている。いくつかの国は，児童労働によって生産された物品の購入を今なお拒否している。児童の権利についての国際条約への言及は頻繁になされている。しかし，この問題の真の解決は，児童を労働から切り離し，補償金を支払うことによっ

てではなく，大規模な開発計画，とくに灌漑事業によって土地を保有している親の側の経済的状況を改善し，これに基づいて児童を搾取的労働の場から抜け出させることによって達せられるだろう。児童労働の問題は，これが資本主義の発達と国際的関係とに結びつく現状にあっては，司法積極主義のみによって解決できるものではない。また，データが全く存在しないことが，児童の雇用主の訴追を困難にしている。

## 5 連邦人権委員会の役割

### 1 その構成

連邦人権委員会は，外圧もあって，1993年9月23日に公布された大統領令に基づいて設置された。この大統領令は，1994年1月に大統領の認証を得た1993年人権保護法に置き換えられた。連邦人権委員会委員の任命は，首相を委員長とし，下院議長，内務大臣，上下両院それぞれの野党指導者，上院副議長からなる委員会の助言に基づいてなされる[54]。連邦人権委員会は，最高裁長官であった者をその委員長とし，委員には，最高裁判事又は以前最高裁判事であった者の中から1名，高裁長官又は以前高裁長官であった者の中から1名，人権に関して学識のある者又は実務経験がある者の中から2名選出する。上記の者に加えて，連邦マイノリティ委員会委員長，連邦指定カースト及び指定部族委員会委員長，連邦女性委員会委員長が職務上その委員となる[55]。委員は，最高裁の調査に基づいて不正行為又は不適格が立証されたときにのみ，大統領により解任される[56]。

### 2 その職務，権限及び手続き

委員会の職務は，人権侵害についての申立てを調査することである。また，人権侵害申立ての司法手続きへの関与，公共施設への訪問，人権についての研究の促進，人権意識の普及，社会における積極主義の強化，並びに現行人権関係法律の見直し及びこれら法律の実効措置のための提言などもその職務である[57]。委員会は，人権保護法に基づく申立てに関する審問に際して，民事裁判所と同等の権限を持つ[58]。また，委員会は，調査権限を持つとともに，政府調査機関を利用することもできる[59]。

人権侵害の申立てを審問するにあたり，委員会は，関連する政府機関又はその他の機関に対して情報提供又は報告を要求することができ，当該問題について政府が

とった措置によって審問を終了させることもできる。関係政府機関から報告がない場合には，委員会自身が調査を行うことができる[60]。

人権保護法に基づく調査終了の後，委員会は，以下の措置をとることができる[61]。
ⅰ）被疑者である公務員の訴追を勧告
ⅱ）最高裁若しくは高裁に適切な命令を出すよう請求，又は
ⅲ）被害者若しくはその家族に対して暫定的補償を行うよう勧告

委員会が法的拘束力のある決定を下すことができないことは，明らかである。委員会は，最高裁，高裁又は関係政府機関に依存せざるをえない。その勧告は，法的効力を持たない。委員会は，個人又は人権団体から数千もの申立てを受理しており，その多数について関係政府機関からの情報提供又は報告を要求している。多くの場合，いわゆる「郵便局手続き」，すなわち政府機関に人権侵害事件についての調査を求め，措置に関する報告を要求するという手続きを踏んでいる。場合によっては，中央調査局に調査及び報告を求めている。委員会自身が持つ調査権を行使することはほとんどない。

## 3　その実績

1995年から1996年度版の連邦人権委員会年次報告書の内容を分析することによって，人権保護についての連邦人権委員会の有効性が明らかになると思われる。

(1) テロリズム及び暴動

ジャンムー・カシュミール州，北東諸州及びパンジャーブ州など，テロリズムや暴動が頻発している地域の訪問に関しては，委員会の役割は限られたものであった。委員会は，パンジャーブ警察の関与したJ.S. Khalra失踪事件についての調査を行った中央調査局とは「緊密な連携」をとった。また，軍による拘束中の死亡事件に関する報道がなされ，委員会は，この報道に基づいて国防省に通告し，その結果裁判所による調査が命じられた[62]。

(2) 拘禁中の死亡，レイプ及び拷問

委員会は，すべての県治安判事又は警察署長に，拘禁中のいかなる死亡事件又はレイプ事件についても委員会に報告することを要請した。これは，歓迎すべき措置ではあるが，法的拘束力を持つものではない。利用しうるデータを援用しつつ，委員会は拘禁中の死亡事件が増加していることを指摘している。委員会は，インドが1984年拷問等禁止条約に加入すべきであると勧告している。政府がこの勧告を受け

入れる姿勢を持つようには見えない。また，委員会は，拘禁中のすべての死亡者に暫定的補償金を支払うことを勧告している。さらに，委員会は，証拠法及び刑事訴訟法の改正も主張している[63]。

(3) 制度的改革：警察，監獄及びその他の拘留施設

報告は，警察の政治的介入からの完全独立を提言した1979年の警察改革委員会報告の実施に賛成している。人権委員会が全国のさまざまの拘置所を訪問したところ，収容人数の大幅超過，劣悪な環境及び不適切な管理運営などが明るみに出たので，1984年インド監獄法の改正を提言した。少年向け施設の状況も同様に改善を要すべき状態にあることが明らかとなった[64]。

## 4 不服申立ての扱い：代表的な事件

報告書には，連邦人権委員会が扱った代表的な事件が報告されている。連邦人権委員会の職務は，表1から把握することができよう。

連邦人権委員会が扱った上記の事件を概観してみると，多くの事件が，いわゆる「郵便局手続き」，すなわち，通告を発し，報告を求め，補償又は容疑者の処分を勧告するという手続きを踏んでいることが判明する。報告書によれば，委員会が自らの調査権を行使することはほとんどない。ある事件では，チャクマ難民の問題について最高裁に移送している。チャクマ難民は，バングラデシュから流入してアルナーチャル・プラデーシュ州に定住した人々であり，彼らは武装グループからの攻撃によって生命の危険にされされていた。最高裁は，州政府に対して，これら難民の生命と自由を保護するよう命じた[65]。1999年4月，連邦人権委員会は，ラージャスターン州政府に対して，誘拐された児童が警察の救出活動中に死亡した事件について，両親に2,50,000ルピーの補償金を支払うよう勧告している[66]。

1999年6月，カシュミール峡谷から退去させられた人々が，警備隊による暴行はカシュミール人の長老を排除するためのものだと申立て，受理された。連邦人権委員会は，中央政府に対し，カシュミール地方からの移住者支援策を強化するよう勧告した[67]。

このように，全体的にみると委員会の活動は，法的な意味のない提言や勧告のレベルにとどまっている，と言うことができる。

## 表1 連邦人権委員会が扱った代表的な事件

| | 場　　所 | 事　　件 | 経　　過 |
|---|---|---|---|
| 1 | 1994年<br>南ゴア | 拘禁中の死亡（県治安判事により報告） | 委員会は、情報提供と報告を要求。州政府は、警察官の訴追を決定。 |
| 2 | 1994年<br>ウッタル・プラデーシュ州 | 拘禁中の死亡（アムネスティ・インターナショナルによる報告） | 委員会は、報告を要求。州政府からの報告に基づき、警察官の訴追を勧告。 |
| 3 | 1986—1991年<br>ビハール州 | 拘禁中の死亡（州政府からの報告） | 委員会は事件の起こった都市に調査チームを送り、犯罪を犯した警察官の訴追を勧告。 |
| 4 | 1994年<br>ナガランド州 | 拘禁中の死亡（警察官からの報告） | 委員会の関与により、国防省から被害者の遺族に補償金（1,00,000ルピー）が支払われた。 |
| 5 | 1994年<br>タミル・ナードゥ州 | 拘禁中のレイプ（県長官からの報告） | 州政府は、加害警察官を訴追し、被害者に1,00,000ルピーの補償金を支払う意思のあることを報告。 |
| 6 | 1994年<br>マディヤ・プラデーシュ州 | レイプ（Sakshian, NGOからの報告） | 委員会は、官房長に何らかの処分を要請。その結果、容疑者を訴追。 |
| 7 | 1994年<br>ラージャスターン州 | レイプ（被害者からの通報） | 委員会は、州首相に書簡を送り、第一審で釈放された容疑者について控訴するよう要請。 |
| 8 | マハーラーシュトラ州 | 少女に対する性的虐待（人権団体からの報告） | 人権委員会の職員が現地を訪問。委員会の関与によりレイプ及び虐待の事件でそれぞれの容疑者が告発された。 |
| 9 | ケーララ州 | 警察官による少女の虐待（被害者からの通報） | 委員会の関与により、被害者に補償金が支払われ、警察官は停職処分となった。 |
| 10 | 1995年<br>カルナータカ州 | 警察官の高圧的な態度（野党指導者からの通告） | 委員会の調査チームが当該地域を訪問。州政府は処分を約束。 |
| 11 | 1995年<br>西ベンガル州 | 警察官による虐待（被害者からの通報） | 委員会は、調査を勧告。調査の結果警察官の犯罪行為が明らかとなったため、委員会は彼らの処分を勧告。 |
| 12 | 1993年<br>パンジャーブ州 | 警察官による殺人（人権団体からの報告） | 委員会は、警察官を無実であるとする州政府報告書に憂慮の念を示す。 |

| 13 | 1995年<br>ビハール州 | 警察の発砲による活動家の死亡（被害者側からの通報） | 委員会は，迅速な調査及び被害者の遺族への補償金の支払いを勧告。 |
|---|---|---|---|
| 14 | 1994—1995年<br>アルナーチャル・プラデーシュ州 | チャクマ難民に対する権利侵害（NGOからの通報） | 委員会は，州政府に命令を出したものの，実効性はなかった。そこで最高裁から州政府に命令が出された。 |
| 15 | 1994—1995年<br>マニプル州 | 警備隊によるクキ難民の拷問及び殺害（NGOによる通報） | 委員会は，ナガ族とクキ族との間の紛争を早急に解決するよう勧告。 |
| 16 | 1995年<br>ハリヤーナ州 | 爆竹の暴発による死亡（被害者側からの通報） | 委員会は，州政府に報告を求め，被害者の遺族への補償を勧告。 |
| 17 | 1994年<br>パンジャーブ州 | 警察による拉致（被害者の父親からの通報） | 委員会の調査に基づき警察官への処分を実施。 |
| 18 | 1994年<br>ビハール州 | 対抗射撃による死亡（被害者の妻からの通報） | 委員会の調査に基づき警察官への処分を実施。妻への1,00,000ルピーの補償を勧告。 |
| 19 | 1993年<br>グジャラート州 | 宗派間抗争による死亡（関係者からの通報） | 委員会の調査に基づき州政府からバーブリ・マスジット破壊を契機とする宗派間抗争による死亡者の相続人に2,00,000ルピーの補償金が支払われた。 |
| 20 | 1995年<br>オリッサ州 | 終身刑の囚人への差別的処遇（被害者の妻からの通報） | 委員会の調査に基づきオリッサ州政府は，減刑を行った。 |

# 6　まとめ

　連邦人権委員会の存在は，少なくとも人権侵害の事実を明らかにし，人間の尊厳的価値にかんする公共の意識を高めることに役立ってきた。また，マスメディア，人権セミナー，並びに警察，準軍事組織及び軍人に対する人権教育又は一般教育を通じての人権教育などによって，人権擁護文化を広めるために積極的に活動している。さらには，関係政府機関の人権への関心を呼び起こし，人権侵害者の責任を追及せしめる。

PILは，20年前には確かに驚異的な成果を残した。悲惨な奴隷的労働者，拷問を受けた被疑者及び女性収監者，女性保護施設で虐待された収容者，盲目にされた収監者，搾取された児童並びにその他の多くの人々が司法の介入によって自由になった。しかし，自由になった後，彼らがどうなったのかはほとんど知られていない。
　PILの最大の貢献は，貧しい人々の人権に対する政府の責任を高めたことである。裁判官の活動だけでは，政府の違法行為に有効に対処することは出来ないが，政治権力が人権に敏感になるという文化を創出することは可能なのである。支配層によって民衆の権利が侵害されるとき，PILは，その権利を擁護するための闘いの手段となる。インドの法制度の中でPILが得た正当性は，前例のないものである。PIL積極主義は，権力の正当性を問い，裁判所を民衆のためのものとした。人権が司法の努力によっては十分に保護されないとしても，裁判所は人権のための闘争の場として残るであろう。
　政治的関与とその実績との間のギャップが，正義を達成するために裁判官が長期にわたって関与しつづけなければならない結果を導いた。1980年代初期，PILは，裁判所にアクセスできない人々が，司法に容易にアクセスできるようにするための手段として理解されていた。今日，PILは，インド社会のあらゆる病理を解決するために用いられている。司法の能力を超えたこれらの関与の結果，あらゆる種類の不安，悲惨あるいは不公正な状況からの救済を司法に求める人々が大量にあふれた。日の目を見るありとあらゆるものが，今や司法の関与の対象となった。不衛生な構造物，廃棄物，環境破壊，文化的伝統の保存，政治腐敗，疾病，失業，居住，教育政策及び麻薬政策の失敗，並びにその他の多数の「公益」問題が救済申立ての対象とされた。今日PILで扱われる問題は，虐げられた人々のそれよりは，中間階層の人々の利益に焦点があてられてきたように思われるのである。コーラン禁止令の要求[68]，テレビの連続シリーズの放映[69]，消費者保護法の施行[70]，汚職大臣の罷免[71]，石油ポンプ[72]や官舎[73]の不正な割当の無効確認，海外送金に関連して賄賂やリベートを受け取った政治家や官僚の訴追[74]，下級裁判所職員の労働条件改善[75]，知事の解任[76]，あるいは大学教員選任の無効確認[77]などは，いずれも中間層の利益を守るための厚かましい例であろう。典型的なPILは，いずれもエリートによって始められており，彼ら自身の選好や優先順位が影響している。それぞれの社会活動団体は，異なった目標やイデオロギーを持っている。これらの団体の多くは，被害を被っている特定の集団と永続的に関係を持ちつづけているわけではない。新聞で報道された事件につ

いてのPILなどは，一過性のものということができる。PILをすべての公益問題にかんして濫用することは，抑圧された階層に代わって救済を求めるものという本来の姿を失わせることになると考える。

　また，別の困った傾向も出ている。搾取され，あるいは不利益を受けているグループのためのいくつかのPILは，何年もわたって結論の出ないままである。PILの処理が極端に遅れた場合には，たとえ進歩的な判決であっても単なる学問的な関心をひくものにしかならない。さらに，司法判断が故意に無視されるという問題が存在する。驚くべきことに，裁判所は，自らの命令を怠った者に対して侮辱処罰権を行使して処罰することには消極的なのである。裁判所の命令が頻繁に無視され続けることは，裁判所に対する信頼を失わしめる。PILは，インドで存在し続け，容易になくなることはないだろう。しかしながら，いくつかのPILの成功も，これからPILが人権保障の有効な手段であり続けることを保障するものではない。PILの将来は，これを誰が，誰のために用いるのかにかかっている。

(1) Upendra Baxi, "Taking Suffering Seriously: Social Action Litigation in the Supreme Court of India" in Baxi (ed.), *Law and Poverty*, 387-415 at 389 (1988).
(2) *A.D.M. Jabalpur v. Shivkant Shukla* AIR 1976 SC 1207.
(3) AIR 1979 SC 1360. この事件が最終的に処理されたのは，1995年8月であった。
(4) AIR 1982 SC 1008.
(5) *Kadra Pahadia v. State of Bihar* AIR 1981 SC 939.
(6) (1995) 3 SCC 743, 750.
(7) 1981 (Supp.) SCC 87, 210.
(8) *Upendra Baxi v. State of Uttar Pradesh* 1981 (3) SCALE 1136.
(9) 1986 (Supp.) SCC 576.
(10) AIR 1990 SC 752.
(11) *Veena Sethi v. State of Bihar* (1982) SCC 583.
(12) *Parmanand Katara v. Union of India* AIR 1989 SC 2039.
(13) *Sheela Barse v. State of Maharashtra* AIR 1983 SC 378.
(14) *PUCL v. Ministry of Home Affairs* AIR 1985 Delhi 268. しかし，*R. Gandhi v. Union of India*事件において，マドラス高裁は，1984年のインディラ・ガンディー女史暗殺後の暴動の中でシク教徒コミュニティに対する人権侵害があったとして，補償金の支払いを命じている。AIR 1989 Madras 205.
(15) AIR 1989 SC 1452.
(16) *Delhi Judicial Service Association, Tis Hazari Court Delhi v. State of Gujarat* AIR 1991 SC 2176.

⒄　*PUDR v. Commissioner of Police, Delhi* 1989 (1) SCALE 114 [599].
⒅　*Saheli v. Commissioner of Police, Delhi* AIR 1990 SC 513.
⒆　*Geeta v. Lt. Governor, Delhi* 1998 Delhi Law Times 822.
⒇　AIR 1993 SC 1961.暫定的に金銭による救済を実施するという考えは，以下に挙げる判決で既に示されていた。*Rudol Shah v. State of Bihar* AIR 1983 SC 1086; *Sebastian M. Hongary v. Union of India* AIR 1984 SC 571; *Bhim Singh v. State of J&K* AIR 1986 SC 494.
(21)　(1997) 1 SCC 416.
(22)　*Punjab and Haryana High Court Bar Association, Chandigarh v. State of Punjab* (1994) 1 *SCC* 616, 及び (1996) 4 *SCC* 742.
(23)　*Navkiran Singh v. State of Punjab* (1995) 4 SCC 591.
(24)　(1996) 7 SCC 20.
(25)　*Id*. at 26.
(26)　(1996) 8 SCALE SP6.
(27)　1993年人権保護法第36条2項によれば，連邦人権委員会は，人権侵害を構成する行為が行われた時から1年を超えて申立てがなされたいかなる事項についても審問することはできない。
(28)　(1998) 5 SCALE 219.
(29)　*Ranjit Kumar v. Secretary of Home Affairs, Punjab* (1996) 2 SCALE 51.
(30)　*State of J&K v. J&K High Court Bar Association* 1994 (Supp) 3 SCC 708.
(31)　*Sudip Majumdar v. State of M.P.* (1996) 5 SCC 368.
(32)　*PUCL v. Union of India* 1996 (3) SCALE 5.
(33)　(1995) I SCC 14.
(34)　(1997) 6 SCC 241, この原則は*Apparel Export Promotion Council v. A.K. Chopra*事件においても示された。AIR 1999 SC 634.
(35)　*P. Rathinam v. Union of India* 1987 (2) SCALE 317, 1993 (2) SCALE 126.
(36)　*All India Democratic Women's Association v. State of Tripura* W.P. (C) No. 385 of 1988, W.P. (Cr.) No. 366 of 1988 (Unreported).
(37)　M. Sharma "Bonded Labour in India: A National Survey on the Incidence of Bonded Labour, Final Report 1981" *Academy of Gandhian Studies*, Hyderabad, 1981.
(38)　(1984) 4 SCC 161.
(39)　*Bandhua Mukti Morcha v. Union of India* AIR 1992 SC 38.
(40)　AIR 1984 SC 1099.
(41)　*Mukesh Advani v. State of M.P.* AIR 1985 SC 1363.
(42)　*H.P. Sivaswamy v. State of Tamil Nadu* 1983 (2) SCALE 45.
(43)　*T. Chakkalackal v. State of Bihar* JT 1992 (1) SC 106.
(44)　憲法第15条3項，第24条，第39条(e)号及び(f)号，並びに第45条，1986年少年裁判

法，1986年児童労働（禁止及び制限）法。
(45) *Munna v. State of UP* (1982) 1 SCC 545.
(46) *Sanjay Suri v. Delhi Administration* 1987 (2) SCALE 276.
(47) *M.C. Mehta v. State of Orissa* W.P. (Cr.) 1504 of 1984 (Unreported).
(48) *Sheela Barse v. Union of India* AIR 1986 SC 1773.
(49) *Sheela Barse v. Union of India* AIR 1988 SC 2211.
(50) *SCLAC v. Union of India* (1989) 2 SCC 325. 1989年3月17日，裁判所は改めて各県判事に対し，拘置所における未成年の現状，児童施設，特別施設及び保護観察施設の設置状況について報告するよう命じた。*SCLAC v. Union of India* (1989) 4 SCC 738において裁判所は，連邦直轄領であるアンダマン及びニコバル諸島を除いて児童を拘置所に収容している州は存在していなことに満足の意を表した。
(51) *Bandhua Mukti Morcha v. Union of India* 1986 (Supp) SCC 553.
(52) *M.C. Mehta v. State of Tamil Nadu* AIR 1991 SC 417.
(53) *M.C. Mehta v. State of Tamil Nadu* 1996 (1) SCALE 42.
(54) 1993年人権保護法第4条
(55) 同第2条
(56) 同第5条
(57) 同第12条
(58) 同第13条
(59) 同第14条
(60) 同第17条
(61) 同第18条
(62) National Human Rights Commission: Annual Report 1995-1996; para 3.1-3.13.
(63) 同paras 3.14-3.22.
(64) 同paras 3.23-3.38.
(65) *National Human Rights Commission v. State of Arunachal Pradesh* (1996) 1 SCC 742.
(66) *The Hindustan Times*, Delhi, April 25, 1999.
(67) *The Hindustan Times*, Delhi, June 12 and 14, 1999.
(68) *Chandanmal Chopra v. State of West Bengal* AIR 1986 Cal. 104.
(69) *Odgssey Communications (P) Ltd. v. Lokvidagan Sangathan* (1988) 3 SCC 410.
(70) *Common Cause v. Union of India* (1996) 2 SCC 752.
(71) *D. Satyanarayana v. N.T. Rama Rao* AIR 1988 A.P. 144.
(72) *Centre for Public Interest Litigation v. Union of India* 1995 (Supp) 3 SCC 382.
(73) *Shiv Sagar Tiwari v. Union of India* (1996) 6 SCC 558.

(74)　*Vineet Narain v. Union of India* (1996) 2 SCC 199.
(75)　*All India Judges Association v. Union of India* AIR 1992 SC 165.
(76)　*Kasturi Radha v. President of India* AIR 1990 Mad. 116.
(77)　*Bishwajeet Sinha v. Dibrugarh University* AIR 1991 Gau 27.

　（邦訳にあたって、浅野宜之氏（聖母女学院短大）に大変お世話になった。ここに記して感謝したい。）

# 台湾の民主化における司法創造的立憲主義
―― 大法官会議の役割と個人の権利の保障 ――

黄　昭　元

安　西　文　雄訳

## I　序

　1987年7月,台湾[1]で38年続いた軍政が終了した。それは1980年代初頭以来続いている台湾の自由化の過程において画期的なことがらであった。さらに4年後の1991年5月には,台湾政府は正式に「動員および共産主義的反抗の抑圧の時代」が終了したとし,真の民主化に向けた一連の政治的改革を開始した。この民主化の中心にはさまざまな憲法改革があり,これが1996年3月に行なわれた初の総統直接民主選挙につながるのである[2]。

　真正な立憲主義が開花するためには民主主義が必要である。台湾においてもそうである。台湾がリベラルな民主主義へと移行するにつれて,台湾の司法部も積極化したのであるが,それは特に個人の人権が問題にされる事案において顕著である[3]。もちろん憲法の要請を実現することは,国家の三権が共通に負担することである。しかし司法審査の権限を付与された司法部こそが,市民の憲法上の権利の侵害に対し,救済を与える究極的な存在である。これと並んで重要なことは,実用的な理論（ルールや原則,概念など）をつくりだして,憲法の抽象的な規範を個々の事案にあてはめてゆくという司法部の能力・機能である[4]。この観点からすれば,裁判官がいつ,何を,いかに語るか,ということによって,ある程度,現実生活における立憲主義の意味が規定される。本稿においては,第一に憲法上の権利を実施する大法官会議の役割を検討し,次いでその限界を考察したい。

## II　台湾憲法における大法官会議の位置づけおよび機能[5]

### 1　位置づけ

　大法官会議は,台湾における憲法裁判所の機能を果たすものであり,合憲性審査の権限を持つ唯一の機関である。大法官会議が持ついくつかの権能のうちに,憲法上の争訟の裁決が含まれる[6]。大法官会議は1984年に創設されて以来,司法行政を統

括する司法院のもとに位置づけられている[7]。しかしながら，司法院は大法官会議の権限に正式に介入することはできない。

### 2　組　織

現在，大法官会議は国民大会の同意を経て総統が任命する17名の大法官によって構成される。各大法官の任期は9年であるが，再任が可能である。しかし，2003年から大法官の数は15名に減少し，任期8年で再任はなくなる予定である[8]。現在のところ各大法官には1名のロー・クラークが付されていて，調査または判決執筆の補助にあたっている。

### 3　資　格

過去20年にわたり，ほとんどの大法官は大学で教育を受けた法律家であり，法学教授，裁判官，検察官および政府の公務員から選ばれている。さらに約半数の大法官は海外の大学，特にドイツの大学で博士学位を取得した大学教授である。

### 4　手　続

大法官は，法廷形式よりも会合形式で職務を行なう。大法官の会合の多くは秘密会であるが，稀に公開の聴聞がなされることがある。公開の聴聞においても大法官はめったに質問を発しない。座って両当事者の議論を聴いているだけである。また当事者間において交互尋問はない。

### 5　判決の形式

大法官会議の判断は「解釈」といわれる。憲法に関する解釈をするためには，構成員の3分の2以上の出席があり，かつ，出席者の少なくとも3分の2の賛成が必要とされている。もっとも，すべての「解釈」——それは多数意見であるが——には大法官全員の署名がなされるものとされているが，各大法官には，同意意見または反対意見を表示することが許される。

## III　憲法上の権利の実施における大法官会議の現実の役割

この章においては，大法官会議の果たした機能を概観し，かつその重要な「解釈」のいくつかを検討する。

## 1 大法官会議の果たした役割の概観

1988年から1999年6月までに，大法官会議は全部で3,311件の訴えを受理し，うち3,209件を処理した。3,209件のうち2,843件は手続上の理由により却下され，「解釈」が下されたのは266件のみである。266件の「解釈」のうち236件の事案が憲法上の権利に関するものである。さらにこの236件の「解釈」のうち114件において，法律，規則，または裁判所の先例が違憲であると判断された。この統計からすれば[9]，大法官会議はとりわけ軍政終了後，憲法上の権利の実施にたいそう積極的であると考えられる[10]。

## 2 大法官会議への申立て権能の拡大

台湾の司法審査は明らかに集中型であるが，この20年間に大法官会議自身，申立て権能を相当に拡充してきた。現行の大法官会議手続法によれば，中央または地方における統治の最高部門，立法院の3分の1の議員，諸個人（法人や政党を含む）が憲法解釈を求めて直接に大法官会議に申立てることができる[11]。1995年1月に大法官会議は「解釈371号」を下したが，それは各裁判官に，係属中の訴訟を停止し，適用法律の合憲性審査を大法官会議に求める権能を付与するものであった[12]。この画期的な「解釈」によって，多くの若く新鮮な感覚を持った裁判官が，軍政下以来の時代遅れな法律や妥当性が疑われる法律を俎上にあげることができるようになった[13]。しかし1988年以来，申立てのうち90パーセント以上は市民によってなされている[14]。こういった現象はある面で，1982年に下された画期的な「解釈177号」によっている。この「解釈」において大法官会議は，民事，刑事，または行政事件上の終局判決であっても，もし事案に適用される法律が違憲と判断されれば再審査されなければならないと判示した。この「解釈」によって，敗訴した当事者は，自らの事案に適用された法律の合憲性を争うべく，常に大法官会議に申立てることができることとなった。いったん大法官会議が法律を違憲と判断すれば，当事者は再審査を受けることができる。現実にこの「解釈177号」によって，ますます多くの市民が，大法官会議にこういった非常救済手段を求めうるようになった。1980年代後半以降，大法官会議の取り扱い件数が急増し，たいていの申立てを市民が提起しているのは，こういった理由による[15]。大法官会議は，自らが下した「解釈177号」および「解釈371号」によって，「憲法秩序の擁護者」から「憲法上の権利の擁護者」へと変貌していったのである[16]。

## 3　人権に関わる事案を扱う際の,司法積極主義への傾斜

　大法官会議は個人の人権をより擁護するものへと徐々に変貌しているが,それは人権に関わる事案において大法官会議が司法積極主義へと傾斜している点でも明らかである。1990年代はじめ,人権に関わる事案における大法官会議の判断は,国家の安全や公共的利益との折り合いをつけるものであることがしばしばであった。例えば,国家安全法やその執行のための諸規則は,市民が海外から台湾に帰国する権利を恣意的に制限するものであったが,大法官会議はこれらを合憲であると判断した[17]。また,この法律には,軍法会議で審査された民間人の被告が軍政終了後通常裁判所に訴える権利を侵害する規定が含まれていたが,それを合憲と判断する「解釈」もある[18]。しかし近年,大法官会議は,財産権や,裁判所に訴える権利(とりわけ公務員が実効的な法的救済を受ける権利),そして身体の安全に関する権利などを侵害する法律を違憲とし,より積極化しているように思われる。最近の「解釈445号」において大法官会議は,「表現の自由は,民主政治の展開のために最も重要な基本的権利であると捉えられるべきである」と判示し,いわゆる政治的性格のある権利(表現,集会,および結社の自由を含む)が他の諸権利よりもより保護に値するとまで判断している。こうして大法官会議は,司法審査の権限を行使することに積極的であるのみならず,いわゆる精神的自由の優越的地位の理論を展開しようともしている[19]。この理論は,民主政治に関わる権利である表現,結社および集会の自由は,財産権など他の諸権利よりもより保護に値するとするものである[20]。

## 4　新しい司法審査基準の導入

　大法官会議が新しい司法審査基準を導入しようとしていると思われることは,興味深い。かつて,大法官会議はある種の二重の基準を適用していると思われたが,その基準はアメリカ合衆国連邦最高裁が用いたものとまったく逆の二重の基準であった。アメリカ合衆国の連邦最高裁は長い間,政治的自由を制約する法律に対しては厳しく合憲性審査をするが,経済的および社会的権利が関わる場合,特に平等保護条項に関わるときには緩やかに審査する,という立場であった。驚くべきことに,かつて台湾の大法官会議は,これとまったく逆のことをしていた。財産権を侵害する法律に対しては厳しく審査するが,市民的・政治的権利の関わる事案においては政治部門の判断により敬譲をはらうものであった[21]。最近になってようやく大法官会議は,先に論じた精神的自由の優越的地位の理論の展開にも対応して,かつ

ての立場を逆転させていると考えられる。

　こういった転換がなされるまでは，しばしば「比例原則」が法律の違憲性を判断する主要な審査基準として用いられた。しばしば大法官会議は，中華民国憲法23条に規定されている「必要な場合を除いて」という要請を[22]，次の3つの目的・手段テストとして定式化したのである。(a)法律が用いる手段は，立法目的の実現のために適切なものでなければならない，(b)法律が用いる手段は，権利を最も制約しないものでなければならない（LRM（least restrictive means）の基準），(c)法律によってもたらされる損失と利益を比較したとき，利益の方が大きいものでなければならない(比較考量のテスト)，というものがこれである。大法官会議が，たいそう批判のあった中華民国憲法23条を，法律の合憲性審査のための正当な基準へと事実上変化せしめたことは疑いない[23]。大法官会議はより正確な審査基準を作り上げようと努力しているのであるが，しかし，大きな難点が2つ指摘される。第一には，大法官会議が，立法目的――それが現実のものであろうと推定上のものであろうと――の正当性の審査においてあまりに緩やかな審査をしているという点であり，第二には，おそらくは政治的配慮によるものであろうと思われるが，さまざまな権利の審査において一貫しない立場をとっていることである。例えば大法官会議は，政治プロセスに関わる権利の「優越的自由の理論」を強調しているようであるが，市民の選挙権，被選挙権を制約する法律に関して，アメリカ合衆国にみられる「合理性テスト」と同じようなたいへん緩やかな基準を適用して合憲と判断している[24]。

## 5　憲法解釈の拘束力の定め方

　近年の司法積極主義の高揚にともない，大法官会議と政治部門（立法部と執行部を含む）との対立は，必然的であると思われる。大法官会議がその「解釈」の効果（判断されたものの拘束力）につき，注意深く複雑なモデルを作っていることは注目に値する[25]。

　確かに，憲法に反する法律や規則はすべて無効であるというのが憲法の要請である[26]。しかし，憲法自身も，いかなる法律も，そのような憲法違反の法律が「いつ」執行されなくなるのかにつき明らかにしていない。1980年，裁判所の発する令状なく警察が市民を拘束する権限を認める法律につき，大法官会議は違憲と判断した[27]。しかし1990年1月，大法官会議が新「解釈」を下し，新たに理由を加えてその法律を違憲と判断するまで[28]，立法院はその法律を改正しなかった。この1970年

の「解釈」は，違憲と判断した法律について，たとえそれが改正されなくとも，1991年7月1日以降効力を持たなくなると明示していた。これ以来，大法官会議は，法律や規則を違憲と判断するとき，しばしばこの「将来効的無効」の手法（すなわち「違憲であるが効力はある」というモデル，つまり違憲の法律は将来のある時点に至ってはじめて無効となると判示すること[29]）を用いるようになっている。

　この「将来効的無効」の手法のほかにも，大法官会議は，政治部門との直接的な対立を回避するさまざまな手法を用いている。大法官会議が問題になっている法律を単に違憲と判断するにとどめて，その効力は否定せず，その法律を改廃するか，するにしてもいつするかを，あげて立法部に委ねることもある（「違憲判断のみ」というモデル）[30]。こういったモデルを用いることによって大法官会議は立法部への敬譲を示すのであるが，それはしばしば個人の権利の実現にとってはマイナスとなる。他方，最近の「解釈477号」において大法官会議は反対の方向に歩みだしている。この「解釈」において大法官会議は法律を違憲と判断し（平等保護条項の判断において「過小包含」であることが理由），従って当該法律は即時に無効であるとした。さらに大法官会議は，当該法律の適用から違憲的に排除された人々は，その法律の改正を待つまでもなく「解釈477号」によって直接的に，平等の権利と法律の適用による利益を主張できると明示的に判断した[31]。この「解釈477号」は，台湾の司法審査の歴史のなかにおいて最も顕著な司法積極主義を体現するものといえる。そしてこの「解釈」は，確かに個人の権利には有利であるが，司法部と立法部との境界を不明確にさせるという危惧を明らかに醸し出したのである。

　これまで論じてきたような複雑なモデルに対しては，多くの批判が寄せられた[32]。比較憲法学の見地からすれば，判断の拘束力に関するさまざまなモデルは，明らかにドイツやオーストリアの憲法裁判所の実務を参酌している。にもかかわらずこういった実務は憲法の至高の原則――憲法に反する法律は無効であるとする原則――から逸脱しているといえる。そしてこの至高の原則からの逸脱は，必然的に成文憲法の至高性を弱めてしまうだろう。また，憲法の擁護者であり，人権の擁護者であるという司法部が担う基本的な責務に対して深刻な疑念を投げかけるものともいえる。過去の実例から明らかにいえることであるが，政治部門に対して配慮すれば人権に対して不利になってしまうことが多い。こういう実務を行なう消極的な司法部は，政治的に緊急の必要性があるため個人の権利を制約するのだという便利な口実をみいだす[33]。この観点からすれば，大法官会議はこれまでの実務を，とり

わけ実効的人権保障の見地から，真剣に見なおす必要に迫られるのかもしれない。

## IV 個人の権利保障における司法審査の限界

　1990年代において，台湾の大法官会議が現実に果たした憲法上の権利実現の役割を検討したが，この章においては，この側面における司法の限界についてさらに考察したい。もちろん私は，既に論じた少数の事例から過度にそして性急に一般化することの危険は十分承知しているつもりである。

### 1　司法部の消極的役割
　裁判所は，その性質からして，誰かが事案を持ち込んでくれるまで，事案について判断することはできない。ある法律や規則の合憲性を誰も問題にしないなら，裁判所がそれを職権で論ずることもできない。従って違憲の法律も司法部がそれを無効とするまで何年も効力を持ち続けうるのである。

### 2　事後的審査
　裁判所は事案の事後的審査をなしうるのみである。すなわち裁判所は被害の発生後にしか救済をなしえない。さらに裁判所の救済は将来志向的であるというより過去志向的である。裁判所が被害が生じないよう予防的な措置を講ずることは，まったく不可能ではないにしても，裁判所のマンパワー，取り扱い事案の負担，および制度的な慣行によって制限される。

### 3　事案特定的な救済
　司法部が行なう救済は，その取り扱う事案にとって特定的なあり方でなされるのであり，一般的な救済ではない。法律とは裁判所がこれが法律だというものだ，という言い方には賛成できるが，裁判所それ自身は，執行部や立法部のような，一般的な政策決定者ではない。さらに判決拘束力の限界からして，裁判所の判決の拘束力は当該事案における当事者，主題に限定される。同様の人権を侵害された他の被害者は，自分の事案を裁判所に申立てて法的救済を求めなければならない。

### 4　積極的権利を司法的に救済する際のジレンマ
　裁判所は，消極的性格を持つ個人の自由を侵害する法律を違憲と判断することに

おいては，うまく機能しているかもしれない。法律を否定し無効と宣言すればよいからである。しかし積極的な権利（例えば社会的・経済的権利）については，政府の無干渉ではなく，広範で将来志向的な観点から行なわれる，財政面を含めた資源再配分を要する。専門的知識の違い，組織や判断形成過程の違いを考慮に入れると，積極的権利の実現に関する判断は，政治部門が行なった方が妥当だと論じられるかもしれない。

### 5　集中型司法審査システムの難点

集中型司法審査システムには，その長所と短所に関しさまざまな見解があるが，台湾の大法官会議のような集中型司法審査システムをとるとき，個人の権利の保護への注意が薄れてしまうという，はっきりした難点を伴うことになる。この難点が明らかに現われるのは，判決が遅れるという点である。憲法裁判所またはそれと同等の組織は，法律や規則の合憲性審査をする唯一の憲法上の機関であり，裁判官の数が限定され事案がますます多くなっていることからして，訴訟当事者のために早期に事案を解決することがたいそう難しい。台湾の実例からいえば，大法官会議の取り扱い事案がますます多くなっていることによって，多くの当事者は「解釈」が出るまでに2～3年待たされるのが現状である。さらに悪いことは，台湾のシステムは当事者に暫定的な救済を与えないのである。また，「通常の救済が尽きたこと」という要請があることも難点である。この手続的要請のため，権利を侵害された犠牲者は，現実の救済を求めて大法官会議に申立てるまで何年も憲法上の権利主張を妨げられるのである[34]。

### 6　保守的な法律家が形成する保守的な裁判所

歴史を通じて，法律家が革命家になることは少ない。現代の多くの国においては，優れた法律家であっても体制側の利益を擁護しがちであり，さらには権力者になったりすることがみられる。人権擁護家であるよりも優れたロビイストである法律家の方がはるかに多い。また法学教育や法学の考え方は，「形式」，「法律適合性」，「現存の法秩序との調和，適合性」などにたいそう注意を払うがゆえに，草の根の人権運動としばしば対立してしまうことは，よく知られている。これは法律家一般の保守的性格なのである。

台湾の場合，支配的政党がこれまで大法官のほとんど全員を任命してきたので，

リベラルといえる大法官がほとんどいないが，それは驚くには値しない。大法官の区分けをするならば，それはリベラルか保守的かによるというより，保守的であることを前提としてその度合いによってなされるのである[35]。

## V 結 論

 古くからの格言によれば，「ピアノの演奏者を撃つな。彼は可能な限りのことをしているのだ。」という。この格言を用いるなら，「光栄ある大法官たちは，可能な限りのことをしているのだろうか」と人々は問うべきである。これは確かに簡単には答えられない問いである。

 ある意味では，司法部門は政府全体の一部門にすぎない。裁判所は憲法上の権利の唯一の擁護者ではないし，またそうであってはならない，ということを我々は銘記すべきである。他にも重要な機関が，例えば人権を実効的なものにする人権委員会などがある[36]。また実際上，警察やその他の法実施機関も重要であり無視できない。司法部門の判断を実行に移すために，とりわけ人権が関わっている場合には，立法部門と執行部門という政府の2つの部門との協力に常に依拠することになる。

 しかしながら，司法部門への評価は，憲法の権威によって付与されるというより，事案ごとに判断を積み重ねによって得られることも銘記すべきである。憲法は適法性を付与するのみであり，司法部門自身が，特に個人の権利が関わる事案で努力することにより，正当性を獲得してゆかねばならない。憲法上の権利の擁護者として司法部門（大法官会議）が成功するか否かは，個々の市民の満足によって判断されるのであって，法的論証のうまさによって判断されるのではない。そして人々こそが，光栄ある大法官たちができる限りのことをしているか否かを判断する主体なのである。

(1) 本稿において「台湾」とは，台湾という国（現在の国名「中華民国（ROC）」）をいう。近年，台湾政府は「台湾のROC」または「ROC（台湾）」という言葉を用い，中国（PRCまたは1949年以前のROC政府）と区別している。

(2) 自由化および民主化という視点から憲法上の変化をより詳細に分析したものとして，次の論文を参照されたい。JAU-YUAN HWANG, CONSTITUTIONAL CHANGE AND POLITICAL TRANSITION IN TWAIAN SINCE 1986: THE ROLE OF LEGAL INSTITUTIONS, unpublished S.J.D. dissertation, Harvard University, pp. 100-120, 154-254 (1995).

(3) Sean Cooney, *Taiwan's Emerging Liberal Democracy and the New Constitu-*

*tional Review*, in VERONICA TAYLOR (ED.), ASIAN LAWS THROUGH AUSTRALIAN EYES, Melbourne: Law Book Co., pp. 163-82 (1997)も参照。
(4) Richard H. Fallon, Jr., *Foreword: Implementing the Constitution*, 111 HARVARD LAW REVIEW 54, 56-57 (1997)参照。
(5) この点についての簡潔な議論として例えば，Jau-Yuan Hwang & Jiunn-rong Yet, *Taiwan*, in CHERYL SAUNDERS & GRAHAM HASSALL (EDS.), ASIA-PACIFIC CONSTITUTINAL YEARBOOK 1995, Carlton, Australia: Center for Comparative Constitutional Studies, University of Melbourne, pp. 279, 297-98, 307-08 (1997); Lawrence Shao-Liang Liu, *Judicial Review and Emerging Constitutionalism: The Uneasy Case for the Republic of China on Taiwan*, 39 AMERICAN JOURNAL OF COMPARATIVE LAW 509, 514-523 (1991); Tay-Sheng Wang, *Chapter 4*: Taiwan, in POH-LING TAN (ED.), ASIAN LEGAL SYSTEMS: LAW, SOCIETY AND PLURALISM IN EAST ASIA, Sydney, Australia: Butterworths, pp. 124-61 (1997)など参照。
(6) 1947年中華民国憲法78条によれば，大法官会議には「統合解釈」を下すことによって法律や規則の間に存する抵触を解決するというもう１つの権能がある。1992年の憲法改正によって大法官会議に３つめの権能が加わった。それは政党について違憲と判断し解散させる権能である。中華民国憲法修正５条４項および５項（1992年，1997年改正）。
(7) 　大法官会議と司法院との憲法上の位置関係については，学界において議論がある。中華民国憲法のもとでは，司法院が最高の終審裁判所であり，憲法，民事，刑事，行政に関するすべての事案を扱いうるのであって，それはアメリカ合衆国連邦最高裁になぞらえられると主張する者もいる。この見解においては，大法官会議と司法院とはそれぞれ別の機関ではなく，憲法上同一の機関であることになる。この問題については，さらに次の論考などを参照されたい。Liu, *supra* note 5, at 514-517; Yueh-Sheng Weng, *A Study on the Evolution of the Functions of the Grand Justices*, 23 NATIONAL TAIWAN UNIVERSITY LAW JOURNAL 25 ,26-28 (1993) (in Chinese).1997年７月，司法院は改革プランを発表したが，それは司法院が真の裁判所へと移行する（2009年以降）ことを提案するものである。JUDICIAL YUAN, CONCLUSIONS, ACTION ITEMS AND IMPLEMENTATION SCHEDULE OF NATIONAL CONFERENCE ON JUDICIAL REFORM, Taipei: Judicial Yuan, p. 6 (1999)参照。
(8) 　司法院の院長も副院長も大法官の中から選ばれるのであって，1947年以来行なわれていたように政治的に任命されるのではない。しかし，司法院の院長または副院長である大法官は，８年の任期を保障されない。中華民国憲法修正５条１項および２項(1947年，1997年改正)。2000年４月に国民大会は再度，憲法改正を行ない同意権を立法院に与えた。従って現行規定が効力を失う2003年以降，大法官はすべて，総統が指名し立法院によって承認されることとなる。中華民国憲法修正５条１項（1947年，2000年改正）。
(9) 　大法官会議が近年抱えている事案の統計については，司法院のウェブサイト

⑽　1948年以降，1987年7月の軍政終了以前に下された216件の「解釈」のうち，法律や規則，あるいは裁判所の先例を，明示的または黙示的に違憲と判断したものは8件しかなかった。「解釈」の86号，166号，177号，185号，187号，201号，210号，213号参照。

⑾　大法官会議手続法5節（1958年，1993年修正）。

⑿　「解釈371号」に関する簡潔な検討として，Sean Cooney, *supra* note 3, at 172-73 も参照。

⒀　例えば地方裁判所の裁判官が，大法官会議に対して，死刑の合憲性（「解釈476号」や裁判所の令状なくして検察官が被告人を拘束する権限を持つことの合憲性（「解釈392号」）を審査するよう申立てた。大法官会議は「解釈476号」において死刑の合憲性を肯定したが，「解釈392号」においては検察官が被告人を拘束する前述の権限につき違憲と判断した。

⒁　1988年から1997年まで，申立ての95.48パーセントは個人によってなされている。JUDICIAL YUAN (ED.), ANNUAL REPORT OF JUDICIAL PRACTICE: CASE ANALYSIS, Taipei: Judicial Yuan, p. 69 (1998)参照。

⒂　「解釈177号」が下される前，個人の申立てにもとづいて下された「解釈」は1件しかなかった。

⒃　多くの国の実例によって示されるように，集中型司法審査システムをとる憲法裁判所は，通常，抽象的意味における憲法秩序の調和・一貫性を維持することに熱心であるのに対し，アメリカ合衆国にみられるような非集中型司法審査システムにおいては，個人の権利の保障により熱心である。司法審査システムの一般的な比較法研究としては，MAURO CAPPELLETTI, JUDICIAL REVIEW IN THE CONTEMPORARY WORLD (1971)などを参照。

⒄　1990年10月5日「解釈265号」。

⒅　1991年1月18日「解釈272号」。

⒆　Yueh-Sheng Weng, *Characters and Prospect of Constitutional Review in Taiwan*, in JUDICIAL YUAN, ESSAYS IN CELEBRATION OF THE FIFTY ANNIVERSARY OF CONSTITUTIONAL REVIEW BY THE GRAND JUSTICE OF THE JUDICIAL YUAN, Taipei: Judicial Yuan, pp. 285, 317 (1998) (in Chinese)も参照。この論文においてWeng氏（前大法官であり，現司法院長）は，アメリカ合衆国連邦最高裁のストーン判事が1938年のカロリーヌ判決（United States v. Carolene Products Company (304 U. S. 144)）に付した有名な脚注(4)に依拠しているように思われる。

⒇　光の側面があると同時に，影の側面もある。影の側面として死刑の問題がある。1985年以来大法官会議は死刑の合憲性を肯定している。1回目は1985年3月22日に下された「解釈194号」であり，次いで1990年7月19日に下された「解釈263号」である。最近のものでは，1999年2月の「解釈476号」においても大法官会議は死刑の

合憲性を肯定している。こういった判断は，台湾の人権運動にとって大きな打撃であると考える人が多い。

(21) Chih-ping Fa, *Standards of Review for Property Rights and Other Rights under the Constitution*, 23 CHENG-CHIH UNIVERSITY LAW REVIEW (1981), reprinted in FA, SELECTED ESSAYS ON CONSTITUTIONAL LAW, Taipei: Cheng-Chih University, pp. 227, 264 (1985) (in Chinese)を参照。

(22) 中華民国憲法23条によれば，憲法上列挙された自由および権利は，他の人々の自由に対する侵害を予防するため，差し迫った危機を回避するため，社会秩序を維持するため，公共の福祉を促進するため，に必要である場合を除いては制約されない，とされている(傍点筆者)。この条項が個人の権利に対する一般的制約根拠の主要なものとされている。

(23) 大法官会議がドイツ連邦憲法裁判所から比例原則を導入していることは明らかである。また台湾の法制度全体に大陸法的伝統があることも反映されている。にもかかわらず，近時，大法官会議はアメリカ合衆国憲法上の理論，概念さらには審査基準を導入するようになっている。例えば表現の自由が関わった最近の「解釈」において，大法官会議は明示的にアメリカ合衆国の憲法判例に言及し，「明白かつ現在の危険」(「解釈445号」)，ミラー判決において採用された，猥褻に関する「現在のコミュニティの基準」(「解釈407号」)，「営利的表現は相対的に価値の低い表現であること」(「解釈414号」)などの概念や理論を，判決理由において用いている。

(24) 1992年1月24日の「解釈290号」および1998年10月22日の「解釈468号」。

(25) 1982年から1985年の間に下された「解釈」である177号，183号，185号，188号，193号を参照。

(26) 中華民国憲法171条，172条 (1947年)。

(27) 1980年11月7日の「解釈166号」。

(28) 1990年1月19日の「解釈251号」。

(29) 将来効的無効の技法を用いた最初の「解釈」は，1987年8月14日の「解釈218号」(違憲と判断した命令は6ヵ月後に効力を失うと判断)であり，これに続くのが1988年4月24日の「解釈224号」(2年後に法律が無効となると判断)である。

(30) 例えば，「解釈」410号，455号，457号，485号などを参照。ドイツにおいてこのタイプの判断手法は，*Unvereinbarkeitserklaerung*, *Verfassungswidrigkeitserklaerung*, *blosse Verfassungswidrigerklaerung*などといわれる。

(31) 1999年2月12日の「解釈477号」。

(32) 将来効的無効や違憲性宣言判決については，その正当性を問題にするのみならず，こういった「解釈」の理由づけや猶予期間が，あまりに単純あるいは恣意的であるなどの批判をする論者が多い。例えば，Jau-Yuan Hwang, *On "Unconstitutional But Still Valid" Model of Interpretations by the Grand Justices*, 12 TAIWAN LAW REVIEW 31-39 (April 1996) (in Chinese)など参照。

(33) 例えば大法官会議が，法律について違憲ではあるがなおしばらくの間，有効であ

ると判断すれば，憲法判断を求めた当事者は，自らの事案について直ちに再審査を受ける権利を奪われる。こういった理由によって，このような実務は市民が申立てをするインセンティヴをたいそう減少させてしまう。しかし最近，大法官会議手続法を改正するため司法院が提示した法案によれば，違憲な法律が現実に無効とされる以前に，このような当事者に再審査を受ける権利を保障しようと企図されている。

(34) 台湾においては「解釈371号」は，このような難点をある程度緩和している。注(11)～(12)に対応する本文参照。

(35) このことをよく示しているのは，次のことである。大法官会議は3つの「解釈」（194号，263号，476号）において死刑の合憲性を肯定した。しかも多くの人々が落胆したことには，これら3つの「解釈」において反対意見は1つもなかった。大法官のなかではYueh-Sheng Weng氏（現司法院長）のみ，後に講演においてこの問題につき個人的に後悔の念を表明し再考している。Weng, *supra* note 7, at 48参照。

(36) これまで台湾には国の人権委員会がなかった。1998年からNGOの人権グループ（台湾人権協会）がこの問題についてキャンペーンをはじめた。2000年5月20日，新たに選出された総統Chen Shui-bian（陳水扁）氏は，その就任演説で国際的な人権規範を台湾において実施するため，独立の人権委員会を創設する指針を述べている。

## 第Ⅱ部　ま　と　め

石　村　　修

　「立憲主義」とした表題との関わりで，最も工夫を込めたのがこの第Ⅱセッションである。そのことを意識しながらアジアにおける「課題と展望」を導出できる諸国を選び，そのテーマに沿った講演者を招請することに慎重を期して来た。報告者達が期待に添った形での報告をしていただいたことこそ，われわれの喜びとするところであったといえよう。また主催者である全国憲法研究会としては，1999年度・春の研究総会のテーマであった「アジアと人権保障」に連動させようとする意図があったことも確かであった。「憲法問題11号」に収められた論考は，わがくにの憲法学者を刺激し，わが国がアジアの中で今後いかなるスタンスを取るべきかを改めて提示したことであった。確かに「立憲主義」の母国は欧米諸国であり，これを模倣する—しなければならなかった—ことからアジアの近代化が始まったわけであるが，近代化の歴史を数世紀経て，今やアジアも独自の「近代化・現代化」を志向している。わが国もこの動静を知るべきであり，そのための努力を払わなければならなかった。

　アジアは他の地域と異にして，共通する人権憲章をもっていないが，その憲章を作るための努力を重ねているだけでなく，その国に見合った人権実現の確保も考慮しており，第Ⅱセッションの報告者には，この点を強調してもらうことをお願いしていた。当日司会を担当した江橋崇氏（法政大）が，国際人権法を専攻する山崎公士氏（新潟大）をコメンテーターとして指名したのも，尤もなことであった。

　山崎氏は99年9月にマニラで開催された「アジア太平洋国際人権機関フォーラム」の年次総会に参加され，その会合の意味を紹介された。現在7カ国で構成される同総会は，93年国内での人権実施機関に関する「パリ原則」をガイドラインとして確認することとし，具体的には「政府からの独立，多元的な社会の反映，被害者の直接的訴え，公開性・透明性」を確保する機関の設立を確認した。今回の会合では，とくに，社会権の実施，子どもの権利，女性の権利，NGO・NPOとの連携，等が議論された。そして山崎氏は，わが国にはないこうした実施機関を設けることは，他の諸国でも模索されている新しい潮流であると評価していた。

　司会者はこのコメントを受けて以下の3冊を紹介し，アジアの人権実施状況を知

るヒントとしていた。それは,『パリ原則に関する国内人権機関』(解放出版社),山崎公士編『世界の国内人権機関』(解放出版社),篠原一・林屋礼二編『公的オンブズマン』(信山社),の3冊である。司会者は4人の報告を終わって述べた感想として,各国のそれぞれの努力で人権に関する進展が見られること,さらに,アジアにおいて「地下水脈」があり,この水脈は国連を中心とした各国の協力関係を作り出すものであり,この水脈を見てもらいたかったことを強調した。また,今回のシンポジウムを通じて新たな友情関係を作り出すことができたと評価している。以下,テープに記録された質疑の様子を要約して再現することにする。

　第1報告者のバガランガン氏に対して,近藤敦氏(九州産業大)は,フィリピンでは国籍選択に関し,アメリカと異にし「血統主義」が採用されている理由を質した。その回答は,これが憲法事項ではなく法律問題であるとして,それは保護主義の現れであるとされた。続いて,大内氏は,ワランヨウ氏にも同様に,「人権実施に関してどのような前提条件が必要であるか」と問うた。バガランガン氏の見解では,アジアでは個人的レベルで動くことが多く,効果は法を超えたところで考えなければならない。また,行政や司法への信頼が欠けている点が問題であるとし,今後の発展に期するところが多いとされた。ワランヨウ氏の見解では,次下の3つの条件が必要であり,それは,「一般の国民による参加型民主主義,市民社会の確立,そして憲法に示された教育の役割」であるとされた。萩野芳夫氏(関東学院大)は,フィリピンは立憲主義がアジアでは最も早く進んだ国であり,その人権委員会も最も早く作られたものであるとして,次の2点の質問をした。一は,人権委員会への訴えが減っていることの理由であり,二は,社会権の実効性についてである。これについて,報告者は悲観的に見ているわけではなく,人権委員会が実は法律的な枠を超えて機能していること,その例として,地域社会での啓蒙活動を挙げていた。最近ではより具体的な問題の解決に当っていることが,アジア開発銀行により評価されてもいる。社会権については,制度的メカニズムの変化を指摘し,今後の発展が期待されるとされた。

　ワランヨウ報告には3名から質問が出された。いずれも97年憲法に関わるものであり,高橋氏(早稲田大学生)からは,新しい憲法に「人間の尊厳」が盛り込まれているが,制定過程での反対理由について問われた。その回答は,ワランヨウ氏は委員長から託されて,憲法の「権利・自由」の部分の草案を書き,ヨーロッパ各国の憲法を参照して,大原則を書いたこと,「人間の尊厳」は主観的に解される恐れがあ

り議員の反対にあったが，説明を繰り返すことによって最終的に理解してもらったこと，とされた。今泉慎也氏（アジア経済研究所）からは，タイがアメリカ型の違憲審査制から，大陸型の制度に変えた理由，および「人権委員会」の独立性・中立性を確保するための措置が問われた。第一について，従来のCourt of Justiceはシビル・ローを解釈して来たに過ぎず，公法の解釈権をもっていなかった。そこで，特別の機関を設けて，政治や社会学の知識をもった独立の審査機関が必要になったことが，その設立の理由であるとした。第二の質問については，任命制の過程で議会が国民の参加を認めたこと，予算独立権をえたこと，調査権限を付与されたこと，を付言している。山崎氏は，タイでは人権侵害に対して草の根レベルでどのようなことがなされているかを問うた。NGOが海外から資金をえていることの批判もあったが，政府もその活動を認めつつあり，とくに，公衆衛生や教育の面で多大な役割を演じていることが紹介された。

　シン氏には，インド最高裁の活動に感銘を受けたことを前提として，3名からの質問がまず紹介された。まず孝忠延夫氏（関西大）からは，PIL（公益訴訟）への高い評価は今後とも維持されることが期待されるであろうか，また，拡張された憲法解釈が，新しい人権解釈として一般化できるのであろうか，と問われた。次に五十嵐二葉弁護士からは，元来イギリスでできなかったことが，どうしてインドで可能となったのかという点が，最後に，徐氏（ソウル大）からは，PILと司法権の独立との関係が問われた。

　これらの質問はほぼ重なっていた関係から，シン氏は一括して以下のように答えていた。インドのPILは独自の発展を遂げて成立してきたものであり，70年代の始め有能な判事，法曹会，大学教授の支援を受けて，政府の役人の人権侵害に対向しようとしたものである。インド国内での宗教対立等による複雑な人権対立を背景にしており，PILは汚職を暴き，政府をコントロールする役割があるのである。その意味でPILの有効性はあったのであり，アメリカもこれを政府援助との取引で支援してきたことが説明された。しかし，人権対立の根深さを最後に強調していた。シン氏には同様の視点から，石埼学氏（亜細亜大）は，インドのような多様な社会において，同質性をどのように実現するか，カッパ氏（カトマンズ大）からは，インドにおける少数者の人権は真に護られているのか，という本質的な質問が出されていた。時間の関係で回答はされなかったが，上記の説明の中に一部は含まれていたように思われる。

このセッションの最後に登壇した黄氏に対しては，安西文雄氏（立教大）からは専門的な二つの質問が出された。その一は，表現の自由の優越的地位課題が現実に活かされているのか，第二に，違憲の法律の将来効か即時無効の選択は，大法官会議の選択によるのであろうか，である。その回答は明快であった。台湾では最近での印刷法廃止のように，1980年代から表現の自由擁護のために戦われた経緯が有る。その意味では，立法も司法も他の国の例を跡追いしてきたことになる。第二の点について，それは大法官会議での裁量によると説明された。最近では2件あるが，ケイス・バイ・ケイスに判断されている，とされた。

　司会者は最後のまとめの言葉として，四つの報告から判断して，アジアの諸国における人権対応やその成熟度のおける差を認めつつも，同一の方向性を確認している。来る21世紀において，アジアにおいて真の意味で「人権」を定着させたいという全ての参加者の気持ちを代弁していた。そしてアジアの法学者の間に形成された「友情・ネットワーク」を知り得て，司会者としても大変ハッピーであった，と結んでいた。

# 第 III 部
日本国憲法とアジア

# 日本の憲法改正問題[1]
―― 戦後日本における憲法改正論議と立憲主義 ――

岩　間　昭　道

1　はじめに
2　50年代の憲法改正論議
3　90年代の憲法改正論議
4　むすび

## 1　はじめに

　この報告は，アジアとオセアニアの人々に対して，日本国憲法のもとでの憲法改正論議を紹介し，戦後日本の立憲主義と憲法状況の特徴の一端を明らかにすることを目的とするものである。周知のように，日本国憲法は，制定以来，今日にいたるまで一度も改正されていない。しかし，憲法改正をめぐる論議はこれまで活発に行なわれてきており，のみならず，今後，憲法改正問題は最大の政治問題となることが予想される。また，この憲法改正をめぐる論議には，戦後の我国の立憲主義と憲法状況の重要な特徴が示されているように思われる。そこで，本報告では，まず，50年代の憲法改正論議を紹介し，次に，90年代の論議について概観し，最後に，戦後日本の立憲主義の特徴と，今日の憲法改正論議に関連しての私見をごく簡単に述べることにしたい。

## 2　50年代の憲法改正論議

　日本国憲法制定後，憲法改正が精力的に主張されるようになったのは，50年代に入ってからである。すなわち，1951年に日本の占領が終了するとともに，保守党の側から憲法改正が公然と主張されるようになり，憲法改正の是非をめぐって激しい論議が展開されることになった。ところで，この時期の憲法改正をめぐる論議には，次のような特徴がみられる[2]。

1　第1に，この時期の憲法改正要求の中心は，第9条の改正にあったことである。すなわち，日本国憲法は，個人の尊重を中心とした基本的人権の保障，国民主権主義及び平和主義を基本原理としており，天皇主権を基本原理とする明治憲法とはその内容を根本的に異にしていた。そして，以上の基本原理のうち，平和主義，特に第9条についていえば，それは，戦争の放棄のみならず，一切の軍備の保持を禁止した点で，国家の安全保障史上画期的意義を有するものであった。もとより，こうした第9条は，様々な政治的判断の所産であった。しかし，同時に，同条は，戦争と文明は本質的に矛盾するという正当な認識にもとづいていたほか[3]，我国が侵略戦争を行ったことの反省にもとづくものでもあったことは看過されるべきではない。したがって，こうした第9条は，戦後の日本にとって，新しい理想を意味していたと同時に，国際社会，とりわけアジア・オセアニア諸国の人々に対する道義的意義を有するものであった。

　しかし，1950年の朝鮮戦争の勃発とともに，連合国最高司令長官マッカーサーの指令にもとづいて，警察予備隊とよばれた準軍事組織が創設された。当時の政府は，第9条第2項が禁止する「戦力」は「近代戦争を有効に遂行するに足る程度の装備・編成を備えたもの」を意味し，警察予備隊はそうした「戦力」にあたらないから第9条に反しないと主張したが，我国の再軍備は，実質上，この時から開始されることになった。そして，1954年に創設された自衛隊はまぎれもなく軍隊，すなわち，「戦力」としての性格を備えるにいたった。このため，自衛隊が第9条に反しないと説明することは最早困難となり，かくして，当時の保守党内閣は，第9条の改正を目指すことになったのである。

2　第2に，しかし，この時期の憲法改正要求は，第9条の改正にとどまらず，憲法全体の改正をも目指していたことである。周知のように，日本国憲法は，連合国の占領下で，いわゆるマッカーサー草案をモデルにして制定された。もとより，このことは，我国が受諾したポツダム宣言のもとでは維持することができなかった明治憲法に，当時の我国の政治的指導者達が固執したために主として生じたものであったが，いずれにしても，こうした制定事情の結果，占領の終了とともに，保守党の側から，日本国憲法は占領軍によって「押しつけられた」ものであるから，我国が独立を回復した今日，改めて憲法を自主的に作り直すべきだとする主張がなされることになった[4]。もっとも，こうした人々が問題としていたのは，制定過程だけ

ではなく，日本国憲法の内容，特にその基本原理でもあったということは注意されなければならない。すなわち，こうした人々は，天皇を国の元首と定め，個人よりも国家や「家」といった団体を重視する憲法の制定を，つまりは，明治憲法の復活を目指していたのであった。

　3　第3に重要なことは，保守党の側から主張されたこうした改正要求は激しい反対にあって結局実現されなかったことである。その原因は様々であった。直接的な原因としては，1955年の衆議院議員選挙と翌56年の参議院議員選挙で，憲法改正の発議に必要な3分の2以上の議席を保守党が獲得できなかったことにあった。しかし，憲法改正が挫折した根本的な原因は，当時の国民の多くが，厳しい戦争体験から，日本国憲法と平和主義を強く支持していたことにあったといえる。さらに，当時の支配的憲法学説が果たした役割も軽視することはできない。すなわち，当時の支配的憲法学説は，個人尊重の原理と基本的人権の保障を重視して，憲法擁護の主張を展開した。また，平和主義についても，第9条の普遍的意義を強調して改正反対の立場に立ち，自衛隊は第9条に反しないとする政府の解釈を厳しく批判したのであった。

　4　しかし，第4に，注意されるべきことは，このように憲法改正の試みは挫折したものの，第9条の改正によって目指された事柄は，その後，かなりの程度において，政府の9条解釈の変更によって実現された，ということである。すなわち，第9条の改正の試みが挫折した後，政府は，我国は国家固有のいわゆる個別的自衛権を有すること，したがって，「自衛のため必要最小限度の実力」，すなわち「自衛力」は第9条第2項で保持を禁止された「戦力」に該当せず，自衛隊の保持は第9条に反しないとする新しい解釈を採用した。そして，こうした新しい解釈にもとづいて，政府は，以後，軍備を増強していったのである。また，関連して注目されるのは，自衛隊がその後世論に受け入れられていったことであり，政府がこれ以後しばしば憲法解釈の変更によって政治目的を達成するようになっていったことである。いずれにしても，我国の立憲主義に対する国民の信頼感は，この時から低下していくことになったといっても過言ではない。

## 3 90年代の憲法改正論議

　憲法改正をめぐる論議は，90年代に入って，冷戦の終結，湾岸戦争の発生，環境汚染の深刻化などをはじめとした国際及び国内情勢の著しい変化を背景にして，再び活発化することになった。この時期の改正論議の特徴は，以下の点にある[5]。

　1　第1に，90年代の改正論の中心も第9条の改正にあることである。もっとも，50年代と比べて，90年代の9条改正論には，次のような違いが見られる。すなわち，後述するように，個別的自衛権とそれにもとづく「自衛力」は現行憲法上認められていると今日では広く解されるようになったこととも関連して，90年代の9条改正論は，個別的自衛権の明示的な承認よりも，むしろ集団的自衛権の行使や国連軍への参加の承認に重点を移しつつあるようにみえることである。そして，集団的自衛権についていえば，保守党の内部では現行憲法上集団的自衛権の行使も認められているとする立場も有力ではあるが，政府は，現在のところ，集団的自衛権の行使は現行憲法上認められていないとする解釈をとり，かつ，集団的自衛権の行使を認めるような憲法改正には慎重な立場をとっているようである。しかし，99年に制定された周辺事態法は実質的に見れば集団的自衛権によってのみ正当化することが可能であり，したがって，立憲主義に忠実であろうとするかぎり，集団的自衛権の行使を憲法改正によって承認することは，政府にとっても喫緊の課題であるように思われる。また，90年代の第9条改正論の特徴は，国連憲章43条にもとづく正規の国連軍への参加を可能にするための憲法改正が，野党の一部を含めて主張されていることである。正規の国連軍に対して今後どのような形で協力すべきかという問題は，第9条を擁護しようとする人々にとっても，今後検討されなければならない問題であろう。

　しかしながら，この時期の9条改正要求の核心は，なお個別的自衛権の明示的承認と自衛隊の正式の認知にあるといえる。現行憲法上個別的自衛権は認められており，自衛隊もそうした個別的自衛権にもとづくものとして憲法に反しないとする解釈は，たしかに今日では，政府のみならず多くの野党によっても承認されており，そうした意味では，憲法改正によって個別的自衛権を明文上承認することは，今日では第二義的な重要性しかもたないように見える。しかしながら，第9条の明文からすれば，第9条は「自衛力」を含む一切の軍備の保持を禁止しているとする憲法

学説の解釈の方が政府の解釈よりも合理的であること，また，自衛隊の保持は憲法の基本原理である平和主義の根幹に関わる変更であるが，そうした変更は，憲法全体の趣旨からすれば，主権者である国民の明示的な同意によってのみ，つまり，憲法改正の方法によってのみ正当性を獲得することができること[6]からすれば，第9条改正の中心問題は，今日でもなお個別的自衛権の明示的承認と自衛隊の正式の認知にあるとみるべきであろう。なお，今日，憲法改正によって個別的自衛権を認めることは，主権国家の軍事力を国家の防衛と国際社会の平和と安全を維持するための基本的手段とする伝統的な安全保障政策を今日の時点で改めて選択することを意味する，ということも注意されなければならない。

　2　第2に，右に述べたように，今日の改正要求の中心は第9条の改正にあるといえるが，しかし，改正要求は今後憲法全体の改正へと移っていく可能性が高い，ということである。その理由は，ひとつには，自衛権を明示的に認めれば，付随して，宣戦布告・自衛隊の指揮権・緊急権・緊急事態にさいしての基本的人権の制限・国民の国家防衛義務に関する規定の新設等憲法の全体に及ぶ改正要求が生じることにならざるをえないことにある。しかし，より注目されることは，こうした要求とは別に，今日，改正論議が憲法の全体にわたって展開される傾向を示していることにある。こうした傾向は，たとえば，2000年に両院に設置される予定の憲法調査会が憲法について「広範かつ総合的に調査を行う」こととしていることや，99年の7月に発足した21世紀臨調の「新しい日本をつくる国民会議」が戦後の憲法体制の包括的な見直しを行う方針を固めていることにみられるほか，これまで公表されてきた私的な憲法改正案にもみられる。たとえば，1994年に公表された読売新聞社の憲法改正試案では，自衛のための軍備の保持及び国連の平和維持活動への自衛隊の参加の承認のほか，基本的人権と公共の福祉の調和，環境権等の新しい人権の明文化，憲法裁判所の設置等がめざされており，このように改正要求は憲法の全体に及ぶ傾向を示している[7]。

　ところで，今後，改正論議の重点が憲法の全体に移っていくことになるとした場合，問題はどのような改正要求が憲法調査会，とりわけ世論において支配的となるかにある。この点について，これまでの改正要求は，大別すると，次の三つに分けることできるように思われる。すなわち，第1は，憲法の基本原理を承認したうえで，環境権条項の採用等時代の要求に応じた改正を目指す立場，第2は，憲法の基

本原理を承認したうえで，時代の要求に応じた改正と同時に，部分的にせよ日本の伝統や文化に憲法を適合させるような改正をも目指す立場，第3は，極端なナショナリズムの観点から，憲法の基本原理，特に個人の尊重原理をも含めた憲法全体の改正を目指す立場，である。このうち，少なくとも，第2と第3の立場は，同時に第9条の改正も目指すことになる可能性が高い。憲法調査会では，現在のところ，第1ないし第2の立場が有力となるのではないかと予想されるが，我国の近時の政治動向にかんがみると，第3の立場も軽視することはできないであろう。

3　第3に，以上のような今日の様々な改正要求は，部分的にせよ実現される可能性が高い，ということである。その主たる理由は，今日の政党の動向のほか，最近の世論調査によると，国民の多数が憲法改正自体に対して強い反対を示していないということ，というよりもむしろ，環境権等を明文化するための憲法改正に対しては積極的に賛成する傾向を示していることにある[8]。

## 4　むすび

以上，日本国憲法の下での憲法改正論議を概観してきたが，最後に戦後日本の立憲主義の特徴と，最近の憲法改正論議に関連しての私見をごく簡単に述べておきたい。

1　第1に，日本国憲法のもとでの立憲主義の特徴のひとつは，解釈の変更によって憲法を時代の変化に適応させてきた，ということである。もとより，こうした対応の仕方には―とりわけ人権に関しては―必ずしも理由がなかったわけではない。しかし，日本国憲法が憲法改正の最終決定権を主権者たる国民に委ねた趣旨にかんがみれば，「自衛力」の保持のような憲法の重要な変更は，憲法所定の改正手続により，国民の明示的な決定によって行われるべきであり，憲法解釈の変更によって，つまりは最高裁判所の憲法解釈の変更によって行われるべきではないであろう。たしかに時代の変化に対するこのような対応の仕方には，民主主義が十分定着していない我国ではリスクが伴うかもしれない。しかしながら，このように憲法の重要な変更の是非について国民が自ら決定することによってはじめて，憲法は国民によって支えられたものとなり，民主主義もまた定着していくことになるように思われる。

**2** 第2に強調しておきたいことは，日本国憲法が採用した立憲主義の原理，すなわち，個人の尊重原理を核心とする基本的人権の保障のために公権力を憲法によって拘束するという原理は，人類の貴重な遺産として今後も維持されなければならない，ということである。そして，重要なことは，我国の歴史にかんがみると，一切の軍備の保持を禁止した第9条は，しばしば指摘されているように，我国において立憲主義がよく機能しうるために必要な条件を定めたものであるように思われることである。したがって，第9条の命運がアジアの平和の維持に大きく依存しているとすれば，アジアの平和の維持こそ我国の立憲主義が機能しうるための不可欠な条件ということになろう。

**3** 最後に，第9条を擁護しようとする憲法学説は今日の憲法改正論議に対してどのように対応すべきかという問題に触れておきたい。この点については，まず，次のような立場が考えられる。すなわち，かりに日本国憲法に改正されるべき点があるとしても，第9条を擁護するためにはいかなる憲法改正の提案にも断固として反対すべきだという立場である。この立場は，今日の政治状況にかんがみるとたしかに十分な理由がある。しかし，他方で，これとは異なった立場もありうるように思われる。すなわち，「あるべき憲法像」の観点から，内容に応じて個別的に改正論の是非を判断するという立場である[9]。そして，もしこうした立場にたって「あるべき憲法像」を構想する場合には，憲法の編別について，第1章を憲法の基本原理，第2章を基本的人権，第3章を象徴天皇に変更するよう提唱した1949年の東大憲法研究会の改正案[10]は今日でもなお参照に値するであろうし，また，西欧諸国のみならず，アジアやオセアニア諸国の最近の憲法の動向も積極的に参考にされるべきであろう。

(1) この小稿は，全国憲法研究会の主催により，1999年9月に早稲田大学で開催されたアジア・オセアニア立憲主義シンポジウムで行った報告である。
(2) 1950年代の憲法改正論議の概要については，ジュリスト73号（1955）所収の諸論文（宮沢俊義「憲法改正問題の考え方」，鵜飼信成「憲法改正論の2つの型」，芦部信喜「憲法改正問題の概観」），芦部信喜・憲法制定権力（1983）217—311頁，佐藤功「憲法改正問題の発展とその論点(1)」法律時報26巻7号（1954）68頁以下，同(2)法律時報26巻8号（1954）78頁以下，同「憲法改正論の系譜と現状」ジュリスト638号（1977）44頁以下。

(3) 憲法改正草案を審議した帝国議会で，幣原国務大臣は，次のように戦争と文明は根本的に両立することができないと主張している。「改正案の第9条は戦争の放棄を宣言し，我国が全世界中最も徹底的な平和運動の先頭に立って指導的地位を占むることを示すものであります。今日の時勢に尚国際関係を律する1つの原則として，ある範囲の武力制裁を合理化，合法化せむとするが如きは，過去に於ける幾多の失敗を繰返す所以でありまして，最早我が国の学ぶべきことではありませぬ。文明と戦争とは結局両立し得ないものであります。文明が速かに戦争を全滅しなければ，戦争が先ず文明を全滅することになるでありましょう。私は斯様な信念を持って此の憲法改正案の起草の議に与ったのであります」（清水伸編著・逐条日本国憲法審議録（増補版）第2巻（1976）21―22頁）。

(4) 日本国憲法は占領軍によって「押しつけられた」かどうかを判断するにあたっては，マッカーサー草案をモデルとした憲法改正案が帝国議会で保守党議員を含む圧倒的多数の賛成（衆議院で賛成421（反対8），貴族院で賛成298（反対2））で可決されたということ，そして，そうした保守党議員の賛成は，一定の制約のもとでのものではあったにせよ，次の宮沢教授の文章に示されているように，自主的な選択という性格をもっていたという事実は軽視されるべきではない。すなわち，1946年2月，「幣原内閣がマッカーサー草案を受け取って，これに非常な反発と抵抗を感じたにもかかわらず，結局において，それをだいたいにおいてそのまま政府案として採用することにしたのは，マッカーサー草案に定められたような天皇に関する制度が，それが幣原内閣にとっていかに不満なものと考えられたとしても，当時の国際情勢のもとにおいては現実に望みうる最大限―もちろん幣原内閣の立場から見て―の天皇制であったこと，言葉をかえていえば，マッカーサー草案の定めた天皇制よりも天皇に有利な天皇制を新しい憲法に定めることは，当時の国際情勢のもとにおいては，まったく不可能であり，マッカーサー草案に協力しないことは，おそらくは天皇制そのものの全面的否定をもたらしたであろうと考えられること，にもとづくのであろうとおもわれる」（宮沢俊義（芦部信喜補訂）・全訂日本国憲法（1978）9頁）。

(5) 90年代前半の憲法改正論議の概要については，さしあたり，佐藤功「最近における改憲論議」ジュリスト1020号（1993）105頁以下参照。また，この時期の憲法改正問題に対する憲法学の対応については，中村睦男「憲法改正論50年と憲法学」法律時報66巻6号（1995）76頁以下。なお，最近の憲法改正の主張としては，小沢一郎「日本国憲法改正試案」文芸春秋1999年9月号94頁以下，鳩山由紀夫「自衛隊を軍隊と認めよ」文芸春秋1999年10月号262頁以下。

(6) この点については，岩間「最高裁判所の憲法解釈の限界」憲法裁判と行政訴訟（園部逸夫先生古希記念論集）（1999）65頁以下参照。

(7) もっとも，読売新聞社の憲法改正試案について，奥平教授は，同試案は「9条の『改憲』を本来の基本的なねらい」としたもので，第9条関係以外は，「迷彩効果のはたらき」と「『改憲』のムードを醸成するという触媒効果のはたらき」を期待され

たものにすぎないとする（奥平康弘「『改憲』アングルからみた『憲法50年』」法律時報68巻6号（199）8頁。
(8) たとえば，1999年3月に読売新聞社が行った世論調査によると，憲法を改正するほうがよいと答えたものが53％，改正しない方がよいと答えたものが31％，人格権・環境権の明文化に対する賛成は7割に達している（読売新聞1999年3月22日朝刊）。
(9) 第9条を擁護しつつ，「あるべき憲法像」の観点から内容に応じて個別的に改正論の是非を判断すべきだとする立場は，これまでも時折主張されてきた。たとえば，1967年に，池田教授は，国民の福祉充実のための改正と第9条の改正のいわゆる「抱合わせ改憲の確率が高い場合には，護憲勢力は，憲法改正はタブーである，という魔法から解放されねばならない」と説いていたほか（池田政章「憲法改正はタブーか―『護憲』の意味を考える」同・憲法社会体系Ⅲ（1999）145頁以下所収），比較的最近では，奥平教授は，「いまの憲法をその本来の性質において十分に活か」すべきだとする立場に基本的にたちつつ，「もとより憲法は不磨の大典」ではなく，「国民の自由と福祉をさまたげ，世界の人びととの連帯を害する条項が摘示されたばあいには，これを改めるのにはばかるものであってはならない」と述べ，そうした条項の例として，「第1章　天皇」を指摘し（奥平康弘・コメンタール改憲論者の主張（岩波書店・1983）62頁），小林直樹教授も，戦後の我国の護憲運動は保守派の憲法改正は阻止してきたが，「改憲を前提とする政策の定立には極めて消極的であった」と述べつつ，「急速に展開する現代社会の要請に対応し，憲法の根本理念により適合した政策を樹て，必要ならば憲法改正をも積極的に計ることが，民主的な国民の課題となる」と説き，憲法改正を要する政策的検討のテーマとして環境権を挙げている（「憲法政策論序説1」法律時報62巻4号（1990）49―50頁）。なお，樋口教授は，今日の憲法改正論議にどう対応すべきかという問題に関して，樋口教授自身としては，「今は日本国憲法を変えることに反対」だが，憲法調査会については，1957年の憲法調査会の場合と異なって，「今回は憲法調査会の設置に反対した議員の人びとも，そこに入って大いに議論をしてほしい」と述べ，そうした議論の対象として，たとえば，通常の立法についての国民投票制導入の問題，外国人の国政レベルでの参政権の問題，男女平等の問題などを指摘している（樋口陽一「現代の改憲論と有事法制」世界1999年11月号38頁以下）。ちなみに，最近の学説上，憲法改正による環境保全条項の採用を推奨するものとして，青柳幸一・個人の尊重と人間の尊厳（尚学社・1996）166，214―5頁，岩間「環境保全と日本国憲法」ドイツ憲法判例研究会編・人間・科学技術・環境（信山社・1999）225頁以下。また，1970年に大阪弁護士会の人々が新しい人権として環境権を提唱したさい，その憲法上の根拠をさしあたりは25条と13条に求めつつ，将来は独自の規定を設けることが望ましいとしていた（大阪弁護士会環境権研究会編・環境権（1973）87頁）。いずれにしても，戦争こそ最大の環境破壊の原因だとすれば，今日，戦争の廃絶を基礎づけるうえでも環境保全の理念は不可欠なものといわなければならないであろう。

⑽　東京大学憲法研究会「憲法改正の諸問題」法学協会雑誌67巻1号（1949）1頁以下。同研究会は、註解日本国憲法を執筆したメンバー（田中二郎、鵜飼信成等）で構成されおり、同研究会の改正案では、本文で紹介した編別のほか、天皇の「国事に関する行為」を「この憲法に定める行為」に改めること、6条が定める天皇の内閣総理大臣及び最高裁判所長官の任命権・7条が定める天皇の国会召集権及び衆議院解散権を削除すべきこと、大臣という名称は「封建的君臣関係を象徴する名称」であるから他の表現（たとえば、国務長官等の表現）をもちいるべきこと等が提案されていた。また、1949年に、辻清明、有倉遼吉等の憲法・政治学者によって構成された公法研究会が発表した憲法改正意見では、現行憲法の「民主主義の原則を深化・発展」させることを目指して、第1章には「人民主権の宣言を含む基本的人権の規定」を定めるべきこと、皇位の継承は国会の承認にもとづいて行われるものとすること、第9条については、第1項の「国際紛争を解決する手段としては」を削除し、第2項の「前項の目的を達するため」を「如何なる目的のためにも」と改めるべきこと、圧制に対する人民の抵抗権を明文化すること等が提唱されている（法律時報21巻4号（1949）56頁以下。同改正意見を紹介したものとしては、中村睦男・前掲論文72頁以下。ちなみに、中村教授は、同改正意見を、「今日にあっても、将来なされうる憲法改正にとって十分参照に値する貴重な提言を行っている」ものと評する）。なお、1994年の読売新聞社の改正試案では、憲法の編別として、第1章に国民主権主義、第2章に天皇、第3章に安全保障が規定されるべきことが提唱されている（読売新聞社・憲法―21世紀に向けて―（1994）31頁以下）。ちなみに、奥平教授は、前述したように、こうした読売新聞社の改正試案に対しては批判的な立場をとり、編別についてもあえていま改正しなければ困るというものではないとするが、同時に、「日本国憲法の中枢は国民主権の原則、民主主義の原理にあり、これと両立するかぎりでのみ、天皇制は憲法適合的である」とし、「こうした観点からすれば、『第1章　天皇』という現行憲法の体裁は、もともと──おかし」く、「第1章は、国民主権の原則・市民的自由と権利尊重主義・平和主義といった日本国のありよう（ナショナル・ゴール）を謳うものでなければならない道理である」と主張する（奥平・前掲論文11頁）。

（2000年1月脱稿）

# 日本国憲法9条と国際法

龔　刃韌

中村睦男訳

1　国内立憲主義と国際立憲主義
2　平和憲法のジレンマ
3　国際法および平和憲法の危機
4　条約と憲法との関係
む　す　び

## 1　国内立憲主義と国際立憲主義

### 1　国内立憲主義の変化

(1)　伝統的立憲主義の欠陥

　伝統的立憲主義は，はじめに西側諸国において形成された憲法体制に関する原則体系あるいは価値である[1]。外見的立憲主義を別にして，伝統的立憲主義は主として権力の濫用を阻止するため[2]，政府権力の制限と権力の分立に重点を置いたのである。これらは現在でも立憲主義の重要な原則であるが，伝統的立憲主義はそれ自身の重大な欠陥もあると指摘されるべきである。それは，すべての人の基本的権利の尊重が伝統的立憲主義の核心的内容になっていなかったということである。

　確かに近代市民革命の時代に，自然法に基づく人権宣言は現われたが[3]，しかし，当時個人が自然権をもつといっても，すべての人は人間として平等な基本的権利を有するとは考えられなかったのである。実際に，近代市民革命以後の長い間に，西側諸国においていわゆる個人の権利とは，新しい特権として見なされたことを指摘できる[4]。これらの特権は，まず男性の特権として現れた[5]。次に有産者の特権であった。第三の特権としては，白人の特権であった。そのほか，以上の諸特権と関連し，宗教，文化および植民地主義の特権もみられた。このように，近代市民革命の時代から第二次世界大戦までの間に，個人の権利あるいは自然権という用語は実際上いろいろな特権の代名詞でもあった。

### (2) 現代的立憲主義の特徴

現代的立憲主義と伝統的立憲主義との根本的相違は，人権主体の普遍性および人権の最高価値を認めることである。人権，性，言語，または宗教による差別なくすべての人は人間として基本的権利を有すべきという認識は，第二次世界大戦後になってはじめて一般的に認められることになった。これは，いうまでもなく第二次世界大戦中，ファシズム，ナチズムと軍国主義の国家による人権侵害の残虐な行為に対する深刻な反省の結果であるほかはないのである。

このような文明の進歩は，伝統的立憲主義から現代的立憲主義への変容を導いた。すなわち，すべての人に人間として人権と基本的自由を尊重することは，立憲主義の最高の価値と目的になったことである。立憲主義のその他の原則は，この目的を達成するために機能しなければならない。したがって，現代的立憲主義は，すでにいわゆる西洋文明を超えて，普遍的な原理となっている。このような立憲主義は「人権立憲主義」と呼ばれることもある[6]。

ところで，最近いわゆる「アジア立憲主義」という概念も聞かれる[7]。しかし，文化，経済および政治的な多様性をもつアジア地域に対して，その一つの価値観としてアジア立憲主義を提唱することは，アジア地域の多様性を無視することになるのみならず，現代的立憲主義の普遍性を否定する恐れもあると思われる。

### 2 国際立憲主義

国際立憲主義という概念は，あまり使われていないようにみえる。というのは，国内社会と異なって，国際社会は現在190以上の独立国家によって構成され，また，超国家的な世界政府も存在していないからである。しかし，国際社会はまったく無組織の状態でもない。19世紀末から国際社会の組織化の程度はますます高まってきている。とくに，第二次世界大戦後に成立した国際連合は，最も重要な国際組織として，世界の平和と安全を維持するため，その他のいかなる国家あるいは国家集団によっても代わることはできない重要な役割を果たしてきた。国際連合の加盟国は現在188ヶ国であり，ほとんど全世界のすべての国家を含んでいる。

国際社会において，条約の数は数え切れないほど多いのであるが，国連憲章はもっとも重要な条約であるといえる。国連憲章103条によれば，「国際連合加盟国のこの憲章に基く義務と他のいずれかの国際協定に基く義務とが抵触するときは，この憲章に基く義務が優先する」と規定されている。こうして，国連憲章はある意味にお

いて国際社会かつ「国際共同体」の憲法と見なすことができる[8]。

　国際立憲主義の目的は国家間およびその組織的な構造の実体法連帯関係を固めることによって，国際協力を養成することであるといわれる[9]。国際社会の構造を考えると，国連憲章に定められている目的と基本的原則は，国際立憲主義の基本的価値であるべきと思われる。国連の目的は，簡単にいえば，平和維持と人権尊重である。この目的を達成するため，国連憲章第2条は，主権平等，憲章義務の誠実履行，国際紛争の平和的解決，武力使用の禁止，国内管轄事項干渉の禁止などの基本的原則を定めている。ここで平和主義は国連の目的だけでなく，国連の原則およびこれらの原則の基本的精神でもある。したがって，平和主義は国際立憲主義の核心的内容ではないかと思われる。

## 2　平和憲法のジレンマ

### 1　日本国憲法の進歩性および意義

(1)　現代的立憲主義の産物

　日本国憲法は，日本を占領したアメリカ人の法律家によって起草されたものであるので[10]，とくに権力の分立，司法審査などの領域においてはアメリカ憲法の影響が強いといえる。しかし，日本国憲法は単なるアメリカ憲法の複製品というわけではない。

　18世紀に制定されたアメリカ憲法は，近代的意味での最初の成文憲法として，人類文明に対して巨大な貢献をなしたといえる。しかし，時代の制限により，アメリカ憲法および権利章典には，欠陥があることも指摘されるべきである。たとえば，アメリカ憲法でいう「人民」には，財産としての奴隷はもちろん，自由になった黒人，女性および貧乏な白人男性などが含まれなかった。そのために，奴隷制度は保存され，人種差別も禁止されなく，また平等な投票権も保障されなかったのである[11]。刑事手続においても，無罪推定および拷問を禁止する原則などに関する憲法上の規定もなかったのである[12]。

　実際に，日本国憲法起草当時のアメリカ社会において，人種差別あるいはアパルトヘイトは依然として合法的制度として存在していた。アメリカ社会の平等権を本格的に推進する市民権運動は，そのあとに起こったのである。このように，日本国憲法に対して，アメリカの影響は主に伝統的立憲主義に限られているようにみえる。

　ところで，日本国憲法は，国民主権，人権尊重および平和主義という基本的原理

に基づくので，アメリカだけでなく，第二次世界大戦後に現れた民主主義，平和主義および人権尊重という国際社会の新しい認識を吸収した成果である。このように，日本国憲法は人類文明の進歩と成果を反映し，現代的立憲主義に立って制定されたものであるので，アメリカ憲法を超越するところもあるといえる。

(2) 最も徹底した平和憲法

各国憲法のなかで，特定の戦争の制限するという平和条項は，昔からあった。ところで，諸国の憲法の平和条項は，いずれもいわゆる「征服戦争」，「侵略戦争」，「国策の手段としての戦争」という特定の戦争を放棄することにとどまる。戦争遂行の戦力の制限に関する規定はほとんどにみられない[13]。ただ，1949年のコスタリカ憲法12条によると，常設制度としての軍隊は廃止されるが，大陸協定もしくは国の防衛のためにのみ，軍隊を組織することができる。

以上の諸国の憲法に比べると，日本国憲法の平和条項は最も徹底したものであるといえる。日本国憲法9条は，国権の発動たる戦争，武力による威嚇または武力の行使を永久に放棄すると定め，1年前に発効した国連憲章の原則をよく反映している。さらに，戦争と武力の行使を放棄するため，日本国憲法は，戦争遂行の戦力，つまり陸軍空軍とその他の戦力を保持しないとはっきり言明し，また国の交戦権をも認めないと定めているので，コスタリカ憲法より一層徹底的である。このように，日本国憲法9条は，国内立憲主義に対しても，国際立憲主義に対しても貢献しているといえる[14]。

(3) 戦後日本経済繁栄の基礎

敗戦後，日本の本土は戦争の廃虚となり，また狭い島国として資源も少ない。このような状況のなかで，日本はわずか数十年間のうちに，アメリカに次ぐ，世界第2位の経済大国になった。この日本の経済奇跡の原因について，各国の学者から，日本の企業経営，文化，国民性，社会構造などさまざまなことが挙げられていたが，日本国憲法の意義を見逃しているようにみえる。

私見によれば，日本国憲法こそ，戦後日本の経済奇跡の最も基本的な原因ではないか。つまり，日本は戦後の新しい憲法の制定によって，まず民主主義のもとで長期的に安定した社会環境を作り出した。このような社会環境はまさに経済発展の最も基本的な条件である。

そして，戦後日本の経済繁栄に，日本国憲法9条はとくに重要な役割を果たした。東西冷戦時代に，米ソなどの軍事大国が高額の軍事費を投入し，軍備競争をしてい

た間に，日本はこの9条のおかげで，軍事費が他の諸国と比べて，少なくとも対GDP比においては格段に低く押さえられてきた。それに応じて，日本は抜群の投資率や生産性の伸び率を示してきた[15]。

## 2　平和憲法と安保体制の並存
### (1)　再軍備から軍拡へ

日本国憲法は最も徹底した平和条項をもっているが，現実に徹底して適用されたことはない。その最初の原因は，米ソ冷戦の開始による，日本を占領するアメリカの極東政策の転換である[16]。そのために，戦後の日本では民主改革は徹底的に行われなかっただけでなく，日米安保体制のもとで，平和憲法の発効したあと，まもなく日本の再軍備のコースも始まった。まず朝鮮戦争の間に，1950年の警察予備隊の創設をへて，1952年，旧日米安保条約の要請にこたえて，警察予備隊を陸上部隊としての保安隊に改編し，また海上整備隊が設けられ，この両者を統合する保安庁が設置された。1954年，日米相互防衛援助協定（MSA協定）に基づき，自衛隊法と防衛庁設置法の防衛2法が，国会で強行的に成立した。そして，同年7月1日から，防衛庁，陸上，海上，航空の3自衛隊が発足し，日本の再軍備は本格的にスタートした[17]。1960年の新しい日米安保条約は，依然としてアメリカ軍の日本駐留をみとめ，日本の防衛力を増強する義務を定めている。この条約は軍事同盟の性格を強めたが，日本の対米従属的地位は変わっていない[18]。

新安保条約が調印された後，集団的自衛権の問題に集中してくる[19]。集団的自衛権は，軍事同盟をむすび，戦争の正当化をはたす危険性もある[20]。日本政府の一貫した見解によれば，集団的自衛権の行使は認められないという[21]。それにもかかわらず，日本はアメリカと集団自衛的かつ軍事同盟的な安保条約を維持してきている[22]。さらに，1978年の「日米防衛協力の指針」「旧ガイドライン」は，日本に対する武力攻撃がなされた場合のみならず，このような攻撃がなされる恐れのある場合の対処行動なども問題とされ，現行日米安保条約の枠組みを突き破っているようにみえる[23]。

1990年代にはいってから，東西冷戦が終わった。国際関係の構造的変化は，本来ならば，日米安保体制の存在理由を弱めるあるいは失うという結果になるはずであったが，実際には，日米安保体制のもとでの日米軍事協力は一層強化されてきている。とくに，1997年9月23日に日米安全保障協議委員会により共同発表された「日

米防衛協力のための指針」「ガイドライン」および1999年5月24日成立した「周辺事態法」(新ガイドライン関連法) によれば，従来の「極東」という地理的概念に代えて，これより広くまたあいまいな「周辺事態」という新概念が提出された。このように，新ガイドラインおよびその関連法は，これまでの日米安保体制および旧指針をさらに超え，「専守防衛・個別的自衛権」を建前とする従来の防衛政策から，「先制攻撃型日米同盟協力」を軸とする，アジア地域安保体制へ変容したのである[24]。このように，日本周辺事態における日本に対する武力のありなしにはかかわりのない独立した軍事協力体制の整備が行われたのである[25]。

新ガイドラインは，アジア地域に対するアメリカの軍事支配体制を維持する前提として，日米の戦時任務をはっきりさせ，地域安全のため日本に財政と軍事を分担させることは，アメリカの外交政策の重要な一環である[26]。しかし新ガイドラインおよび周辺事態関連法の制定は，たんに日本政府がアメリカの軍事戦略に追随した結果だけでなく，日本自身の経済・政治的利益に基づいて推進されていることも注意されるべきである[27]。

(2) 平和憲法と現実との矛盾

戦後の日本は最も徹底した平和憲法をもつにもかかわらず，現実にはすでに世界有数の軍事力を保持している国になっている。日本に比べて，コスタリカ憲法はそれほど徹底した平和条項をもっていないが，戦力制限条項の履行について，コスタリカのほうがはるかに誠実であるようにみえる[28]。

日本国憲法と現実の矛盾に対して，どのように憲法9条の解釈を行うのかは，戦後日本における憲法論争のもっとも重大な焦点であるといえる。そして，興味深いことは，憲法9条に関する解釈をめぐって，日本では憲法学者の多数説あるいは通説と政府見解との立場の対立，裁判所の「中立」的な立場，という，いわゆる「三方鼎立」という日本の特別な風景を見せていることである。

まず，9条による戦争の放棄および自衛権について，日本の憲法学者の通説は，9条は自衛戦争と制裁戦争を含めて，一切の戦争を全面的に放棄するという立場である[29]。自衛権の行使について，日本の憲法学者の通説は，「武力なき自衛権」という立場をとっている[30]。これに対して，日本政府は自衛戦争を含む一切の戦争を放棄するという戦後初期の立場から，1950年の「武力なき自衛権」という立場に変え，さらに1955年から，「武力による自衛権」を主張しはじめた[31]。

次に，「戦力」に関して，日本の憲法学者の通説は，「警察力以上の実力説」であ

る。これによれば，現在の自衛隊は，その人員・装備・編成などの実態に則して判断するかぎり，「戦力」に該当するといわざるをえない[32]。そして，一切の戦力保持が認められないとする立場からは，駐留米軍も違憲と解される[33]。これに対して，憲法制定の時に日本政府の立場は憲法学者の通説とほぼ同じであったが[34]，1952年に，近代戦を遂行しうる実力に達しないものは憲法の禁止する戦力ではないという立場に変更した。さらに，1954年に自衛隊の発足にともない，日本政府は自衛のために必要最小限度の実力，「自衛力」「防衛力」をもつことも憲法上禁止されておらず，自衛隊は違憲ではないという新たな立場に再び変更した。また，日本の駐留米軍について，1951年に，日本政府は，憲法9条2項により禁止されたものではないとした[35]。

このような場合に，日本の裁判所の関連する判決は特に注目される。ところが，日本の最高裁判所は，いままで日米安保条約および自衛隊について，違憲論も合憲論もはっきりいわずに，憲法審査の対象から除外し，回避的な方針をとってきた。要するに，日本の裁判所は，「憲法判断回避」の判決例を重ねているので，9条の判例は形成されていないといえる[36]。

このように，日本国憲法9条と現実との矛盾は，政府の立場と憲法学者の立場との対立および最高裁判所の回避的政策によって，簡単に解決することはできない難問となっている。

## 3　国際法および平和憲法の危機

### 1　武力使用の禁止原則の逸脱

国連憲章2条4項が定める武力の行使を禁止する原則は，国際立憲主義のもっとも基本的な原則である。国連国際法委員会は条約法の法典化作業の過程で，この原則がユス・コーゲンス（強行法）であるとの見解を表明した[37]。そして，国際司法裁判所は，1986年のニカラグアに対する軍事的活動事件で，武力行使の禁止原則は，慣習法としての法の信念を表明したものであるとした[38]。したがって，この原則は，国連加盟国だけではなく，すべての国家，国際組織および地域的機関に対して，法的に拘束力があるということである[39]。武力行使の禁止原則は，それ自身が重要性をもつだけでなく，既存の国際法の諸原則にも大きな影響を与えた[40]。

武力行使の禁止原則には，2つの例外がある。1つは，国連憲章51条による個別的または集団的自衛権の行使である。もう1つは，憲章第7章によって，国際の平

和および安全を維持しまたは回復するために，安保理自らかあるいは安保理の許可によって，軍事的措置を行使することができる。

ところが，1999年4月からの，アメリカが主導するNATOのユーゴに対する空爆は，自衛権の行使でもなかったし，国連安保理の許可を得なかったので，武力の不使用原則に違反するというべきである(41)。このNATOの武力行為の違法性については，ヨーロッパの代表的な国際法学者も認めざるを得ない(42)。しかし，この事件は欧米先進諸国の武力行使の禁止原則から逸脱しようとする動きを表し，国際関係における危険の先例になるおそれがあることも否定できない。

## 2 地域紛争に巻き込む危険性

自衛隊の濫用を制限するために，国連憲章51条は加盟国に対して武力攻撃が発生した場合を前提としている。ところが，1997年の日米間の新指針および1999年の周辺事態法は，日本に対する直接の武力攻撃が加えられない周辺事態が発生する場合にも，日米軍事協力のために自衛隊が武器使用およびアメリカ軍への後方地域支援を行うことができることを定めた(43)。これは，集団的自衛権と本質的に異なる地域的「取極体制」へ転換したといえる。国連憲章53条によれば，「いかなる強制行動も，安全保障理事会の許可がなければ，地域的取極に基いて又は地域的機関によってとられてはならない」としている。しかし，新指針も周辺事態法も国連安保理の許可を軍事的行動を行う要件としていない(44)。

新指針および周辺事態法が日本の安全に寄与するどころか，日本および地域の安全に対して高い危険性を与えることも予想されうる。安保体制の日本に対する危険性については，30数年前ベトナム戦争の時に日本の国際法学者田畑茂二郎教授がすでに指摘したことでもある(45)。この危険性は現行日米安保条約の枠組みを超えた新しい指針および関連法によって，アジア地域の武力紛争に巻き込まれる可能性を一層高くしている。たとえば，朝鮮半島問題や，台湾問題などいわゆる周辺事情が起こり，万一アメリカと関連国との武力衝突が発生する場合に，アメリカに軍事基地を提供している日本は，新指針および周辺事態関連法に基づいて，アメリカ軍に後方地域支援をしなければならない。現代戦争では，前線と後方地域との区別は難しいので，結局，日本もこのような武力紛争に巻き込まれ，交戦国になり，新しい戦争が起こる可能性がないわけではない。

## 4　条約と憲法との関係

　戦後日本の実質的再軍備は，主にアメリカ側のイニシアティブと圧力によって推進されてきた[46]。日本の軍事力である自衛隊の形成および強化は，日本国憲法上に根拠を見つけられないが，日米安保条約上に根拠が見られる。したがって，日本平和憲法のジレンマの起因は，憲法と条約との関係にあるといえる。

### 1　各国の立場の比較

　条約の国内法における法的地位は，国際法上統一の規則がなく，主として各国の憲法によって自ら決められる[47]。そのために，条約と国内法との関係について，各国の実行もそれぞれ異なるのである。たとえば，日本，フランス，スペイン，ロシアなどのように，条約が普通の国内法より高い地位をもつとされる国があるし，アメリカ，ドイツ，イギリスなどのように，条約が普通の法律あるいは連邦法と同一の地位を定める憲法もあるし，また，中国のように条約と国内法との関係について法律上の規定がない国もある[48]。

　条約と憲法との関係については，世界の多数の国では条約に対する憲法の優位性が認められている。国際協調主義を特に重視するオランダも，必ずしも憲法に対して条約の優位性を認めているとはいえない[49]。1983年に修正されたオランダ憲法91条3項によれば，憲法に違反する，あるいはこの結果を導く条約規定の通過は，議会の3分の2以上の多数の賛成を経なければならないとしている。そのほかのいくつかの国においても，憲法に違反する条約を批准するため，まず憲法改正を行わなければならないか，あるいは憲法改正と同じ手続で承認しなければならないということである[50]。したがって，これらの諸国においては当然に憲法に対する条約の優位性を認めるものでなく，その国会での承認にあたっては，実質的に憲法改正と同じ手続と要件を充たすことを義務づけている[51]。そのほか，最近の国際的な傾向として人権条約は特に高い国内法上の地位が与えられているが，憲法に対する人権条約の優位性は認められていない[52]。

### 2　日本政府の特別な立場

　条約と憲法との関係について，日本政府の立場は非常に特別である。日本国憲法98条2項は「日本国が締結した条約及び確立された国際法規は，これを誠実に遵守

することを必要とする」というあいまいな規定を定めることに留まるので，条約と憲法との関係について，学説上も慣行上も争いがあり，一定しないようにみえる。

条約に対する違憲審査権，とくに条約の実質審査をめぐって，消極説と積極説とに分かれるが[53]，日本の憲法学界においては憲法優位説が支配的学説であるといえる[54]。そして，日本の国際法学界においても，条約締結手続が憲法改正手続に比べていちじるしく簡略であるという理由から，憲法優位説が有力である[55]。

ところが，1959年第33国会における内閣法制局長官の答弁によれば，普通の2国間の政治・経済的な条約については憲法が優先すると考える，しかし「たとえば降伏文書あるいは平和条約というよな一国の安危にかかわるような問題に関する件におきましては，これは……憲法と条約とを比較してみた場合には，やはり条約が優先する場合はあろう」と述べている[56]。ここで，国際条約の種類によって，憲法優先か，それとも条約優先かという特別な立場がとられた。ところで，日米安保条約は，政治・経済的な条約ではなく，日本の安全にかかわる軍事的条約であるので，先の答弁および日本政府の一貫してきた慣行に鑑み，「一国の安危にかかわる」というような種類の条約に該当すると読み取れるようにみえる。そうだとすれば，日本国憲法に対して日米安保条約が優位するという結論を導くことになるといわざるをえない。これがおそらく戦後日本において，憲法を超える効力をもつ日米安保条約と平和憲法との並存局面の基本的な原因ではないか，と思われる。

しかし，先に述べた諸国の憲法と本質的に異なって，日本では憲法規定と一致しない安保条約について，事前の憲法改正手続を経ずに，憲法改正より著しく簡易な手続で批准することができたということである。しかも日本のいわゆる国際協調主義は，いままでアメリカに対する軍事協力を中心にしてきたので，一般的意味での国際協調主義ではない。ここで，もし日米安保条約の日本国憲法に対する優越性を確認することができれば，憲法に対する軍事的条約の優越性を認めるのは，世界で日本しかないことになる。しかし，日本の平和憲法に対して，これ以上皮肉なことはないであろう。

## むすび

人類史上最も徹底した平和条項をもって，また戦後日本の民主主義，平和および経済繁栄に重要な役割を果たしてきた日本国憲法に対して，高く評価することができると思われる。しかし他方において，日米安保体制のもとで，憲法によって放棄

された「戦力」は不断の強化をともない，憲法の平和条項もますます空洞化してきている。とくに，最近日米の共同指針および周辺事態関連法によって，専守防衛という枠組みさえ超えて，軍事大国になる障害としての憲法の平和条項を廃止する動きも一段と強くなっているようにみえる。憲法改正手続を経ないうちに，法的規範としての憲法9条を，日本の内閣あるいは行政機関の解釈によって事実上改正ないし廃止することは，日本の立憲主義および平和主義に対して非常に危険なことである。したがって，いま日本の平和憲法は歴史の交叉点にあるといえる。

　21世紀に向って，人類文明は進歩と滅亡とに同時に直面している。もし日本がほんとうにアジア地域の平和と安全に貢献することを望むならば，また日本の国民の平和と安全を考えれば，国連憲章に従い，平和憲法を守って，非軍事同盟的な平和国家としての役割を果たしていく道が最も賢明ではないか。もちろんこれは最終的に日本国憲法の国民主権原理に基づき，平和を愛好する日本国民の良知に訴えるべきことであると思われる。

(1)　立憲主義は3つの思想源流，つまり自由主義（liberalism），合理主義（rationalism）と個人主義（individualism）があるといわれている（Car. J. Friedrich, *Constitutional Government and Democracy*, Blaisdell Publishing Co., 1967, pp. 6-7.）

(2)　杉原泰雄『憲法　立憲主義の創設のために』（岩波書店，1990年）3―4頁。

(3)　宮沢俊義『憲法II［新版］』（有斐閣，1974年）8―19頁。

(4)　拙文：Gong Ren Ren, "International Human Rights, Comparative Constitutionalism and Features of China's Constitution", *Human Rights: Chinese & Canadian Perspectives*, Edited by E.P. Mendes and A-M Traeholt, University of Ottawa, 1997, pp. 75-77.

(5)　男性の特権に対抗するために，フランスにおいてもアメリカにおいても女性の権利宣言がわざわざ提出されたわけである（辻村みよ子＝金城清子『女性の権利の歴史』（岩波書店，1992年）38―41頁，66―68頁）。

(6)　L.M. Beer (ed.), *Constitutional Systems in Late Twentieth Century Asia*, the University of Washington Press, 1992, pp. 7-20.

(7)　韓大元『亜洲立憲主義研究』（中国人民公安大学出版社，1996年）。

(8)　B. Fassbender, "The United Nations Charter As Constitution of the International Community", *Colum. J. Transnat I.L.*, Vol. 36, 1998, p. 542.

(9)　Ibid., pp. 552-553.

(10)　筒井若水＝佐藤幸治ほか編『日本国憲法史』（東京大学出版会，1976年）383―392頁。

(11)　L. Henkin, *The Age of Rights*, Columbia University Press, 1990, pp. 91-92, pp. 114-115.
(12)　Ibid.
(13)　芹田健太郎『憲法と国際環境［補訂版］』（有信堂，1992年）132―133頁。
(14)　L.W. Beer, "Peace in Theory and Practice under Article 9 of Japan's Constitution", *Marquette Law Review*, Vol. 81, 1998, p. 815.
(15)　杉原泰雄『憲法Ⅰ　憲法総論』（有斐閣，1987年）420―421頁。
(16)　藤原彰『日本近代史Ⅲ』（岩波書店，1977年）198頁。
(17)　藤原彰・前出注(16)，220―221，198頁。
(18)　渡辺洋三『日米安保体制と日本国憲法』（労働旬報社，1991年）183―188頁。
(19)　国際司法裁判所は，1986年のニカラグアに対する軍事的活動事件において，集団的自衛権の行使について，武力攻撃を受けた国家が自ら宣言すべきであり，さらに，武力攻撃の犠牲者であるとみなす国家による援助要請がないかぎり，その他の国家は集団的自衛権を行使することはできないという要件を明確にした（ICJ Report, 1986, pp. 104-120.）。
(20)　渡辺洋三『憲法と国連憲章』（岩波書店，1993年）37頁。
(21)　安藤仁介「国際法と日米――日本の憲法と国際協調主義」佐藤幸治＝初宿正典＝大石眞編『憲法50年の展望Ⅰ』（有斐閣，1998年）287―305頁。
(22)　冷戦時代にアメリカと日本，韓国およびフィリピンとそれぞれ締結した軍事同盟の条約は，ともに典型的な集団的自衛権型条約であると指摘された(G.K. Walker, "Anticipatory Collective Self-Defense in the Charter Era: What the Treaties Have Said", *Cornell Int'l L.J.*, Vol. 31, 199, pp. 366-367.）。
(23)　杉原泰雄『人権の歴史』（岩波書店，1992年）214―215頁。
(24)　山内敏弘「新ガイドライン関連法上の問題点」ジュリスト1160号（1999年）39頁，森英樹「逐条コンメンタール・周辺事態法」法律時報71巻9号（1999年）53頁。
(25)　松田竹男「新ガイドライン・周辺事態措置法案の国際法的検討」法律時報71巻1号（1999年）48頁。
(26)　C. Ajemian, Comment: "The 1997 U.S.-Japan Defense Guidelines under the Japanese Constitution and Their Implications for U.S. Foreign Policy", *Pacific Rim Law & Policy Journal*, Vol. 7, 1998, p. 337.
(27)　渡辺治「日本の軍事大国化・新自由主義改革の世界史的位置」法律時報71巻9号（1999年）18頁。
(28)　コスタリカは，軍隊をもたず，1万人程度の治安警察隊を設置している。そして，国連や米州機構に加盟しても，軍事的協力は留保し，難民受け入れなど中米平和に貢献するような積極的平和外交を展開している（沢野義一『非武装中立と平和保障　憲法9条の国際化に向けて』（青木書店，1999年）45頁）。
(29)　芦部信喜『憲法学Ⅰ　憲法総論』（有斐閣，1992年）258―260頁。

(30)　芦部・前出注(29)266頁，中村睦男『論点憲法教室』（有斐閣，1990年）260―262頁．
(31)　山内敏弘＝古川純『憲法の現状と展望［新版］』（北樹出版社，1996年）37―41頁．
(32)　芦部・前出注(29)270頁，伊藤正己『憲法［第3版］』（弘文堂，1995年）177頁．
(33)　樋口陽一・森英樹・高見勝利・辻みよ子編『憲法理論の50年』（日本評論社，1996年）65頁．
(34)　たとえば，当時日本文部省から中学1年生向けにつくった『新しい憲法のはなし』があった．
(35)　杉原泰雄・前出注(2)34―42頁．
(36)　森英樹「9条裁判と憲法学」法律時報68巻6号（1996年）67頁．日本の最高裁の回避の基本的理由として，「統治行為論」のほか，各事件ごとに具体的な法技術上の理由が挙げられた．日本の最高裁の司法消極主義の原因について，戸波江二「日本の違憲審査」前出注(33)114―115頁，拙著『現代日本司法透視』（世界知識出版社，1993年）68―70頁，67―78頁．
(37)　*ILC Yearbook*, 1963-II, p. 52.
(38)　*ICJ Report*, 1986, pp. 98-102.
(39)　B. Simma, "NATO, the UN and the Use of Force: Legal Aspects", *EJIL*, Vol. 19, 1999, p. 3.
(40)　杉原高嶺＝水上千之ほか『現代国際法講義［第2版］』（有斐閣，1995年）9頁．
(41)　拙文「北約対南連盟使用武力没有合法根据」時代潮（1999年第5期）33頁．
(42)　B. Simma, op. cit., p. 14.; A. Cassese, "Ex Iniuria ius oritur: Are We Moving towards International Legitimation of Forcible Humanitarian Countermeasures in the World Community", *EJIL*, Vol. 19, 1999, p. 23.
(43)　山内敏弘・前出注(24)38頁．
(44)　日本政府によれば，日米安保条約，新指針およびその関連法に基づく日本の行為が国際上常に「合法」であるという前提は，アメリカ軍が国際法上違法な武力行使を行うことはありえない「公理」が存在しているといわれる．しかし，このような「公理」は，国際法上の常識に違反するのみならず，戦後アメリカが外国で武力行使を行った記録をみれば，歴史の事実をも無視しているといえる（森川幸一「国際法から見た新日米防衛協力関連法等」ジュリスト1160号（1999年）50頁）．
(45)　芦部・前出注(29)289頁．
(46)　深瀬忠一『戦争放棄と平和的生存権』（岩波書店，1987年）312頁．
(47)　F.G. Jacobs, S. Roberts (ed.), *The Effect of Treaties In Domestic Law*, 1987, Introduction, p. 23.
(48)　拙文「国際人権紛争と中国」杉原高嶺編『紛争解決の国際法』（三省堂，1997年）280頁；A. Cassese, "Modern Constitutions and International Law", *Recueil des Cours*, Tome 192, 1985-3, pp. 363-364.
(49)　*Akehurst' Modern Introduction to International Law*, Edited by P. Malanc-

zuk, 7th Edition, 1997, Routledge, pp. 67-68.
(50) たとえば，1958年のフランス憲法（54条），1978年のスペイン憲法（95条），1992年のモロッコ憲法（31条），1993年のペルー憲法（57条），1996年のウクライナ憲法（9条），などである。
(51) 山本草二『国際法［新版］』（有斐閣，1993年）112頁。
(52) 拙文・前出注(4)。
(53) 佐藤幸治『憲法［第3版］』（青林書院，1995年）345頁。
(54) 芦部・前出注(29)93頁，伊藤・前出注(32)678－688頁。
(55) 田畑茂二郎『国際法新講上』（1990年，東信堂）60頁，山本草二・前出注(51)111頁。
(56) 谷内正太郎「国際法の国内的実施」広部和也＝田中忠編『国際法と国内法』山本草二先生還暦記念（勁草書房，1991年）112頁。

［付記］本稿は，中村睦男教授と高見勝利教授のご推薦で1999年9月23日，24日に全国憲法研究会の主催により早稲田大学で行われた「アジア・オセアニア立憲主義シンポジウム」第Ⅲセッション〈日本国憲法とアジア〉において，「日本国憲法と国際法――憲法9条を中心にして」という表題で行った報告の報告原稿をもとに作成したものである。ここで，私は北海道大学留学時代（1980年代）から国際法と憲法学の良師益友，深瀬忠一，中村睦男，高見勝利および帰国以後に知り合になった杉原泰雄などの諸教授の学恩と友情に深い感謝の意を表したい。

# 日本国憲法と周辺事態法
—— 日本国憲法の平和主義に対する評価を中心に ——

鄭　　萬　喜

清野幾久子 訳

## I　はじめに

　1999年5月24日，日本では，新たな日米防衛協力のための指針（新ガイドライン）を施行するための国内法として，周辺事態法案，自衛隊法改正案，日米物品役務相互提供協定改正案が参議院で可決され，ここに日米安保体制は新段階に入ることになった。なぜなら，新ガイドライン関連法案によって，日本は，日本における有事の際だけでなく，日本の周辺で起こる地域紛争に出動する米軍を支援するための法的根拠を，初めて設けたからである。すなわち，日本政府が日本の周辺で起こった武力紛争等の周辺事態において米軍を後方支援し，物品役務を提供することにより，日米安保体制は，「アジア太平洋安保」へ，さらには「周辺事態」の解釈如何によっては全世界にも適用され得る「世界安保」へ変質する可能性を含むことになったのである[1]。

　しかし，新ガイドラインの根拠になる現行の日米安保条約は，5条で，日本国の施政の下にある領域における，自国の平和及び安全を危うくする，いずれか一方に対する武力攻撃に対して共同で行動することを定めており，6条では，極東における国際平和及び安全の維持に寄与するため，アメリカ合衆国軍隊の日本国内での施設及び区域の使用を認めている。この防衛条約により1978年に策定された日米防衛協力のための指針（旧ガイドライン）も日本に対して武力攻撃がされた場合の日米両国の共同対処方針を定めていたのであり，日本以外の極東における事態で日本の安全に重要な影響を与える場合の日米間の協力に関しては，いかなる言及もしていなかった（旧ガイドラインのIII）。このような日米安保条約は主に冷戦体制下でソ連の攻撃を前提にしたものであるが，ソ連の崩壊でその前提は喪失してしまい，日米両国は，日米安保の新たな定義をしなければならなくなった。そこで，日米両政府は，1996年に東京で，日米安保条約の実質的改定を意味する「日米安保共同宣言」を発表し[2]，そのなかで，日米安保の目的を日本防衛からアジア太平洋地域の平和と安全

の維持へと再定義した。そして，1997年9月には，この共同宣言を具体化した「日米防衛協力のための指針」(新ガイドライン)を策定し，アジア太平洋地域を含む，日本以外の地域における有事(周辺事態)にも対応ができる，日米軍事協力体制の構築を促進した。このような一連の動きが今回の周辺事態法成立につながったのである。

　日本の軍事大国化に繋がりかねないこのような現実政治の展開は，戦争の放棄と戦力不保持を規定した日本国憲法の平和主義に矛盾するものであり，新ガイドラインに対する批判と反発・憂慮の声は日本国民の間でも高まった。日本の学界のなかでも，とりわけ全国憲法研究会は，この問題に対して深刻な憂慮を表明した[3]。また，この新ガイドライン関連法に対しては北東アジアの周辺諸国も著しく敏感な反応を見せており，特に，中国，北朝鮮及びロシアは強い非難を表明した。中国は，新ガイドライン関連法が成立した直後の外交部論評を通じて，「(新ガイドライン関連法は)時代の潮流に逆らうもので，極東地域に否定的な影響を与える」と述べ，さらに「直接的であれ間接的であれ，台湾を周辺の範囲に含めることには断固として反対する」と表明している。また，北朝鮮は新ガイドライン関連法の審議過程の段階ですでに，戦争法であると非難しているし，ロシアも中国のように強くはないが，憂慮を表明している[4]。ところで，韓国政府は，マスコミの大書特筆にもかかわらず，即座に反応することなく沈黙を保ってきた。なぜならば，韓国にとって，新ガイドライン関連法の成立は，対北朝鮮安保能力の強化につながると同時に，日本の軍備増強に対する社会的憂慮の増大という2つの側面をもつのであり，この相反した視点が韓国政府の見解を明らかにすることを難しくしたからである。

　ともかく，このような新ガイドライン関連法の成立による日本の対米協力は，日本政府自身が従来違憲であると解釈してきた集団的自衛権の行使に当たるだけでなく[5]，日本および極東の平和と安全のための基地提供を規定した，現行の日米安保条約にも反することになる深刻な問題を提起するのである。したがって，例えば日本の周辺事態として想定される「韓半島問題」や「台湾問題」において，アメリカが軍事的介入を行い，これに対して日本が軍事的協力をすることになると，このような日本政府の行動は，日本自身が武力攻撃を受けているのでない以上，日本国憲法に違反することはもちろんのこと，現行の安保条約にも抵触するといわざるをえない[6]。

　韓国の立場からみても，新ガイドライン関連法は，韓国の対北朝鮮政策や統一政策に少なからぬ影響を与え得るということから，大きな関心を持たざるを得ない問

題である。韓半島の統一は国家的・民族的課題であり，その統一の方法は，武力によらずに，あくまでも平和的統一政策により推進することを，韓国憲法は明文化している（4条）。このような平和的統一政策の推進のため，1991年には南北間の和解と協力のための合意書が採択されており，現在の金大中政権は，「太陽政策」という対北朝鮮包容政策を積極的に行っている。したがって，現時点で日本がとるべき方策は，山内教授が適切に指摘しているように，韓半島有事を想定し，アメリカとの軍事的共同行動をとることではなく，韓半島の統一が平和的に解決されるように，日本がいかなる外交的努力を行うべきかを顧慮することである。これは，日本の周辺と北東アジアの平和と安全のためにも望ましいことである[7]。

　本論文で筆者は，韓国の憲法学者の一人として，日本国憲法の平和主義について，その規範と現実の乖離という観点から考察を加え，特に最近の新ガイドライン関連法の問題点を批判的に検討する。そして，現在韓国政府が採っている対北朝鮮太陽政策と関連させながら，日本の新ガイドライン関連法を分析し，韓半島と東アジアの平和のための方案を，韓日両国憲法の平和主義に立脚して模索することを試みる。

## II　平和主義と憲法

### 1　平和主義憲法の歴史

　2度の世界大戦を契機に，各国は憲法上，平和主義の原理をとり入れるに至った。特に，第2次世界大戦の惨禍の経験とそれに対する反省は，世界人類をして平和を希求させることになり，各国国民の平和希求の精神は，対外的には国家間の侵略戦争防止のための条約の締結で，国内的には憲法上の平和主義の採択という形で現れた。

　近代における国際平和主義の歴史は，思想的にはカントの『恒久平和のために』（Zum ewigen Frieden, 1759年）から始まるといえるが[8]，第1次世界大戦直後の国際連盟規約（1919年），1928年の不戦条約等が重要な意味を持つ。第2次世界大戦以後の国際連合憲章は，国際平和維持のために侵略戦争の禁止，武力行使または武力による脅威の禁止はもちろん，紛争解決手段としての戦争または武力に訴える行為を禁止し，これを集団的安全保障体制によって担保している。国際連合体制下の，集団的安全保障の理論は，特定の加盟国による他の加盟国に対する攻撃や武力行使に対しては，他のすべての加盟国の共同防衛という対抗措置をもって対処し，世界秩序の安全と平和を維持するという理論である。すなわち，この体制に違反する侵

略国は，大規模な集団的対抗措置をうけるという圧力により，戦争を抑止するという原理である[9]。このような国連の国際平和主義精神にのっとり，各国の憲法は平和主義を多様な形態において採択している。特に憲法上に平和主義を直接的に宣明している国として，ドイツ，日本，韓国等のように戦争の惨禍を経験した国々，またはスイスのように中立政策を採用している国々があげられるが，近年の憲法としては，南アフリカ憲法が平和主義を強調している程度である。このように，憲法上に平和主義を直接的に規定した国家は一部に過ぎないが，これは平和と戦争の問題が国際法の領域に属するからである[10]。そしてこれらの国家の平和主義の内容をみると，旧西ドイツ基本法（1949年）は武器の製造，輸送，取引を制限し，平和錯乱行為の処罰を定め，良心的兵役拒否権を認めている。スイス憲法（1948年）とオーストリア憲法（1955年）は永世中立を宣言し，イタリア憲法（1947年）は国際平和秩序のための統治権の制限を定めている。

## 2 日本と韓国における平和主義憲法の制定

### (1) 日本国憲法における徹底した平和主義

第2次大戦後の日本国憲法上の平和主義に関する規定は，徹底した平和主義を採択することで，平和主義を掲げる憲法の中でもきわだった意味を持つ。日本国憲法の平和主義は，国家の根本規範により，戦争の放棄と戦争の手段である戦力の不保持を定めることで，自己抑制という「自己完結型平和主義」を取っている[11]。戦争の放棄に関しては沿革的には1791年のフランス憲法の侵略戦争の放棄規定にその例をみることができるが，日本国憲法の場合，他国を侵略する手段さえも放棄していることから，これは歴史的にもその類例をみることができない規定といえる。このような日本国憲法の平和主義は，憲法施行後半世紀を経る間，改正されずに存続してきたという点から，肯定的に評価される一方，平和主義の空洞化が批判的に指摘されてきた。なるほど，日本の平和主義規定は日本とアジアの平和維持に一定の寄与をしてきており，日本社会における自由と民主主義のために積極的な役割を遂行してきたといえる。また，戦後日本の経済発展のための役割をも担ったという見解も妥当であると考える[12]。しかし，冷戦の終焉後，日本国憲法の平和主義は混迷をきたし，非暴力的に平和を構築するという規範に対する確信の喪失がみられる。平和主義を巡る混迷の解消は，究極的には日本国民の政治的選択にかかるのであるが，現時点においては，日本国憲法の平和主義をいかに再構築するかが重要な課題であるといわざるをえない[13]。

## (2) 韓国憲法と平和主義

韓国憲法は，前文で「外においては恒久的な世界平和と人類共栄に貢献することによって」と謳い，5条1項は「大韓民国は国際平和の維持に努め，侵略的戦争を否認する」として国際平和を標榜している。このように韓国憲法は，一切の戦争を否認しているのではなく，正戦論に立脚して侵略戦争だけを否認し，防衛戦争ないし自衛戦争は肯定している[14]。さらに6条1項は国際平和主義の実現と関連して「憲法に基づいて締結，公布された条約及び一般的に承認された国際法規は，国内法と同等の効力を有する」とし，国際法秩序尊重の原則を明らかにしており，6条2項では「外国人は，国際法と条約の定めるところによって，その地位が保障される」とし，外国人の法的地位が相互主義の原則により保障されることを明らかにしている。

また，平和主義と関連して，韓国憲法は平和統一の原則を規定している。韓国では，第2次世界大戦以後の分断国家として，南北分断以来今日まで，統一問題が民族の最大課題として引き継がれてきており，憲法上にも統一条項を設けているのが特色である。建国の初期には平和統一政策を標榜していなかったが，1970年代に入り，国際緊張が緩和される状況のなかで，1972年の歴史的な「南北共同声明」が発表されたが，これが最初の平和統一方針となった。こうして，1972年の憲法で平和統一条項が新設されることになり，現行憲法にはより詳細な規定が置かれている。憲法前文は「祖国の平和的統一の使命」を明示し，憲法4条は「大韓民国は，統一を指向し，自由で民主的な基本秩序に立脚した平和的統一政策を樹立し，これを推進する」としている。また，66条3項は，「大統領は，祖国の平和統一のための誠実なる義務を負う」と定めている。このような憲法上の平和統一の原則にしたがい，政府は積極的な平和統一政策を推進することになり，1990年8月には「南北交流協力に関する法律」を制定しており，1991年9月には南北が国連に同時加盟することをもって，韓半島の平和と安全及び平和統一を実現させる基盤を形成することとなった。また，同年12月には「南北間の和解と不可侵及び交流・協力に関する合意書」が採択された。

ところで，韓国の学界では，従来から北朝鮮の存在を法的に如何に見るべきかについての議論が，韓国憲法3条の領土条項の解釈を巡って展開されてきた。すなわち，3条の「大韓民国の領土は，韓半島およびその付属島嶼とする」の解釈については，学説が分かれている。第1説は，憲法3条は，現実的に韓国の統治権は北朝

鮮の領域には及んではいないが，韓国の憲法と法律上においては認められているという説である。つまり，大韓民国が，韓半島における唯一の合法政府であり，北朝鮮の領域は，いわゆる朝鮮人民共和国が不法に占領している未修復地域であるという。これは，「韓国唯一合法政府論」，「北朝鮮未修復地域論」とも言われるもので，地理的・歴史的概念として，従来の支配的な概念であった。第2説は，近年の学説であり，1972年以降の，平和統一条項の憲法へ盛り込み，南北の国連同時加入，「南北合意書」[15]の交換などの一連の動きを顧慮し，北朝鮮を事実上の国家として認めるべきであるという説である。したがって，祖国の平和統一を成し遂げるためには，これからは北朝鮮を事実上の統治体制として認め，北朝鮮の領域までも韓国の領土として解釈するような非現実的な冷戦時代の論理から脱皮すべきであると主張する[16]。この説が，現在の有力説である。これに対して韓国の憲法裁判所は，「北朝鮮政権の2重性論」を展開し，一方では憲法の領土条項を根拠に北朝鮮を「反国家団体」としながらも，他方では平和統一条項を根拠にして，北朝鮮を「対話と協力の同伴者」とし，両条項の憲法上の規範調和的解釈を試みている[17]。

## III　日本国憲法の平和主義——その規範と現実の乖離

### 1　平和主義の成立背景

日本国憲法は，徹底した平和主義をその規範内容としている点から，平和主義を標榜する世界各国の憲法のなかでも先駆的な意義をもっている。このような平和主義が成立した歴史的な背景としては，一般的には「戦争の違法化」という国際的潮流と共に，政府の行為によりもたらされた「戦争の惨禍」に関する国民の体験とそのような体験を通じた反戦感情の高まりが挙げられる[18]。

すなわち，日本政府による「アジア太平洋戦争」は，アジア諸国の民衆に多大な惨禍をもたらしただけでなく，広島・長崎の原子爆弾による被爆が端的に明らかにしているように，日本国民に対しても多大な被害を与えたのである。このような悲惨な戦争体験が，多くの国民の反戦意識を涵養させたのである。この点で日本国憲法の平和主義規定は，「核時代の歴史的な刻印」[19]としての意味を持ち，悲惨な戦争を体験した日本国民の「総意の結晶」ともいえる[20]。

しかし，このような戦争の違法化と国際平和主義の潮流，戦争の惨禍に対する反戦感情だけが，日本国憲法9条に端的に示されている非武装平和主義を採用することとなった背景とみることはできない。憲法9条は，連合国の立場からはポツダム

宣言により提示された日本に対する「非軍事化」政策の一環としての意味を持ち，当時の日本政府の立場からは「国体守護の避雷針」としての意味を持った。すなわち，憲法9条が生みだされたもう一つの要因は，天皇制存続のための天皇の戦争責任回避にも見出しうるということである[21]。しかし，だからといって9条がマッカーサー総司令部により一方的に強要されたものであるとみることは，決して9条の成立背景としては妥当な見解であるとはいえないという主張もみられる[22]。要するに，日本国憲法が掲げる平和主義・戦力不保持の規定は日本国民の平和への希求と平和主義思想を前提としながら，最終的にはマッカーサーの決断により作られたとみるのが妥当である。いわゆる敗戦後の日本は，非軍備の形で再出発しなければならなかったのであり，当時の一般国民の反戦意思およびそれらを反映したマッカーサー草案により，戦争放棄条項が具体的に条文化されたという点からして，9条は日米の合作の意味が強いとみることができる[23]。

## 2 平和主義の規範構造と解釈

(1) 憲法上の平和主義に関する規定

日本国憲法の平和主義に関する内容は9条に規定されている。1項では，国権の発動である戦争だけでなく，事実上の戦争である武力による脅威または武力の行使をも，国際紛争を解決する手段としては永久に放棄すると規定している。また2項では，1項の掲げる理念を達成するため，陸海空軍その他の戦力の不保持を規定し，国の交戦権を否認している。すなわち，9条の内容を一言で要約すると，戦争・武力による国際紛争解決のためのすべての戦力と交戦権の放棄を規定したものといえよう。このような意味を持っている条項は，制定当時には明快に解釈されたが，その後，日本が事実上の戦力を持つにつれ，解釈は揺れ始めており，後述のような新解釈が提起されることになった。また，日本国憲法は，平和主義を構成する要素として，9条以外に，憲法前文でいう「平和のうちに生存する権利」という「平和的生存権」を定めているのが特色である。この平和的生存権は，個人の人権保障の大前提であり，平和の問題を人権の観点から捉えるという点で，政治の実践においては重要な役割を果たすといえるが[24]，現実には平和的生存権が侵害された場合の法的権利性ないし裁判規範性の有無について，日本の学説と判例は未だに理論的に定着していないようにみうけられる[25]。

### (2) 政府解釈の変遷

　憲法制定時の9条に関する政府解釈は，一切の軍事力を保持せず，また戦争あるいは武力によらずに国際平和に寄与するという，徹底した平和主義を内容としていた。当時の唯一の争点は「自衛のための戦争」までも放棄することが，9条の解釈に合致しているのかについてであった。本来国家の自衛権は，国際法においてはその実現手段である軍事力の保持・行使と一体的に理解されてきたからである。これに関する日本政府の公定解釈は，自衛戦争を含む一切の戦争が不可能であるということで，この論理は「軍備のない自衛権論」といわれることになった。このような政府の解釈は，当時の国民にも抵抗なしに受け入れられたのである。

　しかし，1950年の再軍備開始からこの政府解釈の破綻が始まった。1950年発足の「警察予備隊」は，それが軍隊であることを曖昧にするための苦肉の命名であったが，1952年の「保安隊」には国内の秩序維持だけでなく，日本の平和を維持するという対外的な軍事目的も登場し，1954年の「自衛隊」の創設によって，日本はついに日本を防衛することを主な任務とする紛れもない軍隊を持つことになり，ここに憲法との矛盾は決定的なものになった。さらに，在日占領米軍がそのまま駐留する日米安保条約の締結は，「政府の行為によって再び戦争の惨禍が起こることのないようにすることを決意し」たという憲法前文にも背馳することであった。安保体制・自衛隊発足に連動して，支配層において憲法改正が主張され，それを政治目的の筆頭に掲げた保守一党化，つまり自由民主党の結成が行われたことは，上記の政局の方向が憲法と正反対であることの表れであった。しかし，憲法の改正に失敗した政府・自民党は，それ以降憲法の解釈を変更していく。すなわち，従来の，一切の戦力放棄による戦争放棄という解釈の枠は維持しながらも，憲法上否定されていない自衛権を根拠にして，その自衛権の手段である自衛力は合憲であるという論理を採ることになった。ただし，戦力の保持は禁止されているので「自衛のための必要最小限度の実力としての自衛力は，戦力に至らない限り合憲」であるとした。結果的にこのような解釈は「軍備のない自衛権論」が，正反対の「軍備による自衛権論」に変質したことを意味する。ここで問題となるのは，戦力に至らざる程度というのはいかなるものなのかについてであった。しかし，政府解釈が，自衛力の限界は国力・国際情勢・科学技術の進歩に対応して変化しうると明言されたことにより，「戦力に至らざる程度」の基準は，最初からなかったも同然であったといえる。

　1960年に日米安保条約が改正され，日本は防衛力の増強をより明白に約束させら

れることになり，日本の施政下にある米軍が攻撃を受けた場合には，アメリカと共同で武力行使を行えるようになった。この新安保条約の運用において大きな転機になったのは，1978年の「日米防衛協力のための指針（ガイドライン）」の策定であった。これにより，日本は専守防衛の枠を超え，「日本以外の極東における安全に重要な影響を与える場合」においてもアメリカに協力することになった。このような新安保体制下での自衛隊の増強には，さらに拍車がかかることになり，その後の日本の軍事費は急速に増加している[26]。

　1989年のベルリンの壁の崩壊と1991年のソ連の解体による東西冷戦構造の終焉は，安保体制と自衛隊の存在に大きな影響を与えた。冷戦の終結にともなって，国連の機能が活性化するにつれ，日本では，国連の活動に，自衛隊を軸にして軍事的に協力することこそが国際貢献であるという新たな論理が登場することになった。日本政府は，1990年8月のいわゆる湾岸危機の勃発に際して，アメリカの強力な要請を受け入れ，30億ドルの財政支援と共に湾岸地域に自衛隊の小艦船を派遣した。そして，1992年には自衛隊の本格的な海外派遣を可能にするPKO法を強行成立させた[27]。日本は同法に基づいてカンボジアとモザンビークに自衛隊を派遣しており，1994年には，人道的援助という名目でルワンダ周辺地域に自衛隊を派遣した。同時に，在外日本人の輸送などのために自衛隊機を海外に派遣することができるように，自衛隊法の改正も行われた。このような国連協力を理由とする自衛隊の海外出動については，日本政府は合憲であるという新たな解釈を示している。すなわち，憲法が禁止する戦争及び武力は侵略を目的とするもので，とくに戦争は国権の発動としての戦争を意味しているから，国際共同体である国連の平和活動は憲法に抵触しないという論理である。憲法が禁止していない国際活動のために，政府解釈として合憲の行政組織である自衛隊を活用することは，憲法上いかなる問題もないとみるのが国連活動における自衛隊の参加を認める，最近浮上した憲法解釈である。その後，今回の新ガイドライン策定と関連法の制定で，憲法上の平和主義の解釈はもう一度変更されるという運命に遭遇することになった。これは，新ガイドライン体制の本格的な構築が憲法との矛盾を最大限に激化させていることを意味する[28]。そして，最近憲法改正の主張が声高に叫ばれているなかで，国会の「憲法調査会」設置は，とうとう国会が憲法改正に向けた足場を形成することになったことを示すのである[29]。

## (3) 学説と判例の立場

　日本国憲法9条1項は，戦争の放棄について定めているが，そこでは，「国権の発動たる戦争」だけでなく，事実上の戦争行為ともいえる「武力の行使」及び「武力による威嚇」をも放棄するとされている。ところで，この戦争行為の放棄には「国際紛争を解決する手段としては」という文言がついていて，これを巡っては学説が分かれている。まず，戦争全面放棄説（第1説）は，自衛戦争をも含めたすべての戦争が放棄されているとする。これに対して，多数説である侵略戦争放棄説（第2説）は，国際法上の慣例に習い，9条1項で放棄されたのは侵略戦争のみであるが，9条2項で，自衛戦争・制裁戦争が禁止されていると解する。この説は，結論的には戦争全面放棄説と同じになる。要するに，日本国憲法は，まず9条1項で，侵略戦争を放棄し，次に9条2項ですべての戦争を放棄するという仕組みであると考えられる。

　ところで，上記のような9条の憲法規範と日米安保条約及び自衛隊法等の下位法との間で現れる乖離現象に対する厳格な法的判断を行えば，憲法学界の多数説が述べているように，違憲の判断を下さざるをえないだろう。しかし，日本の最高裁は，いわゆる砂川事件で，下級審における安保条約の違憲判断を否定して，同条約は高度の政治性を有しているので，司法審査になじまないという，意図的な「憲法判断回避」の立場を採ったのである[30]。ここには，一方では裁判所は憲法判断を回避しながら現実を追認するという側面と，他方では正面からの合憲判断には躊躇するという側面が表れている。これについては，法律家として正面から憲法判断を要求される場合に，違憲であるとしか判断しえない程度に現実の違憲性は明白である，という分析もなされている[31]。最高裁は，安保条約のように「高度の政治性」を有するものは，一見，明白に違憲無効であると認められない限り，司法判断に適合しないという統治行為論による判断回避の立場を採ったのである[32]。このような日本の裁判所の司法消極主義的な傾向は，違憲審査制度の形骸化を招来し，立憲主義の発展を阻害する要因になりうるといわざるをえない。

## IV　新ガイドライン関連法をいかに見るべきか

### 1　新ガイドライン関連法と平和主義

　新ガイドライン関連法の核心をなす周辺事態法は，日本国憲法9条の平和主義に照らしてみて，根本的な問題を内包していることは，すでに全国憲法研究会の声明

をはじめ，多くの学者らにより指摘されたところである[33]。周辺事態法によると，「周辺事態」が発生した場合には，政府は適切かつ迅速に，後方地域捜索救助活動，船舶検査活動その他周辺事態に対応するために必要な措置を実施し，日本の平和及び安全の確保に努めるものとすると規定しているが（2条1項），ここでいう周辺事態とは，「日本周辺の地域において日本の平和および安全に重要な影響を与える事態」（1条）であるとされている。したがって，同法には，「日本の平和及び安全に重要な影響を与える事態」と「日本周辺地域」が何を意味しているのかに対する明白な判断基準を設けなければならない。周辺事態法の規定のこのような曖昧性については，今後日本が周辺事態に軍事的に対応することを選択することが正しいとしても，周辺事態の概念が曖昧なままに放置されているため，無原則的な濫用あるいは拡大の危険性が存在するという問題点が深刻に指摘されている[34]。

いずれにせよ，この法によると，日本が直接攻撃を受けない場合にもアメリカの軍事力の行使に協力しなければならなくなり，それは日本の防衛という名目で締結された日米安保条約や，専守防衛のために設置された自衛隊を変質させ，日本と直接関係のない戦争に関与することを認めて，日本の戦争参加に道を開くことになるのである。これは，これまで自衛隊の海外派兵の禁止と集団的自衛権の否認などにおいて規範力を保ってきた憲法9条の平和主義にとって「試練の時代」を意味するといえる[35]。また，新ガイドライン関連法は，自治体の協力を通じた後方地域支援と捜索を行うことを定めており，地域住民を戦争の砲火のなかに巻き込む危険性を有しているこれは，戦後ずっと日本の各自治体が独自に育ててきた平和への願望，つまり，日本国憲法前文と9条により保障されている平和的生存権を侵害することでもある。したがって，現時点で，日本の学界には日本国憲法の平和主義と平和的生存権の意味を再確認する作業が切実に要求されているといえる。

## 2 新ガイドラインの真の意図は？

日本政府はなぜ国内外の反対世論と学界の批判にもかかわらず，国会多数派の工作によって新ガイドライン関連法を成立させたのか。日本政府は新ガイドラインの目的を，日本に対する武力攻撃ないし周辺事態が発生した場合に，より効果的で信頼性ある日米協力を行うための堅固たる基礎を築くためと説いている[36]。日本本国の平和及び安全のためという根本的な目的以外に，他の目的と意図はないのか。この点に関して，渡辺教授は「新ガイドラインによる日米軍事同盟の強化の背景には冷戦終焉後のアメリカ側の戦術変換と日本側の要因が結びついている」とし，日本

側の要因としては，日本資本主義が構造的に変化し，1980年代後半以降の「日本企業の多国籍化」の結果，軍事大国化への要求が切実になったと分析している[37]。すなわち，日本企業がアジア全地域に進出し，危険を排除して輸出産業に集中するためには，やはり自国の強力な軍隊の支援が必要であり，この点で世界戦略を市場原理中心に展開しているアメリカの論理と日本のそれは相通じる点があるとみているのである。したがって，昨今の日本の動きは，単なる民族主義や軍隊を保有した普通の国家建設だけからきているのではなく，むしろ市場保護の論理に基づいて，進出アジア諸国の政局不安による自国企業と産業基地の損失に対する憂慮から導かれるものであるという分析は注目に値する。要するに，新ガイドラインによる日米軍事同盟の強化は，日本企業の多国籍化に基づいた日本の新たな軍事大国化の要請からなされており，その軍事大国化の方式は，日米軍事同盟の強化を基本としながら，国際連合という旗の下で，自衛隊の海外出動体制を追求することを選択したものといえる。しかし，日本企業の保護という経済的理由のために，政府が憲法違反の問題を抱えている行動を強行するということは，日本の立憲主義の擁護という観点からしてもゆゆしき問題である。そして，新ガイドラインに対して，「憲法第9条に基づく平和主義を実現するには，その経済的基礎となっている多国籍企業本位の経済構造を改革し，他国を侵害しない国民経済の再建を展望する中で，はじめて可能であると思われる」という渡辺教授の指摘は[38]，大変説得力があると考える。

### 3 新ガイドライン関連法と韓国の「太陽政策」

日本の周辺事態法上の周辺事態が北朝鮮体制の変化あるいは北朝鮮との戦争の危険を主な対象として想定されていることについては，国内外に異論がないところである。国際政治における北朝鮮問題は，ヨンビョン核施設査察を契機に起きた1994年の韓半島危機にひき続き，1998年のデポドンミサイル発射事件，1999年3月の北朝鮮船舶の日本領海侵入，金蒼里核施設疑惑などで一層深刻さを増し，韓半島の再びの危機的状況は，極東アジアの主要イッシューとして浮かび上がっている。このような状況のなかで，日本は北朝鮮との一連の関係悪化をむしろ絶好のチャンスであるかのようにとらえ，新ガイドライン関連法を制定し，自衛隊の活動範囲と武力使用の正当化を図ったのである。ところで，この新ガイドライン関連法に対しては，日本の再武装，軍事大国化への懸念という観点から，韓国側から厳しい批判が噴出するだろうという予想は，みごとに外れてしまった。韓国政府の公式見解の表明は出されていないし，各マスコミもそれ程敏感な反応は見せていない。このような韓

国の態度の背景には次のような要因があると考える。第1に，IMFの経済援助を受けている昨今の経済危機により，安保問題に対する国民の関心の低下が挙げられる。第2に，金大中政権の統一政策に基づいた，いわゆる「太陽政策」との関連である[39]。特に，太陽政策という対北朝鮮包容政策を堅持していくためには，韓国としては日米の軍事力による対北朝鮮の軍事抑止力を必要とするため，この点からは反対する理由がないといえる。むしろ，この新ガイドライン関連法は，北東アジアにおける日本とアメリカの地域安保の役割を可能にするという点で，肯定的に評価する見解も見られる[40]。

しかし日本の軍事大国化は，韓国に対して少なからず脅威となり，韓半島の平和統一政策に負担となることも看過しがたいことである。過去における日本帝国の侵略戦争によってひきおこされた韓国民族の日本に対する反感と不信は，大多数の韓国人をして，日米間の安保協力が韓国の安保にも役立つという認識にもかかわらず，日本の地域安保の役割が増していくことに対しては，賛同を躊躇させている。また，北朝鮮の戦争挑発を前提にした新ガイドライン関連法の制定は，今後の韓国の対北朝鮮政策にも否定的な影響を与える可能性があると考える。1999年6月13日から15日までの3日間，北朝鮮のピョンヤンで南北首脳会談が開かれた。55年間の対立を超えて開かれたこの歴史的なトップ会談は，太陽政策が韓半島の緊張緩和を導く正当で効率的な方法であること，また南北の平和的な再統合を容易にするものであることを証明している。韓国人の対日本不信の解消は韓国人だけの問題ではないから，究極的には日本の対外政策が解決すべき課題であるし，日本は，韓半島の分断と軍事的対立を前提にしている近視眼的な新ガイドライン関連法の制定で軍事的プレゼンスをするのではなく，むしろ韓半島の統一を前提にした東アジアないしアジア・太平洋地域の新たな安全保障システムを構築することに関心を持つべきである[41]。すなわち，日本は韓半島における有事を想定して，アメリカとの軍事的共同行動に邁進するのではなく，韓国民の念願である韓半島の平和的統一のために積極的に努めることが，結局は日本が北東アジアの平和と安全保障に寄与する道なのであり，日本国憲法上の平和主義原理にも合致する方策なのである[42]。くり返すと，韓半島の緊張緩和と平和統一は，北東アジアの平和維持に必須なのであり，北東アジアの平和を維持することが，世界平和と直接結びつくという点を深く認識し，日本は韓半島の平和統一の実現に積極的に努めなければならないと考える[43]。

## V 結　語

　日本の現実政治における新ガイドラインの策定とその関連法の制定が，日本国憲法上の平和主義原理に違反する深刻な問題点を抱えていることは否定し難い。しかし，日本とアジアにおける平和の定着のためには，日本国憲法制定時の徹底した平和主義理念を今後も続けて維持しなければならず，そのために日本は，アメリカとの軍事同盟強化によって軍事大国化の道を進むのではなく，平和的な外交努力に力をいれ，アジアにおける地域安保体制を構築することが重要である。特に，北東アジアにおける平和は，韓半島の平和統一が重要な鍵となるゆえに，日本は韓半島の平和統一に向けて，周辺国家との国際的な協力を怠ってはならない。

　冷戦の終焉後，国際社会における唯一の覇権国家の地位に立ったアメリカは，地球上の至るところで起こっている地域紛争に，人道主義と人権外交という名目で軍事介入をしているが，最近のコソボ紛争におけるアメリカの軍事行動に対して，ロシアや中国等は，アメリカの対外政策を非難する立場をとっている。アメリカ国内においても，ヘンリー・キッシンジャーは，コソボ紛争と関連して，アメリカの外交戦略を批判しながら，人道主義的介入（humanitarian intervention）と人権を掲げた外交政策は，再検討されるべきであると指摘している[44]。したがって，日本は，このようなアメリカの傲慢で独善的な対外政策にただ追従するのではなく，「対米一辺倒から日本の主体性を回復するために，アメリカの核の傘から離れて，地域安保へと進むべきである」という，酒井氏の主張[45]は，評価すべきであると考える。

　日本国憲法の平和主義を特徴づける，非軍備平和主義と平和的生存権の保障は，世界平和を実現するための方向と内容を先駆的に示してきたという点で，高く評価するに値する。したがって，平和主義の現実的状況が憲法9条と大きな差異があるということをもって，憲法を改正し，「普通の国」への方向転換を試みようとするよりは，憲法制定当時の理念である徹底した平和主義を堅持していくことが正しい道ではないかと考える。

　一方，憲法理論的な側面から憲法9条をみる時，憲法規範と現実政治との間の乖離は，立憲主義の発展を阻害するおそれが大である。新ガイドラインの策定と関連法の制定は，日本国憲法の平和主義条項の名目化を招来し，憲法の規範力の喪失を意味することになる。この点で，日本の議会は立法の過程において党利党略からはなれ，民意の忠実な反映をはかり，政府の対外政策に対する統制機能を強化すべき

である。最近の日本の政治改革が，日本社会の保守勢力による国会多数派形成を図り，改憲のための議員数を確保するためのものであるならば，これは日本の健全な議会制民主主義の発展を困難にするといわざるをえない。

　最後に，筆者から見た日本国憲法の特徴は，憲法の解釈において，裁判所より政府が最高の有権的解釈機関として機能しており，裁判所は消極的な立場から違憲審査に臨んでいるのではないかということである。日本国憲法9条の解釈において，政府の解釈により日米安保条約やガイドラインおよび関連法等が正当化される一方で，最高裁はそれらに関する憲法判断を回避していることが，果たして日本の立憲主義の観点から正しいことであるか疑問である[46]。

　平和主義条項に局限された問題ではないが，憲法の擁護のためには，窮極的には主権者である国民による国政に対する批判と監視が不可欠であり，そのためには，国民の世論形成に主導的役割を果たしうる学会の現実問題に対する積極的な意見表明と方向提示は大変重要であると考える。このような観点から，日本の全国憲法研究会の憲法擁護のための努力は高く評価されるべきである。

(1)　山内敏弘・太田一男『憲法と平和主義』(法律文化社，1998年) 50頁。
(2)　この日米宣言は，両国首脳の共同宣言の形でだされた。しかし，現行の日米安保条約を実質的に変更することを意味するこの共同宣言は，日本国憲法73条3号の規定に反し，国会の承認なしにされたもので，日本の議会制民主主義に違背する問題を含むといえる（山内敏弘・太田一男，前出注(1)46頁）。
(3)　日本の全国憲法研究会は，1999年3月16日，「周辺事態法案等を憂慮する憲法研究者の声明」を発表した。その中で，同研究会は「周辺事態法案は，憲法九条の平和主義に照らして根本的な問題を含み，さらに憲法上の多くの問題をかかえている」と指摘し，憲法に基づく政治が行われるよう，立憲主義の尊重を訴えた。全国憲法研究会編『憲法問題10』(1999，5) 186頁。
(4)　週間韓国，1999. 5. 4 参照。
(5)　日本政府は，従来，集団的自衛権の行使は憲法9条に反すると解釈してきたが，近年，憲法解釈を変更して，集団的自衛権の行使も憲法上可能であるとしている。その根拠としては，国連憲章51条が国連加盟国に個別的自衛権と共に，集団的自衛権を承認していることや，集団的自衛権は個別的自衛権と共に主権国家の固有の権利であるということを挙げている。このような政府の見解に対して，学説は正面から批判していて，多数説は，憲法上の自衛権の存在自体は肯定しているが，ここでの自衛権は武力なしの自衛権で武力行使を伴う権利は自国の防衛のためにも認められておらず，他国の防衛のための武力行使はなお認められないとする（山内敏弘・

太田一男，前掲注(1)・60-64頁)。一方，国際法的観点からも，集団的自衛権は国家に固有の権利ではなく，国連憲章により創設された新たな権利であり，一般的な見解によれば，国際法上確立された自明な権利としては認められない（山本草二『国際法（新版）』（有斐閣，1994年）736頁。藤田久一『国際法講義2』（東京大学出版会，1994年）402頁)。

(6) 山内敏弘・太田一男，前掲注(1)・51頁。
(7) 山内敏弘・太田一男，前掲注(1)・51頁。
(8) カントは，戦争を道徳的に罪悪であると見て，戦争を行ってはならないという実践理性の要請として恒久平和の理念を確立している。また，国際平和のための条件として，国内法と国際法及び世界市民法による実践を提示している。これについての詳細は，金哲洙『現代憲法論』（博英社，1979年）96頁以下，カントの恒久平和論に対する評価としては，Karl Jaspers, Kants zum ewigen Frieden, 1958; Carl J. Friedrich, Inevitable Peace, 1974.
(9) 集団的安全保障システムに関しては，藤田久一『国連法』（東京大学出版会，1998年）314頁以下。
(10) Cheryl Saunders, World Peace and Constitutional Law, 国際憲法学会韓国学会『世界憲法研究』第2号（1997年）71頁。
(11) 最上敏樹「冷戦後国際社会における日本国憲法の平和主義」全国憲法研究会『憲法問題』第10号（1999年）38頁。
(12) 山内敏弘「平和主義の現況と展望」前掲注(11)・76-78頁。
(13) 最上敏樹・前掲論文（注11）47頁。
(14) 権寧星『憲法学原論』（法文社，1999年）169頁。
(15) 1991年12月31日に合意された南北合意書1章1条は「南と北はお互いに相互の体制を認めるとともに，これを尊重する」と規定している。
(16) 許営『韓国憲法論』（博英社，1999年）185頁。
(17) 憲法裁判所は，「……現段階において北韓は，祖国の平和的統一のための対話と協力の同伴者であると同時に，対南赤化路線を固守しながら，我が自由民主主義体制の潜伏を画策している反国家団体という性格も，ともに持っているのが厳然たる現実である点に照らし，南北交流協力に関する法律等が公布施行されたといっても，国家保安法の必要性が消滅したとか，北朝鮮の反国家性がなくなったとはいえない。」としている。憲裁決1997．1．16「憲バ6．26．93　憲バ34．35．36（併合)」，憲法判例集第九巻一集2頁。
(18) 山内・太田，前掲注(1)3頁。
(19) 水島朝穂「平和主義」大須賀明編『憲法』（青林書院，1996年）46頁。
(20) 戸波江二『憲法』（ぎょうせい，1996年）87頁。
(21) 大久保史郎「韓半島の統一と日本の役割」前掲注(10)194頁。
(22) 山内・太田，前掲注(1)5頁。
(23) 田中英夫『憲法制定過程覚え書』（有斐閣，1979年）90頁以下，小林直樹『憲法第

九条』（岩波書店，1988年）23頁以下，芦部信喜『憲法（新版）』（岩波書店，1997年）55頁．

(24) 戸波江二・前掲注(20)同頁．

(25) 詳細は，浦田一郎『現代の平和主義と立憲主義』（日本評論社，1995年）108頁以下．

(26) 日本の自衛隊費用を始めとする防衛費は，おおよそ毎年の国民総生産（GNP）ないし国内総生産（GDP）の1％を超えてはいないが，政府の一般会計歳出の6％を超過している．1998年の防衛関係費は総額4兆9千3百億円で，GDPの0.95％，歳出の6.36％に該当する．防衛庁『防衛白書』（1998年）375頁．

(27) 1992年6月15日に国会を通過したPKO法は，国際連合の平和維持活動への参加という名目で戦後初めて武装した自衛隊の海外派兵を法律上可能にしたが，日本国憲法の平和主義に照らして，この法律は根本的な疑問があるとわざるをえない．詳しくは，山内・太田，前掲注(1)，18頁以下．

(28) 和田進「安保体制のグローバル化と国民意識・運動」法律時報71巻1号30頁．

(29) 日本の参議院は，1999年7月26日，翌年の通常国会で憲法問題を総合的に議論するために「憲法調査会」を各院に設置する国会法改正案を通過させ，戦後初めて国会で憲法改正議論が行われることになった．朝日新聞1999年7月27日参照．

(30) 最（大）判，昭和34．12．16 刑集13巻13号3225頁．

(31) 森英樹「非軍事平和主義」『現代憲法講義1』（法律文化社，1993年）87頁．

(32) この判決に対して水島教授は，批判的立場から，条約に対する違憲審査権の行使を主張している．すなわち，条約に関する国会の承認手続（第61条）と憲法改正手続（第96条）の困難性の差異を考えるとき，手続が比較的容易である条約によって実質的に憲法改正が行われるのを避けるためには，条約に対する違憲審査は認められるべきであると主張する（水島朝穂・前掲書（注19）317頁）．

(33) 代表的な文献としては，山内敏弘編『日米新ガイドラインと周辺事態法』（法律文化社，1999年）．

(34) 横田耕一「周辺事態の問題性」山内・前掲注(33)58頁．

(35) 大須賀明，全国憲法研究会主催の憲法記念講演会（1999．5．3）での代表挨拶から．

(36) 防衛庁『防衛白書』（1988年）231頁．

(37) 渡辺治「安保体制のグローバル化を促するもの」法律時報71巻1号（1999年）7－9頁．

(38) 渡辺治「日米新ガイドラインの日本側のねらい」山内・前掲注(33)36頁．

(39) 金大中大統領の統一論は，「3原則3段階統一方案」で知られている．ここでの3原則とは，「平和共存」「平和交流」及び「平和統一」を意味しており，3段階は，第1段階の「一連合二独立政府の共和国連合制」→第2段階の「一連邦二地域自治政府」→第3段階の「一国家一政府」への経路を漸進的に追求していくことを意味する（金大中『私の道，私の思想』（ハンギル社，1994年）343-350頁）．このような

統一論は，金大中政権の対北朝鮮政策にも反映されており，政府は対北朝鮮政策の目標として「平和・和解・協力」を掲げている。さらに，対北朝鮮政策の3大原則として，①平和を破壊する一切の武力挑発の否認，②吸収統一の排除，③和解・協力の積極的な推進，を打出している（これに関しては「"国民の政府"対北政策推進基調」(http://unikoreago.kr/kr/load/c31/c313.htm (99/07/27)を参照）。

(40) 新ガイドラインに関して，肯定的に評価するものとして，金瓊元「新日米安保指針と韓国」（コラム）朝鮮日報1999．5．5参照。

(41) このような観点から，大久保教授は，日本の新ガイドライン策定を批判し，韓半島の統一のために日本は憲法上の平和主義原則を遵守すべきであると主張する。詳細は，大久保・前掲注(21)167頁以下。

(42) 同旨，山内敏弘・太田一男，前掲書（注1）51頁。

(43) これに関連して金哲洙教授は，韓半島の統一はドイツの統一のように南北と周辺強大4国（アメリカ・日本・中国・ロシア）のレベル（two＋four）で決定され得ると述べ，韓半島と東アジアの平和も，周辺強大4国と南北を含む相互安全保障を締結する方案を提示している。金哲洙「東北アジアの平和と韓半島の統一」国際憲法学会韓国学会・前掲注(10)35頁以下。

(44) Henry A. Kissinger, "New World Disorder", Newsweek, May 31, 1999, pp. 22-24.

(45) 酒井新二「地域安保こそ日本の目指す道」（論壇）朝日新聞，1999．6．16。

(46) もちろん，日本の違憲審査制は，アメリカ型の司法審査制（judical review）を採用しているから，ヨーロッパ型の憲法裁判制度のように，憲法訴訟のみに専従し，積極的に政治的問題に対して司法的判断を行うことが期待されにくいということは理解できる。しかし，アメリカ連邦最高裁判所の司法審査制が憲法の最高規範性を確保し，アメリカの立憲主義を確立するのに決定的な原動力になっている事実に照らすと，日本の司法審査制もより積極的に活性化されることが期待されると考える。これに関連して，樋口教授は，日本国憲法下での違憲審査の運用は，きわだった違憲判断消極主義と，合憲判断の積極主義によって特徴づけることができると指摘しつつ，政治部分に対する抑制と正統化という二つの機能の微妙な均衡にこの制度の妙味があるとすれば，日本の違憲審査制度の運用は成功しているとはいえないと評している。樋口陽一『憲法Ｉ』（青林書院，1998年）541頁。

# 日本国憲法の意義と全国憲法研究会

植 野 妙 実 子

 はじめに——フランスにおける立憲主義
 Ⅰ 日本国憲法
  一 日本国憲法の意義
   1 日本国憲法と立憲主義
   2 日本国憲法の基本原理
  二 日本国憲法の課題
   1 天皇制の連続性と非連続性
   2 第9条をめぐる状況
   3 その他の問題
 Ⅱ 全国憲法研究会
  一 全国憲法研究会の組織と活動
   1 組織と歴史
   2 活動
  二 全国憲法研究会の課題
   1 政治状況の変化
   2 活動の重要性
 まとめにかえて

## はじめに——フランスにおける立憲主義

 フランス公法を学ぶものにとっては，立憲主義というと，フランス1789年人権宣言第16条を想いうかべる。そこには「権利の保障が確保されておらず，また権力分立が定められていないすべての社会は，憲法をもたない」と述べられている。そこから，フランスにおける立憲的社会は，人権保障と権力分立を不可欠にしていると理解される。
 しかしながらフランスでは，立憲主義ということばは憲法上定着していかない。人権宣言はシェースとルソーの思想を混同しているといわれるが，シェースの考え方によると，次のようだという。個人が政治的権利を有するにしても，主権を保持するナシオンの枠内で国民代表を通じてにすぎず，ナシオンが総体としての権利を有する。そしてナシオンが主権の伝統的な標識である法律を制定する。…ナシオン

が，権力分立を内容とし，個人の権利を保障するような憲法を規範化する[1]。

結局1789年人権宣言から導き出される結論は，憲法の実現を法律中心主義にゆだねるということで，「社会が法律を介して個人の権利を保障する」という意味であった。他方で権力分立は当時においては「国王からの立法権の奪取」を意味していたという[2]。

阪本昌成は立憲主義の2つのモデルとして，民意を統治過程に統合するための憲法構造を理論的に追求するフランス型と，多元的な民意を統治過程に多元的に反映させる，憲法構造を伝統のなかから発見しようとするアメリカ型と分けるが，いずれにしても両者の起点は同じではない[3]。

フランスで立憲主義がその意味として意識されるようになるのは，現行1958年第五共和制憲法になってからであるし，より詳しくは，憲法院が法律の合憲性審査を実質的に担うようになる1970年代に入ってからといえるであろう。ただし例えばルイ・ファボルーなど7人のフランスの教授による『憲法』の索引にはconstitutionnalisme（立憲主義）や，supériorité de la Constitution（憲法の最高法規性）のことばはみられない[4]。またフランスにおける最近の著作についても立憲主義と題するものはなく，わずかに憲法政体をという意味で『ジャコバン憲法政体とソヴィエト憲法政体』があるにすぎない[5]。

エリザベート・ゾレーはパリ第2大学の憲法の教授でもありアメリカ法の研究者でもあるが，彼女の著した『憲法』においては，憲法の2つの概念を明らかにし，1789年人権宣言第16条をキーワードとして，「規範としての憲法の一般理論」「権力の組織」「権利の保障」についての説明を行なっている[6]。

まず憲法の概念の第1は，憲法が一国家の政治体制を示し，政府と識別できないものであることを示していること，第2は，憲法が政府の上に存在する法，すなわち政府より優越する法規範の総体であること，としている。そしてこれらの概念を，叙述的憲法，規範としての憲法にそれぞれ対応させて説明している。規範としての憲法の定義として，「憲法は自由な人民が手にする基本的かつ最高の法である」と述べ，基本法であるというかぎりにおいて，憲法は政治社会の基礎である，最高法であるというかぎりにおいて，規範としての憲法はすべての他の法律に優越する法律である，規範としての憲法は「自由な人民」の成果であると述べる。さらにアメリカにおける規範としての憲法という創造を説明して「合法性」と「合憲性」の区別を明らかにした後，フランス革命時の憲法観は，法律に基づく国家という意味で法

治国家を確立したが憲法に基づく国家を確立したのではないと述べる。フランスで確立していくのは，シェースが望んだように，フランスにおける主権は純粋に排他的に国民に存するという考え方であり，今日においても適用されている1789年人権宣言第3条は「あらゆる主権の原理は本質的に国民にある」と述べている。シェースによればこうした国民主権は「国民は憲法の下におかれないばかりではなく，おかれることはできず，おかれてはならない」のであり，もし国民が憲法やあらゆる他の実定法の下におかれるなら，もはや国民は主権者ではないということになるという。同時に法律は一般意思の表明であり，憲法的法律と通常法律の区別がないことも示している[7]。

　ヨーロッパ全体の憲法的伝統もアメリカ的伝統からは遠いものであって，第2次世界大戦以前には議会の権限を制限するという考えは散発的にはあっても具体化されなかった，と述べる。しかしながら今日では状況は大きく変わり，多くの国が憲法の規範的概念に賛同している。具体的にはこのような進展は，議会に徐々に効果的に，法律の合憲性の審査を通して国家の憲法を尊重させるようになっている事実が示している。フランスもヨーロッパ全体のこうした動きに呼応している[8]。

　このようなヨーロッパの憲法についての新しい概念は，理論的，政治的要因によってもたらされた。理論的要因としては，法の純粋理論（純粋法学）に基づくハンス・ケルゼンの教義によるところが大きい。その考え方は，憲法を頂点とする法のピラミッド的体系に通じる法段階説というものである。ケルゼンは法規範の本質的な2つの性格を有効性と実効性とし，その双方が法体系の頂点に位置する憲法から発するという。かくしてアメリカ型に対応するヨーロッパ型憲法裁判所が，ケルゼンの発想に基づき，世界で初めて1920年にオーストリアで実施される。この憲法裁判所のヨーロッパ型とアメリカ型は，既にルイ・ファボルーが明らかにしているように，前者は，合憲性審査の効果を確保するために特別に構成される専らこれにのみ関わる裁判所であり，後者はこうした憲法裁判が司法体系のそれぞれの裁判官の手のうちに，たとえ下級審の裁判官であったとしても，あるものをいう[9]。

　政治的要因としては，第2次世界大戦の勝利者であったアメリカ人の制度や伝統によって，アメリカの連邦制がヨーロッパ共同体の建設に大いに影響を及ぼしたことと同時に，アメリカの立憲主義がヨーロッパの政治思想や権利や自由の保護の方法に影響を及ぼした。とりわけ連邦制国家における合憲性審査の果たす役割が認識された。しかしながら決定的要因となるのは人権の保障の必要性であった。アメリ

カと同様ヨーロッパにおいても，議会は専制に対する防壁とはならない。また法律は法的には一般意思の表明とみなされ，革命的イデオロギーの中では，一般的融和の成果とされてきたが，今日ではもはや，多数派によって承認された政府の意思の表明にすぎないと認識されるようになっている。議会内多数派が存在するヨーロッパの国において憲法裁判所が発達したのも偶然ではない，という[10]。

　また代表性の観念や政治的イデオロギーも変化した。アメリカ人はヨーロッパの政治文化と異なる政治文化をもたらした。一般意思や共和制的友愛の崇拝を賞賛する満場一致主義者でないとするなら，満場一致の民主主義に多元的民主主義がとってかわることになる。多元主義者であっても少数派の権利を尊重し，多数派の過度の専制に厳格であるべきである。こうしたやり方で，多くの者にとって市民的権利を保障するもっともよい方法は，マディソンによると自由社会を特徴づけるという「利益の多様性」において探究されるべきだということが明らかになる。フランスの憲法院でも，多元主義の尊重が「民主主義の諸条件の1つ」を構成することを判示した際，この新しいアプローチを確認した[11]。

　このようにして，ヨーロッパ諸国における憲法の規範としての観念に向けての進展は，大きな変化をもたらした。公法の性格の変化であり，その基本は以降憲法であり，立法ではない。さらに憲法の性格の変化であり，憲法が政治的規範としての法から裁判規範としての法となる傾向にある。すなわち裁判官によって語られる法だということである。フランスにおける憲法院の判例の効果のもとで生じたこうした変化はいわばあらゆる期待に反してなされた，とゾレーは述べる[12]。あらゆる法の源は一般意思であるとする共和制の伝統に反してなされた。次に第1及び第2帝政のセナのような政治的な形態の下でしか合憲性審査を知らなかった憲法的伝統に反してなされた。さらに憲法院を権利と自由の守護者にしようとは考えていなかった1958年憲法制定者のそもそもの意図に反してなされたのである[13]。憲法の「法を語る」憲法院の権利から，今日のフランスでは政治制度と異なる憲法という法un droit constitutionnelが存在する。常に変わらぬものとして政治制度の研究は政治学の分析方法以外では行われない。反対に憲法はもはや政治学の方法に尽きるということはない。憲法は政治学から離れて，公法の第1の学問，公法の礎となったのである。これにより昔のように公法は合法性の原則から始めるのではなく合憲性の原則から始めることになった。フランス憲法も，一方では権力の組織や権利の保障に関わる形式上の憲法と，他方では市民的政治的権利の内容に関わる事実上の憲法と

に分解される[14]。

かくしてゾレーは今日において初めてフランス人権宣言第16条は実質化されたとするのである。実際，フランスでは今日，法治国家や法の支配が憲法院の合憲性審査を中心として説かれるようになった[15]。アメリカにおける立憲主義との融合がみられるのである。

## I　日本国憲法

### 一　日本国憲法の意義

#### 1　日本国憲法と立憲主義

日本国憲法はむしろルーツにおいてアメリカの影響を受けているといえる。1946年11月に公布，翌年5月に施行された日本国憲法は，第2次世界大戦中の政治のあり方を反省して，日本においてはじめて名実共に立憲主義の名にふさわしい憲法として成立した。既にみたように，当初においてそのような意味でとらえられなかったとしても，立憲主義とはまさにフランス1789年人権宣言第16条が示すように，その基本は，人権保障と権力分立ということであり，その意味で，人権保障も権力分立も不十分であった大日本帝国憲法は外見的立憲主義といわざるをえないのである[16]。他方で，民主主義がすすめば，立憲主義をあえて述べる必要はないとされるが，それは，立憲主義の目的も民主主義の目的も人々の自由や権利を保障するところにあるからである。しかしながら，現在の日本において，真に憲法に基づく政治が行われているかどうかは問題となるところである。したがって民主主義の内容が問われるといえよう。

立憲主義はまた，個人の尊重を前提とするものである。その意味で個人主義に基づくもので全体主義を否定する[17]。自立した個人の自己選択，自己決定による社会の運営，すなわち自治が保障されていなければならない。その点で，日本国憲法第13条は個人の尊重を定め，第14条に法の下の平等を定めている。

こうした人権の保障，民主主義，立憲主義はいずれも，平和であるとき，最大限にその意義を発揮することができる。人権の十分な保障と平和は，不可分に結びつき，人権保障の前提は平和だともいえる[18]。その点に気づいたのか，フランス1791年憲法は，前文に人権宣言を掲げ立憲君主制を採用するものであったが，世界でははじめて征服戦争の否定を明確化していた。

日本国憲法はさらにすすんで，侵略戦争の否定を明言するのみならず，戦力の保持自体を否定し，戦力によらない平和の確立と維持を強く訴えるものである。

日本における立憲主義としてさしあたり次の点が問題となると指摘されている。第1に，情緒をこえた論理的な思想として立憲主義が日本に定着しているのか。第2に，日本人の精神構造は西欧の立憲主義を受容する素地があるのか。第3に，立憲主義を国民の中に強く根付かせる条件は何か，である[19]。しばしば，当然のように日本の特殊性が西欧で誕生した立憲主義を受容できないかのように語られる。しかし立憲主義の目的そのものは人類にとって普遍的価値を有し，さらに日本国憲法は人権の歴史性を認めていること（第97条）も忘れてはならない。

**2　日本国憲法の基本原理**

日本国憲法の特色として通常次の3原理が挙げられる。基本的人権の保障，永久平和主義，国民主権である。なかでも基本的人権の保障が中心である。その理由は，大日本帝国憲法下における法律の留保を前提とする人権の保障とは異なり，日本国憲法は「侵すことのできない永久の権利」として自然権的性格を人権に認め，さらに「人類の多年にわたる自由獲得の成果」として人権の歴史の普遍性を確認しているからである。量的にも第3章（10条〜40条）が人権規定にあてられているが人権規定はそれにとどまらず，憲法の大きな部分をしめている。

これに対し，人権保障の前提として永久平和主義の重要性を認め，人権保障の最もふさわしい手段として国民主権を定めている。国民主権が天皇制との関係で付随的に本文では第1条にしか表現されていないのに対し，永久平和主義の理念は明示されている。しかも，憲法の構成においても，第3章の「国民の権利及び義務」の前に第2章の「戦争の放棄」がおかれて，人権保障の前提としての平和の必要性が確認されている。さらに日本国憲法は，既述したように文言上非常に厳しい平和主義を謳っている。当然こうした3つの基本原理の設定は，憲法改正の限界の議論も惹起するものである。すなわち，西欧において，共和政体の変革が許されないと示している場合があるが（例えば，フランス，イタリア），日本においてはこの三原理を根本的に変革することは許されないであろう[20]。

二　日本国憲法の課題

**1　天皇制の連続性と非連続性**

日本国憲法はその意義も大きいものではあるが，克服すべき点も少なからずある。

その第1は天皇制の問題である。大日本帝国憲法下の万世一系の天皇主権をはばからなかった天皇制から日本国憲法下においては国民主権と並存する，そして「主権の存する日本国民の総意に基づく」地位による象徴天皇制となった。大日本帝国憲法下の天皇制は，また神権天皇制でもあり，日本国憲法下では厳格な政教分離主義（第20条3項）に基づき，信教の自由を個人に保障すると同時に国教の設立も認めず，宗教が直接的，間接的に国または地方公共団体の事項に参与することも，反対に国または地方公共団体が宗教的儀式や行事に参与することも認めていない。

しかるに，天皇制は制度として根本的に異なっているにもかかわらず，実際上同一の天皇が，戦中も，戦後も異なる制度の下で君臨したのである。天皇は新制度の下で現人神ではもはやないことを宣言しても，天皇制の根本的改変は人々にとってはわかりにくいものとなり，新旧体制の連続性が綿々として流れることを許すことになる[21]。また，天皇の戦争責任の追及をぼかすことにもなった。

象徴天皇制は本来，君主制の中でも最も極小化された天皇の権限の状態をさすはずであり，天皇自身の考えや心の動きを問題とせず，すべて内閣の助言と承認に委ねるものである。しかしながら実際上は，第6条，第7条の天皇の国事行為として定められている行為以外のグレーゾーンにあたる行為も多く見受けられている。ここにおいても本来の趣旨と異なった拡大解釈の容認がみられている。

また，戦争中の国体観念の脱却を十分に果たさなかったことが，昨今の「日の丸，君が代」を国旗・国歌法として成立することを許したり，靖国神社法案が模索されて，内閣総理大臣等閣僚による靖国神社の公式参拝を公認しようという問題などを浮上させてくるのである。

そもそも，天皇制は，憲法の基本原理として存在するものでもなく，第1条に述べるように，天皇の地位及び制度は主権者である国民の意思すなわち総意によって可変のものであることを意味している[22]。

2 第9条をめぐる状況

世界的にも画期的，先進的な第9条，とりわけ，戦力の不保持，交戦権の否認を明記する2項が存在しているが，時代を先取りしているその先進性の故に，その趣旨は十分に理解されず，政府による解釈による実際上の改憲が定着している。

第9条は元来，1項の国際紛争を解決する手段としての戦争の放棄の意味は侵略戦争の放棄を意味するにすぎないが，2項において戦力ももたない交戦権も認められない状況でいかなる戦争ができるのか，侵略のみならず自衛のための戦争もでき

ないと解釈するものである。政府においても憲法制定当時（1946年）はこうした解釈によっていた[23]。しかしながら、朝鮮戦争の勃発により日本を極東における軍事基地として利用しようという見方がアメリカ側に出現し、自衛隊が創設され、日米安保条約が締結された。同時に冷戦体制にも突入することとなり、第9条はこうした日米の協調の中で解釈されることとなったのである。

多くの憲法研究者は、第9条2項をその文言通りに厳密に解釈して、戦力によらない平和の確立・維持しか認められないとして、自衛隊、日米安保条約は違憲と判断している。しかし、政府は、戦力に至らざる必要最小限度の自衛力は国家として当然もつことができるとして、世界でその実力を4位ともそれ以上ともいわれる自衛隊を認め、なおかつその防衛力の不足を補う意味で日米安保条約を認めている[24]。それ故、憲法研究者やそれを支持する市民運動家たちと、政府との間には第9条をめぐって解釈の乖離が存在している。

**3 その他の問題**

日本国憲法の規定の趣旨からすると、次のような社会構造自体にかかわる問題も浮かびあがる。

第1は、官僚支配であり、官僚が中心となって政策立案をしている。これは社会の安定性をはかる点では利点と言えるが、時代に即応した大胆な発想や政策が生まれにくい。また企業と官僚の癒着を断ち切ることは難しく、相変わらず天下りなどの問題を生じさせている。

第2は、企業中心社会である。第13条は個人主義を掲げているが、現実には日本の社会は、企業や世帯を中心とする社会であり、個人に基づいてはいない。企業と個人の関係は労働協約に基づくドライな合理的な関係とみるのではなく、企業の大義のために個人が犠牲となり、過労死のような問題を生じさせている。

第3は、不平等社会である。第14条は法の下の平等を掲げているが、現実には多くの不平等が存在する。男女間の平等は国際的な影響もあってかなり改善されてきてはいるが、いまだに表面的であり、人種、民族など外国人に対する差別も散見される。とりわけ後者の点では、基本的に国家主義が拭い去られてはいない。さらに社会的、経済的弱者に対する保護も経済的効率という考え方によって蔑ろにされ、差別的取扱いも多く存在している。

第4は、社会国家としての国家責任の不明確さである。多くの先進国と同様、日本も少子・高齢社会を迎えており、社会保障・福祉の充実は急務である。しかしな

がら，財源の確保も含め，平等が保障されているとはいえず，さらに安易に民間の活力に委ねようとする傾向がある。国家として果たすべき任務は何なのか，国民に対する国家の責任とは何なのかが改めて問われよう。

　日本の社会はこのような多くの問題をかかえているが，これらの多くは憲法の規定を十分に生かしていないことに由来している。したがって，憲法上の規定の意味がどのようなものであるかを，多くの市民に理解してもらう必要があり，その点で憲法研究者の果たすべき社会的任務というものがある。

## II　全国憲法研究会

### 一　全国憲法研究会の組織と活動

#### 1　組織と歴史

　全国憲法研究会（全国憲）は，憲法を研究する専門家の集まりとして1965年4月に全国の憲法研究者112名を結集して，発足した。その前年には憲法調査会の最終報告書が提出され，憲法への危機が高まったことを受けての憲法研究者の行動であった。憲法調査会は，憲法改正の実行をめざすものとして1956年6月に設置された。1957年8月から活動を始め，1964年7月に内閣に報告書を提出して終えている。提出された報告書は改憲についての積極・消極の意見の両論を列挙し，改憲を強く主張するものではなかったが，これを機会に解釈改憲が定着することとなった。しかしながら，改憲の気運は弱まったのではなく，むしろ憲法の実体を骨抜きにする作業が政府によって着々とすすめられていった。三矢研究の存在，建国記念日の設置，長沼ミサイル基地の設置，明治百年記念式典などである[25]。

　全国憲は，当初，憲法問題についての資料の収集，分析，研究成果の公表，意見の発表，他の護憲団体への協力，会員の講師の斡旋などを仕事とし，中堅層の憲法学者を中心として組織され，会長は特に設けず，全国を7地区に分けて若干名の世話人を選んで運営を委ねてきた。学会の折の総会の他，重大な問題が生じたとき，重大な段階に達したときは，全国組織として声明その他の活動を行うことを特色として有する組織であった。こうした対外的な意見発表，意思表示は個人責任を原則とした。

　すなわち全国憲は，憲法問題の理論的研究と討議を第一課題としながらも，民主憲法を護るという姿勢を根本的にとりつつ，必要に応じて，社会的，政治的発言も

全国憲有志という形で団体として表明してきた。設立5年後に，より研究活動が活性化することをめざして，組織と運営の問題点を改めて，全国憲法研究会規約が作られた。その第1条には，「本会は，憲法を研究する専門家の集団であって，平和・民主・人権を基本原理とする日本国憲法を護る立場に立って，学問的研究を行ない，あわせて会員相互の協力を促進することを目的とする。」と定められ，明確に護憲の研究者団体として成立したのである。さらに第2条には，次のように定められた。

「本会は，前条の目的を達成するため，次の事業を行なう。
一　定期的に研究会を開催する。
二　研究成果を公表する。
三　時宜に応じて意見を発表する。
四　前各号のほか運営委員会において適当と認めた事業を行なう。」

護憲という立場から，意見の発表や適当と認められる事業，例えば5月3日憲法記念日の講演会などを行うこととなった。公法の研究者の学会としては，既に，公法学会が存在しているが，全国憲は護憲という立場から，いわゆる学会以上の運動もくり拡げていくこととなった。

ここで，憲法を護るという意味について確認しておく必要があろう。日本において憲法改正の焦点は常に第9条，とりわけその2項であった。その規定の示す平和主義は，世界にも稀な徹底したものであり，第2次世界大戦の反省と悔恨の上にある。この平和主義を中心として，日本国憲法の理念を護るというのが護憲の意味である。その意味では，第9条2項によって，どのような平和を実現するのか明確化する必要もあろう。昨今第9条2項の示す戦力にならない平和の確立・維持という考え方が国際的な動向の中で揺らぎを見せているのも事実であり，全国憲の今後のあり方も問われている[26]。

### 2　活　動

全国憲では，年2回の研究総会の他，設立当初は，部会における研究会やシンポジウムも行なっていた。憲法理論研究会や弁護士との合同研究会も行っていた。憲法記念集会（現在は，憲法記念講演会）は1967年から始められており，1977年からは5月3日（日本国憲法施行日）に開催するようになった。全国憲設立後10年間のあいだには比較的頻繁に声明，アピールを出していた。しかし最近はむしろ，全国憲有志として声明を出すことよりも，全国憲を母体としながらも別個の形で，憲法問題を提起して検証する形の憲法フォーラム開催に力が注がれるようになってきた。そ

の点では学会としての位置づけはより強まってきているといえる。

　1989年からは『憲法問題』という研究会誌を発行するようになり，活動内容の記録のみならず，政治における憲法問題の動きも明確に検討できるようになった。

　1999年5月現在の会員数は，420名以上であり，もはや以前のような中堅の研究者を中心とする団体ではない。専任もしくは専任でなくても，また大学の博士後期課程に在籍するのなら学生であっても，2名の推薦人をもって入会が受けいれられる。憲法研究者の独自の学会として期待されることが多くなった分，設立当初の目的である学問の立場から必要に応じて政治に発言するということはうすめられてきているといえよう。

## 二　全国憲法研究会の課題

### 1　政治状況の変化

　政治状況における最近の大きな変化は，憲法を護るという政治勢力が変化したことである。1994年6月，社会党，自民党，さきがけが支持した社会党の村山富市氏が衆議院で内閣総理大臣に指名され，連立内閣が発足した。社会党は既に1993年の「93年宣言」の中で自衛隊合憲を認め，従来からの護憲政党としての基本的なスタンスが疑われていたが，自民党との連立によってそれはますます強まった。1996年1月村山内閣が終わり，1月に社会党は社民党へと党名を変更したが，9月に結成された民主党へ社民党から党籍変更する者も相つぎ，社民党自体の支持者は激減した。他方で民主党には自民党から党籍変更した者も含まれ，とりわけ第9条についての護憲政党であると評価することはできない。

　第2次世界大戦中の大日本帝国の加害者としての反省からも，また初の原爆投下の被害者としての経験からも，また多数の戦争犠牲者を産み出したという体験からも，日本国民の平和への希求は根強く，平和運動は市民運動として定着していた。しかし，こうした運動と直結していた護憲政党の変節は，拠り所を失うことを意味した。労働運動の大きな柱も平和であったが，労働組合自体も明確な支持政党を失っている。周辺事態法は日米安保をさらに拡大強化するものであるが，こうした社民党の凋落の中で強行された[27]。

　最近では，自民党が自由党，公明党と連立を模索し，その前提において，既述したように懸案の，国旗・国歌法の制定や通信傍受法，住民基本台帳法の改正などを成立させた。しかし，これらは十分に審議を尽くしたとはいえず，また国民の根強

い反対をおしきって採択されたものである。

　周辺事態法をめぐる憲法フォーラムは1999年3月に開催されたが，400名以上もの市民，学生がつめかけ議論をたたかわした。また，周辺事態法案等を憂慮する憲法研究者の声明には216名の全国憲有志が賛同している。しかしながらこうした反対が政党のレベルでは生かされなかった。

　他方で若年層の政治的アパシーは増大している。そしてこうした政治的アパシーに乗じて改憲をもくろむ政治勢力が拡大しつつある。

　日本の現在の政治状況は，自己実現の拠り所を失った市民運動を虎視眈々と改憲のチャンスをうかがう保守政党勢力が食いつぶそうとしているようにみえる。

　1999年7月に国会法の一部を改正する法律が成立して憲法調査会の設置が決まった。この前身として1997年5月に発足した憲法調査委員会設置推進議員連盟が存在していた。その設立趣意書には「21世紀に向けたわが国のあり方を考え，新時代の憲法について議論を行う絶好の機会」といい，「国家の基本問題について真摯に論議することこそが，われわれ政治家に課せられた最大の使命」としていたという。実際は憲法改正を視野にいれて，現行憲法の制度等について調査・検討をする常任委員会として「憲法制度調査委員会」の設置を目論んでいたという。

　設置された憲法調査委員会は，「日本国憲法について広範かつ総合的に調査を行う」（国会法102条の6）という曖昧模糊とした目的をもつものにとどまり，申し合せとして，憲法調査会には議案提出権がないこと，調査期間をおおむね5年程度を目途とすることなどが行なわれた[28]。

　既述したように憲法調査会なる設置は既にあり，その活動の影響を受けて，全国憲法研究会が立ちあがったことを想いおこさせる。しかし状況は同じではなく，世代交代によって憲法の意味や意義をどのようにとらえるのか若干の違いが生じてきているのも事実であろう。

　日本が戦争で失ったものは大きかったが，代償として得た，平和，自由や権利，民主主義は，その意義を忘れることなく大切に育てなければならないものである。こうした状況下にあって全国憲の憲法を護る活動が問われているといえる。

　2　活動の重要性

　全国憲には確かに独自の憲法学会としての活動も期待されている。しかしその活動は，純粋学問的なものではない。なぜならそもそも憲法は不断に政治と結びつくものだからである。憲法は最高法規であり根本規範である。憲法に則って国の政治

が行なわれなくてはならないことは当然である。しかしながら，憲法の文言を拡大的に解釈することによって本来の趣旨からはずれた政治が行なわれているとすれば，憲法研究者として，政治に警鐘をならし，再検討を求めることも当然のことといえよう。

また憲法は法社会学的にも考慮されるべきものである。憲法の述べるあるべき姿が国民の中に定着しないとするならそれはなぜか。あるいはどのような形で憲法を生かすべきなのか，検討していかなければならない。憲法は国民の生活の中に定着してこそ意味をもつものである。

その点では憲法の解釈について認識の違いが存在し，その違いがまさに全国憲の活動の拠って立つところを示している[29]。全国憲には学会としての活動もさることながら，市民の側からのこうした考察や活動に対する期待に答える必要もある。

まとめにかえて

結局，全国憲に課せられている重要な1つの使命は，憲法識字ということであろう。憲法のもつ意味を市民や政治家に知らしめることこそ，重要な役割である。憲法は政治と深く関わっている。しかしながら，法律の制定一つをとっても，第41条の述べる「国会は，国権の最高機関であって，国の唯一の立法機関である」ということが十分に生かされているとはいえない。法律案の審議は委員会中心で行なわれ，しかも審議未了で委員会での強行採決もあり，ときとして国会が通過儀礼となっている点もある[30]。このようなとき，憲法が議院内閣制のどのような理念に拠って立つのかをあらためて認識することは重要であろう。

憲法識字を広めるためには，全国憲自体も実務家，裁判官や弁護士などと交流をはかり，実態に即した提言ができるようにすることも必要である。全国憲の研究総会においては，他の学問分野の専門家からの発言を設けることはあるが，実務家からの発言を設ける機会は最近少なく，個別の裁判のテーマにそって，小さな研究会をもつようなこともしていない。これは憲法研究者がさまざまな場所でさまざまな問題についての発言を求められるため，忙殺されていることとも関わっているが，憲法研究において実務軽視の面があることも否めない。

ところで日本人は，高学歴であるにもかかわらず，選挙の際の投票率は低く，決して政治的意識が高い方とはいえない。96年の短大・大学への進学率は女性48.3％，男性44.2％であるが，投票率については，衆議院(96年小選挙区)で女性60.23％，男

性59.03％，参院（95年選挙区）で女性44.37％，男性44.67％だった。投票率の低下傾向はますます強まっている。自らの政治的選択や決定が日本の命運をきめる重要な行為であることが認識できていない。他の先進国と同様日本も高齢・少子社会を迎え，きめ細かな政策が要求されているにもかかわらず政治への関心は高まらない。このような閉塞的な状況を打破するためにも，憲法研究者による憲法政治についてのわかりやすい解説や分析は重要だといえよう。

　最後に，日本国憲法は，そもそも第2次世界大戦の反省と悔恨を踏まえて制定された。特に平和の尊さを謳っている点に特色がある。その日本国憲法の趣旨や理念を損なう行為は許しがたいといえよう。アジアに危機や分裂をもたらしたり，疑心暗鬼をかきたてたりするのではなく，アジアの平和の確立に力を尽くし，豊かな社会の創出に力を注ぐべきである。国際会議の開催や交流によって互いの法文化や政策を知ることも重要である。全国憲がアジアの平和の確立と人権保障のためにすべきこともまだまだ多くある。したがって，全国憲が発足した経緯をふり返り，全国憲が憲法政治に果たしてきた役割を検証し，日本国憲法の意味をとらえ直すことは今日十分意義があることといえよう[31]。

(1) ミッシェル・ガンザン＝横尾日出雄訳「人権宣言」中央大学社会科学研究所研究報告12号（1993年）449頁以下。

(2) 同論文462頁。ちなみに第16条は元々第6部会第24条が原案でそのまま採択されているが，第6部会案が人権宣言の基礎案とされたのは「穏健な自由主義的立憲派から右の議員たち，人権宣言に消極的な保守派を含めた議員らにより，第6部会案が比較的無難であるため承認されたもの」という。深瀬忠一「1789年人権宣言序説（三）」北大法学18巻3号482頁。

(3) 阪本昌成『憲法1 国制クラシック』有信堂2000年27頁。同「立憲主義の歴史とその展開」阪本昌成編『立憲主義―過去と未来の間―』（有信堂，2000年）2頁以下参照。

(4) Louis FAVOREU et alii. Droit constitutionnel, 2$^e$éd, Paris, Dallez, 1999.

(5) Achille MESTRE, Constitutionnalisme jacoban et constitutionnailsme sovietique, Paris, P.U.F., 1971.

(6) Elisabeth ZOLLER, Droit constitutionnel, Paris, P.U.F., 1998.

(7) Ibid., pp. 9 ets..

(8) Ibid., pp. 44 ets..

(9) Cf., Louis FAVOREU, Modèle américain et modèle européen de justice constituionnelle, AIJC., vol. IV. -1988, Paris, Economica, 1990, pp. 51 et s.

この翻訳についてはルイ・ファボルー＝植野妙実子訳「憲法裁判の比較」『フランス公法講演集』（中央大学出版部，1998年）147頁以下。
(10)　Elisabeth ZOLLER, op cit., p. 48.
(11)　Ibid., p. 49. cf. Déc. 93-333 DC, Autorisation d'emission, 21 janv. 1994, cons. 3, RJC, I, 569
(12)　Elisabeth ZOLLER, op. cit., pp. 49 et 50.
(13)　そもそも憲法院は，第五共和制憲法の第34条の法律事項の監視であり，議会の活動を統制することであった。François LUCIAIRE et Gérard CONAC, La constitution de la république française, 2$^e$ed., Economica, 1987, pp. 1085 et s.
(14)　Elisabeth ZOLLER, op. cit., p. 50.
(15)　ジャン・リベロは次のように述べている。「法治国家とはすなわち我々の政治体制のように今日民主的で自由でありたいと願うすべての政治体制が主張する呼称である。19世紀のドイツの偉大な法律家たちが『警察国家』に対置させて用いたことばであるが，その出現以来，そのことばの意味は内容を拡大させてきている。法治国家とは，尊重され続けている法規範の中にすべての権力がその限界を見い出すような国家である。すべての制度と同様に法治国家も目的に答えるものであるがその目的は確かなものである。それは専制に対する市民の保障である。」Jean RIVERO, État de droit, état du droit, in L'état de droit; Mélanges en l'honneur de Guy BRAIBANT, Paris, Dallaz, 1996, p. 609. 樋口陽一『憲法』（創文社，1992年）9頁以下も参照。
(16)　野中俊彦「日本の立憲主義と天皇制」『憲法と憲法原理』ジュリスト臨時増刊1987年5月3日号（884号）13頁以下。
(17)　江橋崇「立憲主義にとっての『個人』」前掲ジュリスト臨時増刊号2頁以下。
(18)　しばしば立憲平和主義ということばも立憲主義の発展型として用いられる。上田勝美「日本の立憲平和主義に関する理論と課題」杉原泰雄先生古稀記念論文集刊行会編『21世紀の立憲主義―現代憲法の歴史と課題』（勁草書房，2000年）201頁以下。
(19)　野中俊彦・前掲論文19頁。
(20)　なお次のものも参照。山内敏弘「立憲主義を無視した改憲試案」軍縮問題資料172号（1995年）64頁以下。
(21)　樋口陽一「比較憲法論的に見た日本国憲法」『日本国憲法―三〇年の軌跡と展望』ジュリスト臨時増刊1977年5月3日号（638号）65頁以下。
(22)　芹沢斉「第一条」小林孝輔・芹沢斉編『基本法コンメンタール・憲法［第4版］』別冊法学セミナー149号（1997年）15頁以下。
(23)　長谷川正安「第九条」有倉遼吉・小林孝輔編『基本法コンメンタール憲法［第3版］』33頁以下。
(24)　1997年国防支出総額では，アメリカ合衆国，ロシア，フランス，日本，中国，ドイツの順で多い。財団法人矢野恒太郎記念会館編『世界国勢図会1999―2000』。（国

勢社，1999年）506頁以下．
(25)　さしあたり，渡辺治「憲法調査会設置」『法律事件百選』ジュリスト1988年1月1日―15日合併号（900号）100，101頁．
(26)　渡辺治他『「憲法改正」批判』（労働旬報社，1994年）75頁以下（三輪隆担当部分）参照．
(27)　山内敏弘編『日米新ガイドライン周辺事態法』（法律文化社，1999年）．
(28)　前原清隆他「憲法調査会を調査する」法学セミナー2000年5月号48頁以下，森英樹他「憲法調査会／憲法論議の行方」法律時報72巻5号（2000年）5頁以下の各特集参照．
(29)　植野妙実子「憲法解釈について」法学セミナー2000年4月号87頁以下．
(30)　大山礼子『国会学入門』三省堂1997年94頁．
(31)　芦部信喜「憲法学50年を顧みて」杉原泰雄・樋口陽一編『日本国憲法50年と私』（岩波書店，1997年）134頁以下参照．

　なお，全国憲法研究会の組織と活動については次のものを参照した．『全国憲法研究会の10年―活動の記録』全国憲法研究会（1975年）『全国憲法研究会1975―1986―活動の記録』全国憲法研究会（1987年）全国憲法研究会編『憲法問題』1～10号（1990～1999年）三省堂
　※　予備研究会において杉原泰雄教授から日本学術会議法第2条，すなわち日本学術会議の目的を定めた条文についてご示唆をいただいたことを付記しておきたい．それには次のように記されている．
　　第2条　日本学術会議は，わが国の科学者の内外に対する代表機関として，科学の向上発達を図り，行政，産業及び国民生活に科学を反映浸透させることを目的とする．
　日本学術会議とはいわば，学会の頂点に位置づけられるものであるが，そこでは「行政，産業及び国民生活に科学を反映浸透させること」が目的の一つとして掲げられている．

# 第Ⅲ部　まとめ

大須賀　明

　まず岩間報告に対して、コメンテーターの小林武氏（南山大）は、岩間報告が「あるべき憲法像」の観点から、個別的に改憲論に応じてもよいのではないかとした点について、今日の憲法改正論は、憲法裁判所の設置、新しい人権の明文化の提唱などが特徴となっているが、これらは「目くらまし」にすぎず、中心的なターゲットはやはり9条であるので、憲法改正に対してはより警戒的であるべきだという指摘を行った。

　このような小林氏の指摘に対して、岩間氏は以下のように答えた。今日の改憲論では、環境権等が「目くらまし」的に使われており、改憲論に賛成すれば結局9条も改正される可能性があり、それゆえに全面的に改正論には応じないという立場もよくわかる。ただ、それとは別に憲法9条擁護という前提のもとで、憲法の基本原理をさらに発展させるために「あるべき憲法像」を追求するという選択肢もあるのではないか。支配的学説は13条および25条を環境権の根拠としているが、人間と自然の共生という新しい哲学に基づく環境権というのは、人間中心主義を採ってきた13条及び25条を根拠とすることはできないのではないか。最初に環境権を主唱した人たちも、差し当たりは解釈で基礎づけるが、将来的には憲法改正により取り入れるべきだと言っていた。このように、人権保障という観点から積極的に対応するために憲法改正が必要であれば憲法改正を行うべきではないか。

　2番目の龔報告に対して、コメンテーターの中村睦男氏（北海道大）から、現在の日本の憲法改正の論点の一つとして、日本が正規の国連軍に参加するのを可能にする規定を設けるかどうかの問題があるが、国際立憲主義の立場からこのような憲法改正の考え方はどう評価されるかという質問が寄せられた。それに対して、龔氏は、国際法上、あるいは国際立憲主義の観点からは何ら問題はないとした。ただし、日本国憲法の問題としては、平和憲法を改正せずに国連に対しても非軍事協力をしていくか、あるいは今までのアメリカとの軍事同盟を明文上否定した上で国連に対して積極的に協力するか、の2つの対応が考えられるとした。

3番目の鄭報告に対して、コメンテーターの國分典子氏（愛知県立大）から、新ガイドライン関連法が韓国ではどのように評価されているのかという質問が寄せられた。それに対して鄭氏は、韓国の国際政治学者のなかでは、アジアの平和のために周辺事態法を肯定的に評価する人もいるが、公法学会では多くの会員は日本の軍事大国化に敏感な反応を見せていると答えた。

　最後の植野報告に対して、浦田一郎氏（一橋大）は以下のような感想を述べた。改憲論、あるいは政府の解釈改憲論がどのような構造を持っているのかということは、例えば国会の憲法議論のような便利な資料が整理されていないこともあり、意外と厄介な仕事である。解釈改憲論をめぐってどう考えるかという時に、そもそも解釈改憲論がどうなっているのかということは、我々の重要な研究課題である。こういった浦田氏の感想に対して、植野氏も同感であるとし、解釈改憲で一括りにできない問題もあるし、また改憲論と言われるものの中身も多岐にわたるのであって、それらを一つ一つ詳細に検討すべきであると述べた。

　最後に小沢隆一氏（静岡大）から、ガイドライン関連法と自衛権との関係についての質問が岩間氏になされた。岩間氏は、この質問は後ほど考えてみたいとしつつも、集団的自衛権とは、我が国と密接な関係にある国家に対する武力行使が発生した場合に、同時に軍事行動に入るという概念であるが、周辺事態法で後方地域支援を行う場合、それは実質的軍事行動の一環であるから、その限りでは集団的自衛権で説明でき、かつ憲法で禁止されていると答えた。

　以上のような討論の締めくくりとして、司会の浦田賢治氏（早稲田大）は、第1に各国のナショナルな問題、第2にアジア立憲主義の成立の可否、第3に新しい秩序をどう捉えるか、つまり国連憲章と日本国憲法の平和原則に対してグローバルな観点からの攻撃があるが、それに対してローカルに、ナショナルに、オリジナルにどう対応していくか、という3つの問題が提起されたと述べて本討論を締めくくった。

# 第 IV 部
## アジア立憲主義の総括

## アジア，オセアニアと立憲主義

シェリル・ソンダーズ
阪口　正二郎　訳

1　アジア・オセアニア地域の特徴
2　憲法の比較
3　立憲主義という概念
4　立憲主義に対する挑戦
5　立憲主義にとっての文脈の変化？
6　アジア・オセアニアにおける立憲主義

　本書において，アジアおよびオセアニアの異なった地域から集まった憲法学者たちが，理論と実践の両面から自国の憲法上の仕組みに言及しながら，立憲主義の現状や未来に対する展望を提示している。諸論稿の多様さと広範性は，相互理解，問題関心と問題を共有しようとする協働という観点から見て，よりシステマティックで継続的な地域をまたがる比較研究が有する利点を示している。本稿の主たる目的は，諸論稿を通じて現われている幾つかのテーマを総括し，それらが立憲主義の基準と実践に対して有する含意について考察することにある。またそうすることで，オーストラリアおよびそれと同様な憲法に関する伝統を有する他の諸国の立憲主義にとっての幾つかの問題に関する展望を示すことにしたい。

　総じて，本稿における議論の概略は以下の通りである。アジア・オセアニア地域の法および憲法システムは，歴史的な経験，現在の状況，文化，伝統に関連する理由から著しく多様なものである。この特徴は，アジア・オセアニア地域を憲法学者にとって特に興味深い対象にするものではあるが，同時に本シンポジウムにおける試みを複雑なものにもしている。この地域全体における統治に対するアプローチの多様性は，立憲主義を特定的な形で定義することを困難にしている。過度に厳密な定義を用いるならば，不注意に文化的ヴァイアスを持ち込んだり，不適切に焦点を限定することになってしまう。そこで，さしあたり，ここでは，立憲主義という概念をもっと一般的な形，すなわち，それぞれは異なった形で満たされることがありうる2つの要素の組み合わせとしてとらえることにしたい。第1の要素は，憲法に定められた基準と手続にしたがった制限政府である。第2の要素は，一般的には人

民の同意を通じて客観的な形で認定される公益にしたがった統治である。

　どのように定義しようとも，立憲主義というものは決して容易に維持できるものではない。それぞれの要素は傷つきやすいものであるし，さらに，両者の間のバランスもしばしば不安定であることがある。

　世紀末の現在，アジア・オセアニア地域を含む世界全体において立憲主義にとって新しい文脈が現われつつある。この文脈に特に影響を与えているのが，国際化，グローバリゼーション，国際的な経済競争などの諸力であり，これらの力が立憲主義に対して及ぼす影響は肯定的なものもあれば否定的なものもある。アジア・オセアニア地域における憲法システムも，これらの力によって影響を受けており，その帰結も肯定，否定の両面がある。全般的には，憲法や憲法原理の形式や実体へのコミットメントが強くなるという意味において，立憲主義が強まっているという一定の兆候が見られる。さらに，憲法や政府の仕組みの設計においてもますますの刷新が見られる。一般的には，このことは，もっぱら植民地時代にその正統性が由来する制度や実践が拒否され，別のところから創造的な形で制度や実践を輸入したり，ローカルな文化や伝統をより詳細に考察する，という最近の傾向のうちに現われている。こうしたことから，アジア・オセアニア地域の状況を反映した立憲主義というものが現われつつあると期待することができるかもしれない。しかしながら，そのような希望を持つにはまだ時期尚早であり，反証も多い。この地域における立憲主義は，多様な人々のためになるような形で展開し繁栄するようになるためには，依然として注意深く育まれねばならない。

## 1　アジア・オセアニア地域の特徴

　憲法あるいは他のことを考える場合にも，アジア・オセアニア地域は世界において最も多様な地域の1つであることに注意すべきである。地理的に見れば，西はインド亜大陸，東はキリバスその他の太平洋諸国，北は中国、日本，南はニュージーランドまで及ぶ地域である。しかも，この広大な地域の中には，世界で最も人口が過密な幾つかの国もあれば[1]，逆に比較的少数の人しか住んでいない世界で最も小さい島国もある[2]。またこの地域の人々の状況は，社会的，文化的，政治的，経済的に極めて異なっており，憲法典や統治システムに求められる要求もそれに応じて異なっている。

本稿の関心からみてより重要なのは，この地域における諸国家の歴史的経験の多様性である。大半の国は，中には何千年にも及ぶほど，長くて豊かな文化的発展を享受している。しかしながら，より最近の時代においては，大半の国はヨーロッパ権力による植民地化という経験を有している。植民地化を免れた国家であっても，ある時期または複数の時期において，西洋の影響をいやおうなしに受けている。この地域においては，異なった時期に異なった西洋権力が関わってきた。顕著な影響を与えているのは，イギリス，フランス，オランダ，ポルトガル，スペイン，アメリカであり，ある観点からすれば，そこにオーストラリアを含めることさえできよう。植民地化を行った権力の側でも，その内部において，法や統治，また植民地政策や植民地化の実践に対するアプローチの著しい違いが存在していた。幾つかのパシフィック・アイランドの共同体のような[3]，一部の例外を除けば，大半の国はずっと以前に脱植民地化したが，他の場合と同様に憲法や法システムにおいて植民地化権力の影響は現在でも残っている[4]。

　こうした結果，アジア・オセアニア地域はヨーロッパそれ自体よりは遥かに多様な憲法上の仕組みの組み合わせを提示している。大陸法の基礎を有するシステムとほぼ同じ割合でコモン・ロー・システムが混在している。必然的に，これらのシステムは，特に法源や裁判所の役割や構造に関して，一般的にもまた特に憲法に関わる事柄についても，コモン・ローと大陸法の原理や方法の違いを反映している。他に重要な違いとしては，国際条約の締結や批准の仕方や，国内法における国際法の地位が挙げられる[5]。さらに，現在のアジアには世界の他のどの地域よりも多くの社会主義または共産主義統治システムが集中している[6]。

　アジア・オセアニア地域におけるそれぞれのシステムは，何らかの形で他から派生したものである。しかし，それぞれの場合において，オリジナルのモデルは，現在の社会的，経済的必要性だけでなく，ローカルな歴史や文化によっても相当程度修正されてきた。どれ1つとってみても原型に忠実なものはなく，1つの国家のシステムの中に異なった法的アプローチが混在しているのがふつうである。憲法の仕組みに関しては特にそうである。

## 2　憲法の比較

　アジア太平洋地域は，比較憲法学という新しい学問分野にとって宝庫である。本

稿は先に，この地域には，異なった法的，理論的基礎を有する多様な憲法システムが，極めて接近しながら併存していることを指摘しておいた。また，急速な経済的，環境的、社会的、政治的な相互依存関係の進展があいまって，統治の質というものを共通の関心を有する問題にしている。このこと1つをとっても，他国の憲法の仕組みに関する信頼しうる理解を持つ必要があろう。また，他から移植された憲法に関する概念同士が互いに混在していること，またそれらがローカルに発展してきた概念とも混在していることは，その存在形態と現実の働きの両面において，憲法というものの究極的な性質に影響を与えている要因を詳細に検討する絶好の機会を提供してくれる。

　すべての憲法学者は，憲法典とその歴史，憲法典の制定に影響を与えた憲法理論と，憲法典が現に作動する文脈の間には密接な関係があることを理解している。本書に寄せられた論稿において，杉原泰雄教授は，これらの要因が憲法典や立憲主義にも時を越えて影響を与えることを示している[7]。この憲法の偶発的な側面が，他国の憲法の研究やそれらの比較という作業を有効で信頼しうる形で行うことを著しく難しくする。憲法制度の原理やルールや作用を大雑把に理解するだけでは不充分なことは明らかである。各々のシステムは，それ自身の文脈的要因に照らして理解されねばならず，それらの文脈的要因というものは，歴史的，経済的，文化的，社会的なものであろう。これらの要因の方が，憲法典のルール自体よりも，認定し評価することがはるかに難しいものであろう。このことは，当該国家の外部にいる者にとっては特に深刻である。なぜなら，統治システムが実際にどのように作用しているのか理解するためには，生涯にわたってそのシステムと接触を持つ必要があり，当該国家の外部にいる者にとってそれは不可能だからである。異なった国の憲法学者が協働して研究を行うことが重要である理由の1つはこれである。

　これらのことを，私にとって最も馴染み深いオーストラリアの憲法システムを例にとって説明することができる。

　第1に，アジア・オセアニア地域の他の憲法の場合と同様に，オーストラリアの憲法にも，多様な影響が混在している。オーストラリアの場合，主たる影響を与えたのはイギリスとアメリカであり，また憲法の変更に関するレファレンダムという形で少しばかりスイスの影響も受けている[8]。アメリカからは，連邦制，司法権の他の権力からの厳格で憲法上のものである分離[9]，そして基本法を表わす成文憲法という概念をオーストラリアは輸入した[10]。イギリスからは，議院内閣制と立憲君主

制を，権利を憲法上保障することに対する嫌悪といっしょに輸入した[11]。他の多くの国とは異なって，オーストラリアは，植民地時代に，自らの憲法の仕組みを制約を受けることなく自由に採用した。しかも，たしかに2つが混在していることから生じる緊張もなかったわけではないが，2つの主要なアングロ・サクソンの憲法伝統から圧倒的にアングロ・ケルトなオーストラリアに憲法上の概念を首尾よく移植するのに，その障害となるような文化的要因は比較的少なかったのである[12]。

全ての国の場合と同様，オーストラリアの場合も，憲法典の条文を見ただけでは実際の憲法のありようのごく一部しか理解することはできない。司法権による解釈[13]，実際の政治[14]，慣習や共通の理解[15]を含む，多様なプロセスを通じて，憲法典は現実の世界に適応するものとされたり，何かが付け加えられたりしてきたのである。そのことを示す劇的で，時宜にもかなった1つの例を挙げておこう。

1901年にオーストラリア憲法が施行された当時，オーストラリアはまだ植民地であった。オーストラリアの憲法典は幾つかの形で依然としてこの歴史的事実を反映している。文面上は，イギリスの女王は強力な存在であり，またオーストラリアは依然としてイギリスに従属している[16]。しかしながら，現実には両方とも正しくない。1901年にあってすら，君主は，オーストラリアもしくはイギリス政府の助言に基づき，憲法慣習や不文の慣行にのっとって，「立憲的な」形で行動するよう期待されていたのである[17]。50年以上も前に，オーストラリアが独立した際，オーストラリアとの関係におけるイギリス政府やイギリス議会のいかなる権威も失われたが，これは憲法典の変更を何ら伴わないプラグマティックな過程を通じて行われた[18]。このどちらかと言えば無頓着な形での調整を可能にしたのは，オーストラリア自体の対内的安定と，憲法に関わる事柄に関するプラグマティックで，ほとんど散文的とも言えるアプローチであった。しかし，このアプローチの限界は，1999年のレファレンダム提案の拒否に至った共和制への移行に関する論争においてついに露呈されることになった。その論争において争点となったのは，オーストラリアにおいて選出された大統領が，イギリス女王および女王を代理する者に代わってオーストラリアの元首とみなされるべきかどうかということであった。オーストラリア国民に対して，現在のシステムがどのようなものか説明することが困難であるほど，憲法典の実際の運用は条文から逸脱しており，国民は現在のシステムに対して提示された変更の重要性を評価することができないほどであった[19]。共和制という問題が将来再燃することはほぼ確実であろう。仮に共和制への移行が承認された場合には，そ

の時はじめてオーストラリアの憲法は，オーストラリアの統治のこの側面の実際のありようを現在以上に反映することになろう。

第2に，オーストラリアの事例は，一国の憲法の形態や作用に対して制憲時の理論が有する重要性を示している。その例として，オーストラリア憲法典は人権の明示的な保障を事実上欠いているということが挙げられる。哲学的には，これはA.V.ダイシーの遺産が引き継がれているということであり[20]，オーストラリア憲法内部におけるイギリス的伝統とアメリカ的伝統の対立点の1つである。しかしながら，憲法上の権利というものが欠如しているからといって，オーストラリアの憲法システムにおいて権利が重要ではないというわけではない。また，いくつかの重要な留保が必要ではあるが[21]，オーストラリアにおいて権利が不当に危殆に瀕しているというわけでもない。裁判所を通じて解釈、執行される憲法上保障された権利というものに代えて，オーストラリアはコモン・ローや[22]政治文化，そしてこれまでのところリベラルで民主的な価値にあまり負担をかけることがなかった一連の社会的、経済的環境に頼りがちである。憲法が作用する文脈が変化して，権利は一般的には尊重されるべきであるとの現在の安易なコンセンサスが崩壊するようなことがあれば，その時はより規範的な権利の保障体制が求められることになろう。

最後に，オーストラリアの事例は，文脈というものが，移植された憲法上の仕組みが作用する際にいかに影響を与えるものであるかということも示している。1例を挙げれば，それは，オーストラリア憲法のいかなる変更もレファレンダムによる承認が必要であるという要件である[23]。オーストラリア憲法はこの要件をスイスから輸入したわけだが，スイスにおいては，レファレンダムという制度は，大小の公共的な決定への直接的な参加というものに慣れた，概して教養のある人民によるコンセンサス型政治というものと符合している。これに対して，それ以外の点では，互いが非常に敵対的な形で向き合うウェストミンスター型の政治文化における代表制に全面的に依拠しているオーストラリアにおいては，レファレンダムはそれほど自然なものではない。したがって，オーストラリアにおいてレファレンダムを有効に使うためには，ふだんの政治的実践を相当程度変える必要がある[24]。これまでオーストラリアがこれをうまく実現できなかったからこそ，憲法を改正しようとする提案の多くが挫折してきたのである[25]。

オーストラリア憲法を文脈との関係において理解しようとすれば見えてくるこうした複雑さは，アジア・オセアニア地域における全ての国においても同じ形で現わ

れる。

## 3　立憲主義という概念

　アジア・オセアニア地域の多様性という事実は，一方ではこの地域を比較憲法という研究にとって極めて興味深い地域にすると同時に，本書の主題である立憲主義の分析を複雑なものとする。立憲主義の意味は，法や統治に関する多様なシステムの間で異なっているかもしれないし，多様なイデオロギーの間でも異なっているかもしれしれないし，また時代によっても異なっているかもしれない。しかし，本稿の目的からすれば，一定の共通点を見極める必要がある。その際に厄介なのは，立憲主義という概念を定義しなければならないが，その定義は文化特定的ではなく一定中立的なものであり，しかもアジア・オセアニア地域と同じくらい多様な地域を包摂するに充分包括的なものでなければならないということである。

　最低限，立憲主義は，憲法の手続と規範にしたがった統治というものを意味する。しかし，立憲主義についてまわる法の支配の場合と同様に，これは必要条件であって充分条件ではない。憲法典という形式的な入れ物はその中味に注意を払わなければ，空虚で意味がない。立憲主義の内容に関する見解は時代ごとに変化してきたが，このことについては争いがあるかもしれない。それにもかかわらず，20世紀後半においては，真に立憲的な体制であると言えるためには，それが少なくとも2つの特徴を有していなければならないということについて広範な同意がある。第1の特徴は，統治は公益に仕える民意に基づき，民意に答えるものでなければならない，というものである。一般的に，このことは，全ての市民，もしくは国家の完全な構成員は平等に取扱われねばならない，ということを意味する。また大半のシステムにおいては，これは選挙によって選ばれる代表による統治という意味での民主主義を要請すると考えられている。立憲主義という体制の第2の特徴は，公権力は制限されねばならず，公権力の行使は恣意的であってはならず，それは一定の規範的な基準を満たすものでなければならない，ということである。過去50年の間にますます，これらの規範的な基準は人権に関する国際的に承認された基準と関連づけられるようになってきた。他の地域と同様，アジアやオセアニアにおいても，多様なカテゴリーの権利を重視することとそれらの権利の実現方法が現在の立憲主義にとっての主要な問題である[26]。

立憲主義に関するこうした見方は，意思すなわち「政治（gubernaculum）」と法すなわち「司法（jurisdictio）」を，「自由を愛する全ての人が依然としてそれを確保するために闘わねばならない，立憲主義の相互に関する2つの基本的な要素」[27]だとしたチャールズ・マックルワインの仕事に大幅に依拠している。マックルワインは，その著書『立憲主義　その成立過程』を，上の2つの基本的な要素の間の潜在的な緊張関係についての考察に当てたが，この緊張関係はその後の時の経過にもかかわらず，現在でも依然として明らかに存在している。彼の分析論理は，立憲主義の仕組みの主たる目的をはっきりと押えながらも，それらの目的が達成される方法についてはある程度柔軟性を認める点で，本稿の目的から見て魅力的である。

　立憲主義についてのこのような定義ですら，ある人にとっては厳格すぎ，また別の人にとっては厳格さが足りないものであるかもしれない。自らの伝統に拘束されて仕事をしている憲法学者は，さらなる要件を加味する誘惑に駆られるものである[28]。個々の伝統の内部においては，それはよいことかもしれない。それぞれの立憲主義システムは，内部において特定の特徴が特定の与えられた役割を果たすような，1つの統合されたシステムであるか，もしくはそうしたものでなければならない。たとえば，私自身の伝統からすれば，私は真に立憲的な体制といえる条件として，権力分立，司法権の独立，立法権や執行権の行為に対する司法審査，統治における高度な開放性と説明責任（accountability）というものを付加するだろう。これらの特徴は他の多くの人々によっても受け入れられるであろうが，しばしばその受けいられ方は多様であろうし，強調のされ方もまちまちであろう。

　しかしながら，まずはそれぞれの伝統を横断して協働しようという現段階においては，他の点で立憲主義の最低限の目標が満たされうるのであれば，更に特徴を付加しようという誘惑は斥けられねばならない。定義は厳格になればなるほど，定義をめぐって争いが生じるからである。比較憲法の研究を発展させるためには，広範な合意が可能な何らか一般的な枠内の中で，異なった国家は異なった形で立憲主義の目的にアプローチするものだということをまず最初に認めるほうが有益であろう。

## 4　立憲主義に対する挑戦

　このように定義したとしてもなお，周知のように立憲主義というものは脆弱な概念である。本節において，私は，リベラル・デモクラシーの憲法システムに言及し

ながら，立憲主義に対する幾つかの圧力とその結果として生じる問題について考察しようと思う。そうするのは広範な規模における一般化の試みにつきまとう文化的偏見を避けるためでもある。いずれにせよ，一般にリベラル・デモクラシーと立憲主義が同一視される限り，リベラル・デモクラシーのシステム内部における対立を考察することにより，立憲主義というものの脆弱さをより強力な形で示すことができるかもしれない。

　まず最初に，立憲主義システムとそれが定める統治は公益につかえるもので，その限りにおいて少なくとも人民の支持と同意に基づくものであるよう意図されている，という考え方を取上げて考察しておこう。20世紀後半を通じて，この点に関する大半のリベラル・デモクラシーのアプローチは，人民全体の主権というものを多かれ少なかれ明示的に認めた上で，成人の普通選挙権に基づく自由で定期的な選挙によって選ばれた代表を通じて統治を行う，というものであった。代表制に依拠することの正当化事由の1つは，20世紀の国民国家の規模を所与のものとした現実性であった。もう1つの正当化事由は，代表は理論的に見て共通の利益になるような決定をなす可能性が高いし，実際にもそのように行動するだろうという想定である[29]。

　このモデルは幾つかの鍵となる重要な要素に基いて構築されている。選挙によって選ばれた代表は，自らの正統性の源泉である人民に対して充分な説明責任と政治責任を負わねばならない。また代表は，自らの利益ではなく公益のために行動しなければならない。できれば代表は，賢明で良い統治を行う能力を有していなければならない。

　こうした目的を達成するための伝統的なメカニズムには，公的，政治的な説明責任の主たる媒体である代表によって構成される立法府と，全ての範囲の政府の行動に対して一定の専門性を提供する，立法府より中立的で永続的な公共部門が含まれる。しかし，周知のように，前者の有効性は，組織政党の保身という意識によって損なわれている。けれども，組織政党は代表制が機能するためには不可欠なものである。また，公務員の身分保障は，専門性を維持するためには不可欠だと考えられてきたが，場合によっては，非効率を，また最悪の場合には停滞すらもたらす原因となりうる。もちろん，こうした問題点は，統治に関するアプローチがどのようなものであるかによって変化するし，憲法が機能する文脈の違いに応じて変化する。たとえば，立法府がどの程度うまく機能するかは，その規模や，選出システム，公

益につかえる公務員の伝統，公の野党の存在が政治的，社会的に認められている程度によって変わる。

　法と憲法の定める枠組みにおける制限された統治という第2の立憲主義の特徴に関しても問題が生じないわけではない。憲法システムを通じて制限された統治がどのように確保されるかは，公権力の組織，憲法の規範的ルール，判決の手続と実践いかんによって相当程度変化する。しかしながらリベラル・デモクラシーの体制においては，制限された統治という立憲主義の特徴は，効率を確保し専制的な支配を防ぐという両方の利益のために，諸機関の間での，また時としては政府のレヴェルの間での，公的権力の分立を前提としている[30]。それは少なくとも，政府を含む全ての人が法に服し，当該法自体も人権規範を含む基本的な規範を充足しているという程度において，法の支配を前提にしている[31]。さらに，それは公平な判決システムというものをも前提にしている。多くの国家においては，憲法規範は裁判所の判決を通じて立法府すら拘束することができる，ということが受け容れられている[32]。

　立憲主義が法の遵守に基いている以上，紛争を法にしたがって公平に裁定するというシステムは立憲主義体制にとって必要不可欠なものである。この点に関する主たる問題は，かつてと同様，裁判所やその他の裁定機関が現に充分に独立していること，そして人々がそれらの機関が独立しているとみなせるようにすることである。裁判所は構造上は公的部門の内部に位置しているが，この公的部門こそが裁判所の独立性を最も脅かすものである[33]。実際上も，裁判官の任命，資源，決定の執行に関して裁判所は執行権や立法権に頼らざるを得ない。したがって，他の憲法規範の場合以上に，公平な判決というものは，一方で執行権や立法府の側の自制，他方で裁判所の側の自己主張に基いている。前者の自己抑制と後者の自己主張の両方とも文化や伝統の影響を受けやすい。

　最後に，周知のように，立憲主義の目的だと考えられる効果的な統治と制限された統治はある程度互いに対立する。人民の意思が完全に支配する場合には，法を通じての制限された統治は実現不可能である。しかし制限された統治なくしては，立憲主義は存在しえない。他方で，統治に対する制約は，良き統治がもたらす積極的な社会的利益との間でバランスがとられねばならない。両者の関係が静態的であることは稀である。両者の間の対立は，互いに抑制するという点でよいものであるかもしれないが，どちらかにバランスが崩れれば，問題が起こるだろう。

多くの国家における代表プロセスに関するシニシズムの拡大という状況に，この問題が現時点でも現われていることを見て取ることができる[34]。シニシズムの拡大は，統治がますます複雑なものとなっていること，政党その他の権力保持者による権力の乱用，既存の制度が充分に変化に対応できないでいること，だんだんと教育を受け充分な情報を有する投票者が増えていること，またもちろん権威に対する尊重の失墜，といった様々な理由から説明できる。たしかに場合によっては，シニシズムは正当であり，代表プロセスの乱用それ自体が立憲主義を脅かしている場合がある[35]。しかしながらシニシズムが，実際の事実を反映しているのではなくたんに人々がそう感じているにすぎない場合であってすら，立憲主義が依拠している統治システムに対する支持を掘り崩す可能性があるのである。

さらに，この問題に対する2つの応答も立憲主義内部におけるバランスを試練にさらすかもしれない。第1は，直接民主政をもっと頻繁に利用するという応答である[36]。これに関しては2つの問題点がある。1つは，直接民主政に人々はますます正統性を感じるようになり，その結果法によって制限された政府はますます脅かされということであり，もう1つはパンガランガン教授が，「生の，粗野な権力」だと形容したもの，すなわち代表プロセスによって媒介されない権力という問題である[37]。代表プロセスに関するシニシズムに対するもう1つのよくある応答は，インドの場合のように，代表の権力に対する制約として司法権に今まで以上に頼ることである。しかし，これも極端な場合には，司法権の独立を支えている，か弱く攻撃を受けやすいコンヴェンションに重い荷重をかける可能性がある。

## 5 立憲主義にとっての文脈の変化？

幾つかの歴史的な出来事が重なった結果，20世紀後半には世界中で憲法と立憲主義が新たに注目を集めている。

最も明らかなことは，冷戦の終焉が憲法政治と憲法に関する着想を解放したことである。たまたま，これは，おおむね他国から輸入された独立後の憲法以上にローカルなニーズに対応するような憲法形態を試してみようとする旧植民地の増大しつつあった意向と重なった。これらの理由などから，1990年代は憲法変動の時期となった。時として，変動は新たな原理や実践を生み出すこともあった[38]。しかしたいていの場合には，変動は馴染み深い憲法形式を，異なった状況に適用させたり，組み

替えて用いる形で行われた[39]。概して変動のプロセスはプラグマティックなものであった。20世紀後半の憲法は，抽象的な憲法理論に応答するというよりもむしろ，何が国内で，そして場合によっては国際社会で受け入れ可能であるのか，何が実際に機能しそうかということを評価した産物であった。憲法変動のプロセスはまだ終わっているわけではなく，21世紀初頭まで続くものと思われる。本稿執筆時点で，わずかばかりの例を挙げても，スリランカ，フィージー，パプア・ニューギニア，ソロモン諸島，東ティモール，インドネシアにおいて，積極的に憲法という形で問題を解決しようと模索されている。これらの中の幾つかの場合には，当分変動のプロセスは収束に向かいそうにはない。

また冷戦の終焉はグローバリゼーションと国際化を促進した。筆者は，グローバリゼーションということで，あらゆる種類の私的な取引活動の劇的な増加に言及しているわけだが，コミュニケーション方式の多様性と速度の変化，情報テクノロジーの新たな形式によってもさらに私的取引の増加はますます加速する。対照的に，国際化ということで筆者は，たいていの場合は条約やその他の協定という伝統的な形で進められるものの，時としては新たな国際的な制度や地域的協働を含む新たな国際的な協働という形で表明される，政府間の関係の新たな範囲，量，多様性というものに言及している。

国際化はグローバルというよりも地域的な形で行われるかもしれない。これまでのところ最も成功している地域的協働はEUである。1990年代までにそれはもはや新たな現象とは言えなくなった。しかしながら，地政学的な文脈の変化を含む様々な理由から，ヨーロッパ統合は近年急速に進化し，一国の立憲的な仕組みと国際的な仕組みの中間に位置する混合的な結合形態を生み出してきた[40]。EUは，他の地域も，選択的ではあるにしても，追随するかもしれない1つのモデルを提示している。連合を構成している国家のコモン・ロー・システムと大陸法システムがある程度収束していくということは，同じ法的伝統を有する他の国家全てにおいても感得されることになろう[41]。

国際化とグローバリゼーションは国際的な競争の原因であると同時に，それに対する対応でもある。国際的な競争も立憲主義という主題に幾つかの点で関係がある。

ある観点から見れば，国際的な競争は，一国の生活の経済的な側面に適用される限り，立憲主義を強化する一定の可能性を有している。立憲的な体制のほうが経済活動に対して安定し信頼可能な枠組みをもたらすからである。経済のパフォーマン

スを向上させるために，国家自身が憲法による解決を求めるかもしれないし，他国からそうするよう圧力がかかるかもしれない。グローバリゼーションにともなうコミュニケーション革命も立憲主義にとって関連性を有する。コミュニケーション革命によって，世界の規範からあまりにもかけはなれた憲法の実践は白日のもとにさらされる。コミュニケーション革命は，自国や他国の政府の行為に関する情報と，それを変えるための圧力を課す手段を提供するので，人民にとって解放的な力となりうる。

　しかしながら憲法に関して言えば，これらの現象は負の側面もまた有している。ヨーロッパで顕著な1つの問題点は，古い国家の崩壊や，多数者や少数者のそれまでは抑圧されてきた怒りが再燃した結果としての，民族的な対立の増加である。今日世界にとっての主たる試練の1つは，しばしば問題を永続化させる継続的な分裂状態にまでは至ってはいないものの，民族的に分裂した共同体の統治に対する憲法による解決を見つけることである。ある点では，これはアジアにおける，異質なものから構成されている社会における立憲主義に対するアプローチの強みでもあった。シンガポールが良い例である[42]。しかしながら，時として多文化主義の達成は権威主義の強化という代償をともなうことがあり，それらの社会にあっては権威主義は人種間の調和の維持という必要性と本当に結びついているのか，それともそれは権威主義の側の言い訳にすぎないのかどうかという問題を生み出す。これに対してアジア地域におけるより同質的な社会は，民族的な差異を調整できていない。21世紀の世界において全ての国にとってこれはますます重要な立憲主義にとっての問題となるように思われる。

　経済の競争もまた政府の行為の変更を余儀なくさせてきた。一定の場合には，これは，あらゆるシステムにとって不可欠な刷新とイノベーションのプロセスを反映するものであり，よいことである。しかしながら，充分な予防措置がとられない場合には，憲法上の基準の低下をもたらすこともある。「経済的な立憲主義」という形式は伝統的に理解されてきた立憲主義よりも狭く，より権威主義的かもしれない[43]。国際的な競争の圧力に対応しようとすると国家が社会的，経済的ニーズを充足する能力が減少する。最近よく見られるプライヴァタイゼーションも，異なった形ではあるにせよ，グローバリゼーションが統治の原理と実践に対してもたらす影響を示している。プライヴァタイゼーションの最も明白で即時的な帰結は小さな政府である。国家それ自身がサーヴィスを提供する場合も，民間部門の形で政府は行

動し，営利的なベースに基いてサーヴィスが提供されることになる。公共部門の規模の縮小と政府の行為形態の変化は，これまで伝統的な公私の領域区分の継続を前提にして形作られてきた憲法その他の規範にも影響を与える。またそれらは，公的な説明責任のための伝統的な諸機関の作用や法の支配の原理にも影響を与える。なぜなら，両方とも，統治は主として法という形式における規制を通じて行われるという前提に基いているからであり，契約やその他の取引を通じてのガヴァナンスという概念にはうまくあてはまらないからである。

## 6 アジア・オセアニアにおける立憲主義

　こうした傾向は，西欧からアフリカ，中央ヨーロッパ，東欧，アメリカに至るまで世界中に例がある。しかしながら，本稿の関心は，これらの傾向がアジア・オセアニア地域においてどのような形で現われているのかということにある。
　上述した現象の大半はアジア・オセアニア地域においても見られる。たとえば，タイやフィリピン，台湾，そしてより不確かな形ではインドネシアにおいても，憲法を改正したり憲法を新たに制定することによって問題を解決しようとする動きがあった。中国とヴェトナムでは，国際的な経済競争の圧力への対応ということも一因となって，社会主義的な憲法理論と憲法実践が刷新された。カンボジアでも，まだ脆弱ではあるものの新たに立憲体制が確立された。ASEANの深化とAPECの確立にはある程度意図的なリージョナリズムが見られる。
　しかし同時に，アジア・オセアニア地域でもグローバリゼーションやそれに関連する潮流の負の効果も見られる。そうした負の効果には，国際的な経済活動が諸国家の生活状態に及ぼす劇的な影響や，公益上の決定をコントロールする力が徐々に国際組織や国際財政，多国籍企業へと移り，徐々に一国がコントロールする力を失ってゆくことが含まれる。民族的対立という現象やその帰結は東ティモールにおいて最も悲劇的な形で現われたし，インドネシアの他の地域においても依然として続いている。フィージーやスリランカ，ブーゲンヴィルを含む他のアジア・オセアニア地域においては，民族的・宗教的対立を緩和するのに憲法が失敗したことは明らかである。また，これまでのところアジア・オセアニア地域においては政治腐敗に対する関心が高まってはいるものの，大した改善の兆候は見られない。
　本書に収められた他の諸論稿からはアジア・オセアニア地域における立憲主義の

展開に関するもっと特定的な洞察を得ることができる。

　第1に，予想されるように，大半の論稿は，多様な種類の権利を含む，人権なるものを相当程度強調している。発展途上国に限られるわけではないにしても，そこにおいて特に社会・経済的な権利が有する意義に関して，他の要因も貢献していることは事実ではあるが，世界の論争が持つ説得力というものをこの地域において見ることができる。非常に多くの人々が搾取の結果非常な貧困常態で暮らしており，市民的・政治的権利というものが他の国ほどの意味を持たない地域においては，社会・経済的な権利が重要視されることは明白であり，必要なことでもある。しかしながら，市民的・政治的権利もまた，個人の観点からだけでなく，そうした権利が統治の説明責任，そして場合によっては統治能力をも支える上で果たす役割からしても，人権の充分な体制にとって不可欠な要素である。市民的・政治的権利と社会・経済的権利の間でどちらに力点を置くのかということはこの地域における立憲主義にとっての主要な問題の1つである。

　この地域においてレレヴァントであり，先の問題にも関連する問題は，先住民の権利を含む，集団の権利の正統性とその法的基礎である[44]。他の権利との関係を含む，環境権の性質と範囲は，世界の他の諸地域の場合と同様にこの地域においても，依然として取り組む必要のある決定的に重要な問題である。また周知のように，この問題は，アジア・オセアニアの諸国を含めて，北と南を対立させる問題でもある[45]。

　幾つかの論稿は，第2，第3世代の権利がどのように実現されるのかという論争にもある程度着目している。一般的には，これらのいわゆる積極的権利なるものは裁判所を通じて執行されうるものとは考えられてはいないが，インドや南アフリカの経験はこれを可能にする手段を示している[46]。タイ王国の新憲法は，人民のイニシアティブの利用を通じての第3の道を提示している。積極的権利を執行する仕組みを模索することが人権委員会が台頭している1つの理由であり，私も後にこのテーマに言及しようと思う。社会・経済的権利の遵守をモニターしたり，国際委員会への報告書を審査し，適切な一国の政策的応答を援助し展開するなどの上で，準独立性を有する人権委員会やオンブズマン，その他の調査機関が重要な役割を果たしていることは間違いない。しかし，幾つかの論稿が注意を喚起しているように，制度は自動的な万能薬というわけではない。それらの制度の有効性は，それらの制度の独立性，構成，それらの制度が集めている尊敬を含む，憲法学者の領分に属す

るその他の要因にもよる。

　また幾つかの論稿は，先に言及した，公的な決定作成において人民自身がより直接的な形で発言できるよう求める圧力があることを示している。たとえばパンガランガン教授は，代表のリコール，立法に関するレファレンダム，憲法変動についての直接的なイニシアティブの行使という，フィリピンにおける3つの最近のこの種の刷新を挙げている。教授の論文は最後の暗いパラグラフの中で，こうした展開が立憲主義に挑戦するものであることを認めている。確かにある意味では教授の意見は正しいものだが，これはおそらく飼い慣らすことが可能であり，また飼い慣らされねばならない展開であろう。人民によるイニシアティブは，適切に用いられるならば，理解の改善を通じて，立憲主義に対する人民の支持を強めたり，建設的な憲法変動を余儀なくしたり，政府の説明責任を改善する可能性がある。問題は，潜在的には劇薬である直接民主政に枠組みを与え，それを立憲主義に関して受容された考え方の範囲内に回収することである。アジアにおいては幾つかの実験が試みられてきている。たとえば，ウィサヌ・ワランヨウ博士は論文の中で，タイ憲法の起草に当って人民の参加が有した意義と，5万人の投票者が集まれば国会に対して権利や自由に関する憲法上の規定を実現する法案を審議するよう請願できるとするタイ憲法第170条が持つ効果の重要性について述べている[47]。

　本書に収められた多くの論稿は，司法審査と法の支配という側面にも言及している。この点に関しては少なくとも2つの重要なテーマが現われている。最も馴染み深い第1のテーマは，司法権の役割の射程に関わるものである。諸論稿に示された経験は，自己抑制的な日本の最高裁判所[48]から憲法上の権利の保障を徐々に展開しつつある台湾の大法官[49]，異常な程積極主義的なインドの司法権[50]まで多様である。またインドの経験は，広範な児童労働の利用は一例にすぎない，複雑な社会的・経済的問題の解決において司法権の果たしうる役割の限界を示している。前述のテーマを取上げるならば，司法権の実践が国によって相当異なることは，少なくともある程度は文化および法システムの違いによって説明がつく。

　幾つかの論稿は，人民の権力という台頭しつつある現象と何がしか関連性を有する新しいテーマとの関係で，裁判へのアクセスという問題に言及している。しばしば司法過程は人民からは遠いところにある。伝統的に裁判官は自らの独立性をまもるために形式性，伝統，既存の手続への固執，ある程度の超然性に依拠してきた。しかしながらより平等主義的な時代にあっては，これらの特徴は，裁判所がどの程

度尊敬を集められるかということに影響し，最終的には憲法秩序を維持するのに裁判所がどの程度有効かということにも影響を与える。裁判所へのアクセスのコストやアクセスすることの物理的な難しさも重要な要因である。何人かの論者は，この点に関して司法権の役割に挑戦する，もしくは少なくとも司法権を補完する可能性を持つものとして，人権委員会 (Human Rights Commission) その他の制度といったメカニズムをあげている[51]。こうした展開が望ましいものであることは明らかである。しかしながら，それらは同時に，人権保障の有効性が最終的に依拠している裁判所の独立というものを掘り崩す可能性も持っている。もちろん1つの問題解決の道筋は裁判所が今まで以上に人々にとってアクセス可能なものになることである。この理由から，シン教授が述べている，インドにおいて公益訴訟が対審構造を革命的に変えたということは特に重要である[52]。

　本書に収められた諸論稿から現われる，立憲主義にとっての最後の1つの問題は，もっと最近のものである。それは国際秩序に関わっており，幾つかの異なった側面を有している。第1は国際化が国内的な憲法システムに与える馴染み深い影響である。国際化は適切な国際的な憲法規範の広範な遵守をもたらす場合には望ましい。しかし多くの国家において，そして特にコモン・ローの伝統に立つ国家においては，以下の理由から，それは国内の権力組織をある程度調整する必要性を示唆している。大半のコモン・ロー・システムにおいては，国際的なコミットメントをなす権限と責任を有しているのは執行権のみである。国際関係に主として責任を負うのは執行権であるという前提は，国際関係の領域が比較的限られた時代に形成されたものである。これまでは主として国内的な関心事であった事項にまで国際関係が及ぶにつれて，この種の決定に対する執行権の説明責任を確保するのに既存のシステムで充分なのかどうかという問題が生じる。たとえばオーストラリアにおいては，この問題に関する議論の結果，条約の提案についてよりシステマティックな形で公共情報を提供すること，少なくとも諮問機関という資格で立法府がこれまで以上に関与することになった[53]。

　最後に，国際的な秩序それ自体の憲法化という問題がある[54]。これは，人民の異なった状況と利益を考慮に入れた衡平な根拠に基づいて，国際的な経済活動をより効果的に統制する方法に関わる。またそれは，国際共同体それ自身が機能するに際して準拠すべきルールの枠組みにも関わる。ゴン・レンレン教授は，彼によれば「平和が核である」[55]国際的な立憲主義という概念を議論する際に，このことに言及し

ている。この関係で，確かにこれまでのところ時期尚早であったことを明らかにしてきたものの，日本の憲法9条は重要な国際モデルを提示している。

　他にも国際秩序に立憲主義が適用される，より平凡な方法がある。現在では実際の決定は一国を超えた国際的なレヴェルでなされる以上，同意，法の支配，その他の憲法上の規範と手続に依拠する，公益のための統治という概念が，このますます重要性を帯びている領域にどのように適用されうるのかを考察する必要がある。これらの問題は本書の射程を超えている。これまでのところは，これらの問題は主として国際法学者の領分に属するものだと考えられてきた。しかしながら，国際秩序がその性格において立憲主義的なものになりつつあるので，これらは憲法学者もそれについて何がしか発言しうる事項である。

(1)　1999年7月現在，推定でインドの人口は1,000,848550人であり，中国の人口は1,246,871,951人である。
(2)　たとえば，トンガの人口は109,082であり，バヌアツの人口は189,036である。
(3)　たとえば，ニューカレドニアやグアム。
(4)　Ayesha Jalal, *Democracy and Authoritarianism in South Asia*, Cambridge University Press, 1995.
(5)　有益なケース・スタディとしては，Monroe Leigh and Merritt R. Blakeslee, *National Treaty Law and Practice*, Studies in Transnational Legal Policy No. 27, The American Society of International Law, 1995を参照のこと。
(6)　中国，ヴェトナム，北朝鮮，ラオス。
(7)　Sugihara Yasuo, "Asian Constitutionalism and Japan".
(8)　オーストラリア憲法第128条。
(9)　Cheryl Sauders, "Separation of Powers" in Brian Opeskin and Fiona Wheeler (eds) *The Australian Federal Judicial System*, Melbourne University Press（近刊）.
(10)　当初，オーストラリア憲法はイギリスの議会制定法として他の法律に優越する法的効果を有していた。
(11)　*McGinty v Western Australia* (1996) 186 CLR 140.
(12)　C. Saunders, "A Constitutional Culture in Transition"（近刊）(1999)。
(13)　たとえば，最高裁判所が，憲法51条29節の「対外的事項（external affairs）」によって，オーストラリア連邦政府はオーストラリアが当事者である誠実になされた国際的な取り決めを実現する法律を制定することができると判示した，*Commonwealth v Tasmania* (1983) 158 CLR 1を参照せよ。
(14)　そうした例として，所得への課税権限を事実上連邦政府が独占していること，州政府の間の協働に基づく多くの国家政策などを挙げることができる。

(15) 連邦政府の執行権の機能および，それと連邦議会との関係はほとんどの場合憲法の条文ではなくコンヴェンションに基づくものである。

(16) たとえば，憲法第59条は連邦議会が制定した法律をイギリス女王が「承認しない(disallow)こと」を認めているように思われる。

(17) J. Quick and R.R. Garran, *Annotated Constitution of the Australian Commonwealth*, Legal Books, 1975, 703.

(18) *Sue v Hill* [1999] HCA 30で述べられている。

(19) Cheryl Saunders, "The Head of State- The Australian Experience: Lessons, Pointers and Pitfalls" in Colin James (ed) *Building the Constitution*, Institute of Policy Studies, Wellington, 2000, 276-286.

(20) A.V. Dicey, *Introduction to the Study of the Law of the Constitution*, 10th ed., 1959, McMillan.

(21) 現在の論争の1つは，オーストラリア北部における必要的実刑判決法の問題に関わる：1983年少年裁判所法53条AE—AG。

(22) *Lange v Australian Broadcasting Corporation* (1997) 189 CLR 520.

(23) 128条。

(24) Cheryl Saunders, "The Parliament as Partner: A Century of Constitutional Review"（オーストラリア連邦議会のInformation and Research Services Research Paperとして2000年刊行予定）。

(25) 44回のレファレンダムにおいて承認された提案はわずか8個である。

(26) Kishore Mahbubani, "An Asian Perspective on Human Rights and Freedom of the Press" in Kishore Mahbubani, *Can Asians Think?*, Times Editions Pte Ltd., 1998, 57.

(27) Charles McIlwain, *Constitutionalism Ancient and Modern*, Cornell University Press, 1947, 146.

(28) 英米の主要な学者の見解の集めた最近のものとして，Larry Alexander (ed), *Constitutionalism: Philosophical Foundations*, Cambridge University Press 1998がある。また歴史を概観するものとしては，Scott Gordon, *Controlling the State*, Harvard University Press, 1999がある。

(29) Bernard Manin, *The Principles of Representative Government*, Cambridge University Press, 1997.

(30) M.J.C. Vile, *Constitutionalism and the Separation of Powers* (2nd ed. 1998), Liberty Fund.

(31) 法の支配とその意味に関する最近の議論を知るには，David Dyzenhaus (ed), *Recrafting the Rule of Law:* The Limits of Legal Order, Hart Publishing, 1999を参照のこと。

(32) John H. Garvey and T. Alexander Aleinikoff, *Modern Constitutional Theory*, West Publishing, 1994, 第三章。

(33) Martin Shapiro, *Courts: A Comparative and Political Analysis*, University of Chicago Press, 1981.
(34) James N. Rosenau, "Changing States in a Changing World" in Commission on Global Governance (ed), *Issues in Global Governance*, Kluwer Law International, 1995, 265; John Uhr, *Deliberative Democracy in Australia*, Cambridge University Press, 1998.
(35) Fareed Zakaria, "The Rise of Illiberal Democracy" *Foreign Affairs*, November/December 1997, 22.
(36) Markku Suksi, *Bringing in the People*, Martinus Nijhoff Publishers, 1993; Dick Morris, *The New Prince*, Renaissance Books, 第47章。
(37) Raul Pangalangan, "Why a Philippine Human Rights Commission? Its Place in a Constitutional Order". ポール・パンガランガー「なぜフィリピン人権委員会か？―憲法秩序におけるその地位」。
(38) そうした例としては、香港との関係における中国の一国二制度、(現在では不幸な) フィージーの1997年憲法における先住民とインド系人民の利益の均衡を図ろうとする試み、さらにはタイ憲法における社会・経済的な権利の扱いなどが挙げられる。
(39) たとえば、1990年ニュージーランド権利章典法における議会主権と人権保障との調整がある。
(40) Dietrich Rometsch and Wolfgang Wessels (ed), *The European Union and Member States*, Manchester University Press, 1996; J.H.H. Weiler, *The Constitution of Europe*, Cambridge University Press, 1999.
(41) B.S. Markesinis (ed), *The Gradual Convergence*, Clarendon Press Oxford, 1994; B.S. Markesinis, *The Coming Together of the Common Law and the Civil Law*, Hart Publishing, 2000.
(42) Kishore Mahbubani, "Singapore: Recipes for a Crowded Planet", in *Can Asia Think?*, Times Editions Pte Ltd., 1998, 183, 187.
(43) Kanisha Jayasuriya, "The Rule of Law and Governance in the East Asian State", (1999) 1 *Asian Law Journal*, 107; Kanisha Jayasuriya (ed), *Law, Capitalism and Power in Asia*, Routledge, 1999.
(44) Will Kymlicka (ed), *The Rights of Minority Cultures*, Oxford University Press, 1995.
(45) Mahathir Mohamad, "Regional Challenges", in Mahathir Mohamad and Shintaro Ishihara, *The Voice of Asia*, Kodansha International Limited, 1995, 119, 127.
(46) 1996年南アフリカ共和国憲法第2章。
(47) Vishnu Varunyou, "Human Rights and Constitutionalism in Thailand". ウィサス・クランヨウ「タイにおける人権と立憲主義」。

(48) Gong Renren, "Japan's Consitution and International Law: Focus on the Peace Article". ゴン・レンレン「日本の憲法と国際法―平和条項を中心に」.
(49) Jau-Yuan Hwang, "Judge-Made Constitutionalism in Democratizing Taiwan -The Role of the Council of Grand Justices and Protection of Individual Rights".
(50) Parmanand Singh, "Protection of Human Rights through Public Interest Litigation in India". パーマナンド・シン「インドにおける公益訴訟を通じた人権の保障」.
(51) 特に, ワランヨウ博士, パンガランガン教授, シン教授の論稿.
(52) Parmanand Singh, "Protection of Human Rights through Public Interest Litigation in India". パーマナンド・シン「インドにおける公益訴訟を通じた人権の保障」, また参照, Mario Gomez, *In the Public Interest*, Legal Aid Centre, University of Colombo, 1993.
(53) このメカニズムには, 国内利益分析 (National Interest Analyses), 条約を審議する議会手続, 条約に関する両院合同委員会 (Joint Parliamentary Committee on Treaties) の設置, 条約に関するデータベースの作成, 条約について連邦と州の間で審議する場合の原則と手続の改訂が含まれる.
(54) Commission on Global Governance (ed), *Issues in Global Governance*, Kluwer Law International, 1995.
(55) Gong Renren, "Japan's Consitution and International Law: Focus on the Peace Article". 前掲

# アジアの立憲主義と日本

杉 原 泰 雄

## I　はじめに——2つの気になること

「アジアの立憲主義」を検討するにあたって，私には，アジアの特殊性を説明する，とくに気になる2つの「理論」がある。

1つは，「アジア的生産様式論」，「アジア的専制論」，「アジア的停滞論」である。これらは，アジア諸国のうちの一部の，ある時代における政治，経済，文化にかんする科学理論として，なお積極的な意味をもっているかもしれない。ここではそれらの科学性の有無を検討するつもりはない。しかし，それらによるアジア諸国の近現代にかんする説明には，帝国主義的政策によって植民地・半植民地状態に陥れられかつ政治的，経済的，文化的発展を阻止されてしまったアジア諸国の政治・経済・文化の状況を維持し合理化するためのイデオロギーとしての側面があるのではないかと気にしている。植民地母国の植民地政策をふまえたうえで，植民地母国の優越性・進歩性とアジア諸国の停滞性・後進性を正当化するための「教義」としての役割である。植民地・半植民地段階のアジア諸国における独立運動，独立後のアジア諸国における政治的，経済的，文化的発展および現在のアジア諸国における政治的，経済的，文化的な激変の動向からすれば，これらの「理論」を無制約の前提としないことが肝要と考える。

もう1つは，「西欧立憲主義の普遍性論」（「その優越性・東漸の不可避性論」）とそれに対抗的異質的な「アジア的法文化論」（とりわけ「儒教的法文化論」）である。この点についても，ここで立ち入って検討するつもりはないが，憲法科学的に検討することがなによりも重要と考え，以下の諸点を指摘しておきたい。

第1に，西欧諸国においても，超歴史的超社会的に妥当するような立憲主義議論や市民憲法は存在しないということである。たとえば，近代の段階においても，近代市民革命を経た国に出現する「近代立憲主義型市民憲法」とは別に，近代市民革

命を経ない国には「外見的立憲主義型市民憲法」が存在した。前者は，基本的人権の保障，国民主権，権力分立を原理とし，後者はそれらを原理としていない。また，近代の段階には，基本的人権を保障しつつも，その概念や保障の範囲と程度を「近代立憲主義型市民憲法」と異にする「民衆の憲法思想」も存在した。さらに西欧諸国の憲法は，近代と現代では，その内容を相当に大きく変化させている。その変化は，たとえば，「近代立憲主義型市民憲法」から「現代市民憲法」への変化として示される。後者においては，前者に欠けていた，性差別の禁止，社会権の保障と経済的自由権の積極的制限，直接普通選挙制度の導入，違憲立法審査制度，地方自治の憲法的保障などがみられる。

いずれにしても，西欧諸国においても，どの社会層が主要な担い手であったか，どのような政治的，経済的，文化的諸条件が存在したかによって，立憲主義論や憲法の内容は，異なっている。それらは歴史的社会的に相対的であり，超歴史的超社会的に一枚岩的であるわけではない。

第2に，憲法を含めた法のあり方が歴史的社会的に相対的であることは，アジア諸国においても変わりはない。アジア諸国の法文化を，歴史の段階や国家のいかんにかかわらず，政治的経済的諸条件を超越して，たとえば儒教の立場から説明することには，儒教の影響の限定性やその理解の多様性のみからしても，疑問が残らざるをえない。近時におけるアジア諸国の法と政治の激変の様相を考慮すればなおさらのことであろう。

## II　アジアの近現代と立憲主義

アジア諸国における立憲主義の問題を検討するにあたっては，以下の諸点に留意することが不可欠だと思う。

その第1は，アジアの多くの国が，近現代において，植民地，半植民地またはそれに類する状態を経験し，国によってはその一環として封建的諸制度の温存が強制されたことである。それら諸国においては，植民地・半植民地状態と封建的諸制度の温存がその停滞の最大の要因であり，そこからの脱出（独立）が政治的，経済的および文化的発展の条件となっていた。立憲主義についても同様であった。

この点とかかわって，その立憲主義の優越性・普遍性を誇っていた植民地母国が，植民地母国なるが故に，政治において立憲主義の原則を貫くことができず，立憲主

義と同時に反立憲主義をも堅持するという,「二重の基準」を保っていたことに留意すべきであろう。本国における立憲主義と植民地における非立憲主義である。憲法は,本国では政治の根本準則であったが,植民地には原則として適用されなかった。不可侵の人権や民主主義の保障は,植民地の住民には及ばなかった。植民地母国の立憲主義は,それが植民地に及ぶことを押し止める役割を果していた。

このような立憲主義についての「二重の基準論」は,第2次世界大戦後の「現在」においても,形を変えて存続している。植民地を維持すべく民族解放闘争を阻止する戦争(たとえば1946年～54年の第1次インドシナ戦争),国内における体制選択に介入する戦争(たとえば1961年～75年のベトナム戦争),発展途上国に停滞と経済的植民地化をもたらしかねない大国による武器輸出などは,その代表例である。

その第2は,独立後に本格的な立憲主義の時代を迎えることになるアジア諸国においてもその内容が政治的,経済的,文化的諸条件のいかんによって,とりわけどのような社会層が独立の,従って立憲主義の主たる担い手となったかによって,その内容が異なることである。現に,アジア諸国において制定された諸憲法の政治的,経済的,文化的な多様性がそのことをなによりも雄弁に物語っている。

その第3は,その問題処理の困難性である。アジア諸国の多くは,第2次世界大戦後に政治的独立を達成するが,以下のような難問をかかえている。

① 植民地遺制,封建遺制の克服の問題である。植民地・半植民地段階において第1次産業の特定分野(モノカルチャー)を強要されたり,第2次産業の発展を阻止されたりすることもあった。このことは,独立後においては,経済的に自立することを困難にする条件となる。それは,また,公教育の普及をも困難とし,全国的な規模で植民地遺制と封建遺制を克服する市民の育成を困難とする条件にもなる。

② 政治的独立にもかかわらず,経済的植民地化のおそれをつねにもっていることである。かつての経済状態から経済的に自立するためには,資本と技術の導入を先進国に求めがちとなる。これに武器輸入に伴う債務と「例外なき自由化」による経済破壊が加われば,その経済・財政的な自立の維持はさらに困難なものとなる。

このような状況のなかで,アジア諸国は,立憲主義をはじめとして本格的な法の整備の時期を迎えている。各国民の英知によって,かかえている諸々の困難を克服し,歴史の批判に耐えられる立憲主義を創出することを期待したい。また,そのために,アジア諸国間で,国益と利潤追求に左右されない学術文化交流を強化したいものである。

## III　日本の立憲主義

　日本は，近代化以降，2つの憲法をもった。1つは，1889年の明治憲法（「大日本帝国憲法」）であり，もう1つは，1946年の現行憲法（「日本国憲法」）である。

　日本の近代化は，市民革命の結果としてではなく，外圧による旧特権階級のイニシアチブによっておこなわれた。「上からの近代化」である。それは，おなじく市民革命によらないで近代化したプロイセン等に学びつつも，それより外見制の度合いがはるかに高い明治憲法として具体化されている。日本型王権神授説に立つ天皇主権，法律によればいかようにでも制限できる「臣民ノ権利」の保障，権力分立を外見化する「天皇による統治権の総攬」の体制は，そのことを示している。この明治憲法は，比較憲法学的にみれば，フランス反革命期(1814―1830年)の「憲章」(La Chart Constitutionnelle, 1814) にもっとも類似している。

　この明治憲法下の政治は，「脱亜入欧」とアジア諸国に対する帝国主義的対応を1つの特色としていた。この憲法下において，日本が，アジア諸国に対してどの範囲と程度において加害者となったかを正確に確認することは，現在なお果たされていない日本の根本課題の1つと考える。この課題に誠実に対処することなく，アジアに「真の友人」をえることはできないと思う。

　日本は，第2次世界大戦における敗戦の結果，現行の日本国憲法を制定した。同憲法の特色は，第2次世界大戦の性格に大きく規定されている。それは，「戦争の放棄」（徹底した平和主義），基本的人権の保障，国民主権，権力分立を原理とする現代市民憲法である。その制定は，天皇主権，「臣民ノ権利」，「統治権の総攬」の明治憲法体制を否定し，それとは異質の体制をもたらすものとして，法的には，現代における日本の市民革命というべきものであった。この憲法は，日本の政治に本格的な近代化と現代化を求め，さらにはそれを超える非武装・非戦をも求めるものであった。

　しかし，現実の憲法政治においては，憲法の少なからぬ規定が軽視された。その代表例が，憲法における「陸海空軍その他の戦力」の不保持と「国の交戦権」の否認にもかかわらず，憲法政治における世界有数の軍隊の存在と外国軍隊の駐留およびその両者の軍事的協力関係の強化であることは，あらためて指摘するまでもない。そのような憲法政治は，憲法の基本用語の概念の悪用・誤用，憲法の規定の論理と

趣旨の軽視などの方法をとっておこなわれた。「解釈改憲」の政治である。憲法の規定の文言・論理・趣旨を不可能なまでに歪めて解釈することにより，憲法の規定自体を改正しなければ不可能なはずの意味をその憲法の規定から導き出し，本来は違憲で許されないはずの政治を正当化しようとする政治の手法である。それは，憲法の規定の文言・論理・趣旨を尊重して解釈運用することを求める立憲主義を実質的に否定する憲法政治の手法である。

1997年は，日本憲法施行50周年であったが，その際の検討主題の1つは，「日本に立憲主義があるか」であり，「どのようにして日本に立憲主義を回復するか」の問題であった。

このような憲法を軽視する政治は，新憲法が国民の憲法意識の革命的な転換の結果として制定されなかった国においては，おこりがちなことである。憲法の原理が国民の心のなかに銘記されていない国において，憲法は権力担当者によって軽視されがちとなる。日本国憲法の定着のためには，憲法の制定後に国民が憲法を自己のものとする憲法学習と憲法擁護の運動が不可欠となる。

憲法が現代の必要に応えるすぐれた内容をもっていることが，その学習と擁護のための前提条件となる。日本国憲法は，それに価するものと考える。

① それは，人権の保障においても，民主主義の問題においても，また権力分立においても，現在までに至る人類の歴史的な努力を凝縮しているということができる。現代市民憲法のなかでも，とくに注目に値するものの1つといって誤りではあるまい。ここでは，立ち入って検討するだけの余裕がないので，このような結論的な指摘だけにとどめたい。

② 非武装と非戦を定める日本国憲法の第9条は，とくに注目に値する。それは，日本の戦争責任のとり方の1つを示すものとして（2度と軍隊をもたず，戦争をしない），戦争と文明が非両立の時代に立ち至っていることの自覚を示すものとして，日本の安全保障が戦争を阻止しかつ世界平和を積極的に創造しようとする世界の平和運動の先頭に立つことにあることを示すものとして，また軍事費の再生産外消耗性を示すものとして，第2次世界大戦後の現在においては，とくに積極的な意義をもつものと考えられる。憲法制定の当時においては，政府もそのように説明をしていた。

たしかに，現実の憲法政治は，すでに指摘しておいたように，憲法から大きく逸脱している。とくに，第9条との関係においてはその逸脱が際立っている。近時の

「周辺事態法」は，アジア諸国の不信と疑惑を集めるまでにいたっている。まことに残念なことだと思う。すでに指摘しておいたような，憲法制定時に説明されていた第9条の意義を立ち入って検討することなく，同条からの逸脱を強化することは，立憲主義との関係で問題が残るだけでなく，重大な問題の処理に必要不可欠な検討もしていないという意味で，軽率というほかはない。第2次世界大戦後の50余年の世界史のなかで，①戦争と文明の両立性が再確認され強化されているか，②軍事費の再生産外消耗性が否定されその再生産性が確認されているか，③日本がこのような方向に進むことがアジアに「真の友」を得ることになるのか，等を本格的に検討すべきである。

　①　第2次世界大戦後のどの戦争においても，戦争と文明の両立性は証明されていないのではないか。戦争による人権の否定は，戦争による人権の保障をはるかに上回っているのではないか。戦争は，人権保障の手段としての意義を失ってしまっているのではないか。

　②　東西対立・米ソ軍拡戦争のなかで，軍事費の再生産外消耗性は，弁解の余地のない程に明証されているのではないか。軍拡競争に入り込んだ国は，例外なく経済的にも財政的に苦境に陥り，憲法で謳っている社会国家（福祉国家）や文化国家の保障を弱めるに至っている。ソ連＝東欧型社会主義国は，軍拡を直接の引き金として，その体制自体を崩壊させている。軍事費の再生産外消耗性をもっとも明確に自覚していたのは，「ついに発見された政治の形態」と評された1871年のパリ・コミューンであった。パリ・コミューンは，経済的に負担が重すぎるとして，常備軍の廃止を宣言していた。この点からすれば，その後裔を自認するソ連＝東欧型社会主義国の崩壊は，皮肉なことであった。

　軍事費の再生産外消耗性は体制のいかんを問わない。資本主義・社会主義，先進資本主義国・発展途上国のいずれにとっても，経済・財政の破綻の要因となる。国連開発（UNDP）の「人間開発報告書1996」によると，先進国の経済成長が続くなかで発展途上国の多くは10年前より経済的に後退し，南北の経済格差は強化されたといわれるが，先進国に対する債務とともに，軍事費の問題がどのように関係しているかを知りたいものである。また，日本の財政破綻状況についても，膨大な軍事費の問題を考慮しないわけにはいかない。

　③　第9条から逸脱する日本の憲法政治がアジア諸国との関係でどのような意味をもつか，については，ここに出席しているアジア諸国の研究者の方々から率直な

ご意見をうかがいたい。

　私は，日本国憲法には，人類の多年にわたる歴史的な努力が凝縮されていると考えている。それは，日本人の存続のためにのみならず，人類の存続のためにも必要不可欠な原則を含んでいると判断している。その判断からすれば，一方で，憲法の学習と擁護を強化することが必要となることはいうまでもない。憲法研究者がとくに国民の憲法学習とどのようにかかわるかが，あらためて問われることになる。国民は主権者であり，国民が憲法を理解して自己のものとするとき，国民は政治を動かす「真の主権者」となる。「大事は，真の主権者・国民と一緒にならなければ，なにも実現されない」のではないか。

　他方で，アジア諸国の憲法研究者とともに，日本国憲法の諸原理，とくに戦争の放棄の問題を検討することも必要となる。第9条は，とくにアジアにおける不戦・軍縮・非核化なしには完結しない。その意味でアジアの諸国民が第9条をどうみるかは，第9条の意義に直結する。この点からも，国益と利潤の追求に左右されない学術文化交流の発展を願ってやまない。

# 第Ⅳ部　ま　と　め

樋　口　陽　一

　最終セッションでは、ソンダーズ教授と杉原泰雄教授との報告のあと、あらかじめ定められていたコメンテーターの発言を皮切りに、討論がおこなわれた。
　ソンダーズ報告に対する石村修氏のコメントは、まず、アジアとオセアニアを包括して立憲主義を論ずるこのシンポジウムの枠組そのものが持つ積極的意味を前提としたうえで、アジアとオセアニアの間の相違・多様性について、報告者の見解をたずねた。ソンダーズ氏は、オセアニアの中にもオーストラリア、ニュージーランドと太平洋の島々の諸国との間には大きな相違があり、アジアの中にも多様性が大きいことに、あらためて注意をうながしたうえで、一方で植民地主義の遺産、他方でグローバリゼーションの圧力を、共通する問題として挙げた。彼女はまた、どの地域についてであれ、変化しながらも変わるべきでないものがあるとすれば何か、という石村氏の問への答えの中で、コミュニィや家族の連帯と、そして個人、という要素をあげた。
　杉原報告への笹川紀勝氏のコメントは、西欧立憲主義が国内と植民地に対する態度とで二重基準に立脚していたという報告の強調点に賛意を表したうえで、こう問題を提出した。——例えばダイシーの『憲法論』は、当時のイギリスの諸植民地の法状況にも論及しており、ロンドンの枢密院司法委員会が植民地の最高裁判所としての役割を持つことがのべられている。同じ植民地支配であっても、かつての日本が国内の外見的立憲主義による裁判制度すらオセアニアを含む植民地に及ぼさなかったこととの違いは大きいのではないか。そのことが、戦後の今もなお、立憲主義を自国内だけにとどめ旧植民地から責任を問われ続けていることにつながっていないか。それに対し、杉原氏は、前述の強調点の半面につき補足したいとして、立憲主義の理念そのものがモデルとして有意義であることはそれとして重要だ、とのべた。同氏は、植民地支配一般の中で日本のそれがきわ立って持っていた問題点についての笹川氏の指摘については、それをそのまま受け入れたい、と答えた。
　討論は、そのあと、午前のセッションから持ち越されたいくつかの応答をすませ

たのち、ソンダーズ、杉原両報告者へのフロアからの質問と答えという形で進行した。

　生々しい現実であったオーストラリア主導の東ティモール多国籍軍派遣についての質問に対する、ソンダーズ氏の率直な意見表明を含めて、予定時間をこえた応答がなされた。その中では、とりわけ、杉原報告で言及された憲法学習について、オーストラリアでの多文化主義との関連で、憲法学習の意義、および、その困難さをのりこえるための市民社会とNGOの役割が強調されたことが、印象的であった。

## あとがき——閉会の挨拶

山 下 健 次

　2日間にわたる熱心で活発な「アジア・オセアニア立憲主義シンポジウム」も閉会の時を迎えました。今回のシンポジウムは，オーストラリア，中国，フィリピン，インド，インドネシア，韓国，タイ，台湾，ベトナムの憲法学者をお迎えして開かれました。

　ご存じのように，4年前の1995年にも，アジアの憲法研究者がここ東京に集まって，立憲主義・人権に関する報告・討論が行われましたが，今回のシンポジウムは，それを大きく発展させたものと評価できます。アジア・オセアニア全域からみれば，なお限られた地域からの参加とはいえ，これだけ多くの憲法学者が一堂に会して立憲主義に関する議論を深めたことは画期的といえましょう。その成功をまず皆様とともに喜びたいと存じます。

　さて，欧米に関していえば，東西の対話が1970年代半ば以降進みました。憲法学の領域での象徴的出来事は，80年代初頭の国際憲法学会（IACL）の発足です。やがて，1989年という画期を経て，「ひとつの憲法ゲマインシャフト」（P. ヘーベルレ Haberle）が成立し，進行しているといえましょう。他方で，ヨーロッパに近接する中近東や北アフリカまで広げて見ますと，また欧米社会そのものの内部でも，キリスト教，ユダヤ教，イスラム教などの文化が共存しかつ対立する状況のもとで，またその他の諸要因が作用して民族紛争等が激化するなかで，立憲民主主義の具体化をめぐるさまざまな困難がみられることはご存知のとおりです。

　アジア・オセアニアはどうでしょうか。そこには，東西問題やいわゆる先進国と発展途上国の置かれた異なった位相の問題があり，また宗教文化の面では，世界のあらゆる宗教が混在し併存するという状況の下で，地域紛争の火種が絶えないという状況があります。そこには，欧米的なるものに対するオリエンタルなものとして一括しては捉えきれない複雑さがあります。

　このような状況のもとで，われわれアジア・オセアニアの憲法学者は何をいかに目指すべきでしょうか。抽象的・一般的にいえば，それが立憲民主主義の理念に基づく営為であることに大方の異論はないでしょう。しかし，人権問題を例にとれば，

西欧モデルに対する文化相対主義，発展段階論等々からの主張あるい反論があります。総じていえば，西欧モデルの人権の普遍化に対する異議申し立てといえましょうか。そもそも人類社会の文化と呼ばれるものには，芸術をはじめさまざまのジャンル，カテゴリーがあり，それぞれにそくして地域や民族の独自性が尊重されなければならないでしょう。法文化にも，尊重すべき独自性があることを認めなければなりません。今回のシンポジウムでも，人権保障と民主主義の具体化にあたっての貴重で多様な取り組みが報告されました。しかし，人権・民主主義という共通の言葉で語る以上，国それぞれ，地域それぞれの特殊性を過度に強調して，立憲民主主義の中身を完全に相対化することはできないでしょう。さきほど，シェリル・ソンダース教授も，アジアの多元性を指摘されつつ，立憲主義の共通性の追求について報告されました。この問題についての真摯な論争を通じて，高い次元の普遍性の認識の共有に到達する必要があると考えます。

　先に申し上げましたように，アジア・オセアニアは，欧米世界にくらべて，さまざまの意味で多元的です。したがってそのなかから人権・民主主義の普遍性を創造していく営みは，理論的にも実践的にも，けっして易しいことではありません。しかし，それは，この地域に住むわれわれにとって避けて通ることのできない課題です。のみならず，統合の一方で亀裂の噴出をも生じさせている今日の世界全体の課題でもあります。

　この2日間にわたる討論を通じて，私たちは，ともに立憲民主主義の確立を目指す憲法学者としてのお互いの友情を深めました。中国の古い言葉にあるように，「朋有り遠方より来る，亦楽しからず乎」（論語・学而篇）です。ここに，私たちの同僚の一人がかつてある国際学会で述べた言葉があります。それは，「権力でなく，友情が平和をつくる（Amicitia, non autoritas facit pacem）」でした。これを想起しつつ，「権力ではなく，友情が立憲民主主義を普遍化する」という言葉でこのシンポジウムを閉じることにいたします。

　最後に，遠路をいとわずアジア・オセアニアの各地からご参加下さった諸先生，ご参加のすべてのみなさん，このシンポジウムを準備し運営を支えて下さった事務局のみなさん，そして物心両面での援助を惜しまれなかった学術振興野村財団，日本弁護士連合会，早稲田大学の方々に心から御礼申し上げます。有り難うございました。

資料：シンポジウムプログラム

## アジア・オセアニア立憲主義シンポジウム

**総合テーマ　アジアにおける新秩序と立憲主義**

　日　時：1999年9月22日(水)及び23日(木)
　場　所：早稲田大学国際会議場
　主　催：全国憲法研究会
　　　　　Japan Association for Studies of Constitutional Law
　共　催：早稲田大学大学院アジア太平洋研究科
　　　　　日本弁護士連合会
　後　援：(財)学術振興野村基金


## PROGRAM 1 ―― 第1日

　　　　主催者代表挨拶：大須賀　明（早稲田大学教授）
　　　　　　　　　挨拶：尾﨑久仁子（外務省人権難民課長）


第1セッション　アジア立憲主義の新たな摸索
第1報告：基本法下の香港モデル：中国における『一国二制度』原理
　　　　　甘　　超英（北京大学法律学系助教授）〔中国〕
第2報告：インドネシアの経済危機と新たな立憲政治
　　　　　スリ・スマントリ（1945年8月17日大学学長）〔インドネシア〕
第3報告：ドイモイ体制と憲法
　　　　　ダオ・チ・ウック（国家と法研究所長）〔ベトナム〕
　　質疑・ディスカッション
　　　　司会：吉田　善明（明治大学教授）


第2セッション　アジアの人権保障
第1報告：なぜフィリピン人権委員会なのか：その憲法秩序のなかの地位
　　　　　ラウル・C・パガランガン（フィリピン大学助教授）〔フィリピン〕
第2報告：タイにおける人権と立憲主義
　　　　　ウィサヌ・ワランヨウ（タマサート大学法学部助教授）〔タイ〕

第3報告：社会活動訴訟の性格と展開
　　　　　　パーマナンド・シン（デリー大学法学部教授）〔インド〕
第4報告：台湾憲法と人権
　　　　　　黄　昭元（台湾大学法律学科副教授）〔台湾〕
　質疑・ディスカッション
　　　　　司会：江橋　崇（法政大学教授）


PROGRAM　2 ——第2日
　　　　挨拶：吉野　正（日本弁護士連合会副会長）


第3セッション　日本国憲法とアジア
第1報告：日本の憲法改正問題
　　　　　　岩間　昭道（千葉大学教授）
第2報告：日本国憲法と中国
　　　　　　龔　刃韌（北京大学法律学系教授）〔中国〕
第3報告：日本国憲法と周辺事態法
　　　　　　鄭　萬喜（東亜大学校法科大学教授）〔韓国〕
第4報告：日本国憲法の意義と全国憲法研究会
　　　　　　植野妙実子（中央大学教授）
　質疑・ディスカッション
　　　　　司会：浦田　賢治（早稲田大学教授）



第1総括報告：オセアニアとアジアの立憲主義
　　　　　　シェリル・ソンダーズ
　　　　　　　（メルボルン大学比較憲法研究所長）〔オーストラリア〕
第2総括報告：アジアの立憲主義と日本
　　　　　　杉原　泰雄（駿河台大学教授）
　　　司会：樋口　陽一（上智大学教授）


　　閉会の挨拶：山下　健次（立命館大学教授）

# Perspectives of Constitutionalism in Asia

International Symposium
on
Constitutionalism in Asia and Oceania

## Authers

| | |
|---|---|
| **Akira Osuka** | Professor of Law, Waseda University |
| **Youichi Higuchi** | Professor of Law, Sophia University |
| **Gan Chaoying** | Associate Professor of Law, Peking Law School, Beijing, China |
| **Sri Soemantri Martosoewignjo** | President, The 17 Augustus 1945 University, Indonesia |
| **Dao Tri Uc** | Director, Institute of State and Law, Vietnam |
| **Raul C. Pangalangan** | Professor of Law, University of the Philippines, Philippine |
| **Vishnu Varunyou** | Associate Professor Thammasat University, faculity of Law, Thailand |
| **Parmanand Singh** | Professor of Law, University of Deli, India |
| **Hwang Jau-Yuan** | Associate Professor of Law, National Taiwan University, Taiwan |
| **Akimichi Iwama** | Professor of Law, Chiba University |
| **Gong Renren** | Professor of Law, Peking Law School, Beijing, China |
| **Jeong Man Hee** | Professor of Law, Dong-A University College of Law, Korea |
| **Mamiko Ueno** | Professor of Law, Chuo University |
| **Cheryl Saunders** | Professor and Director, Institute for Comparative and Inaternational Law, The University of Melbourne, Australia |
| **Yasuo Sugihara** | Professor of Law, Surugadai University |
| **Kenji Yamashita** | Professor of Law, Ritsumeikan University |

# Preface

## Akira Osuka

We have witnessed remarkable economic growth and their energy and competence in NIES and in other Asian countries over the past few decades. The isuue of democratization has rised up as the result of economic growth. Democratization is a political matter, not an economic matter. However remarkable economic growth is, democratization does not always entail with it. Democratization generally means that of certain institutions or cultivation of democratic consciousness of the people, but it is the most crutial to democratize political power and to indoctrinate those who possess power with democratic sense and responsidility. But the task of democratization will become so difficult to achieve when those in power intend to protect many kinds of their own interests acquired through economic development under the authoritarian regime.

Constitutionalism plays an important role in such a situation. Constitutionalism enables to establish democratic political systems which include freedom of speech and of the press, free and fair electoral system. People can publicly claim through these systems their distress against the government and their demands that it should fulfill its responsibility and take effective measures for the people. Without constitutionalism, the consequences of the continued economic development under the authoritarian regime will be disastorous: exhaustion of natural resources, starvation, and environmental destruction on one hand, and devastation of the fundamental human rights on the other hand. Such an authoritarian regime, criticized as "developmental dictatorship" for a long time, easily infringes human rights under the pretext of economic development.

Scholars of constitutional law from countries in Asia and Oceania met at the symposium and discussed the creative development of constitutionalism and its application to Asian countries. The symposium participants will greatly contribute to the realization and establishment of constitutionalism in these countries. But each country has different problems tied to many comlex factors such as remnants of the colonial rule by western countries, contemporary demands of the people for democratization, or many kinds of international influence from other countries.

## Preface

Although we must leave respective inquiry of each country to the treatises in this book, we would like to consider generally what constitutionalism should be under the dual task of economic growth and democratization, where undemocratic authoritarian regime is still alive. This book is a result of the symposium on constitutional law held in Tokyo in 1999 when many scholars from Asian and Oceanian countries participated in it.

In Japan there are two large learned societies of Public law. One is Japan Association for Studies of Public law, which has about 1200 members whose majors vary from constitutional law to administrative law. The other is Japan Association for Studies of Constitutional Law (JASCL), which consists of about 500 members, those who are almost all scholars of constitutional law in Japan.

JASCL has developed theoretical activity for protection of the fundamental principle of Japanese Constitution, that is, eternal guarantee of the fundamental human rights of the people, renounciation of war and complete pacifism, and people's sovereignty and democracy. JASCL has positively stood against reactionary amendment to the Constitution, that has been persistently intended by the conservatives in Japan.

JASCL is a well-known learned society of constitutional law in Japan, and I served as the president from 1997 to 1999. This book is founded on the result both in theoretical and practical acticity during that period, and needless to say, is also founded on the devoted contribution of many JASCL members. I should express special thanks to them, but especially to the effort and contribution of Professor Kikuko Seino, Meiji University.

# Foreword

## Youichi Higuchi

Scrutiny and analysis of foreign constitutions are major research area for Japanese academic circles, and increasing numbers of bilateral exchanges between Japan and countries or regions that offer research opportunities have been observed. However, despite this increasing activity with regards to bilateral forums, multilateral academic exchanges have not been so much in evidence. On the global stage, since its inception in 1989, the International Association of Constitutional Law (Association Internationale de Droit Constitutionnel) has held five world congresses and accomplished much with regards to the context of tendency that a "constitutionalism" symbol has become universal in the various territories of "the west", "the east", "the north", and "the south" since 1980s. In the Asian region, the Japane Branch of the Association hosted the "Symposium on Asian Constitutions" in Yokohama, 1989. Although on a small scale this conference produced good results. Moreover, it is notable that of the 208 foreign scholars who attended the IVth World Congress of the International Association of Constitutional Law in 1995 in Tokyo, 79 were from Asia and Oceania, reflecting the increasing significance of the research area in these regions. In contrast, attendees of the former conferences had mainly come from Europe.

It is within this context that the proceedings of the Tokyo Symposium organized by the Japan Association for Studies of Constitutional Law in 1999 are published. Embracing achievement, I would like to emphasize four points encapsulated within the following statement: (1) In 1999, (2) the Japan Association for Studies of Constitutional Law organized the symposium and (3) gathered scholars from Asia and Oceania (4) in order to discuss the actualities and tasks of constitutionalism.

(1) Just before the end of 20th century and at the dawn of the new millenium, 1999 represents the best time to review the first half of the 20th Century, which saw the results of the process of militarization in Japan dating back to the events of 1894-95 and the latter half of that century in which the ideal and the reality of demilitarization are assumed as a basis for national policy after 1945.

(2) The symposium was held by the Japan Association for Studies of Constitutional Law that consists of scholars who study and advocate the Constitution of Japan that declares that the Japanese people pledge "to accomplish these high ideals and purpose with all our resource" (the preamble of the Constitution of Japan).

(3) The symposium was designed to promote dialogue between Japanese participants and the scholars from the regions where Japan had made a serious impact in the first half of the 20th century as "a military power" and in the latter half as "an economic power".

(4) Finally, the message from a forum providing a platform for such dialogue must be one for all people who confront difficulties on a global scale.

This last point requires more detailed explanation. The big change symbolized by the fall of the Berlin Wall in 1989 seemed to be that constitutionalism, which has a historical limitation under Western European origin, won trust as a universal value. However, the reaction against such a vigorous belief is also strong, and now threatens to drag the world into a period of renewed confusion and anxiety. The idea that justifies the market system as a panacea in the name of "democracy" and "human rights", so-called Market Fundamentalism, has found growing acceptance, mainly around the Anglo-Saxon world. The relative success of this ideology has brought with it an over-confidence, fed by retreat of the rival socialist ideology on the one hand, and a fear amongst others in the face of an apparent breakdown of self-discipline on the other. In such a context, there is a growing tendency that "the virtue" of tolerance that is supposed to be the core of the constitutionalism is decreasing not only in the inside of the advanced constitutional nations but also in the arena of international politics with particular regard towards the Third and the Fourth world. As I write this foreword, the countries that rank amongst the advanced constitutional countries have taken unilateral action with the destructive force of overwhelming arms against the international law and order that has been established for the several centuries. Japan has accepted the constitutionalism of Western European origin; moreover, whilst Article 9 in the Constitution of Japan provides great possibilities for the nation to go beyond constitutionalism, Japan has yet to develop these possibilities. If these proceedings contain the foundations of a dialogue amongst Japan, Asia, and Oceania, it is to be hoped that it must make also a meaningful contribution to the worldwide open forum.

# Contents

Preface ················································Akira Osuka  199
Foreword ············································Youichi Higuchi  201

## Part I  Searching for Constitutionalism in Asia

Hong Kong Model under the Basic Law
  ——Practice of the "One Country, Two Systems" Principle in China ···············································Gan Chaoying  207
The Economic Crisis in Indonesia and the New Constitutional Goverment ·····················Sri Soemantri Martosoewignjo  251
The 1992 Constitution and the Institutional Reform in Vietnam ·············································································Dao Tri Uc  259

## Part II  Protection of Human Rights in Asia

Why a Philippine Human Rights Commission? Its Place in a Constitutional Order
  ——An Inquiry into the Power and Limits of Liberal Constitutionalism ·····························Raul C. Pangalangan  285
Human rights and constitutionalism in Thailand
  ·················································································Vishnu Varunyou  301
Protection of Human Rights through Public Interest Litigation in INDIA ·················································Parmanand Singh  309
Judge-Made Constitutionalism in Democratizing Taiwan
  ——The Role of the Council of Grand Justices and Protection of Individual Rights ·······································Hwang Jau-Yuan  333

## Part III  The Constitution of Japan and Asia

Problems of amending the Japanese Constitution
　──The controversy over constitutional amendment and
　constitutionalism in postwar Japan ·····················Akimichi Iwama　349
Japan's Constitution and International Law
　: Focus on The Peace Article —Outline— ···············Gong Renren　361
An Assessment on the Pacifism in the Japanese Constitutional
　Law·······················································Jeong Man Hee　367
The significance of the Constitution of Japan and
　Japan Association for Studies of Constitutional Law
　···························································Mamiko Ueno　385

## Part IV  General Reports

Asia, Oceania and Constitutionalism ···············Cheryl Saunders　405
Asian Constitutionalism and Japan ················Yasuo Sugihara　425


Afterword : Closing Adress ·····················Kenji Yamashita　433

# Part I  Searching for Constitutionalism in Asia

# Hong Kong Model under the Basic Law
## ——Practice of the "One Country, Two Systems" Principle in China

Gan Chaoying

### CONTENT

I. THE RISE OF THE "ONE COUNTRY, TWO SYSTEMS" POLICY
  1. The Rooting Meaning of the "One Country, Two Systems" Policy
  2. The attitude of the Chinese Leading Circle on the Problem of Reintegration since 1950's
  3. The Raise of the "One Country, Two Systems" Principle

II. HONG KONG BASIC LAW AND ITS POSITION WITHIN THE LEGAL SYSTEM OF CHINA
  1. The Birth of the Hong Kong Basic Law
  2. The Legislative Resources of the Basic Law
  3. Rights of Hong Kong

III. THE POLITICAL STRUCTURE PRESCRIPTED BY THE BASIC LAW
  1. The Chief Executive
  2. The Executive Authorities
  3. The Legislature
  4. The Judiciary

IV. THE SUCCESSES AND THE PROBLEMS OF HONG KONG MODEL
  1. The Strengthened Position of Hong Kong in the Financial Storm under the Basic Law
  2. Democratic Development of Hong Kong
  3. Human Rights Protection in Hong Kong
  4. The Matter of Judicial Review
  5. The Prospect of the Development of the Basic Law

V. THE SIGNIFICANCES OF THE HONG KONG MODEL
  1. It's a model for resolving the questions of Macao and Taiwan
  2. The Development of Marxism through the Model
  3. The Development of the Constitutional Theory of China by the Influence of the Model
  4. The Influence of the Model to the International Law

## I. THE RISE OF THE "ONE COUNTRY, TWO SYSTEMS" POLICY

### 1. The Rooting Meaning of the "One Country, Two Systems" Policy

The "one country, two systems" policy is the basic principle of the Chinese government to handle with the problems of the reintegration of the country. As other newly raised policies in China after the crush of the so-called "Gang of Four" in the Autumn 1976, this Policy was originally brought forward formally by Mr. Deng Xiaoping. He said in 1984 that the "one country, two system" means "the people living in Hong Kong and in Taiwan practice the capitalist systems while in the mainland the billion of the Chinese remains in the socialist system but all in the territory of the People's Republic of China".[1]

The meaning of the Policy set forth by Mr. Deng is that the special administrative regions would be founded, if necessary, in areas such as in Hong Kong, Macao or in Taiwan by the Central Government. The regions as such would come directly under the Central Government, under which the regions would be allowed to enjoy a high degree of autonomic authorities on executive, legislative, and judicatory aspects, except for those foreign and defensive affairs. In the special administrative regions it will keep both the given capitalist system and the ways of life untouched for 50 years, that is, the socialist system and policies will not be introduced into the regions at least for 50 years.[2]

To get more accurate perspectives on the Policy or the Principle, the following explanations to it would be necessary and helpful:[3]

> The Principle means firstly the tenets of adhering to the consolidation of the nation and of upholding the sovereignty of the state, under which the relationship of the Center and the regions shall be handled with in a suitable manner. Because of the historical complex, the Chinese Government lost the jurisdictions to Hong Kong, Macao, and Taiwan for years. But that doesn't mean that China lost the sovereign rights upon them. Therefore, the regression of them to China cannot be deemed as the regaining but the resumption of sovereignty instead. Under this precondition, Hong Kong and the like can be given an autonomic position and the rights specialized in a special law. This is what the suitable manner means.[4]

The state allows the special administrative regions to have a high degree of autonomic rights. Except for those powers relating to the sovereignty of the state and those powers for affairs which must be settled through the conducts of the Central Government, the autonomic rights include administrative, legislative, independent judicial and final appeal powers. This kind of autonomic rights are much higher in degree and much more in number than those enjoyed by the self-government of national autonomous areas within the Mainland China, in which the self-governments cannot have at least the jurisdiction on final appeals.

As a special region, the previous capitalist system and way of life will remain unchanged at least for 50 years. The unchanged aspects include mainly the social system, the economic system, and the way of life. There are three things on the meaning of unchangeableness ought to be explained further. The unchangeableness means at first, of course, that the Central Government will not take any measure to change those systems. On the other hand, it doesn't mean that those systems could not be changed by Hong Kong people themselves. Every system will be changed and developed by its own disciplines in the course of time, as it is a natural process of mankind and could not be ordered fundamentally by the will of mankind.[5] It is theoretically to say that these systems will be developed under the willing of Hong Kong people, not of the Mainland. The second thing refers to the manner of the self-change. Apart from the self-change being not allowed for its against the Mainland in Hong Kong, it can neither be changed for socialism at least in 50 years even if there were a strong ambition or appeal from the side of Hong Kong, for the Basic Law has safeguarded to Hong Kong people that the capitalism will remain untouched for that length of time. If there were some Hong Kong people who wanted to change the system as a whole into the socialist one, it is the Basic Law on its Article 18 (4) will block this attempt. Because that clause provides the means to prevent the attempt.[6] The third approach is related to the would-be changes before the regression. If there were some changes before the big day on July 1, 1997, they should not affect the implementation of the articles of the Joint Declaration and the other agreements between China and Great Britain. If the changes impacted these agreements, the Chinese

Government would have rights to response or even to retaliate. There were in fact several such examples happened before the big day.[7] About 50 years period, as Mr. Deng said when he met British Prime Minister, Mrs. Thatcher on December 1984 that if the first 50-year had passed unchanged at the open-door's policy, we could be sure the unchangeableness in the following 50-year, and so was for Hong Kong.[8] That is, it is unnecessary to make changes on the matter of the status of Hong Kong, if it is proved successful in maintaining the existing systems.[9]

The legal system of Hong Kong mostly remains unchanged. This means that the judicial principles and rough structure of the courts will not be changed except for the jurisdiction of final appeal, resources of legal authority, some legal norms and laws in force after 1997. As Article 81 (2) provides: "The judicial system previously practiced in Hong Kong shall be maintained except for those changes consequent upon the establishment of the Court of Final Appeal of the Hong Kong Special Administrative Region". It would be the necessary exception to the 50-year unchangeableness policy. The Mainland laws listed at the Annex III are laws relating to maintaining the national sovereignty which must be implemented in Hong Kong. And some legal expressions in Hong Kong laws must be changed when the British crown has not performed the role of the highest authority of Hong Kong.

The administration and the legislature are formed by the local people of Hong Kong, which is so-called the norm of Hong Kong people governs Hong Kong. This emphasizes the self-restraint of the Central Government not to send missions to take part directly into the executive and legislative jobs in Hong Kong. The local people here include Chinese as well as the residents with nationalities of other countries. Within these two parts of residents Chinese will have a decisive and positive position either by law or by the practice. However, most of those Chinese residents who master the powers ought to be under the patriotic standard or criterion, the main requirement of which is to support the resumption of the Chinese sovereignty to Hong Kong and not to do any thing impairing the prosperous and stable situation of Hong Kong regardless of their political attitude to the socialist belief.[10] In fact, the governance of Hong Kong by its residents is the key guarantee of the self-government, for the continuance of the legal system must have the maintenance of its way of life as basis. Only will the people who live therein have a common sense about their legal and political systems. As Cassirer said, the various forms of human culture would be combined not by their unification in nature but by their uniformity in the basic tasks.[11]

## 2. The attitude of the Chinese Leading Circle on the Problem of Reintegration since 1950's

In 1949, when the Chinese People's Liberation Army swept all the old regime remains out of the country, the troops didn't march into Hong Kong and Macao. Before and at 1950's, there was indeed an idea to go over the Shenzhen River to liberate the people there. But the leaders, such as Mao Zhedong and Zhou Enlai had framed a policy to the question of Hong Kong even before the establishment of the new government. Mao said on January 1949:

> The affairs on the Mainland are relatively easy to handle with, that is, we can simply dispatch the armies to solve them. It is more difficult to deal with the affairs at the islands. It needs another flexible way to manage or by the means of peaceful interim. It is, therefore, in a long run to deal. At such a situation, solving the questions of Hong Kong and Macao in a rash manner has lost its reasonable basis. In contrary, it would be more wise to make the use of the positions of them, especially of Hong Kong, to develop the overseas relations as well as the imports and exports of Mainland. In general, we should make decisions depending on the run of the conditions.[12]

This statement was in fact the significant decision of the Communist Party on the matter of Hong Kong and Macao. On December 19 of the year, Overseas Chinese Daily of Hong Kong had in front page a front title: Mao Zhedong has pledged to the peace of Hong Kong, and British has promised to acknowledge the New Government of China.[13] From the time on, the Chinese Government has shaped a persistent stand on matters of Hong Kong: Hong Kong is a territory belonging to China, China does not accept all the unequal pacts pressed on China by the imperialist powers in the last century, China asserts to solve the questions through negotiations at the proper times, and the current situations should be maintained before the occasions of agreements achieve.[14] In 1960, when some people outside China questioned the attitudes of China to Hong Kong and Macao, the Chinese Government overtly declared this policy to the world.[15]

The policy had its courses in many respects. First, it was the need of politics. On September 1949, Mao Zhedong stated at the first meeting of the National Committee of the Chinese People's Political Consultative Conference (CPPCC) that the Chinese Government would solve the historical questions by peaceful means. To keep this promise and to make it understood by the peoples in Hong Kong and Macao, the peaceful policy was necessary. Secondly, China needed a peaceful international environment to break the anti-China block set by the USA who was the head of that alliance. Hong Kong was a gap at the block while the British Government hoped to maintain its rights in it. So Premier Zhou brought forward a policy to develop the Sino-British relationship and to try for keeping peace and cooperation with the Great Britain.[16] The most importance to carry out the policy was among the economic affairs. When China endured the great pressures out of the USA and the USSR in 50's and 60's, Hong Kong was the sole largest passage of China to the world. China obtained almost all of foreign currencies, techniques, information, capitals and talents it needed through Hong Kong, which couldn't be replaced by other cities for its position at that time.

Therefore, although there were conflicts between Chinese leaders before 1970's, the leading idea of the time was to solve the questions by peace way. After the fulfillment of transformation of the capitalist industry and commerce into socialist forms in Mainland China, Prime Minister made a speech about the relations between Mainland and Hong Kong. He promised that on the basis of diversity China would render the policies to Hong Kong distinct to those in Mainland, and that it could not transfer the capitalist model of Hong Kong into the socialist one, for that didn't profit both China and Hong Kong. In the light of economic development, China would continue the cooperation with the capitalists and businessmen of Hong Kong no matter would it be in the future.[17]

Hence, before the open-door policy was raised, among the Chinese leaders the peaceful choice was the first approach for the reunification. But there was a hindrance on the road: according to the traditional Leninist politics, either the socialism defeats the capitalist or vice versa.[18] The dilemma was then insolvable in the theory. To the first generation of leaders, it was a task far from their reach. They didn't and might be incapable design a model for the coming back of Hong Kong and Macao to Mainland. What they have done was to set up the principle that the two territories must go back under the sovereignty of China by ways of negotiation. In this situation it was deemed that there was no best ways to overcome the difficulties on the road of reintegration of the country except but waiting.[19]

### 3. The Raise of the "One Country, Two Systems" Principle

The dawn came with the crackdown of Gang of Four and the beginning of the new enlightenment that was started by Mr. Deng after the Third Session of the Eleventh Party Congress held on December 1978. The Third Session ascertained the principle of seeking the truth through practice regardless of what theoretical dogmas says. This opened the vast space to let people consider those theories, which had governed the brains of the people for many years, wrong or right, nihilist or practicable.

The principle of truth-in-practice is not only the new tool of the people to build up a good life, but also the key for the Chinese leaders to solve and formulate again the inner and foreign policies. The first spark of the One Country, Two Systems Policy expressed in the National Day Address by Marshall Ye Jianying in 1981, in which he mentioned the possibility of the reintegration by a peaceful way that Taiwan will be a special administrative region of the state, enjoying the high degree of autonomy, allowed to keep its armies, and to remain its social structures and the model of life unchanged.[20] Although there was no explicit expression of one country, two systems in it, the Address contained in reality the content of the Policy. This was the foundation of the peaceful reunification of the nation.

On September 1982, when Mr. Deng met Mrs. Margaret Thatcher, the British premier, he posed formally the One Country, Two Systems Principle out at the first time aiming for solving the problem of Hong Kong. He told Mrs. Thatcher that the question of sovereignty could not be negotiated and the regression of Hong Kong to China was only the question of time. He denied further the proposal to let British continually administrate Hong Kong under the Chinese sovereignty. But he agreed that Hong Kong would keep its systems not to be changed and the interests of British would be ensured.[21]

On such a basis of political stand, the Chinese Constitution promulgated on December 1982 was added at its draft the Article 31, which reads,

> The state may establish special administrative regions when necessary. The systems to be instituted in special administrative regions shall be prescribed by law enacted by the National People's Congress (NPC) in the light of the specific conditions.

This provision gave Hong Kong a constitutional insurance not to become a mimic of the local governments in the Mainland.

On May 5, 1984, the State Council raised formally the "One Country, Two Systems" principle in its Government Annual Message delivered to the National People's Congress. The NPC passed the Message and this made the Principle a basic state policy to Hong Kong with legal force. Furthermore, the One Country, Two Systems Principle has become to a cornerstone of Chinese Government to deal with the whole problem of reunification.[22]

## II. HONG KONG BASIC LAW AND ITS POSITION WITHIN THE LEGAL SYSTEM OF CHINA

### 1. The Birth of the Hong Kong Basic Law

In the light of One Country, Two Systems Principle, it was achieved an agreement between China and Great Britain in solving the historical question of Hong Kong. To handle with the problems during the interim both governments signed the Joint Declaration on the Question of Hong Kong on December 19 1984. According to this Joint Declaration, the Chinese Government will resume the sovereign rights over Hong Kong from July 1 1997. On April 10 1985, according to a specific resolution of the Congress, a committee to draft the basic law for Hong Kong was formed. On April 4 1990, the Hong Kong Basic Law adopted by the Seventh National People's Congress at its third session.[23]

The Basic Law has a preamble, nine chapters, one hundred and sixty articles, plus three attached annexes with legal force. Either from its structure or its content, the Basic Law is essentially the fundamental legal document for Hong Kong. Therefore, it is called to be the "little constitution" or the "constitution for Hong Kong".

It is not, nevertheless, the true constitution for Hong Kong, on account of its drafting and issuing authorities, not as a result of sovereign conduct by the residents. It is not of the prerequisite in formal meaning of a constitution. It was given to Hong Kong by the Central Government of China. The Basic Law has with the Constitution a relationship of offspring and ancestor.[24] It cannot at the beginning of its birth conflict with the Constitution and must follow the guidance of the Constitution. In fact, the source of the force of the Basic Law came from the authority of the Center by powers granting. This relationship is different from what the relations of constitutions within a federal country have, within which the state constitutions are not descended from the federal constitution though they cannot either conflict with the federal constitution. Furthermore, even it is wrong to think that the Basic Law is the highest legal document in Hong Kong. The Constitution of the land possesses that place instead, either in name or in legal structure. If not so, the sovereignty of China over the Region would be in doubt. In another words, the specialty of the Region is in areas of concrete design of the systems, not in the question of one country. There is no beneath the central government such a local government where the constitution of the land could not cover for.[25]

On the basis of the Basic Law, there was a new relationship born-not the relationship under the Constitution of the state by the people as a whole, but under a statute by the Center. And this statute renders duties not only to Hong Kong, but also to the Central Government. This kind of result comes from the reality that the Basic Law is a mutual compromise between two sides of China and Britain who represented the interests of Hong Kong at the negotiations.[26] And the Chinese side considered thoroughly the benefits of the Chinese living in Hong Kong. This compromise doesn't mean the equal position of a local authority and the central authority, but the mutual interests, which guided the peaceful reunification. The relationship of Hong Kong and the Center was formed under the international interference and exposed to eyes of the countries in the world. By the way, because Hong Kong is an international city and is still one of the main open mouth of China to the world, its rights ought to be respected for the purpose of keeping its prosperity.

## 2. The Legislative Resources of the Basic Law

A. The Basic Law was made under the sovereignty of China. This means that the Basic Law must get its legality from the Constitution of the land.

As mentioned above, Article 31 of the Constitution provides that the state shall establish the special administrative regions when necessary. This implies four things at least in the case of Hong Kong: one is that the special administrative region could be erected, which shall be special depending on those necessary demands, and which are different to the existent national autonomous as well as special economic areas. The special demands for a special statute are those different or even contrary ones for and to the other parts of Mainland China. Thus, the second thing is that the special social and political systems could be allowed in Hong Kong, which are permitted contrary to the systems in the Mainland. Although the differences look like a great chasm in essentials, the Hong Kong part is after all in size pretty small compared with the Mainland. The third is that the special systems must be fixed by national law, that is, in the scope of toleration of the Central Government. What the law says is what the rights to be. Fourthly, the right to make such a law shall be endowed to the National People's Congress. This is the final requirement for the legitimacy of the Basic Law for Hong Kong.[27]

Apart from Article 31, Article 62 enumerates the powers of the Congress, granting the legislature the power to "decide on the establishment of special administrative regions and the systems to be instituted there". This establishment power is in nature a supreme legislative power, which is named in Chinese Constitution as "the highest state power" (Article 57). Under the Constitution, the Congress is the highest organ of state power that is included the power of legislation, establishment, nomination, decision, etc. The significance of separating the establishment power from the legislative power would be in order to emphasize the importance and specialty of the problems of reunification. The intent of the constitutional framer indicated that the systems in Hong Kong and Macao were surely different from those in the Mainland, which shall be guaranteed by the divide of legislative power into catalogues.

In fact, there are two establishment power items of the Congress granted by the Constitution. While Item 12 of Article 62 grants the Congress the power to approve the establishment of provinces, autonomous regions, and municipalities directly under the Central Government, Item 13 grants it another power to decide on the establishment of special administrative regions as mentioned above. Therefore, the establishment of special administrative regions should be deemed as different from the establishment of inner local governments in Mainland. It implies that the different political systems in those areas outside Mainland will be allowed by the Constitution.

The constitutional clauses mirror the basic claims of the One Country, Two Systems Principle. As Mr. Peng Zhen, the later chairman of the Congress said in his Report on the Constitutional Draft that if the principles of sovereignty, unification, and state integrity are to be maintained, Taiwan could remain unchanged in almost every areas of the social structure; and that that is "the principal ground for us to deal with matters of similarity". "Matters of similarity" are, of course, indicating the instances of Hong Kong and Macao.[28]

B. The Basic Law for Hong Kong is in the highest rank of Chinese legislations under the Constitution.

Under the Constitution, only the NPC and its Standing Committee shall exercise the legislative power of the state. What the NPC set down are called "the basic statutes", which would concern concerning criminal offences, civil affairs, the state organs and other matters, while what the laws issued by the Committee are called "the statutes", which are beyond the basic matters. This means, in strict sense, that the basic statutes are higher in force than the Committee statutes. Nevertheless, the Standing Committee shall have the revising power and supplements providing power, though the Congress itself surely owns these powers, to the basic statutes when the Congress is not in session. But the amendments or the partial supplements to the basic statutes by the Committee should not contravene the basic principles of those Congress statutes.[29]

Deducing from its enacting process, the Basic Law for Hong Kong is commonly known as belonging to the category of basic statutes.[30] But this Law is a little bit higher in rank than other basic statutes passed by the Congress itself. Such a position gains from the Basic Law. In Article 159 (1) of the Basic Law of Hong Kong provides:

The power of amendment of this Law shall be vested in the National People's Congress.

That means that the revision power of this basic statute is grasped in hands of the Congress itself. And the Congress made here in this Law incapacity of its Standing Committee to revise the Law. Such an arrangement gives the Basic Law a superb status over other basic statutes, which means its revision should be treated with much care than those latter. It is significant that the rights of Hong Kong will get through this arrangement more prudent warranty.[31]

C. Sino-British Joint Declaration ensures the One Country, Two Systems Principle to be written down in the process of drawing up of the Basic Law.

Although the Constitution has confirmed the position of Hong Kong as a special administrative region and ensured in principle the divergent social and political systems from Mainland, it is impossible to numerate details of the institutions. Another legal document-the Joint Declaration signed by the Chinese and British Governments on December 1984-plays thus the role of concluding the details. The Joint Declaration contains mainly such terms as: (1) the Chinese Government will on July 1 1997 resume the exercise the sovereignty, while the British reign ends; (2) the basic policies of the Chinese Government are to found the special administrative region therein; (3) the Center will grant the Region a high degree of autonomy with legislative, executive and independent judiciary powers; (4) the Center ensures the governing by natives; (5) the Region will certify the human rights and customary rights thereof; (6) the Center will leave the financial affairs independent; (7) the Center lets the government thereof guarantee the public security; (8) the Region protects the benefits of the United Kingdom as well as other countries therein not to be touched, etc.[32]

All contents of the Joint Declaration were written down into the Basic Law composing as the framework of it. And these contents constitute the responsibilities of the Chinese Government, for the Joint Declaration itself is a kind of treaty between China and Great Britain within the meaning of international law. To render his responsibility for ensuring the legal rights of Hong Kong, the Basic Law was framed.

D. Article 8 of Hong Kong Basic Law prescribes:

The laws previously in force in Hong Kong, that is, the common law, rules of equity, ordinances, subordinate legislation and customary law shall be maintained, except for any that contravene this Law, and subject to any amendment by the legislature of the Hong Kong Special Administrative Region.

This presumes that, in the Basic Law itself, there are a lot of prescriptions get their origins from the English law, and the traditional Chinese law and customs.[33] These clauses focus on the social, economical, and judicial systems. The judiciary system as a whole, judicial principles and procedures will be remained unchanged on their original principles of common law traditions with tidy necessary adjustments. Allowing Hong Kong under the rule of the common law traditions is important for maintaining the so-called "previous systems" unchanged, because Hong Kong has been long a society of law. However, there are some laws previously in force in Hong Kong has naturally lost their legal basis after the regression, because of their contravention to the Basic Law. For example, the Letters Patent as a fundamental legal document for the British governing power of Hong Kong as well as the Royal Instructions as an organic law during the colonist period was excluded from the list of the laws previously in force in Hong Kong.[34]

There is a problem needs to be clarified more. The question is: Should the Chinese Constitution be carried out in Hong Kong, as mentioned above, when it has its own "little constitution"? Or is the Chinese Constitution the highest law in Hong Kong? The answer is positive yeah. First, the Hong Kong Special Administrative Region founded through the Basic Law is the result of the Principle of One Country, Two Systems. One Country is the aboveground precondition for the existence of the Region. If the One Country norm were denied, there would have been no the Region at all. And if the One Country proposition be recognized, the Constitution of the land must be obeyed by any of its parts. Secondly, the Basic Law was formulated in accordance with the Constitution of China. This means that the Basic Law will lose its ground of existence, if the highest norm becomes null for Hong Kong. As a common dogma says that any subordinate norm cannot get its legal effectiveness just by its own self-prescription. Thirdly, there is an undivided relevance between the Constitution and the Basic Law. If the relative clauses of the latter should be correctly understood, it must find out the core meanings in the former. For example, what is meant the "Central People's Government" in many articles of the Basic Law or the "socialist system and policies" in Article 5 thereof? The original meanings of them ought to be explained according to the Constitution.

Nevertheless, the Constitution of China cannot be absolutely and fully implemented in Hong Kong. The key line of implementation of the Constitution to Hong Kong is if a given matter relates to the question of sovereignty or not.[35] The question of the implementation force of the Constitution might be nicely answered by looking at the attitude of the courts of Hong Kong to the Constitution. We will find out that the Constitution may not be used as a ruler to justify the behaviors of the residents and the government organs in Hong Kong. Thus it is a very interesting phenomenon of the rule of law: the Constitution is the highest law also in Hong Kong, but has no legal effect in courts.

### 3. Rights of Hong Kong

In the relationship between Hong Kong and the Center, Hong Kong is naturally subject to the Center. But beneath the Central powers, Hong Kong has its own rights provided by the Basic Law.

Before we consider the rights of Hong Kong, we should know what the Central Government has, that is, what it could wield to the Region. They might be expressed in five respects: (1) the basic institutions should be decided by the Center through the Basic Law, even if the structure and the principles of the institutions remain unchanged; (2) Hong Kong cannot be endowed the full powers as a sovereign state; and in the scopes of power of Hong Kong some parts of them, which are of the nature of sovereignty, should be performed by the Center, such as the powers of foreign and defensive affairs; (3) the final interpretation power of the Basic Law belongs to the Standing Committee of the NPC and the amendment power of the Law leaves to the NPC itself; (4) the Center has right to postulate that Hong Kong will not be a basis for the force of practicable anti-communism; (5) the Center can keep the supervision power in hand. By the way, the Center is responsible for the defense of the Region and can station the military forces into Hong Kong. The existence of the garrison is a symbol of national sovereignty.[36]

According to the Joint Declaration and the Detailed Explanation to it by the

Chinese Government, Hong Kong will have rights as below:[37]

(1) the socialist system and policies will not be practiced in Hong Kong, which means that the legislature will be legitimated by a universal election, the executive takes responsibility to the legislature, the governmental departments and the courts could use, apart from Chinese, English, and the flag and emblem of the Region could be hung next to those of the Land; (2) the legislature could in accordance with the legal processes enact laws for Hong Kong and report them to the Standing Committee of the NPC for the record; (3) except the final adjudication, the judicial system and principles, such as independence of justice, will be maintained with the power of appointment and removal of judges; (4) the system and the regulations of the civil services will keep the original appearance, except for the positions of highest rank; (5) the financial incomes needn't to turn over to the Center, though the budgets and final accounts should report to the Center for the record; (6) the free trade policy will be continued; (7) the currency and banking system should be preserved, that is, the Hong Kong dollar will be continued to keep its independence; (8) the shipping management system remains its origins, only do the foreign warships should be into harbors of Hong Kong under the approvals of the Center by way of exception; (9) Hong Kong will be furthermore as an aviation center; (10) the educational system will be maintained; (11) the name of "Hong Kong, China" should be used when Hong Kong develops various relations with the other parts of the world, while Hong Kong has a semi-independent position on matters of foreign affairs relating to it; (12) the stationed army, who was dispatched by the Central Government, will not interfere in the local affairs, and the expenditure for the garrison will be borne by the Central Government at the same time; (13) the applicable parts of two international pacts-the International Covenant on Civil and Political Rights, the International Covenant on Economic, Social and Cultural Rights-shall remain in force and will be implemented through the laws of the Region; (14) Hong Kong Government has the authority to decide the problems as passports and visas.

The contents of the Basic Law are, of course, more than those mentioned above. However, all of these 14 points are guaranteed not only by the Basic Law itself, but also by the Joint Declaration——a legal document with international character. This is the reason why we call them as "rights" of Hong Kong.

## III. THE POLITICAL STRUCTURE PRESCRIPTED BY THE BASIC LAW

What the Hong Kong Basic Law offers could be named as the "Hong Kong Model". It could be but expressed simply as "dominance by administrative" principle. All the political structure of Hong Kong was designed to carry out the principle.[38]

### 1. The Chief Executive

To replace the British Governor, the Basic Law provides the highest political position in Hong Kong to the Chief Executive who is the head of Hong Kong and represents the Region. Different to the British Governor, the Chief Executive is not the highest deputy of the Center in Hong Kong, but the highest deputy of Hong Kong people, either to the Center or to the world. This kind of design is to incarnate and symbolize the creed of Hong Kong Governed by Hong Kong People, which is the principal target of establishing the Special Administrative Region.[39]

However, there is a danger for the Center, purely by such a designation, that the Chief Executive were going to do what the Center would not expect to or what would lead Hong Kong divorced from the whole or what the tendency of such a centrifugal would be resulted from. Hong Kong is after all a part within the territory of China in spite of being an area enjoying the autonomy in high degree. For the sake of sovereignty, the Basic Law is contained with three firewalls. One of them is provided at Annex I of the Basic Law, according to which the Chief Executive should be selected by an Election Committee, not by the universal election at least before 2007. The members of the Election Committee come from every corner of Hong Kong, including businessmen, professions, labors, members of the Legislative Council of Hong Kong, Hong Kong deputies to the NPC and to the CPPCC, etc. The composing structure of the Election Committee ensures the rights and the control of the Center will not be breached, for most of them are intimates or patriots of the Center with the belief of reunification, who will select their resemblance to the post of Chief Executive. The second firewall is built at the Basic Law itself. In Article 44, the Law says that the Chief Executive should be a permanent resident of the Region with no right of abode in any foreign country. That this norm was written down in the Law reflected the countercharge of the Chinese Government to the measure adopted by the last Governor Sir Chris Patten that Great Britain gave 50,000 Hong Kong families the rights to live in Great Britain. The counter-measure in Article 44, avoiding the danger of "double loyalty" of the head of the Region, guarantees the legal loyalty of the Chief Executive to the Chinese Government.[40] At last, the Basic Law provides in Article 45 that in 50 years of the Basic Law in effect, the Chief Executive is capable to take office just after he gets the appointment from the Central Government.

Apart from being the head of Hong Kong, the Chief Executive is also the head of Hong Kong Government. He or she owns the paper powers and functions similar like an American president. Article 48 of the Basic Law grants him powers as below:

(1) To lead the government of the Region;
(2) To be responsible for the implementation of the Basic Law and other laws which, in accordance with the Law, apply in the Region;
(3) To sign bills passed by the Legislative Council and to promulgate laws; and to report the budgets and final accounts to the Central Government for the record;
(4) To decide on government policies and to issue executive orders;
(5) To nominate and to report to the Center for appointment or removal the principal officials as Secretaries and Deputy Secretaries of Departments, Directors of Bureaus, Commissioner Against Corruption, Director of Audit, Commissioner of Police, Director of Immigration and Commissioner of Customs and Excise;
(6) To appoint or remove judges of the courts at all levels in accordance with legal procedures;
(7) To appoint or remove holders of public office in accordance with legal procedures;
(8) To implement the directives issued by the Center in respect of the relevant matters provided for in the Basic Law;
(9) To conduct, on behalf of the Hong Kong Government, external affairs and other affairs as authorized by the Central Authorities;
(10) To approve the introduction of motions regarding revenues or expenditure to the Legislative Council;

(11) To decide, in the light of security and vital public interests, whether government officials or other personnel in charge of government affairs should testify or give evidence before the Legislative Council or its committees;

(12) To pardon persons convicted of criminal offences or commute their penalties; and

(13) To handle petitions and complaints.

These prescriptions show that the powers of the Chief Executive mix the powers and functions of American president, British premier, and even French president in one. The Chief Executive can return a bill back to the Legislative Council (Lego) for reconsideration. The Lego can overthrow the executive veto by two-thirds majority. If so, the Chief must sign the bill and promulgate it as the law of the Region. If the Chief Executive refuses to sign a bill passed the second time, or if the Legislative Council refuses to pass a budget or any other important bill introduced by the Government, and if consensus cannot be reached in cases above, the Chief Executive may dissolve the Legislative Council. But he or she may wield the power of dissolution only once in his or her 5-year term of office. The incumbent Chief Executive, Mr. Tong Chee-hwa hasn't exercised this power since 1997.[41] Compared with the former British governors, the authority of the Chief Executive is cut down. He or she has no capability, as the governors have, to dissolve legislative bodies and to refuse bills just through their own wills. Because of such a change in the relationship of the Chief Executive and the Legislative Council, one kind of checks and balances conviction has been set up in Hong Kong.

There is an organ, the Executive Council, subjected directly to the Chief Executive, which plays a very important role in the process of decision-making of the head. It is the successor of the British Executive Council with almost the same functions. The Council is a consultant organ, and its members are appointed and removed by the Chief Executive himself among the principal officials of the executive authorities, members of the Legislative Council and public figures. The office term of it is as long as the Chief Executive who appoints them is. That means that most of them are those trusted followers of the Chief Executive. The composing number of the Executive Council is used to being fixed normally about 15 members. Before the Chief Executive makes important decisions, introduces bills to the legislature, makes subordinate legislation, or dissolves the Legislative Council, he or she should consult the Executive Council. Different from the former relations between the governor and his executive council, if the Chief Executive does not accept the majority opinion of the Executive Council, his or her specific reasons against the majority of the Council should be filed for record. Such a design gives the Council an ability to perform some kind of control to the Chief Executive.[42] To the British governors, however, that discipline was not the legal mandate that meant a potent responsibility upon him after the given negative event.

## 2. The Executive Authorities

The Chief Executive leads the Government of Hong Kong, that is, the executive authorities of the Region. There are three highest departments in the executive authority. They are Departments of Administration, Finance, and Justice, under which are various bureaus, divisions and commissions. The Secretary of the Department of Administration is in fact the head of the executive authorities and the first deputy Chief Executive when the Chief Executive is temporarily out of office. His or her role is much similar as French premier. But the office doesn't not depend on confidence of the Lego.

The Hong Kong Government performs functions as below:
 (1) To formulate and implement policies;
 (2) To conduct administrative affairs;
 (3) To conduct external affairs as authorized by the Central Government under the Basic Law;
 (4) To draw up and introduce budgets and final accounts;
 (5) To draft and introduce bills, motions and subordinate legislation; and
 (6) To designate officials to sit in on the meetings of the Legislative Council and to speak on behalf of the Government.

A special feature of the political system is that the foreigners are now allowed to take in charge of some lower positions in the government, as the Region was a colony of Great Britain. There are a lot of foreigners living in and serve to the Region. The new government has reasonable needs to make use of techniques and experiences of foreign employees. After the regression, British have lost the status of master of Hong Kong and their political importance has been reduced to a role of serving to a government comprised mainly by Chinese. Only are those enumerated positions in the Basic Law, namely the Secretaries and Deputy Secretaries of Departments, Directors of Bureaus, Commissioner Against Corruption, Director of Audit, Commissioner of Police, Director of Immigration and Commissioner of Customs and Excise, being required to be Chinese citizens among permanent residents of the Region with no right of abode in any foreign country. This is unique in the world on the matter of forming method of government.

Although the officials of the Hong Kong Government have duties to answer the questions before the Legislative Council, neither their appointments nor removals rely on the legislature. They are, in truth, the civil servants with high ranks, appointed by the Chief Executive as heads of departments of the government. They will not be removed by political reasons except being charged with a crime or a breach of law. The responsibilities they have are purely legal ones. This design of the Basic Law is to keep the government stable enough for an effective economic consideration.[43]

### 3. The Legislature

The legislature of Hong Kong, namely, the Legislative Council, has 60 members elected separately from functional constituencies, the Election Committee, and direct elections. According to Annex II of the Basic Law, the proportions of each part was in 1998 30-10-20 and will be in 2000 30-6-24. At the third term the part of the members from the Election Committee will be totally merged into direct elections, and the proportion share will be 30-30, that is, 30 members will be elected indirectly by the functional constituencies and at the same time the other 30 members directly by the voters. After 2007, if there is a need to amend the provisions of Annex II, such amendments must be made with the endorsement of a two-thirds majority of all the members of the Legislative Council and the consent of the Chief Executive, and they shall be reported to the Standing Committee of the NPC for the record. This complex is designed for a smooth transition from the arbitrary management under the British governors to a democratic order by the people of Hong Kong. By the way, the design is also for the adaptation of Hong Kong people to the turning of the dominant rights. After the first parliamentary election of 1998, the voice of accelerating the process of direct election has become noisier than before.[44]

The powers and functions of the Legislative Council include:

(1) To enact, amend or repeal laws;
(2) To examine and approve budgets introduced by the government;
(3) To approve taxation and public expenditure;
(4) To receive and debate the policy addresses of the Chief Executive;
(5) To raise questions on the work of the government;
(6) To debate any issue concerning public interests;
(7) To endorse the appointment and removal of the judges of the Court of Final Appeal and the Chief Judge of the High Court;
(8) To receive and handle complaints from Hong Kong residents;
(9) To impeach the Chief Executive;
(10) To summon, as required when exercising the above-mentioned powers and functions, persons concerned to testify or give evidence.

Under the model of executive dominance, the legislature of Hong Kong is designed as an organ with the role of cooperation with the executive authorities. It is indeed a difficult task for it. In the parliamentary system, the relationship between the legislature and the cabinet is a combined one. The government relies on the relevant majority at the parliament. And this is the main reason why the parliament must support the government. However, we cannot see this kind of combination in Hong Kong between the two bodies. Neither the Chief Executive nor the executive authorities gain their seats in office and powers through the sustenance of the Lego. Only in scarce occasions would the Chief Executive be put into the procedure of impeachment by the Lego. Of course, the government officials must answer the questions laid by the members of the legislature. In order to maintain the efficiency of the administration, the Basic Law has to make the legislature at the corner of the spot. Therefore, the Law provides that the legislators may introduce bills which do not relate to public expenditure or political structure or the operation of the government, and that the written consent of the Chief Executive shall be required before those bills relating to government policies are introduced to the Lego. Under this model, the legislative house seems much like a chat room in aspect of government control.

The most important power of the legislature is the weapon of impeachment. It is only formulated for the control of the Chief Executive, because he or she is the soul with importance and capacity to influence the developing trends and prosperousness of Hong Kong. There are four major steps to do so. First, if a motion initiated jointly by one-fourth of all the members of the Legislative Council, that is, 15 members or above, charges the Chief Executive with serious breach of law or neglect of duty, he or she should resign from office. If he or she refuses to resign, the second step of the procedure would begin. The legislature may pass another motion for investigation, give a mandate to the Chief Justice of the Court of Final Appeal to form and chair and independent investigation committee, which shall be responsible for carrying out the investigation and reporting its findings to the Lego. If the report of the committee shows that the evidence sufficient to substantiate such charges, it would step into the final action of the procedure. The Council may pass the third motion for formal impeachment by a two-thirds majority of all its members and report it to the Central Government. The final step is the Central Government decides whether the Chief Executive should be removed from the office or not.

### 4. The Judiciary

The judiciary of Hong Kong is composed of the Court of Final Appeal, the High Court (comprising the Court of Appeal and the Court of First Instance), several district courts, magistrates' courts and other special courts.

Before the regress to the motherland, Hong Kong was under the tradition of common law. Its legal and judicial system is very different to that of the Mainland. After July 1 1997, to fit for the reality of sovereign regression, the judicial system has been changed mainly in three respects.[45] The first change occurs on the power of the final justice, which has been transferred from the British Judicial Committee of Privy Council to the Court of Final Appeal of Hong Kong. It is said that among the public authorities only can the judiciary entirely keep its position of independence. But it is a misunderstanding to the word "final". The final appeal in the context of the Basic Law means that the decisions or the judgements made by the Final Appeal Court will not be allowed to appeal furthermore, and that there is no any other justice above this Court. But the judges of the Court cannot vitally decide what the legal basis for their final decisions and judgements finally is. As Article 158 of the Basic Law says, the power of interpretation of the Basic Law, the highest legal norm for justice, belongs to the Standing Committee of the NPC. The power of interpretation of the Hong Kong courts comes from the grant of the Standing Committee. If the courts of the Region, in adjudicating cases, need to interpret the clauses of the Law concerning affairs which are the responsibility of the Center, for example the foreign and defensive affairs, or concerning the relationship between the Center and the Region, and if such an interpretation will affect the judgments which are not appealable, seek an interpretation of the relevant clauses from the Standing Committee through the Court of Final Appeal of the Region. The courts of the Region must follow the interpretation of the Sanding Committee for their decisions. Thus, the justice of Hong Kong is not fully and absolutely final and independent from the Center.

The second change happens at the area of judges' construction. Under the British supremacy, most judges on chair were British or those foreigners from the ex-colonies of Great Britain. Now, according to the Basic Law, the Chief Justice of the Final Appeal Court and the Chief Judge of the High Court must be Chinese citizens who are permanent residents of the Region with no right of abode in any foreign country. The rest judges could be foreigners recruited from other common law jurisdictions, and could be Chinese citizens with or without right of abode in foreign countries, except those Chinese who are interior ones of the Mainland because of their legal educational backgrounds on the socialist laws or the continental laws. Apart from the standing judges, the Final Appeal Court can temporarily invite judges from other common law countries to sit on the Court and to hear the cases. There are two reasons why foreign residents and the Chinese with right of abode, even those non-residents, except for the Chief Justices of the Final Appeal Court and the High Court, could sit on bench. One is that the Chinese judges are not very familiar with common law precedents because of their short training and less experiences on common law. Another reason is that the judges are in essence the servants of law, not of politics. What the justice pursuits is equality under the law, so it needs not to put strict restraints on the qualifications. The only restraint to those foreign judges is to pursuit to the rule of law which is everywhere the same requirement to a qualified judge. The judges will take office after they swear to be loyal to the Basic Law.[46]

The third change focuses on application of the laws of Hong Kong. Before July

1 1997, all the British statutes and case law, having higher effect than Hong Kong laws, were certainly applicable at the courts of Hong Kong. It is now the Chinese laws applying to the cases, such as the Basic Law and the Chinese laws listed in Annex III. What the courts should obey are those national laws clearly inscribed in Annex III. However, Article 18 of the Basic Law provides that when the Standing Committee of the NPC decides to declare a state of war or, by reason of turmoil within the Region which endangers national unity or security and is beyond the control of the government of the Region, it may at the same time decide the Region is in a state of emergency, while the Central Government may issue an order applying the relevant national laws beyond the list of Annex III to the Region. Of course, this is a necessary exception to the normal situation which will rarely happen. Therefore, this provision has a nature of safeguard to sustain the highest authority of the Central Government.

Finally, apart from the formal legal resources, the precedents of other common law jurisdictions may be used as references to the sentencing, but without the sanction force to the courts. If a court makes its reasoning out of a precedent of the foreign court, the relevant sentence would be overthrown by the higher court. But if this is done by a higher court, how can it be corrected? This is the problem having not been answered.[47] In the light of common law tradition, every common law precedent can be cited by common law courts of other countries. If it is itself a precedent, the problem will be replayed by the NPC. And even the NPC couldn't restrain Hong Kong judges change the principles containing in the foreign precedents into the principles of Hong Kong case law.

## IV. THE SUCCESSES AND THE PROBLEMS OF HONG KONG MODEL

The Basic Law has been implemented in Hong Kong for more than two years. It appears that it is successful at the whole, however there must be some problems coming forth. The One Country, Two Systems Principle, the Basic Law, and the Region itself are all new political phenomena both for China. Here we will consider, under the Basic Law, the strengthened position, the democratic development, the present problems of Hong Kong, and the prospects of the Basic Law itself.

## 1. The Strengthened Position of Hong Kong in the Financial Storm under the Basic Law

The return of Hong Kong to the control of China is itself a successful example of the sovereign transition. It ends in part the humiliated history of China since the Opium War in 1840. To the Chinese people, including those live in Hong Kong, the return of Hong Kong means a symbol of a new begin of reunification of the Chinese nation. It must strengthen the force of China as well as raise the flexibility of Hong Kong on capacity to meet the sudden events around the world. Furthermore, it must lead China to go on in the way of rule of law. The fulfillment of return was not a conquest by using force, but a negotiation under some principles. The result of it is the Basic Law of Hong Kong, which is a bond not only to the Region, but also to the Central Government who issued it, has become a two-edged sword. Under the colonist-like conditions, Hong Kong could not have such a position of law. Generally speaking, Hong Kong is stable, prosperous and vigorous now after the return.

The success of Hong Kong depends on the endeavor of its people, whilst also on the environments it exists. After return to China, Hong Kong gains a nearer backer for its development. In the financial storm throughout East Asia, Hong Kong stays firm in it relying on its well-built banking system and the fiscal support from the Central Government. Just at the beginning of the Region government, the financial crisis has flooded in Hong Kong; the Secretary of Finance Department of Hong Kong went to Beijing to seek support from the Center. The Center confirmed the countermeasures the Hong Kong government resorted to. In fact, Hong Kong is one of the countries where the crisis has had the mild influences to the economy and the society. It is in some respects because of the strong back of the Central finance. It's the common duty of the Center to ensure the stability, politically as well as economically. And the context of the Basic Law presumes such a relationship between the Center and the Region, which would become a political convention.

## 2. Democratic Development of Hong Kong

Before July 1 1997, Hong Kong was a piece of Chinese territory under the reign of British Crown. The British managed Hong Kong by means of colonialist methods. By a well-known reason, the colonialist governing needn't any form of democracy. Hong Kong was a free community, but never a democratic one.

If the colonialist rule could have been sustained further, the democracy in Hong Kong would be nonsense and inconvenient to the British. Therefore, in more than one hundred years, there was no any kind of democratic election happened in Hong Kong. Only when was the British affirmed that their rule in Hong Kong would be soon ended, they then reluctantly introduced the elections into Hong Kong in 1985. This is the beginning of the democratic development of Hong Kong. There were four general elections formed in Hong Kong from 1985 to 1997. In the election of 1991, the direct election system was firstly brought into Hong Kong, which made a progression of democracy. About two thirds of the seats in the Legislative Council were allotted in this direct selection catalogue.[48]

After the sovereign return of Hong Kong to China, the first parliamentary election was held in the Region on May 24 1998. Compared with the voting rate of 35.8% in the 1995's election, which was pursuant to the electoral model that had been brought up, by the last governor of Great Britain, Sir Chris Patten, in a Political Reforms Plan which turned the indirect part of the seats by functional constituencies into the actually direct elected part of the legislature, the election of 1998 had a higher rate of direct votes up to 53.29%.[49] This was achieved even at the weather of a big rainstorm. The fact has illustrated that the people of Hong Kong is much ardent to the democratic development of their own society, whereas they didn't care very much to the democracy set up by a colonialist government.[50] The main targets of the foundation of the Region are to actualize and corporealize the basic policies of the Center for "One Country, Two Systems", "Hong Kong governed by the residents themselves", and "high degree of autonomy". That the Hong Kong people themselves shall govern Hong Kong doesn't mean an oligarchic rule, or an elitist rule. What the Hong Kong people expect is a rule by the majority. It is why the voting rate was so high than the most predictions of the public opinion polls held before the election day.[51] Because of the provisions of the Basic Law, that the public occupations are elected will become the routines of the political life.

Of course, there were still other elements affecting the process of election and its voting rate, such as the political attitudes of the voters, the needs to make the balances between the powers, and the excellent organizing works by the government, etc.

## 3. Human Rights Protection in Hong Kong

As mentioned above, before the establishment of the Region, Sir Chris Patten, the last governor of Great Britain in Hong Kong, took several steps to make some barriers or troubles for the coming Region. They included to pass a bill of human rights, to give fifty thousand Hong Kong families the right of abode in the Kingdom, to raise a political reform plan, and so on.

To protect human rights of the people is the persistent standing on the problem of human rights when drafting the Basic Law. After an all-round consideration, the draft of the Basic Law had been contained a lot of articles on the rights for the residents of Hong Kong. But, just before the draft would be passed at the National People's Congress, the British submitted to the Chinese a draft of Hong Kong declaration of rights on March 1990, to turn the International Covenant on Civil and Political Rights into a Hong Kong law. And on June 5 1991, the draft passed the Lego of Hong Kong as the Hong Kong Bill of Rights.[52]

The Chinese Government protested such a measure having been adopted by the British, not for the Bill of Rights itself, but for the attitude and manner of the action. The reasons of objection are enough to deny the effective force of the Bill in the future Region. First, the Bill would affect the implementation of the Basic Law, for there contained articles similar with those in the Basic Law, which might make some misunderstanding between two laws. Secondly, the passing of the Bill procedurally breached the Sino-British understanding on the arrangements for the smooth transit of Hong Kong, because according to the understanding it required the negotiations between two sides for any effective result of arrangement for Hong Kong. However, if there is no the third reason, the two above won't affect the implement of the Basic Law. The crucial point of passing the Bill was that it contained the clauses with conflict effect to the Basic Law, which made the Bill probably in a legal position higher than the Law. The Article 3 (2) of the Ordinance for implementation of the Bill reads: "All pre-existing legislation that does not admit of a construction consistent with this Ordinance is, to the extent of the inconsistency, repealed". Moreover, Article 4 even provides that all legislation enacted on or after the commencement date shall, to the extent that it admits of such a construction, be construed so as to be consistent with the International Covenant on Civil and

Political Rights as applied to Hong Kong. These two articles is called as the "overriding clauses" that their effects would be higher than other laws in Hong Kong.[53] This might make there have been two highest laws in Hong Kong and the Basic Law might have been bypassed by the courts of the Region in cases concerning with the rights of the residents. This kind of clauses in the Bill inevitably was denied by the Chinese Government. Both Article 2 of the Annex II of the Joint Declaration between Chinese and British governments as well as Article 8 of the Basic Law provide that the laws previously in force in Hong Kong shall be maintained, except for any that contravene the Basic Law and subject to any amendment by the legislature of the Region. Following to these legal norms the Standing Committee of the NPC passed a resolution handling with the legal force of the laws of Hong Kong before July 1 1997. The resolution declared invalid of three clauses of the Bill when the big day of return comes.[54]

In fact, the question of the Hong Kong Bill of Rights is not simply the legal effect of it. Behind the event we can find out the political struggle on the matter of Hong Kong. The human rights protection has been long as a fundamental value of the Hong Kong society. And the Central Government through the Basic Law has solemnly promised that the future Region government will protect the given rights of the residents of Hong Kong. The last governor wanted to use the Bill as a political tool or weapon to fight against the Chinese Government or to make trouble on the powers transferring. The countercharge by the Chinese Government is not surprised. It should point out that the battles between two governments actually have negative impacts to Hong Kong. The Center would be always alert to any event occurred there, no matter is it an important one or a tiny one. This is not certainly good to the degree of autonomy.[55]

### 4. The Matter of Judicial Review

Traditionally, as in the English legal system being, the Hong Kong courts under the governing of British had no power to check the statutes issued by the legislature for their effectiveness. According to the principle of English parliamentary supremacy, as A.V. Dicey stated that no person or body is recognized by the law of England as having a right to override or set aside the legislation of Parliament of England,[56] the Hong Kong courts hadn't the explicit power of judicial review on laws of the legislature. However, is it still the discipline for the Hong Kong courts to obey unconditionally the laws of the Legislative

Council, when now it has a so-called written constitution for the Region? Or if does the Lego have a position as the English Parliament over the judiciary?

Any kind of judicial review to the laws in the world should be set up upon a written constitution, the supreme norm of the land. The legal position of the Legislative Council is not, under the Basic Law, supreme.[57] When the courts of Hong Kong have the duties to watch what the Basic Law means at a special instance, they obtain logically the right to review the statutes of the Lego to check their words and meanings. And when the courts find out that there are conflicts between the laws they are surveying and the Basic Law, the Law will have the authority over the laws. Therefore, the Legislative Council cannot enjoy the status as the English Parliament can. And under the Basic Law, Hong Kong courts have gained the power to review the statutes of the legislature.

But that doesn't mean that a written constitution must be protected by means of judicial review in Hong Kong. The main reason would be the authority of the National People's Congress, which is over the authorities of, not only the laws and the courts of Hong Kong, but also the Basic Law. The authority of the Congress is the highest one all over Chinese territory. This status of the Congress gives it the power to supervise the implementations of all laws and legal documents for their constitutionality. And the other organs in China have no right to challenge the authority of the Congress. The Congress thus has the highest authority to protect the Basic Law not to be violated.

The supremacy of the Congress's authority and the review power of the Hong Kong courts have been found to be involved into an awkward contradiction. On January 29 of this year, the Court of Final Appeal of Hong Kong delivered a judgment on the case Ng Ka Ling and <u>Ng Tan Tan v. the Director of Immigration</u>,[58] in which the Court asserted the appellants had the rights of abode to living in Hong Kong as permanent residents. Moreover, the Court expressed such an opinion,

> What has been controversial is the jurisdiction of the courts of the Region to examine whether any legislative acts of the National People's Congress or its Standing Committee (which we shall refer to simply as "acts") are consistent with the Basic Law and to declare them to be invalid if found to be inconsistent. In our view, the courts of the Region do have this jurisdic-

tion and indeed the duty to declare invalidity if inconsistency is found. It is right that we should take this opportunity of stating so unequivocally.

According to the intention of the justices, the Basic Law, as a "written constitution" for Hong Kong, is the highest norm in Hong Kong to which they must pursuant. And it is the only command they must obey. Because the Basic Law is a basic statute promulgated by the National People's Congress, its legal effective degree is higher than any other legislative acts except for those made by the NPC which have higher effect than the Basic Law. It is the duty and province of the Court to say what the Law is. If the Court finds laws, either passed by the legislature of Hong Kong or by the Standing Committee of the NPC, in opposition to the Basic Law, the Court ought to obey the Basic Law and should clarify that the laws repugnant to the Basic Law, no matter from which level of the law comes. Therefore, the Court has a right to declare invalid of such acts and laws when it finds they are inconsistent with the Basic Law. The Court wanted to establish the jurisdiction of review through this case.

In response to the challenge of the Court to the authority of the NPC, some Mainland scholars have denounced the reasoning of the Court, on the behalf of the Central Government. In their opinion, the NPC is the highest organ to say what the Basic Law means, as Article 158 of the Basic Law provides. As the highest organ of state power, the acts of the NPC and its Standing Committee shall be the highest commands of the sovereign, to which any person or body must obey. The sentence of the Court to the case is thus unacceptable. The Court must take an explicit action to correct its mistake. The Court then on February 26 gave out a complementary judgment:

> The Court's judgment on 29 January 1999 did not question the authority of the Standing Committee to make an interpretation under Article 158 which would have to be followed by the courts of the Region. The Court accepts that it cannot question that authority. Nor did the Court's judgment question, and the Court accepts that it cannot question, the authority of the National People's Congress or the Standing Committee to do any act which is in accordance with the provisions of the Basic Law and the procedure therein.

Although in this judgment the Court did not say whether it still has the right to challenge the overwhelming force of the acts of the NPC and its Standing Committee, the Central Government kept silence to this judgment, to shows that the Center actually has not had the willing to interfere deep into the autonomous affairs of Hong Kong. But the sentence of the Court on January 29 has brought a dreadful result that there would be over one million mainlanders who have gained the legal status to immigrate into Hong Kong. This would be a great burden for Hong Kong, which is above the receiving ability of it. In this situation, the Hong Kong government sought for an interpretation to the articles 22 (4) and 24 (2c) of the Basic Law, which are concerned of the conditions of them immigrating into the Region and the definitions of the Hong Kong residents, from the Standing Committee of the NPC, to endeavor for limiting the amount of immigration. The Standing Committee emitted an interpretation, which is the first time of the kind, for response. The interpretation clarifies the meaning and the scope of the Hong Kong permanent residents and limits the status of immigration to the Region. Furthermore, the interpretation overthrows the judgment of the Court in case of <u>Ng Ka Ling and Ng Tan Tan v. the Director of Immigration</u>, and reaffirms the authority of the NPC and the Standing Committee over the explanation power of the Hong Kong courts.[59]

Because the Standing Committee has enough measure to defend its authority, the true purpose of the interpretation of the Standing Committee is to support the executive authorities of Hong Kong for their capacity to handle with the affairs within their powers. The executive domination principle should not be replaced by the authority of the courts. It is the core of the Basic Law in matters of administration. Tell the truth, the question is beyond the scope of law, but in the political.

If we take a stand on the view of pure jurisprudence, the result would be more different. Before the adoption of the constitutional amendments on March 1999, President Jiang Zhemin said, "In order to erect more higher the authority of the Constitution in the whole society, the most important thing is to restrict and to circumscribe the powers of the state organs in accordance with law. We ought to insure that the public powers are wielded pursuant strictly to the Constitution. ...... The breach of the Constitution is the most serious breach of law. All acts in violation of the Constitution and the law must be investigated."[60] The NPC and its Standing Committee naturally belong to the state organs which have the duty to obey the Constitution and the laws of the land, passed by themselves, because the Article 5 of the Constitution provides that no organization or individual may enjoy the privilege of being above the Constitution and the law. Therefore, the NPC and the Standing Committee must abide by the Constitutions and the laws including the Basic Law until they are revised by the formal amendments.[61] As a result of the procedural regulation of the Article 159 of the Basic Law for its revision, if there is an act in the future passed with the essential revision to the Basic Law and without complying with the Article 159, the act would be declared in breach with the Basic Law and unconstitutional.[62] And as an independent judiciary of the local with the right of final appeal, though the Final Appeal Court has no authority to check the implementation of laws of the land in the areas of the Mainland, it has lawful right to justify the legality of implementation of any laws and acts of the land, except the Constitution, within the boundary of Hong Kong. However, this authority should be under the constraint set by the Article 19 (2) of the Basic Law, which reads that the courts of the Region shall have no jurisdiction over acts of state.

On the other hand, the authority of the NPC and its Standing Committee should not be higher over or even in the parallel position to the authority of the Constitution. The authority of the NPC is not the authority of the written Constitution. And in a state with the creed of rule of law, every authority comes from the constitution of the land, therefore being controlled by the constitution.[63] Thus the NPC and its Standing Committee cannot take any conduct ultra vires which is denied by the spirit of the Constitution and cannot set itself out of the laws it passed.

### 5. The Prospect of the Development of the Basic Law

We have discussed the question of interpretation of the Basic Law. Now we should consider the future development of it. That indicates the possibility of revision of the Basic Law.

The Article 159 of the Basic Law provides that the power of amendment of it shall be vested in the NPC. This regulation makes in reality an informal amendment to the Chinese Constitution, as I have mentioned at the beginning of this paper, for by the Constitution the other basic statutes could be partially revised by the Standing Committee, whereas the Article 159 of the Basic Law actually restrains or prohibits the power of amendment of the Standing Committee to the Basic Law. There bring about two results. Man may ask at first that can the Constitution be revised by an ordinary law of the land, not by the formal procedure provided at the Article 64 of the Constitution. This question could be construed from the supremacy of the NPC. The NPC may make or unmake any law of the Land, including in its authority the power of constitutional amendment, and any organs below it must abide by its command. Because of the Basic Law of Hong Kong being a statute made by the NPC, if the Law implies that the Standing Committee has no right to revise it, the Standing Committee must obey and postpone wielding its power to revise the Basic Law. Automatically reasoned from such a conclusion, the second reasoning is that the Basic Law is in a place a little bit higher than the other basic statutes drafted also by the NPC, such as civil and criminal codes or procedural laws, though in Chinese legal scroll they are in the same level of legal force. Therefore, it could be right that the Basic Law is at least in a special position within the Chinese legal system. Through this status the rights and freedoms of the Hong Kong residents can be much surely guaranteed by the Basic Law.

As a fundamental law for Hong Kong, the stability of the Basic Law is important for the prosperity of Hong Kong. It shouldn't be frequently revised. Only in the necessary occasions can it be amended under the strict procedure and through a wide consensus. However, some of the present clauses of it will lead it to the road of revision. Let us just have a consideration in the respects of political system. The Article 45 (2) exhibits the probability: the ultimate aim for the position of the Chief Executive is the selection of him or her "by universal suffrage upon nomination by a broadly representative nominating committee in accordance with democratic procedures". This indicates the would-be direct election method of the Chief Executive, as mentioned above, after 2007, according to Annex II of the Basic Law. Similarly, Article 68 (2) provides that the ultimate aim for seats of the Legislative Council is "the election of all the members of it by universal suffrage". The change will also happen or start after 2007. At that time, it presumes that the all seats of the Legislative Council will be possessed by direct elections, then a strong parliamentary majority party or parties' alliance must emerge at the legislature. This will cause the strikes to the principle of executive leading role, because no one could assure that the executive and the legislature will keep concurrence on every government policy. If the legislature constantly expresses its different opinions on the policies, how will the executive authorities do? What can the executive do? And will it make what affections to the whole society of Hong Kong? The Basic Law must reply these questions and make itself fit for the requirements under such a political situation.

Let us now give a try to consider some possibilities to answer the questions. The direct elections of the Chief Executive and the Legislative Council will spring two centers of the powers for Hong Kong, which is ugly for a democratic society. To keep the leading position of the executive, there are two ways. One way is to follow the model of English parliamentary government, turning the legislative majority into the executive lead. This needs to change the political system thoroughly, which will not be accepted by the Basic Law. Another way is to learn from the model of American separation of powers, setting apart the executive and legislative powers. This will wipe out the power of the Chief Executive to dismiss the legislature. There will be problems, too. To tell the truth that the principle of the executive lead should be pondered thoroughly, if the problems should be well resolved. In any case, the influence of the political parties should be put into the consideration. Anyway, the Basic Law must be revised to get the system to work effectively. Man cannot live but not express his life.[64]

## V. THE SIGNIFICANCES OF THE HONG KONG MODEL

The Hong Kong model is simply to say that, according to the principle of one country, two systems, the given government of a country establishes, pursuant to a constitutional law of the land, a special administrative region within a territory of the country, within which the social, economic, legal and political systems are allowed different to those of the other parts of the land. Hong Kong is the first of such a region within China, and might be the first instance in the world. The establishment of the Region has, therefore, a far-reaching historical significance both to China and in the world.

### 1. It's a model for resolving the questions of Macao and Taiwan

Although there are different historical backgrounds, the model is, generally speaking, yet applicable to Macao and Taiwan. In the light of Hong Kong model, the Chinese Government and the Portugal Government, on April 13 1987, signed a Joint Declaration to arrange the peaceful transition of Macao back to the control of China. On March 31, the Basic Law of the Macao Special Administrative Region passed the first session of the Eighth National People's Congress. The return will come on December 20 1999. It is the second success of the principle of One Country, Two Systems in solving the question of domain within China.

The remaining problem of the reunification of China is the question of Taiwan. In despite of being the focus concern of Chinese Government since 1950's, it seems that this question will be solved at the last. In fact, the conception of One Country, Two Systems principle came out of the try to persuade the authority of Taiwan to begin negotiations about the unification with the Mainland in early 1980's.[65] The difficulty is that it is the problem between two parts of Chinese who all claim legitimate for the representative qualification of China, though now and then there are hoots about the independence of Taiwan. We are against with steadiness the claim for Taiwan's independence and the possibility of its separation from the dominion of China, while we give the Taiwan's leaders a peaceful choice of reunification under the principle of One Country, Two Systems. Out of this choice there would be only the way of armed liberalization. By the peaceful plan, Taiwan might gain more than what Hong Kong has been given from the Central Government, and vise versa, because its situation is after all very particular compared with the matters of Hong Kong and Macao. For example, the negotiation would be happened between the Mainland and Taiwan in a more equal manner. And the army of Taiwan will be remained mostly untouched as Mr. Deng said.[66]

### 2. The Development of Marxism through the Model

Over one hundred years ago, Carl Marx concluded from the lessons of the failure of the Paris Commune, the first proletarian regime, that the proletarian dictatorship must smash the old state machinery to for the consolidation of the new people's power.[67] Later, Lenin also said that the proletarian couldn't share the state powers with other social classes.[68] While Mao Zhedong expanded greatly the class ally of the proletarian regime, he and his comrades still adhered to the people's nature of the state. In every corner of the country, the government must be red.[69]

It is Mr. Deng Xiaoping, who is entitled as the chief designer of the modern China, that could recognize the present needs and the position of the country from a wider, practicing and changing scope. And based on such an observation, he taught that when the country in a whole is a socialist one, it could promise a special part in it to try a different way of life, which doesn't mean that the country gives up the proletarian principles or changes its nature to a capitalist one. Anyhow, to give citizens of every corner of the land a respected life, the standards of which will be testified by the given people themselves, is the final aim of the rule by the communist party. Therefore, if the Hong Kong people want to live by ways of their being used to, then why should they be disturbed by the need for proving correctness of some pure theory? In opposition to that, the theory must be proved correct by its being useful to the common good of the people and non dangers to the other part of the people of the country. What the Chinese Government or the communist party must sustain are the socialist nature of the country as a whole and the unification of the Chinese nation. Except these two principles, other things are not fundamental to the state nature. Starting from such a philosophical presupposition, the political principle of One Country, Two Systems was framed.

The One Country, Two Systems principle has developed practically and theoretically the state doctrine of Marxism, as a response. It makes the state doctrine established on the reality of the present need, just as Marxism itself appeared and developed for the need of the workers in the nineteenth century. This kind of Marxism with the Chinese character is one of the core standards by the Chinese Government to deal the relationships peacefully with other relevant countries.

### 3. The Development of the Constitutional Theory of China by the Influence of the Model

Because of the theoretical solution of the state doctrine, the Chinese constitutional theory acquires a vast space to be developed. And the implementation of the Basic Law and the establishment of the Hong Kong Special Administration

Region give the research of constitutional theory a great impulse.

The reality of Hong Kong being, within a socialist country, a capitalist community, has made the state structure of China complicated. Now, if man regards China as a unitary country, he must be cautious, for there exist in a traditional consolidated country two legal systems, two political systems, two monetary systems, and two residential qualification systems in one citizenship, etc. If we count Macao and even Taiwan in, China will be found in various respects having multi-choice appearance, much like a federation. But it is also wrong to say China is a federal country, for there is only one constitution, all powers of its units, including Hong Kong, coming from the vest of the central government. The question then is how to justify that China is still a unitary country.

We should answer this question by finding out what is or are the critical element or elements for deciding the nature of the form of state structure. The Article 12 of the Hong Kong Basic Law provides that the Region shall be a local administrative region of China, which shall enjoy a high degree of autonomy and come directly under the Central Government. From this provision, we could presume that there are two elements, the nature and source of the powers or authorities of a lower government as well as the relationship between the central government and the lower governments, which will decide the form of state structure belonging to a federation or to a unitary body. The powers of Hong Kong government come from the granting of the Central Government through the Basic Law, in another word, Hong Kong hasn't its own powers, which means that the powers of the Hong Kong people cannot be enjoyed ahead of the existence of the central powers. Besides, Hong Kong people cannot formulate by themselves a constitution and a government.[70] In contrast, in a federal country, the powers and authorities of the constituent parts of it are their innate and original ones, and the federal government can neither grant nor deprive the powers to or of the people of a constituent part. In a part of a federation, the people therein have natural right to write down a constitution themselves for forming their own government. On the topic of relationship between the central and lower governments, we can see that Hong Kong government is a subordinate unit of the Central Government. It was not and is not an independent part of China. The Chief Executive must be appointed by the Center before he or she could take office. The laws passed at the Legislative

Council must be reported to the Standing Committee for record. And the appointments of the chief justices of the Final Appeal Court and the High Court must be reported also to the Standing Committee for record. But in a federal country, the constituent parts have no such responsibilities to the central government. All these show that China is still a unitary country, that is, China is "one country".

On the other hand, however, under the Basic Law, the Hong Kong people enjoy more rights than the people in a part of a federal country. For example, the final jurisdiction for the disputes belongs to Hong Kong, whereas any case could be appealed to the highest tribunal of the land in a federal country. This is of course because of China promoting the "two systems" in its special parts.

Apart from the development discussed above, there are abundant progresses in the constitutional field. We have now two quite different systems and will have multiple systems exist parallel in one country. In the history of modern China, this situation existed indeed between the central government and the communist controlled parts. But that the two governments survived side by side in the revolutionary period was a political reality, which would change frequently along with altering of the support of the people and the balance of the strength. Whereas the two systems in contemporary situation is a legal or constitutional result, which is founded on the conjunct will of the people as a whole.

The Basic Law has enlarged the field of vision of Chinese scholars. They study now more detailed things as the constitutional interpretation, the legislative power, the nature and resources of the law, the functions of laws, judicial systems, and so on. As mentioned above, the interpretation of the Standing of the NPC to the clauses of the Basic Law for Hong Kong was the first instance of the formal legislative interpretation in the legal history of China after 1949. This must lead to perfect the legislative procedures for wielding the interpreting power by the Standing Committee of the NPC.

The studies to laws of the special administrative regions have gradually shaped a new department of legal science.

### 4. The Influence of the Model to the International Law

At the beginning of this paper, we have noticed that the principle of "One

Country, Two Systems" could be used as a rule to resolve the international disputes through peaceful and negotiation way, especially to those historical remainders. The Principle is in fact a vigorous standard with flexibility. The relevant countries can apply it to many situations on their concrete needs accordingly.

We have noticed that the "One Country, Two Systems" policy has been borrowed by some foreign governments as a choice to handle with the historical questions with other countries. Japanese Premier, Mr. Keizo Obuchi, cited in 1998 the example of Hong Kong as a referring model to negotiate about the sovereign problem of Northern Four Islands with Russia. The principles that China were followed to establish the Hong Kong Special Administrative Region could be referred to as the basis of the negotiation with Russia. As well as this model has been mentioned by Korean President for resolving the question of two Koreas.

But we should get knowledge about what are the similarities and the differences between the Sino-British relations and the Japanese-Russian relations, and so on. That the fact of occupation onto the territory by a foreign power is similar element, which leads to the same demand of territories and attached authority return. Another similarity is that the way to get the question settled will be through a peaceful negotiation. On such recognition, the principle would be fixed on. If the talk between two countries has reached such a degree that the principle for the further talk has been in agreement, the question would have been answered in half. The key phase is the consensus on the principle.[71] After that political settlement, then the legal stage will be followed. The Principle of "One Country, Two Systems" is the best choice for a country to solve the domain problems when it should adhere to the notion of national sovereignty.

[1]Deng Xiaoping, "*One Country, Two Systems*", in *Selected Works of Deng Xiaoping*, Vol. III, 1st ed., 1993 People's Press, p. 58. This article was a recorded summary on the talk by Mr. Deng made to a visiting delegation of Hong Kong manufactory and commercial circle on June 22, 23, 1984. In this talk, it was Deng who raised formally first the concept of One Country, Two Systems. By the way, this policy obviously fits for solving the problem concerning Macao.

[2]The focused meaning of the Policy will be found in *the Explanations on the Basic Law of the Hong Kong Special Administrative Region of the People's Republic of China (draft)*, the officail document reported by Mr. Ji Pengfi, the Vice-Chairman of the

National People's Congress, to the 7$^{th}$ National People's Congress (NPC) at its 3$^{rd}$ Session.

[3] Xiao Weiyun, *Courses on the Hong Kong Basic Law*, 1$^{st}$ ed., 1996, China Broadcasting and Television Press, pp. 2~5.

[4] See *Textbook on Hong Kong*, Ed. by the Hong Kong's Social and Cultural Department at the Office for the Affairs of Hong Kong and Macao, 1$^{st}$ ed., 1997, Central Party School Press, p. 116.

[5] After the regress, the democracy of Hong Kong has developed. This can be explained as the change of political system. See *One Country, Two Systems and the Basic Legal Systems of Hong Kong*, ed. by Xiao Weiyun, 1$^{st}$ ed., 1990 Peking University Press, Chapter 6.

[6] By the Article 18 (4), after the declarations of the state of emergency by the Standing Committee of the NPC, the Central Government may issue an order to apply the national laws in Hong Kong. This clause indicates the events as turmoil affecting national unity or security and being beyond the control of the Region government. Though the clause doesn't sight clearly if the "turmoil" includes the event of attempt to overthrow the government under the Basic Law, it is by the context of the Basic Law and the Joint Declaration that that event shall be included.

[7] In the interim, China and British authority in Hong Kong had fought on matters of the new international airport of Hong Kong, the right of abode, Hong Kong Bill of Rights, the electoral reform, and so on. See Song Xiaozhuang, *Hong Kong Basic Law and the Conflicts at the Later Interim*, 1$^{st}$ ed., 1998 Hong Kong Culture and Education Press, Co.

[8] "China Will Abide by Its Words", in *Selected Works of Deng Xiaoping*, Vol. III, pp. 102~103.

[9] Deng Xiaoping, "The Address to the commissars of the Draft Committee for the Basic Law of Hong Kong Special Administrative Region", in *Selected Works of Deng Xiaoping*, Vol. III, p. 215.

[10] It is as Deng put it, If there are some Hong Kong people scold the Communist Party of China and China after 1997, it will be allowed. However, if the scold alters into action and to change Hong Kong into a basis against the Mainland under the name of democracy, it will beyond the degree of our tolerations and will interfere in to prevent it. See "*The Address to the commissars of the Draft Committee for the Basic Law of Hong Kong Special Administrative Region*", in *Selected Works of Deng Xiaoping*, Vol. III, p. 221.

[11] Ernst Cassirer, *An Essay on Man: An Introduction to a Philosophy of Human Culture*; -Chinese version by Gan Yang, 1985 Shanghai Translation Press, p. 282.

[12] Cited from Li Yuelan, "Three Generations of the Party Leaders Were Care for the Regress of Hong Kong", in *Documents of the Party*, 3$^{rd}$ Vol., 1997.

[13] *Ibid*.

[14] *Textbook on Hong Kong*, pp. 23~24.

[15] *Ibid*. p. 25.

[16] *Ibid*. p. 24.

[17] *Ibid*. p. 25.

[18] See "State and Revolution", in *Selected Works of Lenin*, Vol. III.

[19] *One Country, Two Systems and the Basic Legal Systems of Hong Kong*, ed. by Xiao Weiyun, p. 2.

[20] See *People's Daily*, October 1, 1981.

[21] "Our Prior Standpoints on the Question of Hong Kong", in *Selected Works of Deng*

*Xiaoping*, Vol. III.

[22] See *The Important Documents on the matter of the Basic Law of the Hong Kong Special Administrative Region of the People's Republic of China*, 1990 People's Press, p. 16. Mr. Deng explained further that the way of unification of Taiwan to the Mainland would be quite different to the Hong Kong model, see "*Assumption on the peaceful unification between Mainland China and Taiwan*", in *Selected Works of Deng Xiaoping*, Vol. III, pp. 30~31.

[23] The detailed drafting process was described in *Explanations to the Basic Law of the Hong Kong Special Administrative Region of the People's Republic of China and Other Related Documents*, which was delivered by Mr. Ji Pengfei, the head of the Drafting Committee for the Law on the third session of the seventh NPC.

[24] See Xiao Weiyun, *Courses on the Hong Kong Basic Law*, pp. 73~74.

[25] Although the experts in the Mainland do not accept the idea of little constitution, it is the common viewpoint of the Hong Kong society. As a senior lawyer of Hong Kong said that because of its uniqueness in content, specialty in nature, the Basic Law is not merely a national law passed by the NPC, but also the little constitution for Hong Kong, composing the basis of all Hong Kong laws. See from the Internet of Hong Kong Information Center, *The Basic Law Linking to the Hong Kong Laws*. See also "*Is it correct to say that the Basic Law is the little constitution of the Hong Kong Region?*" in *People's Daily*, June 16, 1997.

[26] It is a strange political phenomenon that the interests of a local were represented not by the sovereign but by a foreign manager. This should be deemed of course the logical outcome of the One Country, Two Systems Policy. However, it showed the true position of Britain at the time-the pseudo-sovereign in the course of negotiation.

[27] Xiao Weiyun, *One Country, Two Systems and the Basic Legal Systems of Hong Kong*, p. 86.

[28] *Constitution of the People's Republic of China*, 1982 People's Press, p. 72.

[29] Article 58, Article 62 Item 3, and Article 67 Item 2 and 3 of the Constitution.

[30] See *Introduction to the Basic Law of the Hong Kong Special Administrative Region*, Wang Shuwen ed., 1997 Central Communist Party School Press; *One Country, Two Systems and the Basic Legal Systems of Hong Kong*, Xiao Weiyun ed.

[31] The restraint to the revising power of the Committee would be regarded as a revision to the arrangement of the Constitution. It is common in the Chinese legislative practices to revise a higher norm by a lower one if there is no repugnancy to the former. In this case, the Basic Law doesn't vest any right or power to the Committee, whereas limit the power of the Committee. And the Congress has the constitutional approach to limit the powers of its Standing Committee. Therefore, this kind of revision to the Constitution shall not be regarded as unconstitutional.

[32] See *Joint Declaration on the Question of Hong Kong by the Government of the People's Republic of China and the Government of the United Kingdom of Great Britain and North-Ireland*, 1984 Beijing Foreign Languages Press, pp. 3~5.

[33] The traditional Chinese law and customs indicate the customary law as mentioned in Article 8 of the Basic Law. Their origins came from the laws of Qing Dynasty and local customs applied in the part of Hong Kong, New Territory, before 1841. They are the only legal norms of Qing Dynasty remained in Chinese legal system. See *One Country, Two Systems and the Basic Legal Systems of Hong Kong*, Xiao Weiyun ed., Chapter III.

[34] Yang Jinghui, Yang Chunfeng, and Shi Hanrong, *Brief Explanations to the Basic Law for Hong Kong*, 1997 People's Press, p. 12.

[35] As Mr. Deng put it, the sovereignty of China to Hong Kong could not be put into the course of negotiation. This is the bottom line of the Chinese Government to handle with the questions of reunification. See *Selected Works of Deng Xiaoping*, Vol. III, p. 12.

[36] See Xiao Weiyun, *Courses on the Hong Kong Basic Law*, pp. 86~88.

[37] See *Joint Declaration on the Question of Hong Kong by the Government of the People's Republic of China and the Government of the United Kingdom of Great Britain and North-Ireland*, pp. 7~19.

[38] See *Explanations to the Basic Law of the Hong Kong Special Administrative Region of the People's Republic of China and Other Related Documents*, in part of "Relations between the Executive and the Legislature".

[39] See Xiao Weiyun, *Courses on the Hong Kong Basic Law*, p. 160.

[40] According to Article 44 of the Hong Kong Basic Law, the Chief Executive will not have or will give up the right of abode in any foreign country before he declares to take part in the election. Compared with this, the Basic Law for Macao adopted in 1993 provides in its Article 49 that the Chief Executive of Macao doesn't allow to have right of abode in foreign countries just in his term of office. That means the Macao Chief Executive could be free to have right of abode before taking office, regardless of his national status in elections. See Xiao Weiyun, *One Country, Two Systems and the Basic Law of the Macao Special Administrative Region*, 1993 Peking University Press, pp. 156~161.

[41] The reason would be duplex. Neither the Chief Executive nor the executive branch of the government relies on the confidence of the Lego. Therefore, there is no division between the parties as government or opposition parties. Furthermore, the electoral provisions in the Basic Law restrain the shaping of the party system. See Cai Ziqiang, *Perspectives on the Electoral System of Hong Kong*, 1998 Mingpao Print, Ltd., pp. 4~6.

[42] *One Country, Two Systems and the Basic Legal Systems of Hong Kong*, p. 259.

[43] *Ibid.* pp. 263~267.

[44] See Lu Feng, "*Mr. Chief Tong, Why Couldn't You Hear the Voice of Democracy?*" In *Apple Newspaper*, Hong Kong, May 26, 1998.

[45] See *One Country, Two Systems and the Basic Legal Systems of Hong Kong*, Chapter 9.

[46] See Xiao Weiyun, *Courses on the Hong Kong Basic Law*, pp. 227~230.

[47] In fact, the final Appeal Court has cited a lot of foreign precedents as reference for deciding the cases. For example, as in case of "right of abode". See *Ng Ka Ling, Ng Tan Tan v. The Director of Immigration*, FACV 14/1998; *Tsui Kuen Nang v. The Director of Immigration*, FACV 15/1998; *The Director of Immigration v. Cheung Lai Wah*, FACV 16/1998.

[48] See Cai Ziqiang, *Perspectives on the Electoral System of Hong Kong*, Chapter II.

[49] See *Wenhui Newspaper*, Hong Kong, May 27, 1998.

[50] Wei Shunji, *Not for the small souvenir*, in Takungpo Newspaper of Hong Kong, May 25, 1998.

[51] The voting rate expected before the election day (May 24, 1998) by the correspondences were from 33% to 67%, but the common sense was the rate would be lower than in 1995. See April 30, May 2, 5, 21, 1998 of Hong Kong Wenhui Newspaper, and May 23, 1998 of Takungpo Newspaper.

[52] "Hong Kong Bill of Rights", in *Hong Kong Lexicon*, Zheng Ding'ou, ed., 1996 Beijing Languages College Press.

[53] It was said that there were at least 5 disadvantages for the implement of the Basic Law if the overriding clauses hadn't been abandoned: first, changing the basis of Hong Kong legal norms; second, changing the review rule of the Hong Kong laws; thirdly, corroding the interpreting power of the Standing Committee of the NPC to the Basic Law; fourth, affecting the efficiency of the legislation and jurisdiction of Hong Kong; fifth, making confusions to the resources of the decisis for the judiciary. See Song Xiaozhuang, *Hong Kong Basic Law and the Conflicts at the Later Interim*, pp. 117~118.

[54] Article 2 (3) about the interpretation and the applying intentions of the Bill, Article 3 about the effect of the Bill to the former legislations, and Article 4 about the interpretation to the future legislations have been abandoned by the *Decision of the Standing Committee of the National People's Congress on the handling to the former legislations in accordance with the Article 160 of the Hong Kong Basic Law*. See *People's Daily*, Feb. 24, 1997.

[55] See *Reading Book on the Problems of Hong Kong*, State Council Office of the Affairs of Hong Kong and Macao, ed., 1997 Central Communist Party School Press, pp. 186~189.

[56] From M. Allen & B. Thompson, *Constitutional and Administrative Law*, 4th ed. 1996, Blackstone Press, p. 52.

[57] Feng Huajian, *The Link-up between the Basic Law and the Hong Kong Legislations*, from http://www.info.gov.hk, April 3, 1998.

[58] The case has been called as the "Case of right of abode". The case concerned to the right of abode of four children who had been residents of Mainland. They live now in Hong Kong with their parents. They claimed to the Court, pursuant to Article 24 of the Basic Law, that they were permanent residents of Hong Kong with the rights of abode. But the Director of Immigration had denied their status, by explanation, based on the Statute of Immigration of Hong Kong and the Mainland regulations issued by the public security. The four children brought the case finally to the Final Appeal Court. FACV 14/1998, Hong Kong.

[59] See *People's Daily*, June 27, 1999.

[60] *People's Daily*, February 1, 1999.

[61] *The opinion of the Hong Kong Bar Association to the jurisdiction of the Final Appeal Court*, February 25 1999, on the Internet of Hong Kong Government Information Service Center.

[62] In fact, the Final Appeal Court of Hong Kong had indicated in its decision on that case that the "act" and the "law" should be distinguished on their effectivities. To the law listed at Annex III of the Basic Law, the Court must stare, while they have no duty to follow the words in an act.

[63] See Edward S. Corwin, The *"Higher Law" Background of American Constitutional Law*, in Harvard Law Review, XLII (1928~1929).

[64] Ernst Cassirer, *An Essay on Man: An Introduction to a Philosophy of Human Culture*; -Chinese version by Gan Yang, p. 283.

[65] This is so called "Marshall Je's Nine Rules". See *People's Daily*, Dec. 31, 1980.

[66] See *One Country, Two Systems and the Basic Law of Macao Special Administrative Region*, Xiao Weiyun, ed., pp. 5~7.

[67] See Carl Marx, *"French Civil War"*, in *Selected Works of Marx and Engels*, Vol. III.

[68] See *"State and Revolution"*, in *Selected Works of Lenin*, Vol. III.

[69] See Mao Zhedong, *"On People's Democratic Dictatorship"*, in *Selected Works of Mao Zhedong*, Vol. IV.

[70] It might be wrong to say that the future powers of "Taiwan Region" come from the grant of the Central Government. The formula of Hong Kong and Macao wouldn't be directly used to the case of Taiwan.

[71] Nevertheless, the more difficult problem might be the nationalities of the residents of the areas.

# The Economic Crisis in Indonesia and the New Constitutional Government

### Sri Soemantri Martosoewignjo

## Introduction

The Indosesian Constitution had been drafted and promulgated by a committee named the Preparatory Committee for the Independence of Indonesia (Dokuritsu Zyunbi Iinkai). The Constitution, which was promulgated on August 18$^{th}$, 1945 by the abobe Committee was valid during two periods, first from August 18$^{th}$, 1945 until December 27$^{th}$, 1949, and second from July 5$^{th}$, 1959 until today.

From December 27$^{th}$, 1949 to July 4$^{th}$, 1959, consecutively the Constitution of the United Republic of Indonesia (R.I.S) and the Provisional Constitution of 1950 (UDD-Sementara) were in force.

When the Provisional Constitution of 1950 was enacted an entity named The Constituent Assembly (Konstituante), was formed through a general election in 1955. The Constituent Assembly was assigned to draft a new constitution to replace the Provisional Constitution of 1950. The Constituent Assembly as a legislative body had their sittings between 1956-1959, who succeeded in drafting a number of articles regulating the material content of the Constitution, but failed to formulate the basic thoughts or basic principles of the State. Therefore the Government proposed to the Constituent Assembly to pronounce the 1945 Constitution permanently, replacing the 1950 Provisional Constitution.

Although all the fractions (groups) of the Constituent Assembly consented to pronounce the 1945 Constitution permanently as required, the Islamic fractions insisted that after the words "the One and Only God……" be followed……" with the duties to perform Islamic "Syariah for their followers."

The proposal to add the above 10 words should be determined by voting. It turned out that the proposal had failed for not being upheld by at least 2/3 of the sitting members of the Constituent Assembly. As such, for the second time the Constituent Sssembly failed to declare a permanent constitution for the Republic of Indonesia.

## The Economic Crisis and the Fall of the President

In the middle of the year 1997, i.e. not long before the General Meeting (Sidang Umum/SU) of the People's Congress (MPR) in March 1998, Indonesia experienced economic and financial crisis, actually until today. The above crisis initially struck some other South-Eastern countries. The value of the Rupiah (Rp) against the US$ Plunged to Rp. 15.000 (US$ 1=Rp. 15.000). The impacts of the devaluation of the Rp were devastating, such as the acceleation of prices especially the 9 main food-stuff. It was also felt on industries and trade, since the prices of imported materials escallated in accordance to the increased dollar's rate.

Hence, the industries were unable to import raw materials and consequently many industries were closed down and lay-offs of labourers were unavoidable. These happenings made the Indonesian people uncomfortable. However, due to the tight control by those in power, the Indonesian people were helpless. The only group, which was courageous enough to oppose the Government, was the students from all universities in Indonesia. The General Meeting of the People's Congress was heavily guarded by the security apparatus. Finally the meeting (as usual) unanimously elected General (retired) Soeharto as president for the 7th five-year term consecutively. By electing Soeharto as President th political situation was even enhanced. The economical and financial atmosphere followed suit. Besides that, students activists were kidnapped.

The political atmosphere became intolerable when 75 students, united in the Communication Forum of the Student's Senate in Jakarta (Forum Komunikasi Senat Mahasiswa Jakarta) occupied the building of the House of Representatives and the People's Congress on May 18th 1998.

The large number of students occupying the building increased immensely the following days of May 19th and 20th. A large numbere of political opponents even joined the students. Finally supported by prominent political figures the students suppressed political fractions and the House Speaker to discharge Soeharto. At the beginning, on May 20th, there were efforts to summon about one million people around the National Monument. However, due to the heavy guardance of the security apparatus, the plan could not be realized.

In such a frightening situation, President Soeharto tried to propose a way out by preparing to form a Reformation Committee and a Reformation Cabinet.

Such was discussed late in the evening of May 20th by President Soeharto with ex Vice President Sudharmono.

Right after the meeting Sudharmono rushed out of the room and met with Vice President BJ. Habibie, carrying a file folder. In the folder there were statements that a number of ministers had submitted their resignation. This was actually the reason why President Soeharto stepped down and based on article 8 of the 1945 Constitution he should be succeeded by Vice President BJ. Habibie as President.

## President BJ. Habibie's leadership and the Reformation Era

Although there were different opinions concerning the resignation of President Soeharto, until now President BJ. Habibie is still the 3rd President of "Republik Indonesia." Article 8 of the 1945 Constitution stipulates as follows:

> "Should the President pass away, resign or the unable to perform his duties during his term of office, he shall be succeeded by the Vice President until the expiry of that term."

After taking the oath of office Vice President BJ. Habibie became the 3rd President, his first step was to appoint ministers of State. This was provided in Article 17 of the 1945 Constitution reading as follows:
(1) The President shall be assisted by ministers of State.
(2) The ministers shall be appointed and dismissed by the President.
(3) The ministers shall head government departments.

From the number of new appointed ministers, there were some from the United Development Party (Partai Persatuan Pembangunan=PPP) and the Indonesian Democratic Party (PDI). Besides that a few persons were from the previous cabinet members, as a.o. The Coordinating Ministers.

Queries arose, whether the BJ. Habibie's government can be pronounced as the New Constitutional Government.

After the new cabinet has been formed, the 3rd President of "Republik Indonesia" started to launch his policy in the field of politics, economics as wwell as law.

In the field of politics, the President and the Speaker of the People's Congress consented in having a Special Meeting of the People's Congress. The above meeting was held for 3 days starting Novermber 10th, 1998. The decisions

resulted from the meeting were pronounced as decrees of the People's Congress, i.e.:
1. The separation concerning the Speaker of the House of Representatives and that of the People's Congress.
2. To annul the Decree of the People's Congress concerning the referendum.
3. Concerning the principles of Reformation and Development.
4. To appoint clean, free from corruption and nepotism government's apparatus.
5. Revoke the Decree of the People's Congress concerning the assignment of a special task and special power awarded to the President/holder of the mandatory power.
6. Concerning the limitation of the President's and Vice President's tenure.
7. Concerning the amendment and addition of clauses to the Decree of the People's Congress concerning the plebiscite (general election).
8. Concerning the provision of the regional autonomy and a balanced finances between the Central Government and the regions in the scope of a unitarian state.
9. Concerning the economic policy in the frame of boosting economic democracy.
10. Concerning the Human Rights.

The above People's Congress Decisions were issued in the attempt to create a new constitutional government. One of the decisions which has been considered very important is the limitation of the reelection of the President and Vice President which is regulated by Article 7 of the 1945 Constitution, which reads:

> The President and the Vice President shall hold office for a term of five years and thereafter shall be eligible for re-election.

The above article fails to state imperatively how many times a President and a Vice President can be reelected.

In fact General Soeharto, who was the first elected President by the Provisional People's Congress in March 1968, become President for 7 terms consecutively. To avoid such occurrence the People's Congress during its special meeting on November 13th, 1998 pronounced:

> "The President and the Vice President shall hold office for a term of five

years and there after shall be eligible for the same period, only for one."

Besides limiting the reelection of the Presidential and Vice Presidential terms of office the Special Meeting also stated about the General Election. While previously the General Election is followed only by 3 parties, according to the new decision of the People's Congress the General Election shall include multi-political parties and shall be arranged democratically, honestly, and justly by voting directly, generally, freely and secretly.

Meanwhile according to the Decision of the People's Congress concerning the establishment of an autonomous region and a balanced finances between the Central Government and the Provinces (regions) regulations concerning the Central and Regional Government and concerning a balanced finances between the Central Government and the Region were also issued. In the above regultions the head of the Region will be given a wide ranging autonomy including a fair and proportional share of finances.

Besides the 2 regulations, the legislators also issued other regulations respectively in relation to political parties, the General Elections, the structure and position of the People's Congress, the House of Representatives and the Regional House of Representatives.

Based on the above regulations there emerged more than 100 political parties. After investigations and selections, only 48 political parties were applicable to be included in the General Election of June 7th, 1999. The above General Election was held to elect members of the House of Representatives and members of Regional House of Representatives I and II.

From the total 500 members of the House of Representatives, 462 members should be elected through the General Election, while the remaining 38 members should come from the Indonesian National Army and the Police who will be appointed by the President. In accordance to the regulation stipulated by Article 2 (1) of the 1945 Constitution.

> The People's Congress (Majelis Permusyawaratan Rakyat) shall consist of members of the House of Representatives (Dewan Perwakilan Rakyat) augmented by delegates from the region and groups, in accordance with regulations as stipulated by law.

As regulated by the Act concerning the structure and the status of the People'

s Congress, the House of Representatives and the Regional House of Representatives, the People's Congress total number cosists of:
1) 500 members of the House of Representatives
2) 135 members from the 27 provinces
3) 65 members from groups

5 Representatives from the Provinces will be elected by the Regional House of Representatives, while 65 representatives from groups will be proposed by respective group.

The election of the President and the Vice President and the problems of the amendment of the Constitution

a) The election of the Presient and the Vice President as regulated by Article 6 (2) of the 1945 Constitution reads:

> The President and the Vice President shall be elected by the People's Congress by majority vote.

Majority vote means at least half of the total plus one member of the People's Congress. Since there are 700 members of the People's Congress, a person could be elected as President and Vice President if he were supported at least by 351 members of the People's Congress.

From the General Election of June 7$^{th}$, 1999, it turns out that not one political party is occupying 251 seats of the House of Representatives.

It is understandable that there willl be no political party holding at least 351 seats. This will cause problems in electing President and Vice President at the General Meeting of the People's Congress in the month of November. What has been affirmed is the emergence of the 5 bigger political parties during the latest General Election, which are the Indonesia Democratic Party of Struggle (PDI Perjuangan), Partai Golongan Karya (Golkar), United Development Party (PPP), National Awakening Party (PKB), and Partai Amanat Nasional (PAN) or the National Mandate (Political) Party.

A Condidate would be elected to become President, if he were supported by at least 3 political parties of the victorious 5 parties from the General Election or when there was one political party, which could exert strength which could collect at least 351 members of the People's Congress. This also applies to the election of the Vice President. Therefore there would be a President and a Vice

President from two different political parties.

b) The problemes of Constitutional amendment

The assumption spreading in Indonesia is the possibility to amend the 1945 Constitution. Such an assumption has been put on discussions by many groups after the People's Congress Decision and the Act relating to the Referendum have been annulled.

As such to amend the 1945 Constitution would be solely the right of the People's Congress. This is in accordance with the regulation stipulated by Article 37, which reads:

(1) To amend the Constitution, at least two thirds of the total number of the members of the People's Congress shall be present.

(2) A resolution shall be adopted with the consent of at least two thirds of the total number of the members present.

The basical thought in amending the 1945 Constitution is the very dominant position and power attributed to the President in the above Constitution. This is also enhance by launching a reformation in every field of life of the Iindonesian people as well as the State. The proposed substance to be amended a.o. is as follows:

1. The limitation of the terms of office of the President and the Vice President to be reelected.

2. To strengthen the positions of the House of Representatives and the Supreme Court, to provide: a check and balances between the legislative, executive and judicial powers.

3. To strengthen the position and the power of the People's Congress.

Besides that by adhering to multi-party system, the election of a President and a Vice President will be difficult, unless there is a compromise between some political parties in the People's Congress. Therefore there is a wish that a President and a Vice President be elected straight by the Indonesian people.

# The 1992 Constitution and the Institutional Reform in Vietnam

Dao Tri Uc

## Part I

### The 1992 constitution
### —The Constitution of Vietnam during the renovation period.

The 1992 Constitution of Vietnam was passed on April 15th 1992 at the 11th session of the eight legislature of the National Assembly.

The 1992 Constitution contains the following.

(a) Provisions on the political powers in our society and the features of the State and society. The Constitution contains provisions on the political regime (Chapter I), economic regime (Chapter II), social policies in the fields of culture, education, science and technology (Chapter III), defense of the Socialist Republic of Vietnam (Chapter IV);

(b) Provisions on the legal status of persons in our society, the legal relationship regarding rights, obligations and responsibilities amongst the society, State and citizens (Chapter V);

(c) State structure, system of state bodies and their legal interrelationships in a system of unified power (Chapter VI, VII, VIII, IX, X);

(d) Provisions on the National Flag, National Emblem, National Song, Capital and the National Day (Chapter XI)

(e) Provisions on the effectiveness of the Constitution and its amendments (Chapter XII)

The format and substance of the above provisions of the Constitution indicate that these are constitutional provisions, *but not merely provisions of a State system*. A State may exist without a Constitution. *The State must be based upon a Constitution and operate within the Constitution. This is the hallmark of a State governed by the rule of law*.

The provisions of the Constitution were formulated on the basis of constitutional principles. The 1992 Constitution were based on major viewpoints and principles, including the following principles and viewpoints:

1. National sovereignty, territorial unity and integrity;
2. Solidarity amongst the entire people;
3. All the State power is vested in the people. The unified power derives from the people, works by and for the people.
4. Developing a socialist oriented multi-sectoral market economy regulated by the State.
5. Implementing democracy and hurnanity, recognizing and respecting human rights, ensuring basic freedoms of citizens, implementing the social role of the State.
6. Ensuring civil equality before the law.
7. Managing the society and the State pursuant to the law, ensuring legality and discipline in the social life and State administration.
8. Coordination between state bodies in exercising three functions: legislative, executive and judicial.
9. Organizing powers on the basis of administrative territories, ensuring a balance between unified power and creativeness and activeness of the localities.

The 1992 Constitution clearly shows the renovation policy, firstly economic renovation. This was reflected in the amnendments of the second chaptel "economrc regime ". Out of 15 articles of this chapter, 10 articles are completely new and 5 articles were fundarnentally amended. A lot of obsolete provisions were deleted and new provisions were inserted as appropriate to the economic development and management. The Constitution provides for economic policies. This means, "The State develops a socialist-oriented multi-sectoral commodity economy driven by the State-regulated market mechanism. The multi-sectoral structure of the economy with diversified types of production and business organization is based on ownelshrp, of which the first two are the cornerstone" (Artrcle 15). The State expands external economic activitles and assumes their unified administration, expands different forms of economic relations with all countries and international organizations on the principle of respect for independence, sovereignty and mutual benefit, and of appropriate protection for domestic production (Article 24). The State encourages foreign organizations and individuals to invest capital and technology; The State creates favovable conditions for the Vielnamese who live abroad to invest in the homeland (Article 25).

The Constitution points out that the purpose of economic development is to "build a strong country with prosperous life its people, and aimed at erer better satisfying the material and spiritual needs of the people by releasing all productive capacities, bringing into full play the potential of the various economic sectors···" (Article 16).

The Constitution defines clearly the form of ownership and their legal status (Article 17-23). These are entire people's ownership, collective ownership, private ownership, the first two being cornerstones. The economic sectors include state owned sector, collective sector, private sector, private capitalists and state capitalists.

*The 1992 Constitution confirms the social role and functions of our State.*

During all the phases of its development, our State always considevs people as the purpose of and momentum for social development. Therefore, the role of the State is required to protect the people in a new market economy. Different views exist regarding the social role of the State in a market economy.

Questions were raised: Will the State ensure a society for the people or should we let the market influence? Should the State regulate distribution? Should the State use taxation to support social programmes? Business freedom may lead to inequality and should the State intervene to abolish such inequality? How will principles and ideas about equality, fairness, civilization and ethics wovk in a market economy?

Such issues have been raised in history. Two distinct schools of thought have been formulated.

Implementing its social role, our State clearly defines its specific duties vegarding national policies (Article 5), culture, science and technology (Chaptev III) and the basic social and economic rights of citizens (Chapter V). The State through investment develops trade, encourages and supports family and private sector, soletraders, develops small industries, restores and develops traditional trades, creates new mdustries for employment, attracts employment through foreign inverstment exports labour.

Laws on Labour and trade unions and other laws must pvotect interests of employees while encouraging investment and limiting social injustice.

Our State and Party look at social justice from different perspectives. Social justice first exists in the allocation of capital and resources between different regions of the country, creating equal opportunities for people to develop their careers, allocation in business such as in the forms of shares.

Social justice is also achieved by poverty elimination programmes. The State assists poor people to progress and become rich. Developed areas must assists poor areas to develop. Rich people should be encouraged to get richer, assist the State in supporting the poor with capital, means of production, resources and know-how.

Our State implements its social function by way of policies aimed at developing and preserving national culture, humanity, developing literature, arts, nurturing the fine personality of Vietnamese people, developing the mass media, publications, considering education and training as the foremost policies of the State, uniformly managing the national education policies in terms of objectives, curriculum, plans, teacher qualification, examination rules and degree systems. The State develops science and technology, invests in development, It manages a healthcave system for the people, takes care of mother and children, implents population and family planning programmes, develops athletic programmes and sciences for the people.

*The 1992 Constitution is an important basis to develop democracy, reinforce the political system, ensure demeocracy of the people, respect and protect civil rights, reform the state system, build a state governed by the rule of law for the people, by the people of the people.*

As the society develops, people become move aware of their status and the right to be ownevs, to involve in state administration in respect of economic and social management. People become more sensitive to the quality and efficiency of the exercise of administvative powers.

*The 1992 Constitution, to reform the political system, lays the fundamental legal ground for the course of administrative reform in our country.*

This requirement has been formulated in order to achieve a new economy. The administrative system of the centralized economy has a lot of features of that system. It was inconsistent, fragmented, not synchronized and not complete. Therefore, that system pvoves to be inefficient in the new regime. Administrative veform does not mean red tape, indiscriminate interference into the business activities, which have their own rules. Therefore, elimination of red tape and reinforcement of the administrative system are both necessary in order to create the indispensable environment for business and production activities and a stable society.

When we talk of admininistrative reform, we must define the strong points of administrative institutions for the social life. On that basis, we can formulate correct renovation policies.

As part of the state power system, the professional administvative system is closed connected with political factors. This system realizes that behind political and legal decisions lie specific social forces.

Therefore, the role of the adiministrative system is to create harmony between social interests. Some authors look at this cynically, saying that the executive branch may override certain interests, not recognizing political influence, wishing to put political factors in an administrative system. This viewpoint was once raised by the German sociologist Max Webev. However, Weber not only referred to the relative independence of the executive fvom politics but also emphasized its professionalism.

In fact, the tie between the executive and politics oviginates from the executive's function in regulating production, labour, and distribution of capital, which require high consent of social forces, especially when regulating long term and short term economic and social programmes. An administrative system not only controls and directs but also organizes and is closely connected with a lot of social aspects. Administrative activities have therefore changed in their approach, trying to reform the social economic system. Therefore, it is highly political.

Therefore, the hallmark of the current administrative system is no longer a traditional official who works from nine to five. The hallmark now is the social efficiency. Therefore, the current administrative system stvesses negotiations, discussions organization and persuasion. The Constitution provides the Vietnam Fatherland Front includes within it a lot of important social organizations such as the Vietnam Confedevation Labour, Youth Association, Women's Association and other professional bodies (Article 9 of the Constitution). In fact, these organizations are important in assisting state bodies in exevcising state function, including adiministrative activities.

The Constitution provides for the responsibilities of state bodies. State officials must respect and listen to people and must be supervised by people (Article 8). Organizations within the Vietnam Fathevland Front may table law drafts before the National Assembly (Article 86 of the Constitution). The Chairman of the Central Committee of the Vietnam Fatherland Front, the Chaivman of the Vietnam Confedevation of Labour and Heads of associations ave invited to meetings of the Government when it discusses relevant matters (Article 111 of the Constitution). One of the powers and vesponsibilities of the Government is to coordinate with the Vietnam Fatherland Front and people's associations in its activities, enabling such associations to work efficiently (Article 112.11 of the Constitution).

The Constitution provides similarly for local activities. The Chaivman of the Vietnam Fatherland Front and Heads of local people's associations are invited to meeting of the People's Councils at the same level when they discuss velevant matters. People's Councils and People's Committees report on all aspects to the Front and people's associations, listen to recommendations of these associations on how to formulate the system and develop the economy and society in the locality.

## Part II

## Renovation policy, the Constitutions and institutional veform in Vietnam.

### I. The activities of the legislative body and its structure.

It's obviously that the legislative regulations of the National Assembly—The representative organization selected by people, has a long historical development, which was made at the same time with the establishment of the Vietnam Government in 1945. The first Constitution—The 1946 Constitution stated "The people parliament settles all the common problems throughout the country and enacts the laws". The following Constitutions of Vietnam in 1959—1980 and in 1992 also regulate that the National Assembly is the ultimate body, which has constitutional and legislative power.

In addition to the constitutional and legislative authority of the National Assembly, the 1980 Constitution had an article acknowledged: The Standing Committee of the National Assembly is vested to interpret the Constitution and codes, and to make the ordinance.

The research on the procedure for promulgating the ordinance of the Standing Committee shows this proceeding as follows: After the draft ordinance is approved by the Standing Committee, it is submitted to the National Assembly in its next Congress to be passed ov rejected.

In comparison to the previous constitutions, the 1992 Constitution has some more important provisions to centralize the legislative to the National Assembly and to reduce the sphere of making ordinance of the Standing Committee "The Standing Committee of the National Assembly only makes the ordinance on the issues when it is delegated by the National Assembly".

### Delegation of legislation

Thus, in fact, in our country the provision of Delegation of legislation has been already established: The National Assembly delegates to the Standing Committee of the National Assembly to promulgate some ordinances. Throughout the development of this legal document, the ordinance enactment has been essential due to some majov following reasons:

(a) Up to now, the National Assembly has not been a regular-operating ovgan. It has actually two sessions annually. Recently, the numbev of meetingdays had been raised, evevy session lasts for over a month consecutively. In such conditions, to ensuve the accomplishment of the proposed legal plans and programmes, there needs to be a standing organ of the National Assembly with the power of ordinance making to regulate the social relations on time. However, theve must be two conditions for that mandate to assure satisfactory ordinance.

—Firstly, to minimize the mandate of the legislative authority.

—Secondly, the National Assembly Standing Committee's ordinances must be ratified in the immediately successive session of the National Assembly.

From those mentioned above, the mechanism of implementing the National Assembly's legislative power must be considevd to be worked out on the principle: National Assembly is the uppermost State organ and the unique one that has the legislative and constitutional power.

**First of all**, it is a matter of organizing and appointing adequate specialized cadres for the National Assembly's organs and assuring the working conditions and improving the quality of consultative and researching works in the service of National Assembly representatives' activities.

**The second**, by current regulation: The Standing Committee of the National Assembly promulgates ordinances on issues entrusted by the National Assembly and makes cleav the sphere regulated by law and ordinance.

**The third**, there should a strategy for the legislation and implementing laws and the legislative authority of the National Assembly such as the plan of law making and ordinance of the National Assembly. It is said that the law planning programme, started in 1981, is a real breakthrough. Nowadays, the National Assembly works out the law making programme and ordinance annually and for its whole term. However, the law making preparation is confusing, passive and the programme has less feasibility.

According to Article 83 in the 1992 Constitution, the National Assembly, firstly, is the highest representative organ for the people. Through direct election, the National Assembly is founded and becomes the representative organ to implement the authority entrusted by its people. For it is a representative institution, it can't be a centralized entirely authority organ. People also implement their authority directly through elections, self-determination in the National Referendum, the supervision of state machine's opevrtion and selected people's representatives. The National Assembly only implements tasks and authorities entrusted by its people and ensured by Constitution in Articles 83, 84 of the 1992 Constitution. Comparing to the 1959 and 1980 ones, the ideology, that the National Assembly defines more specific authority for itself or offers itself with the right tO delegafe more poweers to the Standing Committee of the Ngtional Assembly or the Government, was completely abolished in the 1992 Constitution. This is a positive tendency, marked an important renovation in the organizing and dividing the authority in our Country.

According to Article 83 in the 1992 Constitution, the National Assembly is also the State's hightest legislative organ however, is it the unique authovized organ? Turning back to the concept of authority and power, the Central State mechanism in Vietnam includes 5 power organs: *The National Assembly, the President, the Government, the People's Supreme Court, the People's Supreme Procuracy*. Each of this has its own legislative status and implements its authority defined by the Constitution and Laws. Therefore the National Assembly should not be considered as the sole authorized organ and thus, the National Assembly has the right to assign or devolve its power to high-ranking state institutions. Comparing the tie between the National Assembly and the Goverument within the Constitutions assesses accurately the authority sphere of the National Assembly.

According to article 104 in the 1980 Constitution, the Ministerial Council is the Goverument of the Socialist Republic of Vietnam, the highest executive and administrative state body of the highest state powered organ. Within this relation, the legal status of the Government is consideved as a National Assembly Committee. This is the typical authority structure applying the ideology of a both legislative and executive Commune-State model. Up to the 1992 Constitution, our State has made remarkable adjustments in the the between the National Assembly and the Government. According to Article 109 in the 1992 Constitution the Government is the executive body of the National Assembly, the highest administrative organ of the Socialist Republic of Vietnam. The Governmnt, one hand depends on the National Assembly, it on the otherhand has held a rather independent status from the National Assembly.

This offers the Government with more flexible and sensitive abilities to operate its adminlstrative management throughout the Country adapted the multi-sectional commodity economy.

In three authority functions of the National Assembly, its inspectoration has shown the weakest in action and the less effectiveness. We considev that one of the amendments in the 1992 Constitution is to constantly pevfect the current mechanism so that the National Assembly implements better its inspectoration, simultaneously that is also the best way to heighten the National Assembly's practical power, but it shouldn't regulate the power supplementation.

## II. The perfection of the Government structure in renovation peviod.

Simultaneously, reforming political system, reforming and perfecting the Government structure is priority challenge to our Country to *build a democratic, pure, dynamic and strong admnistration, operating effectiveky within its functions and executive rights*.

The Government is the executive body of the National Assembly, the highest administrative organ of the Socialist Republic of Vietnam. Reforming and perfecting the govemment structure is always of political and current events. This issue "*affects not only the structure and function of the Government but also legislative, judicaial activities, and rules the devolution of the power from the Central to the Local*".

In our Country, perfecting the Govervument structure is one of the entive perfection of the other institutions in the political system (the Party, the political and Social organizations), in which the Government and the government administration that implement political, economic, social, defense and security tasks, have to get priorities to perfect in the whole comprehensive system.

Current structure of the Government requires a huge Administration. Governmental membevs (under the 1992 Constitution, they aren't compulsorily members of the National Assembly), but in practice 2/3 of the governmental members and heads of the governmental institutions are those of the National Assembly. Consequently, structuring the governmental mechanism is challenging, because of taking too many Government and the National Assembly works, somne governmental members are unable to fulfil their task" reporting to the National Assembly and the Standing Committee of the National Assembly on behalf of the Government", but devolve that upon deputy ministers.

Functions and tasks of the administvative organs have not been clearly defined; The specialized Ministries and general Ministries don't have substantive and clear criteria; sectors and branches haven't classified; several ministries that have the same duty, which is necessarily abolished. For example: there exists overlapped control on export-import tax between the Ministry of Finance and General Department of Customs; overlapped advertising management of the Trade Ministry and the Culture and Information one.

The assignment and. devolution between ministries and ministry-level organs governmental institutions and provincial administrations ave not clear-cut. Ministries and governmental institutions intend to "centralize" the important tasks, even projects that should be carried out by Localities are gained by the Central Organs. Waiting for the Ministries proposing the projects, budget plans … of the Localities is occurred regularly. This obviously slows down the implement of some governmental policies and projects.

Despite not be longing to the governmenlal structure, the consult organizations inlends to expand, some arn even known as "Super-ministries". Actions and effects by various organizations ave of little, but they waste administrative labour source. Many fields of management empowered to these orgaizations are overlapped the authority of the governmental membevs, which reduces the individual roles of Ministers in the Government as the Heads of the state achTLinistvation.

At present, to renovate the structure, executive activities, management, and the administvation (the administrative management in general) of our Government should focus on the following main directions:

1. Defining more clearly the legal status, duties and competencies of the

Government and Prime Minister, the Ministries and Ministers. Studying the 1992 Constitution, we realize that one defect that needs to amend is lack of cleav distinction of responsibilities, duties and competencies between the Government, the Prime Minister and governmental members as well.

The Constitution is needed to append the pvovisions on the substantive responsibility of the Goverument, Prime Minister and Ministers when they don't fulfill their tasks delegated by the National Assembly, ov they seriously vkolate laws, the national inlevests and the roghts and interests of citizen. So the Constitution must regulate clearly the individual responsibility of Prime Minister and Ministers and joint-responsibility of Goverument, Prime Minister and Ministers.

2. Defining the tie of the authority and responsibility within the Government and National Assembly; within the President, the People's Supreme Court, the People's Supreme Procuracy and Local Adimination (the People's Council and the People's Committee at different levels).

For the tie within the Government and the National Assembly, there are not only the provisions that the Goverument is responsible to and reports to the National Assembly but also regulations that: the National Assembly has the power to abolish the Government when the Government loses the trust of the National Assembly. This provision is regulated in order to enhance the governmental responsibility.

For the tie within the Government and the People's Supreme Court, the Constitution should append a provision permitted to establish the Constitutional Court or the Administrative Court system from the Supreme Administrative Court to the District Court. The Constitutional Court or the Supreme Administrative Court given one of authorities is to have the jurisdiction on administrative decisions (administrative management documents) and administrative behaviovs of the Government against the Constitution, laws and decrees of the National Assembly.

For Local Administration, though Article 112 in the 1992 Constitution defines the governmental rights and duties controlling the People's Committee operations' at all levels, building and accomplishing the State unique adiministrative mechanism from the Central to the Local, conducting, supervising, and inspecting the People's Committee in implementing their duties and rights under the laws. In additions, clauses 3, 4 and 5 in Article 114 define the responsibility and authority of the Prime Minister ovev the Local Administrations. For example, Prime-Minister has the rightt to ratify the election, annul the appointmetnt, dismiss the Chairman and Vice-chairman of Provincial People's Committee and City People's Committee controlling by the Central; to cease the implementations of decisions and resolutions of the People's Committee and the Chairman of Provincial People's Committee and City People's Committee controlling by the Central against the Constitution, laws and legaal documents of the senior state organs; to cease the implementations of resolutions of Provincial People's Council and City People's Council controlling by the Central against the Constitution, Iaws and legal documents of the senior state organs, simultaneously propose Standing Committee of the National Assemlbly to remore thevn.

We must grasp thoroughly lhal the authonty lie between the central Government and the local executive organ and local administration is the relation of centralism and decentralism in territory. Thus, we must have a clear view on the role and characteristics of the People's Committee and the People's Council at all different levels. Whethev the People's Council at all different levels is an authority state organ in the Local area ov not.

If it is, the Government-the Central State Administration has a power to cease the implementations of resolutions of Provincial People's Council against the Constitution, laws and legal documents of the senior state organs, conduct, supervise and inspect the People's Council in implementing resolutions and legal documents of the senior state organs, which are regulated in Articles 112 and 114 of the 1992 Constitution, so the Government, the superiov of People's Council at all levels, is an Administrative organ that has the right to run executive state organ at the Local. Move over, clause 3 Article 114 regulate that Prime Minister has the right to ratify the election, annul the appointment, dismiss the Chaivman and Vice-chairman of Provincial People's Committee and City People's Committee controlling by the Central. By the Law on Election People's Council and People's Committee in particulav, by the law on Election in general, the People's Council elects, annul the appointiment and dismiss the Chairnman of the People's Committee; Any organs which hare the right to elect, hare the power to annul the appointment and to dismiss. But its senior organs directly do the ratification of the election result. While analyzing regulations on the relation between Government and localities in the 1992 Constitution, we find it contrary and irrational. So these regulations should be adjusted to suit Vietnamese nature to ensure centralization and democracy principles in the governmental mechanism.

This means in our Country all the State's power is unified, derived from the People and is of the People; The People perform its powers through the National Assembly, the People's Council and other state organ; Simultaneously, there's the assignment, the divided responsibility and the co-operation within the state organs both al the Central level and at the Local levels in implementing the legislative, executive and judicial powers. This viewpoint exists because in our Country not only the National Assembly and the People's Council at all levels implement the state power but all the state organs do as well. As the result of this, the People perform the state power both through the National Assembly and the People's Council, and through all the state organs. From this fact, Article 6 in the 1992 Constitution should be adjusted to suit the practical situations.

3. Building the rational process on making the legal documents and the administrative decision of the Government. The poor quality of structuring the institution and incorrect content and tardiness within the legal documents and its instructed documents remain as a concern. Moreover documents cause troublesome to majority. In institution structuring, the trend to gain more favourable preferences to the Governmet and the Ministries in the administrative management rather than to the People and the enterprises. The co-operation between the Government, Ministries and Branches in solving problems concerned the citizen's rights and interests doesn't often run smoothly, even some problems that must be solved by Ministries, are submitted to lhe Government, the Primee Minister and the Deputy prime Minister to be settled.

The venovation of the governmental control, not only is not only a breakthrough to the administrative reform, but also have influence on creating other breakthroughs and even implementing all the governmental activities and programmes as well.

The position and the role of the Prime Minlster play a strong link in the relation between the Prime Minister, the National Assembly, and the Standing Committee of the National Assembly, the President and other Governmenlal members. This has a lot of renovation m lhe 1992 Constitution.

According to the 1992 Constitution and the Law on Organization of the Government on September 30th 1992, there are some remarkable regulations for the Prime Minister:

*The Prime Minister is the Head of the Government (Article 4 the Law on Organization of the Government) and is responsible to the National Assembly, and reports to the National Assembly, to the Standing Committee of the National Assembly, the President (Articld 110, the 1992 Constitution). The Deputy Prime Minister is responsible to the Prime Minister and to the National Assembly for the duties given by the Prime Minister (Article 4, the Law on Organization of the Goverment); Ministers and other Governmental members are sloso responsible to the Prime Minister and the National Assembly for the fields and the sectors they control (Article 117, the 1992 Constitution).*

The venovation mentioned heve is the responsible relations within the Government, the Prime Minister and the National Assembly, the Standing Committee of the National Assembly, the Pvesident. The Prime Minister becomes more independenl to the governmental power institutions. The responsibilities of the govemmental members to the Prime Minister and the National Assembly as well are defined more clearly, substantively and concentratedly. These create radical differences comparing to those in the 1980 Constitution, which make the position and the role of the Head of the Government a new content and quality.

Highlighting the right and responsibility of the Prime Minister shows the respect for the positlon and the role of the Head of the Government in boosting all the governmental activities, ensuring the governmental functions to be implemented reasonably. By highlighting the individual responsibilities of the Prime Minister and governmenlal membevs, the Constitution forms a basis to establish a *new order* in the government mechanism and *a new incentive* in the management, control and administration of the Governmentt, of the Prime Minister for the challenges and demands of a new period of development In our Country. The incentive, being the combination between the collectively governmental responsibilities and highlighting the individual vesponsibility and right of the Prime Minister as well as the governmental membevs to fulfill the tasks and 10 use the slale authorities defined by the Constitution and Laws, is nol as shmple as being the combination between the administrative, economic and educationa] measures to play their roles and authorilies like they used to do in the old mechanism.

Pursuanl to new provislons, the Government works collectively on the issues within their authorities under the collective decision and leadership to ensure the role of the Prime Minister as the general consensus conductor and to make the governmental activities more dynamic, flexible in an effective way.

Implementmg the govelnmental renovating activities in the way mentioned above, not onliy makes the Governmental collective and the Prime Minister do adequately their works and authorities defined by the Constitution that are to take care of the vadical issues in macro-contvol, but also gives a new clearer view on the Government in the new mechanism. The governmental function is *to plan and conduct the National policies*. The Government has the role of managing the National policies. Ministries and the Local Adiministrations are responsible to control those policies. The Ministries become the administrative organs—the principal conductors play the functions of the administvative managemenl of the Government and the responsibility of the Ministers in deciding the issues undev their authorities to be strengthened. The Ministers become the Heads of the administrations of the fields and the sectors that they control.

This signal shows the Government itself Is endeavoring to get out of the "steel fiame" hierarchy of the traditional administration to a new decentralized administrative mechanism, more dynamic, flexible and effective one bases on a highly devolved mechanism to adjust the tavgets and labour resources .

## II.3. The structure of Vietnamese court system and its intended renovation.

*The Supreme Court* includes the Council of Judges of the People's Supreme Court; Judge Committee of the People's Supreme Court; National Militavy Court; Criminal Court; Civil Court; Economic Court; Labour Court; Administration Court and Appeal Court of the Supreme Court; the court assistants. For some indispensable cases the Standing Committee of the National Assembly decides to set up the other specialized courts following the proposal of the Chief Judge of the People's Supreme Court.

*The pvovincial court* conslsts of judge committee criminal court, civil court, economic court, labour court, administration court and the court assistants. As il is essential, the Standing Committee of the National Assembly decides to establish other specialized courts following the proposal of the Minister of the Ministry of Justice after having discussion with the Chief Judge.
**The distvict coul't;**

**The militavy coul't;** Central militavy court; Militavy zoned court and the same level court; Regional militavy courts.

The central military court is vested to form the committee of judges and it is opevated in a similav way of a specialize court.

Due to the role, the duty and the adiministvative mechanism of the Vietnamese Army, the Minister of the Ministry of Justice after having discussion with the Minister of the Ministry of National Defense and the Chief Judge of the Supreme Court, decides to establish or vemore the militavy zoned courts and the regional militavy courts.

It's the first time in the legislative history our Government promulgates a particulav legal document on judges and the jury of the People's Court. This ordinance was passed on 14th May 1993 by the Standing Committee of the National Assembly and it has substantive provisions on the criteria, the roles and the responsibilities of a judge and the jury at the different levels of the court system. The appointment of judges that was abolished many yeavs ago is now being maintained.

The article 127 of the 1992 Constitution states that "The Supreme Court, the local court, militavy court and other courts acknowledged by law are the judicial organs of the Socialist Republic of Vietnam". Thus, the Court is the only governmental organ that exercises the juvisdiction.

Undev the law on enterprise bankruptcy passed on Decembev 30th 1993, Pvovincial courts and the Supreme Court are in charge of settlement of the request for bankvuptcy declavation.

Besides' regulating the Supreme Court has the jurisdiction and settles the question of bankrupt declaration, the 1992 Constitution defines that "the Supreme Court directs the jurisdiction of the local court and militavy courts. It is also the director of the decision of the specialized and other courts, except the case when the National Assembly makes other decisions before the court is set up".

The Supreme Court guides the other courts in implementing the unified law, sums up the judicial experiences, writes draft law to submit to the National Assembly and drafts the ordinance submitting to the Standing Committee of the National Assembly.

Base on the nature, the functions and the duty of the State, and through the practical operation of the courts in many years we think that the people's court system at present is suitable.

## II.4. The Administration Court in Vietnam.

Vietnam has chosen for itself an administvative arbitvation tribunal from experience of the international community and the country realities, therefore, it is adapted the transitional period stage and its social developmenl. The reseavch for the project on drafting the Administrative Arbitration commenced in May 1993, which was based on the models and the experience of the developed countries, and the real situations in settling the citizens' petition and accusation ov in settling the litigation of the individual, companies and organizations in the country.

The IX National Assembly Congress, in its 8th session approved a resolution to set up the Administrative Court system belonging to the people's court. At the same time, the Standing Committee of the National Assembly passed the Ordinance on the Proceduve for Settlement the Adiministrative Cases, which comes into effect from 1st July 1996 and it was amended on 5th, Januavy 1999. The people's courts at different levels, by this ordinance, hare the power to settle 09 administrative litigation as follows:
—Litigation on the decision of administrative fine.
—Litigation on the administrative decision and behaviov in enforcing to collapse a part or/all of the house and other architecture works.
—Litigation on the administrative decision and behavior in implementing or applying one of these administrative measures: compulsory local education;

compulsory school education; compulsory vocational education; compulsory disease treatment; administrative surveillance.
—Litigation on the decision to sack the staffs and govevmment officials including directors of Departments of ministries, the officials at the same rank and undemeath.
—Litigation on the administvative decision and behavior in the land management.
—Litigalion on the administratlve decision and behavior in licensing and revoking the license for basic building, production and business.
—Litigation on the administrative decision and behavior in collecting tax and making a posterior vecovery of tax.
—Litigation on the administvative decision and behavior in getting fees and costs.
—Other litigation by law.

Because theve hare not been good legal propaganda and advice, the various classes in the society understand laws differently.

People mostly think they are able to bring to the Court all the administrative decisions and behaviours they considev to be illegal ov wrongdoing without classlfying the cases and knowing the deadline for litigation.

Many high-positioned officials of the administvative government offices are afraid of being brought to court and being reduced their prestige. In some cases, they react unpleasantly or rudely in court.

There has been a case the defendant was a government institution, whose attitude caused the judge unpleasant and pressured in court.

## II.5. The structure of the People's Procuvacy.

Since the renovation started in 1986 in Vietnam, there hare been many schemes to reform the government mechanism with different point of views on the position and functions of the People's Procuracy. Recently, their roles and functions are widely being concerned and discussed.

All the opinions proposed to look through the position, the functions of the People's Procuracy derive from two main viewpoints: *Firstly*, all those opinions show that the general inspectorate activities (this is no longer use, but the term is still used here for easy understandlng and it now names the inspectorate on applying the law in the administrative, economic, social, security and international spheres) of the People's Procuracy hare overlapped the actvities of the inspecting institutions. To settle this problem, it is necessary to remove the general inspectorate function of the People's Procuracy and to delegate this power to the State Inspectorate. *Secondly*, the others state that the prosecutlon activities are of the executive activities, so lhe People's Procuracy should become the Pvosecution Institution that opevates amongst the executive institutions.

Vietnarn is now integrating into the Asian region and the World and most countries in the Wovld hare the prosecution institution, but no Procuracy and this prosecution institution is a part of the Executive and hence since 1987 many Schemes have been proposed to put the People's Procuracy into the Prosecution Institution undev the control of the Vietnamese Government. Therefore, the People's Procuracy would not be an independent organ among the four governmental organs. The criminal procedure of the countries followed the judicial precedents like the United Kingdom and United States of America is proceeding the case in the open Court on the principle of cross-examination. In these countries, the Prosecution Institution is a part of the Executive governed by the Government. In the countries enacted law, the criminal procedure is included not only the open verdict but also the stage of chavge, omverstigation and prosecution (inquisitorial principle) and the Prosecution Institution is a part of the Court systern (the judicial systern). In the former socialist countries just like Vietnam, the organ exercises the prosecution power must be of neither the Executive nov the Judicial, which must be an independent organ set up by the highest powered govevrnment body and it regularly reports to this body. Thus, for the traditional theory, the prosecution power is not of judicial and executive spheres, but it is of the power of the State: the Procuracy.

It has been noted that recently, there are vavious opinions about the Prosecution power (embodying its definitions, content, sphere and its subject) and the participants who carry out the prosecution. Evevy opinion looks at it at different aspects, in different situations, historical peviods and in different countries, so it is difficult to hare a common definition of the prosecution power for every country in the World. However, the Prosecution nature, its aims, its subjects, its sphere and its activities are the same in all States. Because each country has its own state mechanism, tradition, conditions and history, there must be no similarity for where in the "State machine" the Prosecution Institution is placed, which organs exercise the prosecution power and apart from the practicing the prosecution rights what other rights the Prosecution Institution has.

The People's Procuracy has its functions to examine the legal application and to exercise the prosecution power, so it must operate independently in any case.

## II.6. The real mattel of the Local Administration.

In Vietnam, the Local Administration is the "machine" implementing the state authority at three levels: Village, District and Province (these thvee is called "local"). The Local Adminislration at each level has the People's Council and the People's Committee.

—The People's Council, by recent Constitution, is the goverumental authority organ in the region and the representative of the people, selected by people and responsible for the people and for the superior governmental authority.

—The People's Committee is the Executive of the People's Council and the governmental administration in the region. To carry out the functions and duties the People's Committee embodies the Specialized Department: The Pvovince has departments, boards and branches; the District has boards and offices; the Village only has specialized names for individuals and the machine is not formed.

The local administrative model is regulated by the Law on the Organization and Activities of the People's Council and the People's Committee. Throughout the activities of the local administrations at different level. Besides the strong points and achievements, some main limitations, short coming and weaknesses hare been existed:

*Changing the state-regulated economic mechanism from the subsidized, red-tape, plannd and centralized model into the marketet economy.*

The renovation of the regulated economic mechanism requires the reform of the basic model and the social-economic mechanism, consequently, it is objectively necessary to reform the Sate Machine in general and the structure of the

Local Administration in particular.

New adapted relationship must be created between the subject and object of the management. In the past, in order to manage the planned, centralized economy, a huge cumbvous state machine was required, comprised various highly specialized branches and levels from the Central to the Local areas. At that time, the Government and the Local Adiministration weve involved into the production and business management and *they performed the organism in -charge rather than the state managemnet-* the fundamental of all the States and Govemvnent.

The structure, of the Government and the Local Administration hare not veorganized to adapt the demand of the goverumental management in the new period, in fact, the Local Administration at different levels is basically the same as it was. The renovation heve is restricted to the amendment of the provisions on its functions and duties and reforming some specialized and service offices. The Provincial Administration and especially the District Administration are still vevy blg and cumbrous, wheve as the Village Adminlstvation is small and unilateral as it was, when the large-slzed collective favms existed, and when lhe state management in the region joined in and mixed with the economic management of the collective farms, obviously, the transfev of the economic mechanism is the effective and direct factor, which objectively requires to reform the new basic structure of the Local Administration at different levels, primarily at district and village levels.

*The contents, the devolution of levels and powers from the Central to the Local.*

The model of che Local Administration is built upon the scale, dimension and limit of the devolution of the levels and powers between the Central and the Local Administration and amongst the Local Administration. Our State is a unique State that is organized as a centralized power regime in both the vertical and the transverse. So, the roles, responsibilities and the structure of the Local Administration hare more special features than those do in the decentralized and self-governed or autonomous states. For example, the roles of the People's Councils in Vietnam are different from those of the Local Counc;ils in many countries because the People's Councils cannot decide all the problevns in their regions.

At present, our devolving to central-local levels occuvs several problems needed to be settled; noticeably, the level devolution is not clear or very detail, and devolving to the local level carries too many works and it does the works of the District Adiministration; the lowest level isn't delegated specifically the duties and the most essential powers in implementing the works related to the people in the region.

The renovation of the central-Iocal leveled devolution in the way of strengthening the authority and responsibilities of the Local Administration will affect the structure and activities of the Local Administrative Machine.

*In the future, it is necessary to conduct the Administrative Leadership instead of the recent People's Committee regime.*

The Committee Administration is the Group-Work management, which has the positive aspects, but il comprises some shortcomings that restrict the activeness and the following in the adiministrative management. Without enhancing the individual roles and responsibilities of the header, simultaneously it supports irresponsibility and it covers the negative aspects and standstill of the organ… Thus, the People's Committee has been showing less appropriate to the mechanism of the Public Administration, especially to the developed administration. In the Wcrld, nowadays, the Committee Administration is no longer existed in the State Administrative Management, while the Leadership Administration is replaced such as: *the Province Governor, the Magor, the Village Chief or the Administrative Manager*, etc.

In Vietnam, because of the effect and the influence of the geography, economic and political conditions as well as culture, customs and tradition in its history the Village Administration in the countryside was not organized the same as the other organs in the State Machine.

Before the August Revolution in 1945, the Village Administration (mainly Viet Villages) was organized and controlled as self-governed one. The self-governed regime commenced at the en of the 15th centuvy, after the Le Feudal State abolished the "Village Praetor"- an official who was appointed, paid and sent to the village to rule. it.

The self-gaoverned regime allowed the village admininistrative organ itself to carry out the local works in the region, and simultaneously to be responsible for meeting the demand of taxes, military service, labour service, etc.

All the internal jobs (sphere of village) and external jobs (between the village and another) were delegate to some persons in the village census record to discuss and decide. These people were then called the village praetors.

In the past, Vietnamese Feudal states only paid attention to villaaes and they had, through the village board, communicated with the peopv. Evevy gift and subsidy for people firstly was delivered to the village board and then to the people, in contrast all the responsibilities of the people to the State weve collected and concentrated to become the common duties and responsibilities of the village. In the other words, the State left the control and the management entirely to the village (exactly the headers of village). So the, way to rule the country was through the representatives of the villaae and it was based on joint-responsibility law (one breached the law therefore all members of the village had to submit the punishment). This management made the head of the village vevy powerful, but he then was nobt fully responsible for what he did. This gap of law helped the village leader on behalf of state or village do some extra works for his own interest or for his family's; therefore the people took the consequence.

After the August Revolution in 1945, the Village Administrative was reorganized differently. For this new structure, the state administrative organ in the village is the collective operated as a Committee: all the important issues are discussed by the entire Committee and are decided by the majority, then they are given to the individual in -charge to perform. This is the democratic aspect of the Local Adiministration.

Part II    Protection of Human Rights in Asia

# Why a Philippine Human Rights Commission?
## Its Place in a Constitutional Order
### ——An Inquiry into the Power and Limits of Liberal Constitutionalism

Raul C. Pangalangan[1]

If the central idea is that a constitution is "a machine that would go of itself"[2] and should secure our rights and liberties through a structure of checks and balances, then a Commission on Human Rights (or CHR) should be superfluous. Yet the Philippines' post-Marcos Constitution deliberately created a CHR in recognition of the human rights problems that arose during the Marcos years. This essay attempts to situate the CHR as a rights-based institution within constitutional theory, and also in relation to non-traditional rights claims arising from the normative and directive principles of the Constitution. It further notes yet another check on government, namely, the direct exercise of the popular power through recall, referendum and initiative. In the end, I ask: how can we reconcile these new mechanisms with the counter-majoritarian strain of constitutionalism, which says that rights are claims insulated from "ordinary" politics, and which elevates them to a "higher" (i.e., constitutional) politics which constrains the popular power?[3]

### Background

Since its independence, the Philippines has had three[4] constitutions: that of 1935, which provided for independence from American colonial power and which was patterned expressly after the American constitution, with three branches of government and a bill of rights; that of 1973 (as amended in 1976 and 1981), whose transitory clauses Marcos used in order to justify perpetuating his emergency powers; and the present constitution of 1987. Philippine constitutional history suggests that U.S. notions of constitutionalism, transplanted to the Philippines, has begun to yield to Third World and Asian realities.

The central idea of American-style constitutionalism was of a constitution that "would enable government to control the governed; and in the next place oblige it to control itself."[5] Its interpreters would later say that a "constitution is not intended to embody a particular economic theory, whether of paternalism…or of *laissez faire*"[6], and that the ideal was the "procedural republic", providing merely a neutral framework which "enabled the citizens to pursue their own ends…govern[ing] by principles that do not presuppose any particular conception of the good.'"[7] Yet no sooner did that new republic adopt amendments that would form its Bill of Rights, expressly limiting the powers of that government and establishing the bases, however bar, of certain normative commitments. This was the model that the Philippines adopted when it became independent.

In this essay, I examine the implications of three constitutional innovations built on top of that structure of separated powers and an explicit bill of rights, and instituting further mechanisms to promote human dignity.

First, the 1987 Constitution provides for an independent Commission on Human Rights, in a separate article entitled Social Justice and Human Rights, with investigative, monitoring, educational and advocacy functions. In this section, I look at the CHR mainly in terms of its enforcement function. (I will not inquire into its separate monitoring function vis-à-vis international human rights treaties, which is a matter more of international law.)[8]

Second, successive Philippine constitutions have provided directive principles, a "constitutional inventory of fundamental community values and interests"[9], the equivalent in human rights discourse of non-traditional, "aspirational" and "programmatic" claims. These "principles" have been declared prominently in Article II of each Constitution, and were expanded in 1973 to include "state policies" as well, and today includes the right to health[10], to a balanced and healthful ecology[11], the duty of the state of economic protectionism[12], to pursue a nuclear weapons-free policy[13], and to promote social justice[14], and guarantee human rights.[15]

Third, the 1987 Constitution institutionalizes the direct exercise of "people power" through the power of recall of elective officials, of referendum on legislative matters, and of "direct initiative" to amend the Constitution.

## A. The CHR and Rights Discourse

### The CHR: Duplicating the Courts?

Several Supreme Court decisions have diminished the powers of the CHR, leading a member of the Court to state, in a dissenting opinion, that the CHR is thus a tiger with no teeth and no claws. The core problem lies in the inevitable overlap of jurisdiction since both institutions are dedicated to redressing rights violations. On the hand, the Constitution vests jurisdiction in the Supreme Court over

> actual controversies involving rights which are legally demandable and enforceable, and to determine whether or not there has been a grave abuse of discretion amounting to lack or express of jurisdiction on the part of any branch or instrumentality of the Government.[16]

### On the other, the CHR has jurisdiction to

> investigate, on its own or on complain by any party, all forms of human rights violations involving civil and political rights.[17]

In *Cariño v. CHR*,[18] the Supreme Court rejected the attempt by the CHR to adjudicate a dispute between the Secretary of Education and public school teachers, who were fired from their jobs after they went on strike to protest unpaid wages. Public officers are barred from labor strikes, the Secretary said. We were fired summarily, without due process of law, said the strikers. The striking teachers sought relief from the Supreme Court, but were rejected.[19] The CHR ordered the Secretary to explain. The Court held that the CHR had no power to compel such process.

> The Commission evidently intends to itself *adjudicate*, that is to say, determine with character of finality and definiteness, [these] issues....
>
> The Court declares the [CHR] to have no such power; and that it was not meant by the fundamental law to be another court or quasi-judicial agency in this country, or duplicate much less take over the functions of the [courts].
>
> The most that may be conceded to the Commission in the way of ad-

judicative power is that it may *investigate*, i.e., receive evidence and make findings of fact as regards claimed human rights violations involving civil and political rights. But fact-finding, [i.e.,] the function of receiving evidence and ascertaining therefrom the facts of a controversy, is not a judicial function [. Judicial power entails in addition] the authority of applying the law to those factual conclusions to the end that the controversy may be decided or determined authoritatively, finally and definitively...This function, to repeat, the Commission does not have.

In this case, the strikers had a plausible human rights claim but which clearly overlapped, too, with claims that may be vindicated before the Courts and administrative agencies. As the Court concluded: "The Commission on Human Rights simply has no place in this scheme of things." (emphasis supplied)

This was affirmed by the Supreme Court in yet another case wherein the CHR issued an order temporarily barring a government agency from the eviction of "squatters" or illegal dwellers from land they were occupying. In *Export Processing Zone Authority v. CHR*[20], the Court held once more that the CHR may not issue such orders which are similar to preliminary injunctions issued by the Courts. The Court proceeded to establish why protective measures, since they aim to preserve the rights of the parties pending litigation, partake of a judicial character.

These decisions demonstrate that the CHR as an institution duplicates the functions of the courts and that "human rights", especially in the sphere of municipal law, are no different from the mass of other rights for which the judicial system is the principal guarantor. The paradox is that the idea of human rights draws its power from rights discourse, yet it is precisely such discourse that confines the place of a CHR vis-à-vis the courts.

**Limiting the CHR to Civil and Political Rights**

The place of the CHR, in this context, should lie in non-traditional rights, or the whole range of "solidarity rights", which can be advanced using the directive clauses of the Constitution or through the International Covenant on Economic, Social And Cultural Rights. On one hand, it is ironic that the CHR must yield to the courts on civil and political rights precisely because these involve "rights", yet as regards non-traditional rights which are not readily susceptible of judicial relief, it likewise possesses no investigative powers. On the other, the CHR is better suited to promote, though not to protect (in the jargon of human rights), non-traditional rights through its broad monitoring, educational and advocacy mandate.

Pursuant to express constitutional provision, the Supreme Court has strictly confined the CHR to "civil and political rights." In *Mayor Simon v. CHR*[21], the Court rejected an order by the CHR, stopping the City Mayor from carrying out a Demolition Notice evicting squatters-vendors from public land, on the ground that the right at stake, e.g., the right to housing and to livelihood, was economic in character and was outside the scope of CHR authority. The evicted residents cited a "right to earn a living" as "essential to one's right to development, to life and to dignity."

The Court inquired into the drafting history of the CHR provisions, and found that the framers of the Constitution had deliberately excluded economic and social claims, recognizing that the evils sought to be precluded were the civil and political rights violated during the Marcos regime and recalling, too, that the Marcos invoked his alleged promotion of social and economic claims as excuses for violating civil and political rights. The Court carefully argued that although international human rights instruments included both sets of rights, and that the Philippines is party to these treaties, the framers of our Constitution decided to economic and social claims from the investigative jurisdiction of the CHR.

Flowing from this, the CHR itself has adopted guidelines on evictions, limiting itself to the manner of eviction (whether it is humane, i.e., if there was prior notice, if there were relocation sites, if there was no use of force), and deferring to the courts on the issue of ownership and title (because these pertained to actual rights). As stated above, the CHR has continued its monitoring, educational and advocacy work in non-traditional areas, although as the examples will demonstrate, these are tied up with the CHR's duty to promote international treaty obligations : the rights of the child, urban evictions, indigenous peoples, the internally displaced, violence against women.

## B. Directive Principles as Constitutional Aberrations

The elaborate list of directive principles has caused tremendous confusion from their inception. Indeed, even during the drafting of the Constitution, some members of the Commission urged their (characteristically, activist) colleagues not to introduce these new-fangled "rights" into the Bill of Rights (a list of what the state cannot do) but instead to insert them in the normative clauses of the Charter (listing what the state must do). I have written elsewhere:

> The Article II "Declaration of Principles and State Policies" reflects an obstinate tendency during the 1986 Constitutional Commission...to ensure a post-EDSA reform agenda by writing it out in agonizing detail into the Constitution itself. Indeed, there were even attempts to smuggle into the Bill of Rights, and thereby reinforce, claims to "education, food, environment and health".[22] To ward these off, it was repeatedly explained that the Bill of Rights was a list of what government <u>cannot</u> do and that the rights therein were accordingly "self-executing". In contrast, social justice claims were "affirmative commands on the State to do something", i.e., what government <u>must</u> do[23]. These required legislative implementation and were more appropriately listed in the social justice provisions[24], as eventually reflected in the final draft.[25]

These principles today continue to wreak havoc in constitutional law debates, which I will proceed to discuss.

### Self-Executing Norms

In one line of cases, the Court has declared some normative clauses directly enforceable or self-executing, and has proceeded to give them legal effect:

a) *The right to a clean and healthful environment, which was deemed to give rise to an actionable claim to stop the issuance of timber-cutting licenses*

In *Oposa v. Factoran Jr.* [26], the broad right to ecology was deemed self-executing, despite its broad, open-ended formulation, namely: the "right of the people to a balanced and healthful ecology in accord with the rhythm and harmony of nature"[27] together with the people's "right to health."[28] A group of minors, represented by their parents, asked a trial court to cancel all existing timber license agreements (TLAs), and to stop issuing new TLAs, citing the "adverse and detrimental consequences of continued deforestation." The Secretary of Natural Resources contended that the suit failed to allege a "specific legal right violated...for which any relief is provided by law", limited as it is to "nothing...but vague and nebulous allegations concerning an 'environmental right'", and that the question of whether logging should be permitted is a political question which should be addressed to either the Congress or the executive branch of government.

The trial court dismissed the case, but the Supreme Court overruled the dismissal, remanding the case to the trial court for proceedings on the merits. The Court said that, on the contrary, there is a "specific fundamental legal right" at stake, namely, the "right to a balanced and healthful ecology."

> While the right to a balanced and healthful ecology is to be found under the Declaration of Principles and State Policies and not under the Bill of Rights, it does not follow that it is less important than any of the civil and political rights enumerated in the latter. Such a right [to ecology] belongs to a different category of rights altogether for it concerns nothing less than self-preservation.

The Court proceeded to state that this right "carries with it the correlative duty to refrain from impairing the environment", a duty codified in revised charter of the environment department[29], the administrative code[30], and earlier decrees[31]. The right is violated when the Government fails in its correlative duty or obligation. Finally, the case raises a justiceable and not political question.

> Policy formulation...is not squarely put in issue. What is principally involved is the enforcement of a right *vis-a-vis* policies already formulated and expressed in legislation.

Besides, the Court added, the political question doctrine is "no longer... insurmountable" in light of the expanded scope of judicial power in the new Constitution which allows the courts to determine "whether or not there has been a grave abuse of discretion...on the part of any branch or instrumentality of the Government."[32]

A leading scholar in the Court, Justice Feliciano, wrote a separate opinion which joined the majority in the result but asked that their doctrines "be subjected to closer examination."

Where substantive standards as general as..."the right to health" are combined with remedial standards as broad ranging as "a grave abuse of discretion...", the result will be...to propel the courts into the uncharted ocean of social and economic policy making.

Therefore, he adds, petitioners must demonstrate, before the trial court, a "more specific legal right—a right cast in language of a significantly lower order of generality", containing "specific, operable norms and standards", and setting forth a "specific, operable legal right, rather than a constitutional or statutory *policy*."

Justice Feliciano found the "right to a balanced and healthful ecology" so "comprehensive in scope" and "generalized in character", failing to identify which particular provision of which code gave rise to a specific legal right. He raised two concerns. The first was the due process concern, i.e., that unless the legal right claimed to have been violated is specified, the defendants will be unable to defend themselves effectively. The second was the "broader-gauge consideration" about the place of judicial power *vis-a-vis* policy-making.

> b) *The right of Filipino nationals to priority in the granting of licenses and state contracts, which was used to invalidate the sale by the state of the historic Manila Hotel to a Malaysian corporation, on the ground that the next-ranking bidder, a Filipino, should be allowed match the winning bid*

In *Manila Prince Hotel v. GSIS*[33], the Court held that the duty of the state to give "preference to qualified Filipinos" in the grant of rights, privileges and concessions gave rise to a direct right of action in courts.

The Supreme Court stopped the sale of the Manila Hotel to the winning bidder, a Malaysian corporation, ordering the seller, a government corporation (i.e., the Government Service Insurance System, the pension fund of government employees) to accept the "matching bid" of the losing bidder, the Manila Prince Hotel corporation. The Court held that the following paragraph of the National Economy and Patrimony provisions of the Constitution were "self

-executory" and "*per se* judicially enforceable."

> In the grant of rights, privileges, and concessions covering the national economy and patrimony, the State shall give preference to qualified Filipinos.[34] (emphases supplied)

The Court ruled that the Manila Hotel belonged to the national patrimony, which encompasses both the natural resources, and the cultural and historical heritage of the nation.[35] Therefore, foreigners could buy the hotel "only if no Filipino qualifies [in the bidding] or if the qualified Filipino fails to match the highest bid tendered by the foreign entity."[36] The Court explained how a normative statement becomes directly enforceable.

> A provision which lays down a general principle, such as those found in [the Constitution's Declaration of Principles and State Policies"] is usually not self-executing. But a provision which is complete in itself and becomes operative without the aid of supplementary or enabling legislation, or that which supplies sufficient rule by means of which the right it grants may be enjoyed or protected, is self-executing. Thus a constitutional provision is self-executing if the nature and extent of the right conferred and the liability imposed are fixed by the constitution itself.... and there is no language indicating that the subject is referred to the legislature for action.[37] (emphasis supplied)

> The mere fact that legislation may supplement or add to or prescribe a penalty for the violation of a self-executing constitutional provision does not render such a provision ineffective in the absence of such legislation.[38]

> [The provision at stake] is a mandatory, positive command which is complete in itself and which needs no further guidelines or implementing laws or rules for is enforcement. From its very words the provision does not require any legislation to put it in operation. It is *per se* judicially enforceable.[39] (emphasis supplied)

> c) *The duty of the state to promote the national interest, which was used to compel an investor not to relocate a petrochemical factory*

In *Board of Investments v. Garcia*[40], the Court reversed the decision of the Board of Investments allowing the Luzon Petrochemical corporation to relocate its proposed plant from Bataan to Batangas, citing the duty of the State to "regulate and exercise authority over foreign investments"[41] and to "develop a self-reliant and independent national economy effectively controlled by Filipinos."[42] A dissent stated:

> [C]hoosing an appropriate site for the investor's project is a political and economic decision which, under our system of separation of powers, only the executive branch, as implementor of policy formulated by the legislature..., is empowered to make.

The Court, she added, "possess[ed neither the] technology and scientific expertise" to make that decision. Another dissenting opinion stated that the majority had "transformed itself into...a 'government by Judiciary.'"

> [The majority has] decided upon the wisdom of the transfer of the site...; the reasonableness of the feedstock to be used...; the undesirability of the capitalization aspect...; and injected its own concept of the national interest as regards a [strategic] industry.

> ...By no means [does the Constitution] vest in the Courts the power to enter the realm of policy considerations under the guise of the commission of grave abuse of discretion.

**Non-Self-Executing Norms**

On the other hand, the Court has also rejected certain normative claims as not judicially enforceable absent implementing legislation:

> a) *The constitutional clauses on economic protectionism, which were cited to oppose the ratification of the WTO Agreement*

In *Tañada v. Angara*[43], wherein the Court held that the World Trade Organization treaty, requiring states-parties to liberalize their economies, was compatible with the "nationalist" clauses of the Constitution. The petitioners contended that the "national treatment" and "parity provisions" of the WTO Agreement placed foreigners on the same footing as Filipinos, in violation of the duty of the State to "develop a self-reliant and independent national economy effectively controlled by Filipinos."[44] The Court held that the normative clauses of the Constitution were not meant to be self-executing.

These principles in Article II are not intended to be self-executing principles ready for enforcement through the courts. They are used by the judiciary as aids or as guides in the exercise of its power of judicial review, and by the legislature in the enactment of laws.

*b) The morality clauses of the Constitution, which were cited to oppose a government-sponsored lottery and the Value-Added Tax*

In *Kilosbayan v. Morato*[45] (upholding a government-sponsored Lotto), cited as well in *Tolentino v. Secretary of Finance*[46] (upholding the Value-Added Tax law), the Court said:

[T]hese were "not...self-executing provisions, the disregard of which can give rise to a cause of action in the courts [because t]hey do not embody judicially enforceable constitutional rights but guidelines for legislation."[47] (emphasis supplied)

Rejecting another challenge to state-sponsored gambling[48], the Court stated that the morality clauses[49] were "merely statements of principles and policies" and as such were "basically not self-executing, [requiring that] a law should be passed by Congress to clearly define and effectuate such principles."

This confusion has in fact triggered frequent calls for constitutional revisions, the latest of which is the current attempt by the incumbent President to amend the "economic provisions" (i.e., the protectionist clauses) to liberalize the economy and, significantly, to exclude economic matters from the courts' power of judicial review.

## C. Institutionalizing "People Power"

The "people's initiative" clauses of the 1987 Constitution have "institutionalized people power"[50]. The Constitution authorizes *first*, "a system of initiative and referendum...whereby the people can directly propose and enact laws or approve or reject any legislative act[51]; *second*, a system of "recall, initiative and referendum" of local officials[52]; and *third*, a direct initiative by the people to amend the Constitution[53]. The mechanisms stand outside the traditional framework of checks and balances amongst the great powers of government, and enhance the ultimate check in a republican government, namely, the sovereign power. In a sense, the "people power" clauses are the final touch in the de-Americanization of the Philippine Constitution: it rejects the anti-populist strain of constitutionalism, confesses openly the folly of trusting institutions to do the checking, and restores the place of raw popular power.

## D. Limits of Constitutionalism

The constitutional developments discussed above are pragmatic responses to historical experience, i.e., the inadequacy of the old model of separated powers and an explicit bill of rights. To the extent that it worked, it led to formal democracy, where the law, in its majesty, allowed rich and poor alike the equal right to sleep under the bridges. To the extent that it failed, it led either to a "soft state" frozen and incapable of governing, or to a dictatorship which legitimized itself solely through positive law.

Persistent constitutional challenges to the CHR demonstrate how oddly the CHR fits into the constitutional order precisely because it aims to vindicate the very same rights already protected by the courts. At the same time, to the extent that the CHR must leave to the courts the traditional judicial function of *post hoc* curative devices, the CHR has demonstrably risen to the project of preventive and structural measures. The irony is that, already, Western legal systems have recognized the limits of limited, court-dispensed solutions, and have begun to explore possibilities of "complex injunctions" that transform social organizations[54].

Conversely, the expanded statement of normative and directive principles has similarly short-circuited the constitutional design. They have elevated affirmative claims to social policy as "rights", and have made them judicially enforceable, as it were, the courts directly exercising the police power. Confusing statements from the Supreme Court provide little guidance. Yet these principles today are addressed squarely through the monitoring, educational and advocacy work ably done by the CHR.

Finally, the "peoples' power" clauses suggest that indeed "[t]here are constitutions [b]ut there is no constitutionalism"[55], and we return to the popular origins of constitutions. Constitutions are created by the people. The people, for their own sake, place certain claims, purposes and longings beyond the reach of ordinary politics, and entrust their guardianship to institutions. In the Philippines, these institutions have repeatedly failed. On one hand, the CHR aims to perfect these institutions, as if to say that, if the three branches of government fail, there will be a fourth, a fifth, a sixth institution, and so on, to meet the situation. But on the other, the enlarged directive principles give up on that hope, and rely instead on the sheer moral power of norms. The "peoples' power" clauses likewise give up on that hope, and allow the people, once again, to take control. But wasn't that what constitutions are all about, namely, holding back the raw, wild power of the multitude and insulating people's rights, our rights? Thus, in the words of the poet, we arrive where we started, and we know the place for the first time. A "machine [indeed] that goes of itself."

(1) Associate Professor of Law, University of the Philippines. A.B., LL. B., University of the Philippines; LL. M., S.J.D., Harvard Law School. Last year, the author was Visiting Professor of Law at the Harvard Law School.

(2) See M. KAMMEN, A MACHINE THAT WOULD GO OF ITSELF: THE CONSTITUTION IN AMERICAN CULTURE (1986).

(3) See R. PARKER, HERE, THE PEOPLE RULE: A CONSTITUTIONAL POPULIST MANIFESTO (1994).

(4) There is actually a fourth, the Freedom Constitution under which Corazon Aquino temporarily governed, from the time she ousted Marcos through the "EDSA people power" in March 1986 to the ratification of a new Constitution in January 1987.

(5) THE FEDERALIST No. 51, at 321 (James Madison) (Clinton Rossiter, ed., 1961).

(6) Lochner v. New York, 198 U.S. 47 (1905) (Holmes, J., dissenting) (striking down as unconstitutional legislated maternity benefits). See parallel ruling in Philippine law, i.e., People v. Pomar, 46 PHIL. 440 (1924).

(7) See, for instance, *M. Sandel*, *The Procedural Republic and the Unencumbered Self*, in COMMUNITARIANISM AND INDIVIDUALISM 12, 13 (Avineri and de-Shalit, eds.) (1992).

(8) CONST., art. XIII §18.7 ("Monitor the Philippine Government's compliance with international treaty obligations on human rights").

(9) F. Feliciano, *The Application of Law: Some Recurring Aspects of the Process of Judicial Review and Decision Making*, 37 The Am. J. of Jurisprudence 17, 46 (1992).

⑽ CONST., art. II §15.
⑾ CONST., art. II §16.
⑿ CONST., art. II §19.
⒀ CONST., art. II §7.
⒁ CONST., art. II §10.
⒂ CONST., art. II §11.
⒃ CONST., art. VIII §1.
⒄ CONST., art. §1.
⒅ Isidro Cariño v. Commission on Human Rights, G.R. 96681, 2 December 1991, 204 SCRA 483.
⒆ Manila Public School Teachers Association et al. v. Honorable Perfecto Laguio Jr., G.R. 95445; Alliance of Concerned Teachers et al. v. Hon. Isidro Cariño, G.R. No. 95590.
⒇ Export Processing Zone Authority v. Commission on Human Rights, G.R. 101476, 14 April 1992, 208 SCRA 125.
(21) Mayor Brigido Simon et al. v. Commission on Human Rights, G.R. 100150, 5 January 1994.
(22) JOURNAL OF THE CONSTITUTIONAL COMMISSION OF 1986, Volume III at 687.
(23) Commissioner J. Bernas, *id.* at 697-98 (social justice claims were "affirmative commands [on] the State to do something" and were not self-executory).
(24) *Id.*
(25) Pangalangan, *Property As A "Bundle Of Rights": Redistributive Takings And The Social Justice Clause*, 71 PHIL. L.J. 141 (1997).
(26) Minors Oposa v. Factoran, 224 SCRA 792, 30 July 1993.
(27) CONST. article II §16.
(28) CONST. article II §15.
(29) Executive Order 192 §4, 10 June 1987, The Reorganization Act of the Department of Environment and Natural Resources.
(30) Executive Order 292, Title XIV, Book IV §1, The Administrative Code of 1987.
(31) Presidential Decree No. 1151 (6 June 1977), Philippine Environmental Policy) and Presidential Decree No. 1152, Philippine Environment Code.
(32) CONST. article VIII §1.
(33) Manila Prince Hotel v. GSIS, G.R. No. 122156, 3 February 1997.
(34) CONST. art. XII §10, para. 2.
(35) Manila Prince Hotel, *supra*, n. 33.
(36) Manila Prince Hotel, *supra*, n. 33.
(37) Manila Prince Hotel, *supra*, n. 33, at 8.

(38) Manila Prince Hotel, *supra*, n. 33, at 10.
(39) Manila Prince Hotel, *supra*, n. 33, at 13-14.
(40) 191 SCRA 288 (1990).
(41) CONST. article XII §10.
(42) CONST. article II §19.
(43) G.R. No. 118295 (2 May 1997).
(44) CONST. article II §19.
(45) G.R. No. 118910, 17 July 1995, 246 SCRA 540.
(46) G.R. 113455, 25 August 1995, 235 SCRA 630.
(47) Kilosbayan, *supra*, at 564.
(48) *Basco v. PAGCOR*, G.R. No. 91649, 197 SCRA 52 (1991).
(49) CONST. article II §§11 (Personal Dignity), 12 (Family) and 13 (Youth); Article XIII §13 (Social Justice); and Article XIV §2 (Educational Values)
(50) Subic Bay Metropolitan Authority v. COMELEC, G.R. No. 125416, 26 September 1996.
(51) CONST. art. VI §32. See also Republic Act No. 6735, the Initiative and Referendum Act, as interpreted in Garcia v. COMELEC, G.R. 11230, 30 September 1994, and Subic Bay, *supra*, n. 50, (upholding a referendum to determine whether a municipality will be included in a special economic zone).
(52) CONST. article IX §3. See also Garcia v. COMELEC, G.R. No. 111511, 5 October 1993 (upholding the law implementing the recall clause); Angobung v. COMELEC, G.R. No. 126576, 5 March 1997 (rejecting as invalid a recall petition) and Evardone v. COMELEC, G.R. No. 94010, 2 December 1991 (upholding a facially defective recall petition, after enough signatures had been collected supporting the petition).
(53) CONST. article XVII §2. See also Defensor-Santiago v. COMELEC, G.R. No. 127325, 19 March 1997 and People's Initiative for Reform, Modernization and Action v. COMELEC, G.R. No. 129754, 23 September 1997 (holding that the Initiative and Referendum Law "inadequately" implemented the Constitution and was not judicially unenforceable, and rejecting a "direct initiative" to amend the Constitution).
(54) See, for instance, the discussion in Harvard Human Rights Program, *Economic and Social Rights and the Right to Health (an Interdisciplinary Discussion Held at the Harvard Law School in September 1993)* (1993).
(55) PARKER, HERE THE PEOPLE RULE, *supra*, n. 3, at 115.

# Human Rights and Constitutionalism in Thailand

Vishnu Varunyou

## Introduction.

If a constitution is a legal framework defining relationship between political institutions on the one hand, and relationship between State and its citizens on the other hand, one has to admit that the Thai constitutionalism has always, until the promulgation of the Constitution of October 11th, 1997, focused utmost interest on political structure to the detriment of rights and liberties of the Thai citizens. But this state of things has changed almost radically with the advent of the present Constitution. Massive popular participation in the process of the drafting of this Constitution in 1996 put the emphasis more on Rights and Liberties and, thus, set a great expectation for the improvement of Human Rights situation in Thailand. In this paper I would like to look at some Human rights problems resulting from constitutional stipulations in the past, and then present an overview of the new constitutional arrangement for Human Rights promotion and protection.

## Problems concerning Human rights in Thailand prior to the advent of the Constitution of 1997.

Human rights in Thailand like elsewhere have always been a political lissue and linked with the country's constitutionalism. So when there are problems with the constitutionalsm, they affect rights and liberties of the people unavoidably.

### Discontinuity of the constitution and instability of human rights.

Constitutionalsation of human rights has the merit of making abstract principles become positive rights, didactic and easy to implement to concrete cases. But this is true only in countries where the change of the Charter does not occur too often. In countries where constitutional discontinuity is their main political feature, human rithts have no basis for their secured existence as well. This is no problem for such country as France where haman rights have a source other than the constitution. i.e. *the Declaration des Droits de l'Homme et du Citoyen* de 1789.

Since 1932 after the June Revolution that transformed the political regime of Siam (Thailand) from the Absolute Monarchy to the Constitutional democracy, the country has experienced nine *permanent* constitutions alternating with another eight *provisional* ones.

Usually the *provisional* constitutions had longer life than the *permanent* ones. In general the drafting of these consitutions was affair of a small group of individuals who gained the confidence of those who succeeded in seizing the power by means of military Coups d'Etat. Provisions of these constitutions were conceiver, in most cases, to perpetuate the power of the military oligarchy who hold the riens of power follwing the coups d'Etat. Rights and liberties of the people were not their main concern.

**Technical problem of constitution-drafting.**

Intentionally or unintentionally, the rights and liberties recognised and guaranteed by the constitutions were limited. This was due to the fact that the constitution-drafters used an *emmerative* method to establish the list of rights and liberties recognised and guaranteed by the constitution. This enumerative, thus limitative, character of the constitutional provisions on Human Rights is aggravated by the general tendency to apply *restrictive* method of interpretation to the constitution. This means that, actually that which was not mentionned in the constitution was *not recognised and guaranteed* by the constitution.

Interestingly, we find different *technique* in the famous constitutional texts of the XVIII Century. For example, Amendment IX of the Constitution of the United States reads

"*The emmeration in the Constitution, of certain rights, shall not be construed to deny or disparage others retained by the people*"

Similar writing appears in the famous French *Decharation des Droits de I' Homme et du Citoyen 1789*. At the beginning of the text it is declared chearly that "*l'ignorance, l'oubli ou le mepris des droits de l'Homme sont les seules causes des malheurs publics et de la corruption des Gouvernements, ont resolu d' exposer dans une declaration solennelle, les Droits naturels, inelienables et sacres de l'Homme.*"

**Rights and liberties are of legalistic nature.**

The legalistic nature of Human Rights was evident in the constitutional provisions as these chauses stipulated that enactment of a law was necessary for the practical implementation of the rights and liberties of the people. Automatically this made the provisions on rights and liberties become only the general principles without immediate application. Most rights and liberties became, thus, dead letters and could not be invoked against any body, even in court, so long as no bill was enacted to implement them.

The legalistic nature of Human Rights also presented another interesting problem.

The law was not only a condition *sine qua non* of the implementation of rights and liberties, it could also set up limits for the exercise of rights and liberties. This is why some legislation, such as the Printing Act, was so limitative on freedom of the press that some wonder whether freedom of the press existed at all.

**Absence of mecanism for the enforcement of rights and liberties.**

In the past rights and liberties were listed in the constitutions as general principles only. Their violation did not give rise to any sanction as the constitution-drafters did not design any enforcement mecanism. This was quite a deplorable situation because some cases were clearly against the constitutional provisions.

**Reforms in the Constitution of 1997.**

The present Constitution on the whole is an attempt to establish a more democratic system in place of the old authoritarian power relations. It guarantees a wide range of rights and liberties not only to individuals but to collective entity and community. These rights and liberties are seen as positive rights in a participatory democracy. Looking at the Constitution and the road towards political and social reform it would seem that the democratic forces of the Thai polity has made quite a big stride. On paper, the decentralisation of state powers, the auditing institutions and the increased participation in political, socio-cultural and economic decision and formulation of public policy in these areas were designed as the driving force towards democratic transformation.

**Recognition of a wider range of rights and liberties.**

By using the technique of *emmerating* the Rights and Liberties of the Thai, although one has to admit that the charter drafters sometimes tried to go into minute details, the past Constitutions made them *limitative* in nature. Jurists, particularly the Courts, refused to recognise such right, inter alia, as community's right to environment preservation simply because it was not mentioned in the constitution.

The new Charter clearly adopts a totally new attitude towards this *technique* of constitution-drafting by stipulating general principle clases which govern the interpretation and application of the constitutional provisions on rights and liberties of the people.

Four clauses are particular importance on this matter:

1) Article 26 "In exercising powers of all State authorities, regard shall be had to human dignity, rights and liberties in accordance with the provisions of the Consitution".

2) Article 27 "Rights and liberties recognised by this constitution expressly, by implication or by decisions of the Constitutional Court shall be protected and directly binding on the National Assembly, the Council of Ministers, Courts and other State organs in enacting, applying and interpreting laws" ;

3) Article 28 "A person can invoke human dignity or exercise his or her rights and liberties in so far as it is not in violation of rights and liberties of other persons or contrary to the Constitution or good morals.

A person whose rights and liberties recognised by the Constitution are violated can invoke the provisions of the Constitution to bring a lawsuit or to defend himself or herself in court" ;

4) Article 29 "The restriction of such rights and liberties as recognised by the Constitution shall not be imposed on a person except by virtue of provisions of the law specifically enacted for the purpose determined by this Constitution and only to the extent of necessity and provided that it shall not affect the essential substances of such rights and liberties.

The said law shall be of general application and shall not be intended to apply to any particular case or person; provided that the provision of the Consitution authorising its enactment shall also be mentionned therein

The same shall apply mutatis mutandis to rules or regulations issued by Virtue of the provisions of the law."

## Mecanisms and measures to enforce the constitutional provisions on Human Rights.

As we have discussed earlier, most of the constitutional provisions on rights and liberties of the people were of legalistic nature and, thus were subject to a prior enactment of legislative measures before they could be implemented. More than often these rights and liberties became dead letters as the Government and the Parliament were reluctant to implement them by legislation.

The Constitution provides three interesting measures to help enforce its provisions
on rights and liberties of the people:

1) The constitutional provisions bind and are directly enforcible. Article 28 stipulates that a person whose rights and liberties recognised by the Constitution are violated can invoke the provisions of the Constitution to bring a lawsuit or to defend himself or herself in the court.

2) Where a bill is necessary to implement provisions on rights and liberties, the people are entitled to initiate enactment of such bill. This is clearly stipulated in article 170 which reads:

"The persons having the right to vote of not less than fifty thousand in number shall have a right to submit a petition to the President of the National Assembly to consider such law as prescribed in Chapter 3 (Rights and liberties of the Thai) and Chapter 5 (Directives Principles of Fundamental State Policies) of this Constitution.

A bill must be attached to the petition referred to in the above paragraph"

3) In stating its policies to the National Assembly, the Council of Ministers must clearly state to the National Assembly the activities intended to be carried out for the administration of State affairs in implementation of the directive principles of fundamental State policies and must prepare and submit to the National Assembly an annual report on the result of the implementation, including problems and obstacles encountered.

**Institutions with a mission of protecting and promoting Human Rights.**

According to the new Constitution, three constitutional institutions are set up with a mission of promoting and protecting the rights and liberties of the people.

-The National Human Rights Commission.

The National Human Rights Commision consists of a President and ten other members appointed, by the King with the advice of the Senate, from the persons having apparent knowledge and experiences in the protection of rights and liberties of the people, having regard also to the participation of representatives from private organisations in the field of human rights.

The powers and duties of the National Human Rights Commission are defined

in article 200 of the Constitution which reads:
  The National Human Rights Commission has the powers and duties as follws:
   1) to examine and report the commission or omission of acts which violate human rights or which do not comply with obligations under international treaties to which Thailand is a party, and propose appropriate remedial measures to the person or agency committing or omitting such acts for taking action. In the case where it appears that no action has been taken as proposed, the Commission shall report to the National Assembly for further proceeding;
   2) to propose to the National Assembly and the Council of Ministers policies and recommendations with regard to the revision of laws, rules or regulations for the purpose of promoting and protecting human rights;
   3) to promote education, researches and the dissemination of knowledge on human rights;
   4) to promote co-operation and co-ordination among Government agencies, private organisations, and other organisations in the field of human rights;
   5) to prepare an annual report for the appraisal of situations in the sphere of human rights in the country and submit it to the National Assembly;
   6) other powers and duties as provided by law.
  The National Human Rights Commission also has the power to demand relevant documents or evidence from any person or summon any person to give statements of fact including other powers for the purpose of performing its duties as provided by law.
  -Ombudsman.
  The establishment of the Ombudsman as an institution whereby the people can submit their complaints concerning the maladministration or negligence by the Administration to take into account their rights and liberties has been discussed for quite a long time. Public debate about this institution can be traced back to the years 1970's. It takes nearly years for the Ombudsman to find its place among constitutional institutions in 1997.
  Article 196 of the new Constitution provides that the Ombudsment shall not be more that three in number, who shall be appointed, by the King with the advice of the Senate, from the persons recognised and respected by the public, with knowledge and experience in the administration of the State affairs, enterprises or activities of common interest of the public and with apparent integrity.

The Ombudsmen have the powers and duties as follows:
(1) to consider and inquire into the complaint for factfindings in the following cases:
   b) failure to perform in compliance with the law or performance beyond powers and duties as provided by the law of a Government official, an official or employeed of a State agency, State enterprise or local government organisation.
   c) performance or omission to perform duties of a Government official, an official or employee of a State agency, State enterprise or local government organisation, which unjustly causes injuries to the complainant or the public whether such act is lawful or not;
   d) other cases as provided by law;
(2) to prepare reports and submit opinions to the National Assembly.

In the case where the Ombudsman is of the opinion that the provisions of the law, rules, regulations or any act of any person begs the question of the constitutionality, the Ombudsman shall submit the case and the opinion to the Constitutional Court or Administrative court for decision in accordance with the procedure of the Constitutional Court or Administrative court for decision in accordance with the procedure of the Constitutional Court or the law on procedure of the Administrative Court, as the case may be.

-The Constitutional Court.

This jurisdiction inspired by the German model is of utmost importance. It consists of a President and fourteen judges appointed by the King upon advice of the Senate from the following persons:
(1) five judges of the Supreme Court of Justice holding a position of not lower than Judge of the Supreme Court of Justice and elected at a general meeting of the Supreme Court of Justice by secret ballot;
(2) two judges of the Supreme Administrative Court elected at a general meeting of the Supreme Administrative Court by secret ballot;
(3) five qualified persons in law elected by the Selective Comminttee;
(4) three qualified persons in political sciences elected by the Selective Committee.

Apart from its role in the contral of the constitutional conformity of legislation, the Constitutional Court has a very important normative power in the field of human rights. By its decision, the Constitutional Court can create rights and liberties that are not written down in the Constitution and make them positive rights with a binding force upon all constitutional institutions. Article 27 of the Constitution stipulates "Rights and liberties recognised by this Constitution expressly, by implication or *by decisions of the Constitutional Court* shall be protected and directly binding on the National Assembly, the Council of Ministers, Courts and other State organs in enacting, applying and interpreting laws."

**Master Action Plan for the promotion of Human Rights.**

Another recent development on the issue of the promotion of Human Rights in Thailand that needs to be mentionned here is the preparation of the Master Action Plan. This will be a sort of *vademecum* of public policy-making for the Goverrnment and the Parliament. The preparation of this Master Action Plan which is actually in process calls for a large participation of all parties concerned, from the government agencies to those who work in the people-based organisations.

**Conclusion**

It may be too soon, after only almost two years of the application of the present Constitution, to conclude that Human Rights under the new constitutionalism are a success or a failure. Lots of measures need to be put in place. But participatory democracy according to the Constitution shows good and positive signs of people getting more and more concious of their role and their power to protect their rights and liberties. The only worry that one has is actually whether this Constitution will have a long life!

# Protection of Human Rights through Public Interest Litigation in INDIA

## Parmanand Singh

### I. Introduction

Since the early 1980s the Supreme Court of India has developed a procedure which enables any public spirited citizen or a social activist to mobilize favourable judicial concern on behalf the oppressed classes. The medium through which the access to justice has been democratised is called "Public Interest Litigation" (PIL). Indian PIL is home grown and is the product of distinct social, historical and political forces and has nothing in common with the American Public Interest Litigation. Professor Upendra Baxi, one of India's foremost legal scholar, preferred to describe the new legal phenomenon as 'Social Action Litigation' which was designed to be used only as an instrument of social change to cases genuinely on behalf of the victimised and oppressed classes. American PIL, according to Baxi, was not so much concerned with State repression or governmental lawlessness or with the problems of the rural poor, as with "civic participation in governmental decision-making" and with consumerism or environment[1]. By changing the nomenclature, Baxi wanted to avoid run-away extension of new legal strategy for focusing any conceivable public interest issues. Baxi's anxieties proved to be true because over the years PIL has overwhelmingly been appropriated for corporate, political and personal gains. Today PIL matters focus predominantly on issues concerning environment, consumerism, governmental accountability and political governance. Today it is no more limited to the problems of the poor and the disadvantaged.

This paper avoids the cases which would come within the category of "civic participation" and focuses mainly on the core human rights issues raised through PIL. An attempt has been made here to offer a critique of judicial responses to the issues of governmental lawlessness in general and problems of custodial violence, rape, custodial, death, bonded and child labour in particular. The role of National Human Rights Commission in protecting human rights has also been discussed.

## II. The Evolution of PIL

The British rule bequeathed to India a colonial legal heritage. The Anglo-Saxon model of adjudication insisted upon observance of procedural technicalities such as *locus standi* and adherence to adversarial system of litigation. The result was that the courts were accessible only to the rich and the influential people. The marginalised and disadvantaged groups continued to be exploited and denied basic human rights. The Emergency (1975-1977) period further witnessed colonial nature of the Indian legal system. During emergency State repression and governmental lawlessness was widespread. Thousands of innocent people including political opponents were sent to jails and there was complete deprivation of civil and political rights. The post-emergency period provided an occasion for the judges of the Supreme Court to openly disregard the impediments of Anglo-Saxon procedure in providing access to justice to the poor. The judges also wanted to refurbish the image of the Supreme Court severely tarnished by a judgment[2] given during the emergency which had tacitly supported the repressive regime. Notably two Justices of the Supreme Court, Justice V.R. Krishna Iyer and P.N. Bhagwati recognised the possibility of providing access to justice to the poor and the exploited people by relaxing the rules of standing. In the post-emergency period when the political situations had changed, investigative journalism also began to expose gory scenes of governmental lawlessness, repression, custodial violence, drawing attention of lawyers, judges, and social activists. PIL emerged as a result of an informal nexus of pro-active judges, media persons and social activists.

The first reported case of PIL in 1979 focused on the inhuman conditions of prisons and undertrial prisoners. In *Hussainara Khatoon* v. *State of Bihar*[3], the PIL was filed by an advocate on the basis of a news report highlighting the plight of thousands of undertrial prisoners languishing in various jails in Bihar. This litigation exposed the failure of criminal justice system and led to a chain of proceedings resulting in the release of over 40,000 undertrial prisoners. Rights to speedy justice emerged as a basic fundamental right which had been denied to these prisoners. This litigation also generated public debate on prison reforms, looking to the horrors of prison administration in India.

In 1981 the case of *Anil Yadav* v. *State of Bihar*[4], was more horrifying, depicting barbarity and police brutalities. A news report revealed that about 33 suspected criminals were blinded by police in Bihar through the acid put into their eyes and then their eyes were burnt. In response to a PIL, the Supreme Court deputed its Registrar to visit Bhagalpur and investigate the truth. Through interim orders the court quashed the trial of blinded persons, condemned the police for their cruel act and directed the State government to bring the blinded men to Delhi for medical treatment. It also ordered speedy prosecution of the guilty policemen. The court read right to free legal aid as a fundamental rights of every accused. Sessions judges throughout the country were directed to inform each accused about his fundamental right to legal aid.

*Anil Yadav* signaled the growth of social activism and investigative litigation. High publicity given to the achievement of PIL in this case encouraged more and more PILs on prisons. A social activist moved the Supreme Court on behalf of four tribal boys who had been languishing in jail as undertrials for more than ten years and immediately got them released[5]. The prison cases gave rise to many new rights. In *Citizen for Democracy* v. *State of Assam*[6] the Supreme Court declared that the handcuffs and other fetters shall not be forced upon a prisoner while lodged in jail or while in transport or transit from one jail to another or to the court or back. In this case, a letter was sent to one of the judges of the Supreme Court by a journalist stating that in a hospital in Gauhati, Assam, TADA detenus were kept in one room handcuffed to the bed and tied to a long rope to restrict their movement, inspite of the door being locked from outside and armed policemen guarding them.

The news reports and magazine articles pertaining to children put in jails, employment of child and bonded labour, custodial gangrape, fake encounter deaths, and so on began to form the basis of early PIL. In 1981 Justice P.N. Bhagwati in *S.P. Gupta* v. *Union of India*[7] articulated the concept of PIL as follows:

> Where a legal wrong or a legal injury is caused to a person or to a determinate class of persons by reason of violation of any constitutional or legal right or any burden is imposed in contravention of any constitutional or legal provision or without authority of law or any such legal wrong or legal injury or illegal burden is threatened and such person or determinate

class of persons by reason of poverty, helplessness or disability or socially or economically disadvantaged position unable to approach the court for relief, any member of public can maintain an application for an appropriate direction, order or writ in the High Court under Article 226 and in case any breach of fundamental rights of such persons or determinate class of persons, in this Court under Article 32 seeking judicial redress for the legal wrong or legal injury caused to such person or determinate class of persons.

## III. Features of PIL

It is thus clear that PIL was evolved basically to protect the human rights of the poor, the ignorant and oppressed people who due to lack of resources and knowledge were unable to seek legal redress. It emerged as the most extra-ordinary innovation in the Indian judicial process which has no parallel in the world. Through the mechanism of PIL, the courts seek to protect human rights in the following ways:-

(1) By creating a new regime of human rights by expanding the meaning of fundamental right to equality, life and personal liberty. In this process, right to speedy trial, free legal aid, dignity, means of livelihood, education, housing medical care, clean environment, right against torture, sexual harassment, solitary confinement, bondage and servitude, exploitation and so on emerge as human rights. These new reconceptualised rights provide legal resources to activate the courts for their enforcement through PIL.

(2) By democratisation of access to justice. This is done by relaxing the traditional rule of *locus standi*. Any public spirited citizen or social action group can approach the court on behalf of the oppressed classes. Court's attention can be drawn even by writing a letter or sending a telegram. This has been called epistolary jurisdiction.

(3) By fashioning new kinds of reliefs under the court's writ jurisdiction. For example, the court can award interim compensation to the victims of governmental lawlessness. This stands in sharp contrast to the Anglo-Saxon model of adjudication where interim relief is limited to preserving the *status quo* pending final decision. The grant of compensation in PIL matters does not preclude the aggrieved person from bringing a civil suit for damages. In PIL

cases the court can fashion any relief to the victims.

(4) By judicial monitoring of State institutions such as jails, women's protective homes, juvenile homes, mental asylums, and the like. Through judicial invigilation, the court seeks gradual improvement in their management and administration. This has been characterised as creeping jurisdiction in which the court takes over the administration of these institutions for protecting human rights.

(5) By devising new techniques of fact-finding. In most of the cases the court has appointed its own socio-legal commissions of inquiry or has deputed its own officials for investigation. Sometimes it has taken the help of National Human Rights Commission or Central Bureau of Investigation (CBI) or experts to inquire into human rights violations. This may be called investigative litigation.

## IV. Governmental Lawlessness And Repression

### 1. Custodial Violence

In 1981 two law professors drew the attention of the Supreme Court to the barbaric conditions of the inmates of Agra Protective Home for women. The letter petition, after some initial difficulties, succeeded in securing humane conditions for the inmates[8]. The horrific conditions of institutions for mentally ill in Ranchi and Delhi were chronicled by *R.C. Narain* v. *State of Bihar*[9] and *B.R. Kapoor* v. *Union of India*[10] and in response to PIL, the administration of these institutions was taken out of the hands of local administration and broad guidelines were issued for the better management of these mental asylums. In all these cases commissions were appointed, inquiries conducted and progress had been monitored by Supreme Court judges. The human rights of mentally ill patients were also protected by another PIL which secured release of these patients from jails in Bihar. Many of these patients had been declared sane yet they were kept in jail from 20 to 30 years[11].

In a landmark judgment the Supreme Court ruled that every injured person has a fundamental right to get immediate medical treatment and that a hospital cannot refuse to treat a medico-legal case[12]. Five women prisoners in Bombay city jail were subjected to custodial violence. The Supreme Court issued guidelines applicable to whole of Maharashtra requiring that only police women be used to guard or interrogate women suspects or prisoners[13].

The publicity given to the effects of communal riots, police firings, police excesses, encounter deaths, army excesses, terrorism and insurgency gave rise to a large number of PIL proceedings coupled with mushroom growth of Non-Governmental Organisations (NGOs) and Social Action Groups (SAGs). The response of the courts in handling the cases of police excesses has been mixed one. Immediately after the assassination of Prime Minister Indira Gandhi in 1984 a communal riot occurred in Delhi and other parts of the country in which many members of Sikh community lost their lives. A civil liberties group approached Delhi High Court for appointment of a commission of inquiry and a direction to CBI to conduct an investigation into the role of police. Rejecting these prayers, the High Court, held that in PIL there could be no precedents and directions in PIL could be given only if they were effective. According to the court, there was no need to distrust the police and politicians as they were equally concerned with human rights[14]. The response of the Court was surprising. The statement that in PIL there could be no precedents was false. The judicial response was frustrating in another case brought before the Supreme Court. A PIL was filed about the killing of many innocent people after 'encounters' with police in Uttar Pradesh in 1982 in an attempt to eliminate dacoity. Another PIL related to deaths of innocent people in police 'encounters' in Tamil Nadu in 1980-81 in order to eliminate activists believed to be Naxalites. These petitions were disposed of in *Chaitanya Kalbagh* v. *State of U.P*[15]. In an order passed in 1989 the Supreme Court held that these matters fell within the domain of the state governments and hence in the first instance, the concerned governments should be approached.

In striking contrast to the above approach of judicial reluctance to make police their adversaries, the Supreme Court became very critical about the 'Police Raj' in the country while hearing a PIL alleging police brutalities on a judicial officer in Nadiad, Gujarat. In this case a telegram was sent by an association of Delhi judicial officers to the Supreme Court alleging assault, handcuffing and brutal torture of the Chief Judicial Magistrate, Nadiad, in the streets by certain police officers. The Supreme Court condemned the police brutalities in strongest terms and ordered their punishment in the exercise of its contempt power[16]. A civil liberties group drew the Supreme Court's attention to the police atrocities committed against poor people who were forcibly taken to a police station in Delhi to work there without wages. One person died in police beating. The court awarded Rs. 50,000 as interim compensation to the next of kin of the deceased and ordered the recovery of the amount from delinquent policemen[17]. A nine year old child was beaten to death by police. In response to a PIL the mother of the child got Rs. 75,000 as interim compensation[18]. Illegal detention of a boy aged 21 years was reported to Delhi Police Commissioner who paid no heed to the complaint. The court ordered an inquiry which revealed 51 injuries on the person of the boy as a result of which he had died in police custody. The High Court of Delhi awarded Rs. 5,50,000 as compensation to the next of kin of the deceased[19].

These are few instances of custodial violence where the only way to protect human rights has been to grant compensation. The compensation jurisprudence was most clearly articulated by the Supreme Court in 1993 in *Nilabati Behera* v. *State of Orissa*[20] in response to a PIL alleging death of a boy of 22 years in police custody. The court evolved the principle of public law doctrine of compensation for violation of human rights. According to this doctrine, liability of the state for violation of human rights is absolute and admits of no exception such as sovereign immunity. In this case the court awarded Rs. 1,50,000 to the mother of the boy as compensation for custodial death. In a landmark judgment of 1997 in *D.K. Basu* v. *State of West Bengal*[21], the Supreme Court has given extensive directions applicable to whole of India as to the procedure to be followed by the police upon the arrest of a person and the minimum facilities available to such persons. This PIL originated in 1986 alleging deaths in police-lockup in Calcutta in July and August 1986. The Chairman of Legal Aid Services, West Bengal addressed a letter to the Chief Justice of India stating that custodial violence was not just restricted to West Bengal but occurred all over the country. The letter requested the Supreme court to call for reports about custodial violence from all over India, suggested that a solatium fund be established to give compensation to victims of custodial violence and that procedural safeguards be ordered by the court.

Compensation jurisprudence for custodial violence is one of the positive achievements of PIL but compensation awards seem to be arbitrary and look more like a charity. There is little evidence that the guilty policemen have actually been punished. Even in those cases where prosecution has been launched, the cases remain pending for years in the absence of judicial monitoring of the proceedings.

### 2. Terrorism and Insurgency

The sovereign remedy of granting compensation has become a judicial commonplace in all kinds of human rights violations. A Punjab advocate along with his wife and two year old child was abducted. Later he was killed. The Bar Association of the High Court of Punjab and Haryana brought a PIL. The inquiry revealed the involvement of Punjab police officers in the abduction and murder. In a series of orders given in 1994 and 1996 the Supreme Court directed the Punjab Government to pay as compensation Rs. 1,00,000 to the parents of the deceased[22]. The kidnapping and elimination of advocates in Punjab became a routine matter. In another PIL the Supreme Court directed the CBI to investigate the kidnapping of advocates. Directions were issued to the government to provide security to the families of the advocates against militants[23].

In 1995 a telegram was sent to one of the judges of the Supreme Court stating that Jaswant Singh Khalra, General Secretary, Human Rights Wing of Shiromani Akali Dal had been kidnapped by Punjab police. Khalra's wife also moved the Supreme Court by way of a petition alleging that her husband was picked up by the police at the instance of a Senior Superintendent of Police who had been threatening her husband with dire consequence if he did not withdraw writ petitions challenging police excesses, custodial deaths and police cremation of unclaimed dead bodies in large scale. In *Paramjit Kaur* v. *State of Punjab*[24] the Supreme Court directed the CBI to investigate into the matter and report. The inquiry revealed the truth in the allegations. Referring to mass cremation of persons labeled as unidentified by the Punjab police, the court remarked:

"Our faith in democracy and rule of law assures us that nothing of this type can happen in this country but the allegations in the press note horrendous as they are need thorough investigation[25]." The Supreme Court directed the Punjab government to grant sanction to prosecute the guilty police officers. The government was also directed to pay Rs. 1,00,000 as compensation to Paramjit Kaur. On December 13, 1996 the court placed on record the report of CBI which confirmed that over 585 bodies of persons who had subsequently been identified had in fact been cremated after being labeled as unidentified. The Court held that the families of those identified were entitled to receive compensation to be determined by NHRC[26]. Later, a technical question was raised about the authority of NHRC to investigate a matter after the expiry of one year from the date of incident[27]. In *Paramjit Kaur* v. *State of Punjab*[28] the Supreme Court declared that in the exercise of its power under Article 32 it was open for the court to ask any authority in India to act in the aid of the Supreme Court as laid down in Article 144. The Supreme Court can direct NHRC to deal with any matter. In such a situation the NHRC would function pursuant to the court's direction and not under the Protection of Human Rights Act 1993. In another PIL the Supreme Court awarded Rs. 2,00,000 as compensation to the parents of a person killed as a result of criminal conspiracy of Punjab police[29].

The human rights problem in Jammu and Kashmir has always remained problematic. The situation of terrorism and armed militancy is more acute in this area than any other part of the country. The violations of human rights in Jammu and Kashmir have not been litigated before the courts. The only available PIL on this matter is Hazratbal episode. The militants laid a siege on the Hazratbal shrine in Srinagar and kept innocent people as hostages. Out of 21 persons the condition of two was reported to be very serious. In response to a PIL the Supreme Court affirmed the judgment of the High Court that the government should not put any hurdle to the supply of food and water to the hostages. In a series of directions issued by the court the authorities were required to prepare food packets and supply them to the inmates at the iron bar fencing of the shrine[30].

There are few cases of army excesses. In one case about 81 tribals lost their lives on account of Army Test Firing Range in a place in Madhya Pradesh. A PIL resulted in the closure of test firing range[31]. Through a PIL the Supreme Court was informed about the loss of life of several villagers due to indiscriminate firing in certain villages in Nagaland by para-military forces. The court ordered a judicial inquiry into the incident[32].

The Assam Disturbed Areas Act 1955 and the Armed Forces (Special Powers) Act 1958 confer wide ranging powers to the Army, preventing judicial intervention in army excesses. Even the NHRC has no power to hear complaints against armed forces.

## 3. Violence Against Women

Women's issues have increasingly been brought before the Supreme Court with the growth of women's movement and investigative journalism exposing harassment for dowry, rape, sexual harassment and discrimination. It is widely perceived that investigation into crimes against women have been unsatisfactory and in some cases even the judges have shown gender bias. Then there are complaints about long delays in final disposal of cases not only in lower courts but also in higher courts. We mention here a couple of PIL proceedings involving gender issues.

In *Delhi Domestic Working Women's Forum* v. *Union of India*[33], the PIL arose out of indecent sexual assault by seven army personnel against six domestic servants traveling in train from Ranchi to Delhi. The Supreme Court, with a view to assisting rape victims, has laid down various broad guidelines. These guidelines include the legal assistance, anonymity, compensation and rehabilitation to rape victims. The National Commission for Women was directed to evolve a scheme for providing adequate safeguards to these victims. In another significant pronouncement, *Vishaka* v. *State of Rajasthan*[34], the Supreme Court declared that sexual harassment of women at workplace constitutes violation of gender equality and right to dignity which are fundamental rights. Taking note of the fact that the existing civil and penal laws in India did not provide adequate safeguards against sexual harassment at work place, the court laid down 12 guidelines to be followed by every employer to ensure prevention of sexual harassment. Most importantly, the court ruled that all courts in India must construe the contents of fundamental rights in the light of international conventions so long as such conventions were not inconsistent with fundamental rights.

Before we conclude this section it would be worthwhile to mention a case to show the deficiencies of the criminal justice system in handling rape cases. One Guntaben was gangraped by policemen of Gujarat. She was stripped naked by policemen before a crowd and subsequently raped by several policemen in the cabin of a truck. An advocate filed a PIL. The incident occurred in 1986. The investigation ordered by the Supreme Court took evidence of 504 persons and even then the CBI took many years to complete the investigation. The hearing was adjourned several times. The CBI report revealed that the State government failed to take action against the policemen despite the report of the inquiry commission appointed by the Supreme Court. The case was heard several times between 1986 and 1993 and two commissions were appointed. Pending the completion of inquiries by the State government, the Supreme Court awarded Rs. 50,000 as compensation to Guntaben by its order in 1993[35]. A news report revealed the rape of 25 tribal women in certain areas of Western Tripura by army personnel of Assam Rifles. In response to a PIL the inquiry report confirmed rape of some of these women. The Assam Rifles and the State government did their best to hush up the crimes. Due to the failure of the State to file a timely reply the case remained pending for long time[36].

The judicial response in addressing the injustices to women has not been satisfactory. Even where the courts have directed inquiries, this has taken many years. Recourse to PIL has been futile in many cases relating to custodial rape. The broad guidelines issued by the Supreme Court on rape trial and sexual harassment have remained largely of academic interest.

### 4. Bonded Labour

In India the bonded labour system continues to be the most pernicious form of human bondage. Under such system a worker continues to serve his master in consideration of a debt obtained by him or his ancestors. Bondage can be inter-generational or child bondage or loyalty bondage or bondage through land allotment. According to an early study there were 26,17,000 bonded labourers only in ten States[37]. Most of these labourers come from lowest strata of the society such as the untouchables, *adivasis* or agricultural labourers. It occurred to the Indian government only in 1976 to pass a central legislation, Bonded Labour System (Abolition) Act 1976. After the Act came into force bonded labour system has been abolished atleast on paper and the practice of bonded labour has been made punishable.

Most of the PIL proceedings on bonded labour seek to implement the Act. The first major PIL on this issue was *Bandhua Mukti Morcha* v. *Union of India*[38], filed in 1981 and decided on December 16, 1983. The action was brought for the identification, release and rehabilitation of hundreds of bonded labourers working in the stone quarries of Haryana. The opinion of Justice P.N. Bhagwati going beyond the Act, defined bonded labour which was forced by economic hardship. The court issued 21 directions to Haryana government. During the proceedings, the court monitored its own directions and appointed a number of commissions of inquiry. Unfortunately most of the directions remained unimplemented for many years. The Court acknowledged its limited capacity in monitoring the schemes of rehabilitation. Ultimately, in 1992 the court recounted the history of the case and was shocked that there was not the slightest improvement in the conditions of the workers of the stone quarries[39]. The litigation ended up with one more warning to the government to be responsive to judicial directions.

In *Neeraja Chaudhary* v. *State of M.P*[40]., a letter was sent to the Supreme Court stating that many bonded labourers who were released by *Bandhua Mukti Morcha* case had returned home but were awaiting rehabilitation even after six month of their release. The Supreme Court directed the appointment of Vigilance Committee for the rehabilitation of these starving people. Despite the initial failure of *Bandhua Mukti Morcha* case in terms of effectiveness PIL were brought before the courts for the liberation of bonded labourer in Madhya Pradesh[41], Tamil Nadu[42], Bihar[43] and other States.

In our view the public interest actions focusing on the plight of bonded labourers have to some extent helped the implementation of the Act. The basic flaw, however, in the implementation this Act is that emphasis is being placed only on the identification, release and rehabilitation of bonded labourers. There is no effort to punish the owners of these labourers. The real emancipation of bonded labourers would be achieved not by cutting them off from the life support system but rather by allowing them to work where they are working. The government must ensure them a reasonable wage and better living conditions.

## 5. Children

Public interest actions on children have sought the implementation of constitutional and statutory obligations towards children[44]. Early PIL cases focused on the children in prisons. In 1981 the Supreme Court's attention was drawn to a news report about sexual exploitation of children by hardened criminals in Kanpur jail[45]. The Court directed the District Judge, Kanpur to visit the jail and report. The report confirmed the crime of sodomy committed against the children. The court directed the release of the children from jail and their shifting to children's Home. No punishment was ordered to the administrators of the jail. Another PIL exposed the inhuman conditions of children in Tihar Jail, Delhi[46]. Sexual exploitation of children in Orissa jails also formed the subject matter of PIL[47].

A major PIL on juveniles in jails was filed by a journalist in 1985. The petition asked for release of children below the age of sixteen and for information on the number of such children. The court was also asked to ensure that adequate facilities were provided for the children in the form of juvenile courts, homes and schools, that district judges should be directed to visit jails and so on. There were many orders from 1985 onwards which remained unimplemented for a long time[48]. In the meantime Parliament passed Juvenile Justice Act 1986. The court's attention was now diverted to the implementation of Act. Being disappointed with many adjournments and repeated non-compliance of judicial directions the petitioner tried to withdraw the petition which was declined[49]. Then the Supreme Court Legal Aid Committee pursued the case. In its final order in 1989 the Supreme Court stressed the need to create juvenile courts, homes and schools. A committee of advocates was appointed to prepare a draft scheme for the proper implementation of the Act. PIL in this case was ultimately effective as of today the country has no juvenile delinquents in jails[50].

We may now briefly address to the problem of child labour. PIL on child labour began in early 1980s in response to a large number of news reports exposing the exploitation of children in fire works and match factories of Sivakasi in Tamil Nadu and in carpet industries in Mirzapur, Uttar Pradesh. The investigative journalism coupled with PIL cases led to the passing of Child Labour (Prohibition and Regulation) Act 1986. This Act prohibits the employment of children in hazardous industries.

In response to a PIL the Supreme Court appointed a commission of inquiry on the child labour in carpet industries in Uttar Pradesh. The report indicated high incidence of child labour. With the help of local administration these children were released[51]. In 1986 a major PIL was brought before the Supreme Court complaining that thousands of children were employed in match factories in Sivakasi, Tamil Nadu[52]. These children were exposed to fatal accidents occurring frequently in the manufacturing process of matches and fire works. The court directed the state government to enforce Factories Act and to provide facilities for recreation, medical care and basic diet to the children during working works and facilities for education. The court also advocated a scheme of compulsory insurance for both adult and children employed in hazardous industries. Every employee had to be insured for a sum of Rs. 50,000. A committee was appointed to monitor the judicial directions. It is rather surprising that although the Child Labour (Prohibition and Regulation) Act 1986 has banned the employment of children in manufacture of matches yet the court in this case permitted the child labour in the process of packing because "tender hands of the young workers were more suitable to the task." The court here failed to recognise that manufacture and packing of matches is inseparable. In a sense, in this case the response of the court on child labour was superficial.

In its final judgment delivered in 1996 the Supreme Court directed that the offending employer of child labour in match factories will pay Rs. 20,000 which would then be deposited in a Child-Labour-Rehabilitation-Cum-Welfare-Fund[53]. The children illegally employed would receive education at the cost of the employer. This is a happy development.

The above discussion shows that in cases involving prisons the PIL actions have ultimately provided impressive results. But the PIL activism on child labour has been unsatisfactory. Some countries still continue to refuse to purchase goods made through the employment of child labour. Frequent reference is being made to International Conventions on the rights of the child. The real solution lies not in the displacement of child labour and pay compensation to them but in launching a massive developmental programme especially in irrigation programmes so that the land owning parents experiencing economic recovery might withdraw their children from exploitative labour. Problem of child labour cannot be eliminated by judicial activism alone in the face of capitalist development and global power relations. Complete absence of data on the prosecution of the employers of the child labour is disturbing.

## V. **Role of National Human Rights Commission (NHRC)**

1. Composition

National Human Rights Commissions came into being through an Ordinance promulgated on 23 September 1993 presumably under some foreign pressure. The Ordinance was replaced by an Act called Protection of Human Rights Act 1993 which received Presidential assent in January 1994. Appointments to NHRC are made with the consultation of committee consisting of the Prime Minister (Chair), Speaker of Lok Sabha, Minister-in-charge of the Ministry of Home Affairs, Leaders of opposition in Lok Sabha and Rajya Sabha, and Deputy Chairman, Rajya Sabha[54]. The NHRC consists of a chairperson who must have been a Chief Justice of the Supreme Court, one member who is or has been, a Judge of the Supreme Court, one member who is or has been the Chief Justice of a High Court and two members to be appointed from amongst persons having knowledge of or practical experience in matters relating to human rights. Besides the above, the chairpersons of the National Commission for Minorities, the National Commission for the Scheduled Castes and Scheduled Tribes and the National Commission for Women are the ex-officio members of the commission[55]. The members of NHRC can be removed by President only on the ground of proved misbehaviour or incapacity on an inquiry by the Supreme Court[56].

## 2. Functions, Powers and Procedure

The function of the Commission is to inquire into complaints of violation of human rights. It can also *intervene* in a judicial proceeding involving allegation of human rights violations, *visit* any state institution, *promote* research on human rights, *spread* human rights literacy, *encourage* social activism, and *review* the existing human rights laws and recommend measures for their effective implementation[57]. The Commission enjoys the powers of the civil court while inquiring into the complaints under the Act[58]. It enjoys investigative power and can utilise the services of any governmental investigative agency[59].

While inquiring into the complaints of violations of human rights, the Commission may call for information or report from the concerned government or any authority and satisfy itself as to the action taken by the government in the matter. It may make its own inquiries if there is no response from the concerned government[60].

After the completion of the inquiry under the Act, the Commission may take any of the following steps[61]. It may;
(i) *recommend* prosecution of the guilty public servant;

( ii ) *approach* the Supreme Court or High Court for appropriate directions; or
(iii) *recommend* the sanction of interim monetary relief to the victim or his or her family.

It is thus clear that the NHRC has no power to take any binding decisions. It has to depend either on the apex court or High Court or the concerned governments. Its recommendations have no legal weight. The commission receives thousands of complaints from individuals and civil liberties groups and in majority of cases it calls for information or report from the concerned government. In most of the cases it uses 'post office' procedure which consists of asking the State governments to investigate the incidents of human rights violations and inform it about the action taken. In some cases it asks the CBI to investigate and report. The investigative power possessed by it is very rarely exercised.

### 3. Performance of NHRC

An analysis of annual report of NHRC for the year 1995-96 would be sufficient to show the effectiveness of NHRC in protecting human rights.

(1) **Terrorism and Insurgency**

The commission's role has been limited to the visit of certain areas of terrorism and insurgency especially in Jammu and Kashmir, North-East States and Punjab. It kept a 'close touch' with CBI investigating into the 'disappearance' of J.S. Khalra in the presence of Punjab police. On reading a press report about the death of a person in army custody the commission issued notice to the defence ministry as a result of which a court of inquiry was ordered[62].

(2) **Custodial Deaths, Rape and Torture**

The commission has required every District Magistrate/Superintendent of police to report to the commission every incidence of custodial death or rape. This is a welcome step but has no legal weight. From the available data, the commission notes the increase in the number of custodial deaths. It has recommended that India should become a party to the 1984 Convention Against Torture and Other Forms of Cruel, Inhuman and Degrading Treatment or Punishment. This is a defferent matter that the government has paid no heed to this recommendation.

The commission has also recommended interim compensation in every incident of custodial death. The report advocates amendments to law of evidence and criminal procedure[63].

(3) **Systematic Reform; Police, Prisons and other centres of Detention**

The report favours the implementation of 1979 report of Police Reforms Commission suggesting complete independence of police from political interference. The Commission's visits to various jails in the country has revealed gross overcrowding, squalor and mal-administration and therefore it suggests the need to amend Indian Prison Act 1894. The conditions of homes for juveniles were found to be equally appalling crying out for reform[64].

### TABLE-I
### Showing Commission's Handling of Cases

1. South Goa     1994
Custodial death (Reported by District Magistrate) – Commission called for information and report. The State government reported its decision to prosecute the police officers.

2. Uttar Pradesh     1994
Custodial death (report by Amnesty International) – Commission called for report. On receiving the report from the state government it recommended prosecution of the guilty police men.

3. Bihar     1986-1991
Custodial deaths (reported by State government) – The Commission sent its investigation team to the concerned cities and recommended action against guilty policemen.

4. Nagaland     1994
Custodial death (reported by a police officer) – Upon Commission's intervention compensation (Rs. 1,00,000) paid to the victim's relatives by Ministry of Defence.

5. Tamil Nadu     1994
Custodial Rape (reported by a Collector) – The state government reported its intention to launch prosecution against the guilty policemen and award of Rs. 1,00,000 as compensation to rape victim.

6. Madhya Pradesh     1994
Rape (reported by Sakshian, NGO) – The Commission wrote to Chief Secretary to take action. Subsequently a case was registered against the alleged culprit.

7. Rajasthan     1994
Rape (Suo moto action) – The Commission wrote a letter to the Chief Minister to file an appeal against the acquittal of the accused by the trial court.

8. Maharashtra

Sexual abuse of a minor girl (reported by PUCL) - The NHRC's investigation officer visited the place. Upon commission's intervention a case of rape and torture was registered against the accused.

9. Kerala
Stripping of teenagers in police-lock up (Suo moto action) - Upon Commission's intervention compensation paid to the victim and the police officers suspended.

10. Karnataka      1995
Police highhandedness (reported by a leader of opposition) - Commission's Investigation team visited the affected area. The state government assured action.

11. West Bengal      1995
Mistreatment by police ( reported by victim) - Commission recommended CID inquiry. Inquiry established the guilt of police officers. The commission suggested action against them.

12. Punjab      1993
Police Killing (reported by PUCL) - The Commission expressed its concern over State government's report about the innocence of the police.

13. Bihar      1995
Killing of an activist in police firing (Suo moto action) - Commission recommended expeditious investigation and payment of compensation to the next of kin of the deceased.

14. Arunachal Pradesh      1994-1995
Violation of Rights of Chakma Refugees (reported by NGOs) - Commission issued directions to the State government which proved futile. Then it moved the Supreme Court which issued directions to the government.

15. Manipur      1994-1995
Torture and Killing of Kuki Refugees by militants (reported by NGO) - Commission recommended expeditious solution of the problem between Nagas and Kukis.

16. Haryana      1995
Killing's by firecracker's blast (Suo moto action) - Commission calls for report from Government. Recommended compensation to the next of kin of the deceased persons.

17. Punjab      1994
Kidnapping by police (reported by victim's father) - Upon the intervention of the commission action initiated against the guilty police officer.

18. Bihar      1994
Encounter deaths (reported by victim's wife) - Upon the intervention of commission action initiated against the police. Recommended compensation of 1,00,000 to the widow.

19. Gujarat      1993
Communal Killings (reported by relatives) - Upon the intervention of the commission compensation of Rs. 2,00,000 sanctioned by the government to heirs of persons killed in communal riot after the demolition of Babri Masjid.

20. Orissa    1995
   Discriminatory treatment to a life convict (reported by victim's wife) – Upon the intervention of the Commission, the Orissa Government remitted the unexpired portion of the sentence passed on a life convict.

## 4. Handling of Complaints: Illustrative Cases

The report gives illustrative cases handled by the commission. TABLE I give the glimpse of the way the NHRC functions.

An analysis of the above cases handled by the Commission shows that in most of the cases it has followed the 'post office' procedure, namely, issuing a notice, calling for a report and recommending the sanction of compensation or action against the culprits. The report shows that the Commission has very rarely exercised its own investigative powers. In one case, it had taken up the case of Chakma refugees to the Supreme Court. The Chakmas who had emigrated from Bangladesh and settled in Arunachal Pradesh were facing threats to their life from a militant group. The Supreme Court directed that the state government would ensure protection of life and liberty of these refugees[65]. In April 1999 the NHRC had recommended to the Rajasthan government to sanction compensation of Rs. 2,50,000 to the parents of a kidnapped boy killed by the police during a rescue operation[66].

In June, 1999 it has taken up the complaints by the displaced persons from Kashmir valley, alleging that the violence perpetrated by the militants was designed to eliminate Kashmiri pandits. The NHRC has recommended to the Central government to enhance the assistance given to Kashmiri migrants[67].

In sum, it may be said that at the level of performance of the commission so much is left at the level of suggestions and recommendations which are devoid of any legal weight.

## VI. Concluding Remarks:

The presence of NHRC has atleast made human right violation more visible and has enhanced the public awareness about the human values. It has also been taking all possible steps to promote a culture of human rights through media publicity, human rights seminars and human rights education for police, para-military and armed personnel and in the system of general education. At times it has drawn the attention of the concerned State governments to be accountable to human rights and bring the human right violators to the book.

PIL has undoubtedly produced astonishing results unthinkable two decades ago. Degraded bonded labourers, tortured undertrails and women prisoners, humiliated inmates of Protective Women's Home, blinded prisoners, exploited children and many others have been liberated through judicial intervention. What happened after their liberation is, however, very little known.

The greatest contribution of PIL has been to enhance the accountability of the governments towards the human rights of the poor. The judges acting alone cannot provide effective responses to state lawlessness but they can surely seek a culture formation where political power becomes increasingly sensitive to human rights. When people's rights are invaded by dominant elements, PIL emerges as a medium of struggle for protection of their human rights. The legitimacy which PIL enjoys in the Indian legal system is unprecedented. PIL activism interrogates power and makes the courts as people's court. Even if human rights have not adequately been protected through judicial endeavours, the courts shall remain the site for human rights struggle.

The gap between political commitments and performance has resulted in chronic over commitment of the judges to enlarge justice. In early 1980s PIL was understood as a medium through which judicial process was made easily accessible to those who were on their own unable to approach the court. Today PIL is being used to cure all ills afflicting the Indian society. The overload of judicial commitments has resulted in massive flow of justice-seekers demanding relief from all kinds of anxieties, miseries and injustices. Almost anything under the sun is now attracting judicial attention. Insanitary structures, garbage, pollution, preservation of cultural heritage, political corruption, disease, unemployment, housing, failure of education and drug policy, and a horde of other 'public interest' issues are demanding remedial attention. It seems that PIL matters today focus more and more on the interests of the Indian middle-classes rather than on the oppressed classes. PIL seeking order to ban *Koran*[68], transmission of T.V. serials[69], implementation of consumer protection law[70], removal of corrupt ministers[71], invalidation of irregular allotment of petrol pumps[72] and government accommodation[73], prosecution of politicians and bureaucrats for accepting bribes and kickbacks through *Hawala* transactions[74], better service conditions of the members of lower judiciary[75], removal of Governor from office[76], or quashing, selection of university teachers[77], are some blatant examples espousing middle class interests. Typically PIL is initiated and controlled by elites and is governed by their own choices and priorities. Different social action groups have different agendas and ideologies. Most of these groups lack sustained commitment to any specific victimised groups. PIL actions are largely episodic and in response to the happening of an event published in newspapers. In my view, overuse of PIL for every public interest matter might dilute the original commitment to use this remedy only on behalf of the oppressed classes.

There is yet another disturbing feature. Some PIL matters concerning the exploited and disadvantaged groups are pending for many years. Inordinate delays in the disposal of PIL cases may rendered many leading judgments merely of academic value. Then there is the problem of willful defiance of judicial directions. Surprisingly, the courts are unwilling to punish the violators of their own orders through the exercise of their contempt power. Frequent defiance of judicial order might also dilute the credibility of the courts. Be that as it may, PIL has come to stay in India and cannot easily be wished away. Some initial successes of PIL, however, cannot certify that it shall always remain an effective instrument for protection of human rights. The future of PIL will depend upon who uses it and for whom.

[1] Upendra Baxi "Taking Suffering Seriously: Social Action Litigation in the Supreme Court of India" in Baxi (ed.) *Law and Poverty*, 387-415 at 389 (1988).
[2] *A.D.M. Jabalpur* v. *Shivkant Shukla* AIR 1976 SC 1207.
[3] AIR 1979 SC 1360. This Case was finally disposed of in August 1995.
[4] AIR 1982 SC 1008.
[5] *Kadra Pahadia* v. *State of Bihar* AIR 1981 SC 939.
[6] (1995) 3 SCC 743, 750.
[7] 1981 (Supp), SCC 87,210.
[8] *Upendra Baxi* v. *State of Uttar Pradesh* 1981 (3) SCALE 1136.
[9] 1986 (Supp) SCC 576.
[10] AIR 1990 SC 752.
[11] *Veena Sethi* v. *State of Bihar* (1982) 2 SCC 583.
[12] *Parmanand Katara* v. *Union of India* AIR 1989, SC 2039.
[13] *Sheela Barse* v. *State of Maharashtra* AIR 1983, SC 378.
[14] *PUCL* v. *Ministry of Home Affairs* AIR 1985 Delhi 268. But in *R. Gandhi* v. *Union*

of India AIR 1989 Madras 205, the High Court of Madras granted compensation for violation of human rights of the Sikh comunity in the riot after the assasination of Smt. Indira Gandhi in 1984.

[15] AIR 1989, SC 1452.
[16] *Delhi Judicial Service Association, Tis Hazari Court Delhi* v. *State of Gujarat* AIR 1991, SC 2176.
[17] *PUDR* v. *Commissioner of Police, Delhi* 1989 (1) SCALE 114 [599].
[18] *Saheli* v. *Commissioner of Police, Delhi* AIR 1990, SC 513.
[19] *Geeta* v. *Lt. Governor, Delhi* 1998 Delhi Law Times 822.
[20] AIR 1993, SC 1961. The idea of awarding interim monetary relief was articulated in early cases of *Rudol Shah* v. *State of Bihar* AIR 1983, SC 1086; *Sebastian M. Hongary* v. *Union of India* AIR 1984, SC 571; *Bhim Singh* v. *State of J & K* AIR 1986, SC 494.
[21] (1997) 1 SCC 416.
[22] *Punjab and Haryana High Court Bar Association, Chandigarh* v. *State of Punjab* (1994) 1 SCC 616, and (1996) 4 SCC 742.
[23] *Navkiran Singh* v. *State of Punjab* (1995) 4 SCC 591.
[24] (1996) 7 SCC 20.
[25] *Id.* at 26.
[26] (1996) 8 SCALE SP 6.
[27] Section 36 (2) of the Protection of Human Right Act 1993 states that NHRC shall not inquire into any matter after the expiry of one year from the date on which the act constituting violation of human rights is alleged to have been committed.
[28] (1998) 5 SCALE 219.
[29] *Ranjit Kumar* v. *Secretary of Home Affairs, Punjab* 1996 (2) SCALE 51.
[30] *State of J & K* v. *J & K High Court Bar Association* 1994 (Supp) 3 SCC 708.
[31] *Sudip Majumdar* v. *State of M.P.* (1996) 5 SCC 368.
[32] *PUCL* v. *Union of India* 1996 (3) SCALE 5.
[33] (1995) 1 SCC 14.
[34] (1997) 6 SCC 241. This principle was reiterated in *Apparel Export Promotion Council* v. *A.K. Chopra* AIR 1999, SC 634.
[35] *P. Rathinam* v. *Union of India* 1987 (2) SCALE 317, 1993 (2) SCALE 126.
[36] *All India Democratic Women's Association* v. *State of Tripura* W.P. (C) No. 385 of 1988 and W.P. (Cr.) No. 366 of 1988 (Unreported).
[37] M. Sharma, "Bonded Labour in India: A National Survey On the Incidence of Bonded Labour, Final Report 1981, *Academy of Gandhian Studies* Hyderabad, 1981.
[38] (1984) 4, SCC 161.
[39] *Bandhua Mukh Morcha* v. *Union of India* AIR 1992 SC 38.
[40] AIR 1984, SC 1099.
[41] *Mukesh Advani* v. *State of M.P.* AIR 1985 SC 1363.
[42] *H.P. Sivaswamy* v. *State of Tamil Nadu* 1983 (2) SCALE 45.
[43] *T. Chakkalackal* v. *State of Bihar*, JT 1992 (1) SC 106.
[44] Article 15 (3), 24, 39 (e), 39(f) and 45 of the Constitution of India Juvenile Justice Act 1986, Child Labour (Prohibition and Regulation) Act 1986.
[45] *Munna* v. *State of UP* (1982) 1 SCC 545.
[46] *Sanjay Suri* v. *Delhi Administration* 1987 (2) SCALE 276.
[47] *M.C. Mehta* v. *State of Orissa* W.P. (Cr) 1504 of 1984 (Unreported).
[48] *Sheela Barse* v. *Union of India* AIR 1986 SC 1773.
[49] *Sheela Barse* v. *Union of India* AIR 1988 SC 2211.

[50] *SCLAC* v. *Union of India* (1989) 2 SCC 325. On 17 March 1989 the court again issued directions to every district judge of report to the court as to the exact position of juveniles in jails, setting up of juvenile homes, special homes and observation homes. In *SCLAC* v. *Union of India* (1989) 4 SCC 738 the Court expressed its satisfaction that except in Andaman and Nicobar, a Union Territory, no State had kept the children in jails.
[51] *Bandhua Mukti Morcha* v. *Union of India* 1986 (Supp) SCC 553.
[52] *M.C. Mehta* v. *State of Tamil Nadu* AIR 1991 SC 417.
[53] *M.C. Mehta* v. *State of Tamil Nadu* 1996 (1) SCALE 42.
[54] Protection of Human Rights Act 1993, Section 4.
[55] Section 2.
[56] Section 5.
[57] Section 12.
[58] Section 13.
[59] Section 14.
[60] Section 17.
[61] Section 18.
[62] National Human Rights Commission: Annual Report 1995-1996 ; para 3.1-3.13.
[63] Paras 3-14-3-22.
[64] Para 3-23-3-38.
[65] *National Human Rights Commission* v. *State of Arunchal Pradesh* 1996 (1) SCC 742.
[66] *The Hindustan Times*, Delhi, April 25, 1999.
[67] *The Hindustan Times*, Delhi, June 12 and 14 1999.
[68] *Chandanmal Chopra* v. *State of West Bengal* AIR 1986 Cal. 104.
[69] *Odyssey Communications (P) Ltd.* v. *Lokvidayan Sangathan* (1988) 3 SCC 410.
[70] *Common Cause* v. *Union of India* (1996) 2 SCC 752.
[71] *D. Satyanarayana* v. *N.T. Rama Rao* AIR 1988 A.P. 144.
[72] *Centre for Public Interest Litigation* v. *Union of India* 1995 (Supp) 3 SCC 382.
[73] *Shiv Sagar Tiwari* v. *Union of India* (1996) 6 SCC 558.
[74] *Vineet Narain* v. *Union of India* (1996) 2 SCC 199.
[75] *All India Judges Association* v. *Union of India* AIR SC 165.
[76] *Kasturi Radha* v. *President of India* AIR 1990 Mad. 116.
[77] *Bishwajeet Sinha* v. *Dibrugarh University* AIR 1992 SC 165.

# Judge-Made Constitutionalism in Democratizing Taiwan
—The Role of the Council of Grand Justices and Protection of Individual Rights

## Hwang Jau-Yuan

## I. Introduction

In July 1987, Taiwan[1] lifted its 38-year long martial rule, which marked a milestone event in Taiwan's liberalization process beginning from early 1980s. Four years later, in May 1991, the Taiwanese government formally terminated the so-called "Period of Mobilization and Suppression of Communist Rebellion" and started a series of political reforms towards a full democracy. At the heart of democratization have been the multiple-stage constitutional reforms, which finally brought about the first direct, popular presidential election in March 1996.[2]

Genuine constitutionalism will be hard to flourish without democracy. Taiwan is no exeption. As Taiwan moved towards a full-fledged liberal democracy, its judiciary soon followed and responded with more aggressive judicial activism, particularly on those cases involving individual rights.[3] No doubt, implementation of constitutional mandates is a common responsibility shared by all threee governmental branches. It is, however, the judiciary, entrusted with the power of judicial review, provides the citizens with fhe final judicial remedy for infringement of their constitutional rights. Equally important is the ability and function of the judiciary to formulate working doctrines (rules, principles and concepts) to implement the abstract constitution on a case-by-case basis.[4] From this perspective, what constitutionalism means in a real life will depend, to a certain extent, on whether, when, what and how the judges say. In this paper, I first examine the role of Taiwan's judiciary (the Council of Grand Justices) on implementing constitutional rights, and then attempt to identity the limits thereto.

## II. Status and Functions of the Council of Grand Justices under Taiwanese Constitution[5]

### 1. Status
The Council of Grand Justices is Taiwan's equivalent of constitutional court,

and has been the only organ that can exercise the power of constitutional review. It has been responsible for deciding constitutional disputes, among others.[6] Since its establishment in 1948, the Council has been a separate organ under the Judicial Yuan, which supervises the judicial administration.[7] Nevertheless, the Judicial Yuan wields no power to intervene the function of the Council, in a formal sense.

## 2. Organization

At present, the Council consists of seventeen Grand Justices, appointed by the President with the consent of the National Assembly. Each Justice serves for a term of nine years and is eligible for unlimited re-appointment. Beginning from 2003, however, the number of Grand Justices will be reduced to fifteen, while each Justice serves for a term of only eight years and no-reappointment is allowed any more.[8] Currently, each Grand Justice has one law clerk to assist his or her in researching or drafting opinions.

## 3. Qualifications

During the past twenty years, almost all the Grand Justices are university-trained lawyers, chosen from law professors, judges, public prosecutors and government officials. Above all, about one half of the total members were full-time university professors, with Ph.D. degrees from overseas universities, particularly Germany.

## 4. Proceedings

The Grand Justices meet and function in the form of conference (council), rather than court. Most conference meetings of the Grand Justices are held in secret, with rare exceptions of public hearings. Even in public hearings, the Justices barely ask any questions. They just sit and listen to the presentations of both parties. There has been no cross-examination by either party.

## 5. Forms of Opinions

The decisions of the Council are calles "Interpretations." It takes an super majority of at least two-thirds votes to pass any constitutional interpretation, with two-thirds of members present. All Interpretations, that is, the majority opinions, are to be signed by all Justices. However, individual Justices are allowed to issue either concurrent or dissenting opinions.

## III. The Real Role of the Council of Grand Justices in Implementing Constitutional Rights

In this section, I will examine the overall performance of the Council and discuss some important Interopretations renderd by it.

### 1. Overall Performance of the Council

From 1988 to June 1999, the Council received a total of 3311 petitions and terminated 3209 petitions. Of these 3209 terminated cases, 2843 petitions were dismissed on procedural grounds and only 266 Interpretations were rendered. Among the 266 Interpretations, 236 cases involve constitutional rights. Furthermore, of these 236 Interpretations, there are 114 cases declaring unconstitutional either statutes, regulations or court precedents. Judged by this statistics,[9] it appears that the Council has been active in enforcing the guarantee of constitutional rights, particularly after lifting of martial rule.[10]

### 2. Wider Access to the Council

Though Taiwan's judicial review is clearly a centralized system, the Council itself has significantly widened access to the Council over the past twe decades. Under the current *Act Governing Proceedings of the Council of Grand Justices of the Judicial Yuan*, any highest governmental branches at the either central or local level, one-third of the members of the Legislative Yuan, or individuals (including legal entities and political parties) may petition for constitutional interpretations.[11] In January 1995, the Council issued Interpretation No. 371, which further allowed each judge to suspend the litigation at trial and to petition to the Council for review of constitutionality of the applicable laws.[12] This milestone Interpretation opened a wide door for many young and untamed judges to challenge many outdated or controversial laws left over from the martial rule period.[13] However, since 1988, private citizens brought about more than 90% of petitions.[14] This phenomenon was partly attributed to the landmark Interpretation No. 177 of 1982. In this Interpretation, the Council expressly mandated any final judgments of either civil, criminal or administrative court be re-tried, if the applicable laws to that specific judgment is declared unconstitutional. With this Interpretation, whoever loses the litigation may always be able to petition to the Council to challenge constitutionality of the laws as applied by the court to his/her case. Once the Council finds that law unconstitutional, the petitioner is entitled to re-trial of his/her own case. In practice, Interpretation No. 177 has significantly induced more and more private citizens to petition to the Council for extraordinary remedy. That explains why the overall caseload of the Council has been rapidly growing, and most petitions are initiated by individuals.[15] With its own Interpretations of No. 177 and 371, the Council did effectively transform itself from a "Guardian of Constitutional Order" to "Guardian of Constitutional Ringhts."[16]

### 3. Increasing Judicial Activism on Individual Rights Cases

The Councils' gradual transformation towards a more effective protector of individual rights is also evident in its increasing judicial activism on individual rithts cases. In early 1990s, the Council's rulings on individual rights cases were still often compromised by considerations of national security or public interests. For example, the Council once upheld constitutional both the National Security Act and its enforcting rules, arbitrarily restricting the citizens' right to return Taiwan from abroad.[17] Another Interpretation also upheld constitutional the same law depriving those civilian defendants, tried by court martial, of their rights to appeal to the ordinary court after lifting of martial rule.[18]. However, in the most recent years, the Council appeared to become more active in striking down those laws infringing property rights, access to the court (particularly the civil servants' right to effective legal remedies) and physical integrity. In a recent Interpretation No. 445, the Council even went further to declare "freedom of expression should be regarded as the most important fundamental rights for developing democratic politics," and the so-called rights of political nature (including freedoms of speech, assembly and association) deserve much more protection. It seems that the Council not only takes up a more active role in exercising its judicial review power, but also is trying to develop a theory of "preferred freedoms."[19] Under this theory, those rights related to democratic politics, namely freedoms of speech, association and assembly, shall receive more protection than shall others, such as propetry rights.[20]

### 4. Introduction of New Standards of Review

It is interesting to note the Council seems to introduce a new set of standards of review. In the past, the Council tended to apply a sort of double standards, which was quite the opposite of that as practiced by the US Supreme Court. In the US, the Supreme Court has long been more rigid on reviewing laws involving political freedoms, while more lenient on economic and social rights, particularly when issues of equal protection are concerned. Quite surprisingly, in the past, Taiwan's Council of Grand Justices was doing exactly the opposite. They tended to be much more active in reviewing laws restricting property rights while more deferent to the legislative and executive branches on other civil and political rights cases.[21] Only in recent years did the Council seem to reverse its previous practice, in part, responding to the development of "preferred freedoms" theory as discussed in the immediately previous section.

Meanwhile, we also observe more frequent use of the "principle of proportionality" as a major standard of review to strike down unconstitutional laws. Quite often has the Council defined the requirement of "except such as may be necessary," provided in Article 23 of the ROC Constitution,[22] as a three-part end-means test: (a) the means must be appropriate for realization of legislative purposes; (b) the means must be the least restrictive means (LRM); and (c) the damages caused by the law must be outweighed by the legal interests pursued by the law (balancing test). Undoubtedly, the Council has in fact transformed the much-criticized Article 23 of the ROC Consitution into a legitimate basis for controlling unconstitutional laws.[23] In spite of all its efforts to build up a more precise theory of standards of review, two major drawbacks are worth noting: (1) The Conucil has been somewhat too lenient on reviewing the legitimacy of legislative purposes, either autual or constructive; (2) The Council has been inconsistent in reviewing different categories of rights, probably out of policy concerns. For example, thought the Council seems to emphasize the so-called preferred freedoms related to political process, it, very surprisingly, applies a very lax standard of review, similar to the so-called "rationality review" of the US, to uphold laws restricting citizens' right to vote and to become candidates.[24]

## 5. Defining the Binding Effects of Constitutional Interpretations

With increasing judicial activism in recent years, collision between the Council and political branches (including both the legislative and executive branches) seems inevitable. It is noteworthy that the Council has carefully built up a complex model to define the binding effects (*res juticata*) of its own constitutional interpretations.[25]

Though the Constitution mandates that any statutes or regulations in violation of the Constitution shall be null and void.[26] Neither the Constitution itself nor any statutes clearly define "when" such unconstitutional laws shall cease to be operative in practice. In 1980, the Council once declared unconstitutional a law, authorizing the police to detain individuals without court warrants.[27] However, the Legislative Yuan failed to revise the law until the Council issued another Interpretation declaring the same law unconstitutional on a new and the previously mentioned grounds in January 1990.[28] This 1980 Interpretation went further to expressly mandate that unconstitutional law should cease to be effective after July 1, 1991, if not revised. Since then, the Council has frequently employed this technique of "prospective voidness" (or "unconstitutional but still effective" model, *i.e.*, declaring a unconstitutional law to become null and void only at some point in the future),[29] when declaring a law or regulation unconstitutional.

Aside from using the above technique of "prospective voidness," the Council also uses a variety of other techniques to avoid direct conflicts with the political departments. In some cases, the Council simply declares unconstitutional the laws in dispute and stops short of expressly negating its validity, leaving it entirely for the legislature to decide whether and when to amend or repeal the law (the "model of "simple declaration of unconstitutionality").[30] With this model, the Council shows its great deference to the legislature at the expense of individual rights. On the other hand, in a most recent Interpretation No. 477, the Council went to the opposite direction. In this Interpretation, the Council declared a statute unconstitutional (because of its being "underinclusive) and therefore null and void immediately. Moreover, the Council even expressly mandated that those people, unconstitutionally excluded from the application of the statute in dispute, may claim the equal rights and benefits granted by this very statute directly on the basis of Interpretation No. 477, without having to wait for any statutory revision.[31] Interpretation No. 477 indicates the most aggressive judicial activism ever seen in the history of constitutional review in Taiwan. Though favorable to individual rights holders, this Interpretation undoubtedly raised the concern of blurring the boundary between the judiciary and legislature.

Such a complex model as discussed above has aroused many criticisms.[32] From the perspective of comparative constitutional law study, these various models of binding effects were clearly borrowed from both German and Austrian constitutional court practices. Nevertheless, such practices have departed from a paramounts principle of constitutional law: any unconstitutional laws shall be null and void. And any departure from this paramount principle will inevitably weaken the supremacy of the written Constitution. It would also cast serious doubt on the fundamental duty of the judiciary to be the Guardian of Constitution or Guardian of Human Rights. Past experiences clearly indicate that being considerate for the political branches often means being harsh on the individuals. A practice of this kind usually lends convenient excuses for the self-restrained judiciary to trade individual rights for political expediency.[33] In this regard, the Council may need to seriously reevaluate its past practice, particularly in light of effective human rights protection.

## IV. Limits of Judicial Review in Protecting Individual Rights

After examining the real role of Taiwan's Council of Grand Justices in implementing constitutional rights in the 1990s, in this section, I will further discuss the possible limits of the judiciary in implementing and enforcing constitutional rights. In so doing, the author is perfectly aware of the danger of over-and hasty generalization from an isolated case as presented above.

### 1. Passive Role of the Judiciary

By nature, no court may decide any case unless and until someone brings a case before it. If no one disputes the constitutionality of a specific statute or regulation, any court is barred from speaking about it, *ex officio*. An unconstitutional law may therefore last for long before the judiciary voids it.

### 2. Post Hoc Review

The court can only provide *post hoc* review of a single case. That means, the court may usually remedy the damage after it is done. Also, the court's remedy is much more backward looking, rather than forward looking. Even though it is not entirely impossible, the court's capability in providing preventive measures to deter damages from happening has been relatively limited, depending very much on the court's manpower, caseload and institutional inertia.

### 3. Case-Specific Remedy

Judicial remedy is rendered in a case-specific manner and not in full-scale, general terms. Even though we agree that the law is what the court says what it is, the court itself is still not a policy-maker of general nature, like the executive or legislative branch. Moreover, considering the limits of *res juticata*, the binding force of a court decision is limited to precisely both the same parties and the subject matter of the despute. Other victims of similar human rights violation may have ot file his/her own case for legal remedy.

### 4. Dilenma of Judicial Remedy for Positive Rights

The court may be good at denouncing unconstitutional a law which is found to infringe the individual liberties of negative nature. To do so, the court only has to negate a law and declare it null and void. But, as far as positive rights go, it requires more than mere "hands-off" of the government and usually involves re-distribution of financial and other resources from a full-scale, forward-looking perspective. Considering the differences in expertise, organization and decision-making process, it may arguably be more appropriate for the political departments to make most decisions regarding realization of positive rights.

### 5. Disadvantages of Centralized Judicial Review Systems

Despite different views on its merits and demerits, most centralized juducial review systems like Taiwan's Conncil of Grand Justices would inevitably entail an obvious disadvantage: less sensitive to protection of individual rights. This disadvantage is evident in its delayed justice. Being the only constitutional organ to decide the constitutionality of statutes and regulations, any constitutional court or its equivalent, consisting of limited number of Justices and faced with increasing number of incoming cases, would find it very challenging to decide a case soon enough for the benefit of petitioners. Taiwan's experience indicates, with the rapidly growing caseload, most petitioners now have to wait for two to three years in order to get an Interpretation on the merits. Even worse, Taiwan's system provides no provisional measures in favor of petitioners. Another disadvantage is the requirement of "exhaustion of ordinary remedies." This procedural barrier may first delay the victims from effectively asserting their constitutional rights for years before they are able to reach the Concil for relief[34].

### 6. Conservative Lawyers Makes Up Conservative Courts

Throughout history, there have been quite a few revolutionaries who are lawyers. The author observed, however, in most countries of modern time, well-trained lawyers tend to associate themselves with those established interests and even become part of "those-in-the power" or "insiders. There are a lot more excellent lawyer-lobbyists than human rights defenders. Also, it is no secret that legal education and thinking, paying too much attention to "formality," "legality" or" harmony and consistency of existiing legal order," are often at odds with grassroots human rights movement. That is the conservative nature of lawyers in general.

In Taiwan's case, as the well-established ruling party thus far appointed almost all the Grand Justices, it is no surprise that we can hardly characterize any Grand Justice as liberals. The distinction among them is more between being very and less conservative than between being liberal and conservative[35].

## V. Conclusion

As an old saying goes: "Don't shoot the piano player; he is doing the best he can." Many should wonder: are our honorable Grand Justices doing the best they can? It is certainly not a question easy to answer.

In a sense, the judiciary is only A branch of the entire government. We shall not forget the judiciary is not, and should not be, the only protector of constitutional rights. There are other important institutions, such as National Human Rights Commission[36], capable of implementing human rights as well. In practice, even the police and other law enforcement departments are far too important to be ignored. Realization of many judicial decisions alway count on cooperation of the other two government branches, particularly when human rights issues are involved.

However, it should be also remembered that the reputation of the judiciary is to be earned case by case, rather than granted by the authority of Constitution. Constitution provides only legality, while the judiciary itself must take pains to earn its own legitimacy, particularly on those individual rights cases. The success of the judiciary (or the Council) as Guardian of Constitutuonal Rights will be better measured by the satisfaction of private citizens, and not by soundness of logical or legal reasoning. And it is a always up to the people to decide whether the honorable Grand Justices are doing the best they can.

**Endnotes**
   (1) In this paper, the author uses "Taiwan" to refer to the State of Taiwan, with the "Republic of China" (ROC) as its current state title. In recent years, the Taiwanese goverment has been increasingly using the term of "ROC on Taiwan" or "ROC (Taiwan)" to distinguish itself from China, PRC or the old ROC government before 1949.
   (2) For a more detailed analysis of constituional change in light of both liberalization

and democratization, see JAU-YUAN HWANG, CONSTITUTIONAL CHANGE AND POLITICAL TRANSITION IN TAIWAN SINCE 1986: THE ROLE OF LEGAL INSTITUTIONS, unpublished S.J. D. dissertation, Harvard University, pp. 100-120, 154-254 (1995).

(3) *See also* Sean Cooney, *Taiwan's Emerging Liberal Democracy and the New Constitutional Review*, in VERONICA TAYLOR (ED.), ASIAN LAWS THROUGH AUSTRALIAN EYES, Melbourne: Law Book Co. pp. 163-82 (1997)

(4) *See* Richard H. Fallon Jr. *Forward: Implementing The Constitution*, 111 HARVARD LAW REVIEW 54, 56-57 (1997).

(5) For a brief discussion of this subject, *see*, *e.g.*, Jau-Yuan Hwang & Jinn-rong Yet, *Taiwan*, in: CHERYL SAUNDERS & GRAHAM HASSALL (EDS.), ASIA-PACIFIC CONSTITUTIONAL YEARBOOK 1995, Carlton, Australia: Centre for Comparative Constitutional Studies, University of Melbourne, pp. 279, 297-98, 307-08 (197); Lawrence Shao-Liang Liu, *Judicial Review and Emerging Constitutionalism: The Uneasy Case for the Republic of China on Taiwan*, 39 AMERICAN JOURNAL OF COMPARATIVE LAW 509, 514-523 (1991); Tay-Sheng Wang, *Chapter 4: Taiwan*, in: POH-LING TAN (ED.), ASIAN LEGAL SYSTEMS: LAW, SOCIETY AND PLURALISM IN EAST ASIA, Sydney, Australia: Butterworths, pp. 124-61 (1997).

(6) Under the 1947 ROC Constitution, the other function of the Council is to render "United Interpretation" to resolve conflicting effects or application of statutes or regulations. *See* ROC Const. Art. 78. A constitutional amendment of 1992 added a third function to the Council: the power to declare a political party unconstitutional and order to disband it. ROC Const. Amend. V, sec. 4 & 5 (1992, amended 1997).

(7) There has been debate among the academia over the constitutional status of the Council *vis-à-vis* the Judician Yuan. Some argues that, under the ROC Constitution, the Judical Yuan itself should be the highest court of final instance, in charge of all cases of constitutional, civil, criminal and administrative law, similar to the Supreme Court of the U.S. In this view, the Council and the judicial Yuan should be the same constitutional organ, instead of two separate institutions oa they have been. For more discussion of this issue, *see*, *e.g.*, Liu, *supra* note 5, at 514-517; Yueh-Sheng Weng, *A Study on the Evolution of the Functions of the Grand Justices*, 23 NATIOANL TAIWAN UNIVERSITY LAY JOURNAL 25, 26-28 (1993) (in Chinese). In July 1999, the Judicial Yuan released a reform plan, which proposed to convert the Judicial Yuan into a real court in the long run (after 2009). *See* JUDICIAL YUAN, CONCLUSIONS, ACTION ITEMS AND IMPLEMENTATION SCHEDULE OF NATIONAL CONFERENCE ON JUDICIAL REFORM, Taipei: Judicial Yuan, p. 6 (1999).

(8) Also, both the President and Vice President of the Judicial Yuan are to be chosen among the Grand Justices, instead of independent political appointments as practiced since 1947. However, both Grand Justices serving as President and Vice President of

the Judicial Yuan shall not enjoy the guarantee of an eight-year term. ROC Const. Amend. V, sec. I & II (1947, Amended 1997).

(9) For a statistics of caselaod in recent years, please refer to the website of the Judicial Yuan at http://www.judicial.gov.tw/juds/EG-IHTM (English version) (last visited August 25, 1999).

(10) Before lifting of martial rule in July 1987 out of 216 Interpretations there were only 8 Interpretations, expressly or implicitly, declaring unconstitutional a statute, regulation or court precedent. *See* Interpretations No. 86, 166, 177, 185, 187, 201, 210 & 213.

(11) Act Governing Proceedings of the Council of Grand Justices of the Judicial Yuan, section 5 (1958, amended 1993).

(12) For a brief discussion of Interpretation No. 371, *see also* Sean Cooney, *supra* note 3, at 172-73.

(13) For example, several judges at various district courts once petitioned to the Council, challenging the constitutionality of both mandatory death penalty (Interpretaion No. 476) and the prosecutors' power to detain the accused without court warrants (Interpretation No. 392).

(14) Between 1988 and 1997, 95.48% of petitions were initiated by the individuals. *See* JUDICIAL YUAN (ED.), ANNUAL REPORT OF JUDICIAL PRACTICE—CASE ANALYSIS, Taipei: Judicial Yuan, p. 69 (1998).

(15) Before the Interpretation No 177, there was only one Interpretation, which was initiated by individuals.

(16) As indicated by practice among most countries, the Constitutional Court under a centralized judicial review system has usually been more enthusiastic about maintaining the harmong and consistency of constitutional order in its abstract sense, while the decentralized judicial review system as prevailing in the U.S. has been more active on protection of individual of individual rights. For a general study of comparative judicial review systems, *see e.g.*, MAURO CAPPELLETTI, JUDICIAL REVIEW IN THE CONTEMPORARY WORLD (1971).

(17) Interpretation No. 265 of October 5, 1990.

(18) Interpretation No. 272 of January 18, 1991.

(19) *See also* Yueh-Sheng Weng, *Characters and Prospect of Constitutional Review in Taiwan*, in JUDICIAL YUAN, ESSAYS IN CELEBRATION OF THE FIFTY ANNIVERSARY OF CONSTITUTIONAL REVIEW BY THE GRAND JUSTICES OF THE JUDICIAL YUAN, Taipei: Judicial Yuan, pp. 285, 317 (1998) (in Chinese). In his article, former Grand Justice Weng seemed to echo the theory as proposed in the famous Footnote Four, written by Associate Justice Stone of the U.S. Supreme Court in the 1938 case of *United States v. Carolene Products Company* (304 U.S. 144).

(20) Despite all the encouraging phenomena, a dark side of the recent judicial activism remains: the death penalty. Since 1985, the Council has twice affirmed the constitutionality of mandatory death penalty in Interpretations No. 194 of March 22, 1985 and No. 263 of July 19, 1990. In a latest Interpretation No. 476, issued in February 1999, the Council once again upheld the constitutionality of mandatory death penalty. It is really a big setback for the human rights movement in Taiwan.

(21) *See* Chih-ping Fa, *Standards of Review for Property Rights and Other Rights under the Constitution*, 23 CHENG-CHIH UNIVERSITY LAW REVIEW (1981), reprinted in: FA, SELECTED ESSAYS ON CONSTITUTIONAL LAW, Taipei: Cheng-Chih University, pp. 227, 264 (1985) (in Chinese).

(22) ROC Const. Art. 23 reads: "All the freedoms and rights enumerated in the preceding Articles shall not be restricted by law *except such as may be necessary* to prevent infringement upon the freedoms of other persons, to avert an imminent crisis, to maintain social order or to advance public welfare." (*emphasis added*) This Article has served as a general limitation on all individual rights.

(23) It is obvious that the Council has imported the principle of proportionality from German Federal Constitutional court. That also mirrors the continental-law history and background of the overall Taiwanese legal system. Nevertheless, in recent years, the Council began to employ more US constitutional law theories, concepts or even standards of review. For example, in three recent Interpretations involving free speech cases, the Council clearly referred to the relevant US constitutional law cases and employed terms or theories such as "*chear and present danger*" (Interpretatin No. 445), "*contemporary community standards*" (Miller test) on obscenity (Interpretation No. 407) and "*commercial speech as low-value speech*" (Interpretation No. 414), in its legal reasoning.

(24) Interpretations No. 290 of January 24, 1992 & No. 468 of Octover 22, 1998.

(25) *See* Interpretations No. 177, 183, 185, 188 and 193, ruled between 1982 and 1985.

(26) ROC Const. Arts. 171 & 172 (1947).

(27) Interpretation No. 166 of Novermber 7, 1980.

(28) Interpretation No. 251 of January 19, 1990.

(29) In fact, the first Interpretation employing such a "prospective voidness" technique was Interpretation No. 218 of August 14, 1987 (delcaring an unconstitutional order to be ineffective after six months), followed by No. 224 of April 24, 1988 (declaring a statute to become void after two years).

(30) *See, e.g.*, Interpretations No. 410, 455, 457 and 485. In Germany, this model of ruling is called "*Unvereinbarkeitserklaerung*," "*Verfassungswidrigkeitserklaerung*" or "*blosse Verfassungswidrigerklaerung*."

(31) Interpretation No. 477 of February 12, 1999.

(32) In addition to questioning the legitimacy of both models of "prospective voidness" and "simple declaration of unconstitutionality," many also critisize the rationals or grace periods given by these Interpretations as either too over-simplified or arbitrary. *See, e.g.*, Jau-Yuna Hwang, *On "Unconstitutional But Still Valid" Model of Interpretations by the Grand Justices*, 12 TAIWAN LAW REVIEW 31-39 (April 1996).

(33) For example, whenever the Council declares a law "unconstitutional but still effective" for some more time, the individual-plaintiff who petitioned for constitutional interpretation will also be deprived of the right to get an immediate re-trial of his/her case. For this reason, such a practice could significantly reduce the citizens' incentive to initiate petitions.

(34) Interpretation No. 371 has mitigated this awkwardness to some extent. *See* the text accompanying notes 11-12.

(35) A good illustration is: the Council affirmend the constitutionality of mandatory death penalty in three Interpretations (No. 194, 263 and 476). To many's disappointment, there were no dissenting opinions in any of these Interpretations. Only one Grand Justice Yueh-Sheng Weng (current President of Judicial Yuan), during one of his public lectures, indicated his personal regret and second thought on this issue. *See* Weng, *supra* note 7, at 48.

(36) So far, Taiwan has no National Human Rights Commission. Only beginning from last year did a NGO human rights group (Taiwan Association for Human Rights) start to campaign on this issue.

# Part III  The Constitution of Japan and Asia

# Problems of amending the Japanese Constitution[1]
## ——The controversy over constitutional amendment and constitutionalism in postwar Japan——

**Akimichi Iwama**

## 1. Preface

Aimed primarily at professors from other Asian countries and Oceania, this report seeks to outline the nature of the controversies concerning proposals to amend the Constitution of Japan and to discuss some characteristics of constitutionalism as well as the constitutional situations that have arisen in postwar Japan.

Since its enactment in 1946, the Constitution of Japan has never been amended. However, from time to time, burning controversies have arisen concerning proposals to amend it, and it seems likely that in the future, the question of constitutional amendment will become a very acute political issue. Furthermore, it seems to me that the controversies to date illuminate significant features of constitutionalism and the changing constitutional situation of postwar Japan. In this report, therefore, I will begin by outlining the controversy of the 1950's and go on to outline that of the 1990's. I will then discuss briefly some significant features of constitutionalism in postwar Japan and end by presenting my views on the present controversy over constitutional amendment.

## 2. The controversy over constitutional amendment in the 1950's

Within a short time after the Constitution was enacted, strong voices were heard, beginning in the 1950's, to the effect that it should be amended. Soon after the Allied military occupation ended in 1951, demands for amendment came to be made so openly by the conservative parties that bitter disputes arose. The controversy at this time was characterized by the following features[2]:

(i) First, the campaign to amend the Constitution was aimed mainly at amending Article 9. The new Constitution advocated as fundamental principles:

1. a guarantee of human rights, at the heart of which is respect for the individual, 2. sovereignty of the people, and 3. pacifism. It differed substantially from the preceding constitution, known as the Meiji Constitution, the fundamental principle of which was the sovereignty of the emperor, or Tennō. With respect to pacifism, Article 9 assumed epoch-making significance in the context of national security, because it not only renounced all types of war, but prohibited the maintenance of any armed forces. It was true that this Article was the product of political maneuvering, but on the other hand, we should never overlook the fact that its formulation was based on reflections about Japan's aggression as well as on a legitimate recognition that war stands in fundamental contradiction to civilization[3]. For the people of postwar Japan, therefore, Article 9 represented not only a new ideal but also a new moral stance to the international community, especially to the peoples of Asia and Oceania.

Nevertheless, as soon as the Korean War broke out, a paramilitary organization called the National Police Reserve was established in accordance with the directive of General MacArthur as the Supreme Commander for the Allied Powers. The Japanese Government maintained that the establishment of the NPR did not violate Article 9 because the "war potential" prohibited by this Article denoted "a force with the equipment and strength capable of effectively conducting modern warfare", and the NPR did not amount to this "war potential". In fact, however, this marked the beginning of the rearmament of Japan. Whatever the legitimacy of this argument, there was no doubt whatever that the Self-Defense Forces established in 1954 amounted to a military organization, i.e. "war potential". Since it was extremely difficult for the Government to demonstrate that the existence of the SDF did not violate Article 9, the ruling conservative cabinet at this time took as its aim the amendment of this Article.

(ii) The second distinctive feature is the fact that the campaign for constitutional amendment at this time did not limit itself to Article 9, but aimed to amend the whole of the Constitution. As is generally known, the Constitution of Japan was modeled on the so-called "MacArthur draft", drawn up during the occupation period. This situation came about mainly because the Japanese political leaders in those days insisted on sticking to the Meiji Constitution, which was incompatible with the terms of the Potsdam Declaration. When the occupation ended, the conservative parties insisted that the Constitution of Japan should be rewritten, signifying the return to independence of Japan, because the existing Constitution was *imposed* on the Japanese by the Occupation Forces[4]. The important point to note is that the conservative parties expressed strong objections not only to the process whereby the Constitution was enacted, but to its basic principles. Specifically, their aim was a Constitution which decreed that the Emperor was the head of state and which valued collective groups such as the state and the extended household or the extended family, above the individual. In short, they wanted to see a restoration of the Meiji Constitution.

(iii) A further important feature to be noted is that the demands for constitutional amendment provoked such intense opposition that the campaign failed. This was due to a number of causes. A majority of two-thirds or more of all the seats in each House was required in order to initiate a constitutional amendment, and the direct cause of the failure lay in the inability of the conservative parties to win this majority, both in the election of members of the House of Representatives in 1955 as well as in the election of members of the House of Councilors in 1956. However, the main reason can be said to lie in the fact that in those days, in the aftermath of their bitter experience of World War II, a large number of people supported the existing Constitution and the doctrine of pacifism. Nor should it be overlooked that in those days, the then dominant constitutional theory played a very important role in preventing any amendment. Laying stress on the essential significance of the principle of respect for the individual as well as on the guarantee of fundamental human rights, the theory developed a series of arguments for the protection of the existing Constitution. With regard to pacifism, it opposed any amendment to Article 9, emphasizing its universal significance, and criticized strongly the official government interpretation which said that the SDF was not in contradiction to the said Article.

(iv) Attention must also be drawn to the fact that the aim of the campaign for amending the Constitution was, to a large extent, achieved, by means of *altering the interpretation* of Article 9, though the attempt to revise the Article itself failed. In 1955, the Government reinterpreted Article 9, maintaining that Japan still retained an inherent right of self-defense, the so-called right of individual self-defense, and that accordingly a minimum potential necessary for self-defense, termed the "self-defense potential", could be differentiated from the "war potential". Since it was only the "war potential" that was forbidden by Article 9, the continuing existence of the SDF did not violate the said Article. Indeed, using this new interpretation, the Government enhanced the strength of the SDF. It is significant to note that the SDF has since gained wide acceptance among the public, and since then, the Government has frequently altered its interpretation of the Constitution, rather than trying to amend its actual wording, in order to achieve its political aims. It would not be an overstatement to say that from this time on, the confidence of the Japanese people in constitutionalism began to decline.

## 3. The controversy over constitutional amendment in the 1990's

As a result of considerable changes in both international and domestic circumstances, including the ending of the cold war, the war in the Persian Gulf, and an intensification of environmental pollution, strong voices were heard, as the nation entered the 1990's, arguing in favor of constitutional amendment. Worthy of particular note in the context of this debate are the following points[5]:

(i) The main focus of those who seek to amend the Constitution in the 1990's is also Article 9. The campaign in the 1990's can, however, be differentiated from that in the 1950's by the following points. Rather than focusing on acknowledgment of the right of individual self-defense, which, along with the maintenance of "self-defense potential", has gained widespread public acceptance as being constitutional, the campaign of the 1990's focuses its attention mainly on the question of acknowledgment of exercising the right of collective self-defense as well as participating in U.N. forces under Article 43 of the U.N. Charter. With regard to the right of collective self-defense, although a few leaders of the conservative parties argue that its exercise is not forbidden by Article 9, the Government has taken the view that exercising the right of collective self-defense is forbidden, and is taking a very cautious approach to questions of constitutional reform concerned with this point. The so-called Guideline Acts in 1999, has involved Japan in the exercise of the right of collective self-defense, so that if the Government were to follow the doctrine of constitutionalism loyally, it would be an urgent matter for it to have the right of collective self-defense recognized by the Constitution. It is also a noticeable characteristic of the constitutional reform debate in the 1990's that those arguing for reform, including some members of the Opposition parties, emphasize the need to make it possible for the SDF to participate in U.N. forces constituted under Article 43 of the U.N. Charter. Those who defend Article 9 will also need to define how Japan can cooperate with legally constituted U.N. forces.

Nevertheless, the core of the demands to amend Article 9 today is comprised of demands for clearer acknowledgment of the right of individual self-defense and for formal acknowledgment of the SDF. It is already the case that not only the Governing parties, but many Opposition parties acknowledge the right of individual self-defense as constitutional and, as a result, approve the constitutionality of the SDF. Hence it can be argued that formally recognizing the right of individual self-defense by means of amending the Constitution is of almost secondary importance. But it cannot be denied that formal acknowledgment of the right of individual self-defense as a constitutional right remains the central problem in the issue of amendment to Article 9. This is because, looking at the express provisions of Article 9, the Government interpretation of the said Article is less reasonable than the constitutional theory which says that Article 9 forbids the maintenance of any armed forces inclusive of "self-defense potential". Moreover, significant modification of pacifism as the principle of the existing Constitution, such as in the direction of allowing the maintenance of "self-defense potential", can gain legitimacy only through the express consent of the people as the body possessing sovereign power, in other words, only by amending the Constitution[6]. It must also be noted that formal acknowledgment of the right of individual self-defense nowadays in fact comes to mean following traditional security policy, according to which the armed forces of the sovereign state are regarded as the basic means of maintaining international peace and security as well as of defending the state.

(ii) Although the question of amendment to Article 9 is central to the current campaign for constitutional amendment in the 1990's, there is a strong possibility that in the future, demands for the amendment of the entire Constitution will become a central feature. The reason for this is that the formal acknowledgment of the right of individual self-defense is likely to be accompanied by demands for addition to the existing Constitution of provisions for the following: the proclamation of war, the right to take command of the SDF, emergency powers, the suspension of fundamental human rights during emergencies, and the obligation of citizens in respect of national defense. Furthermore, independent of the above, it should be noted that the current campaign for constitutional amendment is already showing a tendency to develop into demands to amend the whole of the Constitution. This tendency can be observed in the plan to establish in both Houses of the Diet, in the year 2000, a committee known as the "Kenpō-chosa-kai" (Committee to Investigate the Constitution), whose principal task will be "to investigate the constitution *extensively and all-round*". Another example of this tendency can be seen in the establishment of the unofficial conference, called "the National Congress for Founding the New Japan", whose principal task will be "to review the *whole* of the constitutional system in post-war Japan". We can also note such a tendency in some unofficial drafts of amendments to the Constitution. An example of these is the unofficial draft produced by the Yomiuri Newspaper in 1994, recommending the following: participation by the SDF in U.N. peace-keeping operations and the maintenance of "self-defense potential", the harmonization of fundamental human rights with public welfare, the acknowledgment of new rights such as the right to a comfortable environment and the right to privacy, and the establishment of a constitutional court[7].

However, in the event that the debate on amendment comes to focus on the whole of the Constitution, the central question becomes one of which demand will take the leading place, not only in the committee mentioned above but also in public opinion. The demands made today can be divided broadly into three categories: 1. the demand which is aimed at an amendment to meed the needs of the times, such as the right to a comfortable environment, while preserving the fundamental principles of the Constitution; 2. the demand which is aimed at adjusting the existing Constitution not only so as to meet the needs of the times but also so as to conform, even if only in part, with the traditional culture of Japan, while preserving the fundamental principles of the Constitution; 3. the demand made from a position of extreme nationalism, aimed at amending the whole of the Constitution, including its fundamental principles, such as respect for the individual and the guarantee of human rights. At the very least, there is a strong possibility that both the second and third demands will aim at amending Article 9. For the time being, it may be presumed that, in the Kempō-chosa-kai, the second demand will predominate over the other two demands. However, in the light of political trends in Japan today, the third demand should not be overlooked.

(iii) It is likely that the present demands for amending the Constitution will be met, even if only partially. Besides the current leanings of the political parties, the main reason for this is that according to a recent opinion poll, a majority of the people do not exhibit any determined opposition to the amendment of the Constitution as such. It is rather the case that the people show a tendency to approve of constitutional amendment aimed at formally acknowledging the right to a comfortable environment as well as the right of individual self-defense[8].

## 4. Conclusion

So far, this paper has aimed to give an overview of the controversy concerning proposals for constitutional amendment in postwar Japan. In conclusion, I will state briefly some significant features of constitutionalism in postwar Japan and give my own views on the question of constitutional amendment.

(i) Firstly, one of the noticeable characteristics of constitutionalism in postwar Japan is that adjustment of the Constitution to the changing needs of the times has been carried out by means of *altering the interpretation* of the Constitution. This kind of adjustment, particularly with regard to human rights, did not by any means always necessarily lack reasons. But in the light of the power given by the Constitution in order for the people to make a final decision on constitutional amendment, significant modification of the Constitution, such as the maintenance of "self-defense potential", should be made only with the express approval of the people in accordance with designated amendment procedures, and should never be made by means of altering the interpretation, in other words by interpretations given by the Supreme Court of Japan. Following the route of constitutional amendment on the basis of the will of the people may involve certain risks, since democracy is not yet sufficiently rooted in Japan. However, the Constitution will not be firmly defended by the people and democracy will not plant its roots firmly in the Japanese nation until the

Japanese people make a decision as to whether or not the Constitution shall be amended.

(ii) Secondly, I would like to emphasize that the principle of constitutionalism embedded in the existing Constitution, namely the principle of imposing constraints on the exercise of public powers in order to guarantee fundamental human rights, must continue to be steadfastly maintained in future as the common precious heritage of mankind. What is important is that in the light of Japanese history, Article 9, which forbids Japan to maintain any armed forces, is an essential condition for the successful functioning of constitutionalism in Japan. If we assume that the fate of Article 9 depends to a large extent on the maintenance of peace in Asia and Oceania, it follows that the maintenance of such peace is an indispensable prerequisite for the successful functioning of constitutionalism in Japan.

(iii) Finally, I would like to touch on the question of what attitude the constitutional theory that set out to defend Article 9 should take with regard to the current controversy regarding constitutional amendment. Firstly, there is a school of thought which argues that in order to defend Article[9], any proposal for amendment to the Constitution should be decisively rejected, even if there are points in the current Constitution that need to be reformed. In the light of the present political circumstances in Japan, there is much justice in this argument. On the other hand, there is an opposing view[9], which argues that every proposal for amendment of the Constitution should be judged separately on its merits, measured against an ideal image of what the Constitution should be. If one were in a position of drafting one's own ideal Constitution, it would at least be worth considering the unofficial draft amendment of the Constitution prepared by the Society for the Study of Constitutional Law of the University of Tokyo in 1949[10]. This proposed changing the arrangement of the existing Constitution so as to provide in Chapter 1 the fundamental principles of the Constitution, in Chapter 2 fundamental human rights, and in Chapter 3, the Emperor as a symbol. Also worthy of close consideration are current trends in the constitutions not only of the countries of Europe and the United States of America, but also of the countries of Asia and Oceania.

1   This report was given at the Asian-Oceanic Symposium on Constitutionalism which

was held under the sponsorship of the Japan Association for the Studies of Constitutional Law at the Waseda University on 22 September 19991.

2  For an outline of the controversy over constitutional amendment in the 1950's, see Miyazawa Tosiyosi, Kenpōksaiseimondai no Kangaekata, 73 Jurisuto (1955); Ukai Nobushige, Kenpōkasiseiron no futatuno Kata, 73 Jurisuto Ashibe Nobuyoshi, Kenpōkaiseimondai no Gaikan, 73 Jurisuto Ashibe N., Kenpōseiteikenryoku, 217 (1983); Satō Isao, Kenpōkaiseimondai no Hatten to sono Ronten (1), 26 Hōritsu Jihō 7, 68 (1954); Satō I., Kenpōkaiseimondai (2), 26 Hōritsu Jihō 8, 78 (1954); Satō I., Kenpōkaiseiron no Keifu to Genjō, 638 Jurisuto 44 (1977).

3  In the Imperial Diet, in which the Cabinet Draft of the new constitution was discussed, the State Minister K. Shidehara maintained that war stands in fundamental contradiction to civilization (2 Chikujō Nihonkokukenpō Shingiroku (Zōhoban) 21 (Shimizu Shin ed., 1976)).

4  In judging rightly whether the existing Constitution was *imposed* or not, we should never overlook the fact that the Cabinet draft, which was modeled on the so-called "MacArther draft", was approved by an overwhelming majority of members in the Diet, and that members of the conservative parties also approved it on their own judgment in order to maintain the Emperor System. On this point, see, in particular, Miyazawa T (Ashibe N. Hotei), Zentei Nihonkokukenpō 9 (1978).

5  For an outline of the controversy over constitutional amendment in the 1990's, see, for example, Satō I., Saikin ni okeru Kaikenrongi, 1020 Jurisuto 105 (1993). For the attitude of the constitutional theory over this controversy, see Nakamura Mutsuo, Kenpōkaiseiron no 50 Nen to Kenpōgaku, 66 Hōritsu Jihō 6, 76 (1995). On latest unofficial drafts, see, for example, Ozawa Ichirō, Nihonkokukenpō Kaiseishian, Bungei Shunjū 94, Sept. 1999; Hatoyama Yukio, Jieitai wo Guntai to mitomeyo, Bungei Shunjū, 262, Oct. 1999.

6  For further details of this view, see Iwama Akimichi, Saikōsaibansho no Kenpōkaishaku no Genkai, in Kenpōsaiban to Gyōseisoshō 65 (Sonobe Itsuo Sensei Kokikenen Ronshū 1999).

7  Okudaira points out that the unofficial draft of the Yomiuri Newspaper aims exclusively at amending Article 9, and that its recommendation to amend articles other than Article 9 serves solely as the function of camuflage (Okudaira Yasuhiro, "Kaiken" Anguru kara mita "Kenpō 50 Nen", 68 Hōritsu Jihō 6, 8 (1996)).

8  According to an opinion poll published in the Yomiuri Newspaper in March 1999, a 53 percent majority of the people answering it approved of amending the Constitution and a 70 percent majority approved a formal acknowledgement of the right of privacy as well as the right to environmental protection in the existing Constitution (Yomiuri Shinbun, March 22, 1999).

9   A view has been sometimes maintained, which aims at defending Article 9 and argues that every proposal for amendment of the Constitution except for Article 9 should be judged separately on its merits, measured against an ideal image of what Constitution should be: For example, Ikeda insisted that the constitutional theory aiming at the defense of the existing Constitution should be freed from the taboos on amending Constitution, if an amendment to advance the welfare of the people is proposed (Ikeda Masaaki, Kenpōkaisei wa Tabū ka, in 3 Kenpōshakaitaikei, 145 (1999)). Okudaira takes a basic attitude that the existing Constitution should be adhered to. But, on the other hand, he also argues that an article should be amended without hesitation, when it proves itself to be in conflict with the people in the world as well as to suppress freedom and welfare of people, and gives Chapter 1 of the existing Constitution "Tennō" as an example (Okudaira Y., 62 Konmentāru Kaikenronsha no Shuchō, (1983)). Kobayashi points out that the movement for defending the existing Constitution in postwar Japan has been indeed successful in preventing the conservative parties from amending the existing Constitution, but it has assumed an excessively negative attitude towards policy-making accompanied by constitutional amendment. Emphasyzing that it is the duties of democratic people not only to form policies meeting the needs of a rapidly changing modern society, as well as according with the basic ideas of the Constitution, but also to amend the Constitution, if necessary, he takes the right to environmental protection as an example of such policies (Kobayashi Naoki, Kenpōseisakuron Josetsu 1, 62 Hōritsu Jihō 4, 49 (1990)). Higuchi contends that the existing Constitution should not be amended for the present. But he expects that members of the Diet, who opposed establishing the "Kenpōchōsakai", participate also in it and debate hotly on the problems such as referendum on the enactment of law, the right of foreign residents to vote for a member of the Diet and the equality of the sexes (Higuchi Yōichi, Gendai no Kaikenron to Yūjihōsei, Sekai 38, Nov. 1999). For the opinion recommending the adoption of an environmental protection clause into the existing Constitution, see Aoyagi Kōichi, Kojin no Sonchō to Ningen no Songen, 166, 214 (1996); Iwama A., Kankyōhozen to Nihonkokukenpō, in Ningen Kagakugijutsu Kankyō, 225 (Doitsu Kenpōhanrei Kenkyūkai ed., 1999). When some members of the Ōsaka Bar Association advocated the right to environmental protection as a new fundamental human right in 1970, they based it for the time being on Article 13 as well as Article 25. But they recommended that in future the right to environmental protection should be provided expressly in the existing Constitution (Kankyōken, 87 Ōsaka Bengoshikai Kankyōken Kenkyūkai ed., 1973). Assuming that the most serious environmental disruption is caused by war, we can say that the idea of environmental protection is essential for the abolition of war.

10   Tōkyōdaigaku Kenpōkenkyūkai, Kenpōkaisei no Shomondai, 67 Hōgakukyōkai

Zasshi 1, 1 (1949). In the unofficial draft produced by this Kenkyūkai, which was organized by writers of the well-known commentary on the existing Constitution, the following amendments were proposed in addition to the amendment of arrangement: substituting a phrase "acts provided for in this Constitution" for a phrase "acts in matters of state" found in Article 4, abolishing the power to appoint the Prime Minister and the Chief Judges of the Supreme Court in Article 6, abolishing the power to convoke the Diet and dissolve the House of Representatives, substituting the word like "Kokumuchōkan" for the word "Daijin", for the word "Daijin" symbolizes a feudal relationship between sovereign and subject. In the unofficial draft produced by the Society for the Study of Public Law in 1949, which was organized by younger political and legal scholars such as Tsuji Kiyoaki and Arikura Ryōkichi, the following amendments were proposed in order to promote and strengthen the democratic principles in the existing Constitution: providing in Chapter 1 fundamental human rights and the principle of popular sovereignty, providing that an approval from the Diet was necessary for the succession to the Imperial Throne, eliding a phrase "as a means of settling international disputes" in Article 9 Paragraph 1 and substituting a phrase "in order to accomplish the aim of the preceding paragraph" found in Article 9 Paragraph 2 for a phrase "for all aimes", providing the right of resistance against oppression expressly in the existing Constitution (21 Hōritsu Jihō 4, 56 (1949)). For this draft, see Nakamura M., 66 Hōritsu Jihō 6, 76(1995). In passing, Nakamura comments that it is a valuable draft fully worthy to be referred to in case of amendment to the existing Constitution in the future. In the unofficial draft produced by the Yomiuri Newspaper, the following amendment to the arrangement of the existing Constitution is proposed: providing in Chapter 1 the principle of popular sovereignty, in Chapter 2 the Emperor, in Chapter 3 the national security (Kenpō, - 21 Seiki ni mukete, 31 (Yomiuri Shinbunsha ed., 1994)). Okudaira, who assumes a critical attitude toward the draft of the Yomiuri Newspaper, argues that the arrangement of the existing Constitution needs not to be amended now. But he maintains at the same time that the arrangement providing for the Emperor in Chapter 1 is essentially unsuitable for the existing Constitution, the core of which is the principle of popular sovereignty, and that the national goals of Japan, such as the principles of popular sovereignty, respect for civil liberties and pacifism, should be essentially proclaimed in Chapter 1 (Okudaira Y., op cited., 11).

# Japan's Constitution and International Law
## : Focus on The Peace Article——Outline——

### Gong Renren

1 . National Constitutionalism and International Constitutionalism
(1) National Constitutionalism
(a) Tradtional Constitutionalism

Constitutionalism originated in the West. Carl. J. Friedrich Pointed out that Constitutionalism has three ideological roots: liberalism, rationalism and individualism. In the early days, traditional Constitutionalism involved only the limitations and separation of government powers, and the universality of every person's basic rights had not recognized. In fact, so called natural rights was the only of the replacing word of new privilege, which were the privilege of men, the privilege of the wealthy, the privilege of the white and the privilege of Christian culture.

(b) Contemporary Constitutionalism

Today, promoting and encouraging respect human rithts and for fundamental freedom for all without distinction as to race, sex, language, or religion, has become the foremost goal of contemporary Constitutionalism, and other principles such as limited government, separation of powers and rule of law and so on, should serve this goal. This kind of constitutionalism is also called human rights constitutionalism, which has gone beyond Western civilization, and has an universal value.

(2) International Constitutionalism
(1) International Constitution and International Constitutionalism

International constitutionalism is said a progressive movement which aims at fostering international cooperation by consolidating the substantive legal ties between states as well as the organizational structures built in the past. Since the WWII, the United Nations has become the most important international organization. The UN has played an important role in maintain international peace and security, which can be not replaced by any State or State group. According to the article 103 of UN Charter, the members' obligations under present Charter shall prevail any other international agreement. Since the UN includes almost all states and the few states which remain outside have recognized its fundamental principles, the UN Charter can be regarded as a constitution of international society. The purpose and the basic principles of the UN constitute the contents of international constitutionalism.

(2) Maintaining Peace is the Core of International Constitutionalism

According to the UN Charter, maintain peace is not only the purpose of the UN, but also the basic spirit of its basic principles. Among these principles, the prohibition of the threat or use of force is a ctitical one, which has been seen as a rule of customary international law and jus cogens by the International Court of Justice and International Law Commission of the UN.

(3) The Relationship between Peace and Human Rights

The relationship between peace and human rights is very complicate. Frorm the lesson of WWII, infringing upon human rights in domestic level had special linkage with the invading other countries in international level. However, since the 1945, some democratic countries have used force very often. It is well recognized that peace is the basic condition of human rights, but there is a controversy on whether the right to peace has become a legal right. There are some conflicts between peace and human rights in international society too. One of the most sensitive issues is when there a situation of human rights abuse within a country, whether other countries can use force to intervene that country. Recently, humanitarian intervention has been the focus of debating in international society. But according to the UN Charter, except for self-defense, no matter what kind of excuses, without the authorization of Secutiry Council, using force is illegal in current international law.

2. The dilemma of Peace Constitution

(1) The Progressive Character and Significance of Japan's Constitution

(a) The Outcome of Contermporary Consitutionalism

It is well known there are a strong influence of the United States to Japanese concurrent Constitution. However, this influence mainly limited in traditional consitutionalism. As matter of fact, Japan' constitution is not a simple copy of the Constitution of United States. There are many progressive ideas and provisions in Japanese Constitution, such as in the field of hyman rights and in term of peace article. Therefore, Japan' Constitution can be regarded as an outcome of contemporary consitutionalism

(b) The Most Perfect Peace Constitution

The most prominent feature of Japanese Constitution is the article 9. Althought there are some constitutions which stipulates to waive invasion or conquer war in other countries, only Japanese Constitution declare to waive any forms of wars and not to hold war force anymore. The peace article of Japan's Constitution is an important contribution both to national constitutionalism and international constitutionalism.

(c) The Basis of Economic Prosperous of Japan

Only few decades after WWII, Japan has become the second largest economic country in the world. There had been many explanations about the reasons of economic miracle of Japan, such as culture, national character or the management approach and so on. However, it seems very few scholars attach importance of the Constitution. As matter of fact, it is the current Constitution that makes Japan is one of the world most the stable and peaceful democratic states. Thanks to the article 9 of the Constitution, Japan has spent fewer ofr military purpose, and concentrate to develop its economic strength. So, the current Constitution is the one of most important basis of economic prosperous of Japan.

(2) Exist Side by Side of the Peace Constitution and Japan-United States Treaty of Mutual Cooperation and Security

(a) The Course of Armaments Expansion

in spite of the article 9 of Japan's Constitution declares that the land, sea and air forces, as well as other war potential, will never be maintained anymore, the Japanese military force-Self Defense Force (SDF) has been getting stronger and stronger. Even after the end of Cold War, a new Japan-Unites State Defense Guideline was made in 1997, and the implementing law of the new Guideline was made recently. By clarifying the wartime roles of the U.S. and Japan, the Guideline and the law have promoted the military cooperation of Japan-U.S. from so calles special self-defense system transfer to regional arrangement.

(b) The Conflicts of Peace Constitution and Reality

It is very interesting that there are three kind of different positions on the interpretation of Article 9. Most Japanese constitutional law scholars have been thinking the SDF is unconstitutional, but Japanese government regards the SDF is constitutional. However, Japanese Supreme Court neither said that SDF unconstitutional nor constitutional, and seems take a neurtal position. But as the Supreme Court has been taking a position of avoiding judging this issue, the result seems that the reality or the legality of the SDF or the government's position has been acquiesced by the Court. Generally speaking, Japanese Supreme Courthas proven extraordinarily willing to defer to the political branches, and has generally refused fo find laws duly enacted by the Diet (or other official acts of the government) to have violated the Constitution. The reasons that the Japanese Supreme court has been taking such a position of judicial passivism are complicate, such as diplomatic, political, judicial system, and other cultural and so on.

3. The Crisis of International Law and Peace Constitution

(1) The Tendency of Deviating from the Principle of Non Use of Force

The principle of non use of force stipulated by the UN Charter article 2 (4) is part of jus cogens., which has a legal effect to any country and to any regional level. There are two exceptions of this principle, one is the self-defense according to the UN. Charter article 51, another is the authorization of the Security Council under the Charter atricle 53 in regional arrangements.

The NATO's air-strike against FRY from last April, neither had the reason of selfdefense, nor the authorization of the UN Security Council, therefore breached the UN Charter and general international law. It also could become a dangerous precedent in international relation. As the new Japan-U.S. Guideline and the implementing law have made the military cooperation of Japan-U. S. from selfdefense system transfer to regional arrangement, the danger of breaching UN Charter and the Japanese Constitution has become higher, too, for there is no any provisions both in the New guideline and the Japanese law which stipulating the authorization of the UN Security Council as the precondition of military actions. There is also a danger that Japan could be drawn into a armed conflict with its neighbors, such as with China because of the Taiwan unification issue.

(2) The Relationship of Treaties and Constitution

It is well known that the taking shape and strengthen of Japanese military force has been under the pressures and initiative by the U.S., and the basis of developing Japan's military force is the system of Japan-United States Treaty of Mutual Cooperation and Security. Therefore the relationship between the treaties and the Constitution is the key issue in Japan. There are controversy about this relationship though, the majority Japanese law scholars consider that the constitution is higher rank than treaties in term of the proceedings of making a treaty is much more simple than the constitutional amendment. However, Japanese government has distinguished at least two type of treaties. As the treaties of a bilateral economic or political nature, over which the Constitution prevails. As the treaties that concern matters of "vital importance to the destiny of a nation such as a surrender document or a peace treaty," which shall prevail over the Constitution. The problem is whether Japan-United States Treaty of Mutual Cooperation and Security belongs to the latter type treaties. From the point of view of Japanes government consistent position and practice, it could be said that Japan-United States Treary of Mutual Cooperation and Security prevails the Constitution. Recent years, there is tendency that give human rights treaties a special high rank in many countries by their constitutions. However, with most perfect peace constitution, Japan is only country that give military treaty a higher rank than its constitution in the world!

## Conclusion:

Although Japanese peace Constitution has played a great role for its democratic, peace and economic development, the peace article has becoming a ineffective law, too. Today, the Japanese peace Constitution is on its historical crossroad.

# An Assessment on the Pacifism in the Japanese Constitutional Law

**Jeong Man Hee**

## I. Introduction

The Japanese policy on national security entered upon a new phase when the House of Councilors passed the laws on May 24, 1999 to implement a new set of "the Guidelines of U.S.-Japan Defense Cooperation." The House enacted "the Low Concerning Measures to Ensure Peace and Security of Japan in Siruation in Areas Surrounding Japan (hereinafter referred to as "Surrounding Areas Low"), while amending "the Self-Defense Forses Low" and the Agreement between the Government of Japan and the Government of the United States of America concerning reciprocal provision of logistic support, supplies and services between the Self Defence Force of Japan and the Armed Forces of the United States of Japan. The new laws extended the theater of the military activities far beyond the Japanese territory. As a result of these enactments, the Japanese government obtained a legal foundation for the first time to support the military operations of the U.S. troops for maintaining peace and security in the areas surrounding Japan. Depending on interpretations of the notion of "surrounding areas," it is now feasible that the U.S.-Japan security scheme may cover Asia-Pacific regional security as well as international security[1].

The new Guidelines, however, raises serious questions since the Guidelines come into conflict with the U.S.-Japan Security Treaty, which is the legal foundation of the Guidelines. Article 5 of the Constitution stipulates the cooperation between the United States and Japan to defend Japan when a direct armed-attack on Japan occurs. Under Article 6, the Japanese government shall provide the United States with military bases and other necessary supports in order to assist U.S. operations for maintaining peace and security in the Far Eastern region. Based upon the defense treaty, the Guidelines of U.S.-Japan Defense Cooperation, which came into force in 1978, specified that the two government shall jointly conduct military cooperation only when a direct armed-attack on Japan occurs, without mentioning of possible cooperation in case of any other disputes taking place outside the Japanese territory.

The defense treaty and the original guideline were concluded primarily to cope with the military threat of the Soviet Union during the Cold War era. The end of the Cold War era and breakdown of the Soviet Union made it necessary to newly define the scope of Japanese security under the mutual defense treaty. The United States and Japanese government thus discussed the issue in Tokyo in 1996, and announced the Joint Declaration on the U.S.-Japan Security. Since the Declaration changed the purpose of the U.S.-Japan Defense Treaty from defending Japan to maintaining peace and security in Asia-Pacific region, it was argued that the nature of the declaration was in fact an amendment of the defense treaty[2]. In order to implement the declaration, the new Guidelines of U.S.-Japan Defense Cooperation was adopted in September 1997, and new legislation as well as some changes of the law took place as mentioned above.

Viewing the development as a pursuit of military super power, both academics and Japanese citizens have expressed deep concern for the trend, arguing that it was against the Japanese Constitution, which stipulated the denouncement of war, and disarmament[3]. The new legislation has also excited much controversy outside Japan. East Asian countries, particularly China, Russia and North Korea strongly criticized the new Guidelines and the related laws. Shortly after those laws were passed, the spokesman of the Chinese Foreign Ministry expressed concern over the legislation, commenting that they ran counter to contemporary trends, and would produce a harmful effect on the security in the Far Eastern region. China also protested any attempt by Japan to include, either directly or indirectly, Taiwan with the scope of "the surrounding areas." North Korea had denounced the legislation as a vehicle for war since the legislation was proposed. Russia also showed concern for those laws, although the tone was not so strong as that of China. Taiwan, however, welcomed the development, announcing that those new measures were proper means for the United States and Japan to protect democracy and freedom from potential military threats of undemocratic nations. Taiwan also viewed that such measures would help maintaining security and peace in Taiwan and Asia[4]. Contrary to the neighboring states, South Korean government kept silent on the issue, although the Korean press covered it with heavy headlines. It seemed that it was very difficult for South Korean government to take a firm position on the delicate issue. The government regarded the new measures with favor because the strengthening of the U.S.-Japan security scheme would reinforce South Korea's military capability against North Korea. At the same time, the Korean government concerned that building military power of Japan was regarded with unaffected dislike by the majority of its people.

The enactment of laws related to the new Guidelines and the new policy based on them seem to conflict with the position Japanese government had taken so far. The government had maintained that taking collective self-defense measures by Japan was against the Japanese Constitution[5]. As pointed out earlier, the new policy also runs directly against the existing U.S.-Japan Security Treaty. Japan may provide the United States with military cooperation in case of emergencies in either the Korean peninsula or Taiwan under the new Guidelines scheme, interpreting "the surrounding areas" as including Korea and Taiwan. In these circumstances, the measures taken by Japan would be charged of violating both the Japanese Constitution and the security treaty with the United States[6].

From the perspective of South Korea, the new security measures taken by Japan also raise questions concerning negative impacts on South Korea's policy toward the North as well as its unification policy. The reunification of two Koreas is a national policy goal of the utmost importance. The goal, however, should be pursued not by military forces but by peaceful means, as the South Koran Constitution (art. 4) stipulates. In line with such principle, the governments of two Koreas reached an agreement in 1991 on reconciliation and cooperation. Kim Dae Jung administration has stepped further up, and has been consistently pursuing the so-called "Sunshine Policy." In this regard, the basic proposition of the author is widely shared by Professor Yamauti. He properly agued that the diplomatic efforts of Japanese government should be directed to facilitate the peaceful reunification of two Koreas rather than preparing for military cooperation with the United States in case of armed conflicts in the Korean peninsula[7].

In this paper, the author critically analyzes the new Guidelines and the relevant legislation in the context of the pacifism of the Japanese Constitution. The author in this regard pays much attention particularly on the cleavage between the norm and practice. The author, particularly mindful of "the sunshine policy" of South Korea, seeks to find ideal measures both Japan and Korea can take for the security and peace in Korea as well as Asia. The author in so doing argues against the recent policy changes of Japanese government from the viewpoint of the pacifism embodied in both Japanese and South Korean Constitution.

## II. Pacifism and the Constitution

### 1. The genealogy of the pacific constitution

The aftermath of the two World Wars has brought about the adoption of pacifism by some countries in their constitutional laws. Many nations have also made into international treaties to prevent wars of aggression. Although the origin of modern international pacifism can be traced back to Immanuel Kant[8], most commentators regard the Covenant of the League of Nations in 1919, the Kellogg-Briand Antiwar Pact of 1928, and more directly the Charter of the United Nations as the most influential instruments for such development.

Under the U.N. Charter, all member states are obliged to abandon any acts of aggression, and to seek pacific settlements of disputes. In this regard, the Charter provides the member states with a collective self-defense system to maintain international peace and security. The basic framework of the collective security scheme is that any act of aggression to a member state is regarded as an attack to all member states[9].

The ideals of the United Nations have affected some countries in their constitutions. Germany, Japan and Korea, all of which suffered the ravages of war, stipulated the principle of pacifism in their constitutional laws. Switzerland, as a part of her neutrality policy, also expressly adopted such constitutional provisions. More recently, South Africa emphasized pacifism in her constitution. Although the number of state that expressly announced pacifism in their constitution, it does not mean that a majority of states are ignorant or opposing of the principle. Since the matter of war and peace is widely regarded as a subject of international law, most countries do not seem to deal with the pacifism in their constitutional law[10].

### 2. The Adoption of the Pacifist Constitution in Japan and Korea

(1) The Pacifism in the Japanese Constitution

By drastically adopting the principle of pacifism in 1947, the Japanese Constitution has taken the initiative in pacifist constitutions. The supreme law of Japan stipulated renunciation of war as well as prohibition of armed force.

This type of unilateral self-restraint was termed as "the self-sufficient pacifism" by a commentator[11]. Although the French Constitution of 1791 has a resemblance with the Japan, the Japanese one is very unique and unprecedented in other grounds. In the French, what was prohibited was the war of aggression, but in the Japanese having armed force is prohibited as well.

Some praise the fact that the pacifism in the Japanese Constitution has been unchanged for the half century. Other criticize that the principle has reduced to a mere skeleton. In this regard, the author agrees to the assessment that the pacifist Constitution has contributed for enhancing democracy and economic development in post-war Japan, as well as peace and security in Asia[12]. As mentioned early, the end of the Cold War caused the situation more complicated. It also seems that the faith in the principle of unarmed pacifist constitution is eroding in the Japanese society of today. The eventual determination of the issue is of course a matter of political choice of Japanese people. This paper, however, concerns very much about any changes of the constitutional principle because how to change or reconstruct it is very critical under the current atmosphere of the international relations[13].

(2) Pacifism in the South Korean Constitution

In the Preamble, the Constitution of the Republic of Korea states that the people of Korea endeavor "to contribute to lasting world peace and the common prosperity of mankind." Article 5 section 1 also provides that "[t] he Republic of Korea shall endeavor to maintain international peace and shall renounce all aggressive wars." Unlike the Japanese Constitution, the Korean one therefore allows the war of self-defense or self-preservation based on the theory of just war[14]. In addition, Article 6 section 1 of the Constitution expressly announces the respect for international law and order by providing that "[t] reaties duly concluded and promulgated under the Constitution and the generally recognized rules of international law shall have the same effect as the domestic laws of the Republic of Korea." The following section stipulates that "[t] he status of aliens shall be guaranteed as prescribed by international law and treaties."

As a divided nation after the Second World War, to achieve the reunification has undoubtedly been listed as the top priority of the national policy. The means to pursue the goal, however, has not been so consistent. It was the Constitution of 1972, which followed the historical "Joint Declaration of South and North

Korea" in the same year, which embodied the provisions expressly stating the reunification policy through peaceful means. In line with the new policy, the present Constitution, which was adopted in 1987, has more detailed provisions concerning the peaceful reunification policy. While pronouncing "peaceful unification of our homeland" in the Preamble, Article 4 of the Constitution provides that "[t] the Republic of Korea shall seek unification and shall formulate and carry out a policy of peaceful unification based on the principles of freedom and democracy." Article 66 section 3 in this regard provides that "[t] he President shall have the duty to purse sincerely the peaceful unification of the homeland." Under the policy, the South Korean parliament enacted in 1990 a law concerning the mutual exchange and cooperation between South and North Korea. In September 1991, the two Koreas finally became the member states of the United Nations, adopted an agreement on reconciliation, non-aggression, exchange, and cooperation in December of the same year.

Despite the fact that the South Korean Constitution and relevant laws direct peaceful engagement with North Korea, the judicial definition of North Korea has long troubled South Korean jurists. Traditionally a majority of the constitutional law scholars in South Korea have argued that the government of South Korea is the sole and legitimate government in the Korean peninsula. The theory is based on Article 3 of the Constitution, providing that "[t] he territory of the Republic of Korea shall consist of the Korean peninsula and its adjacent islands." According to the theory, the *de facto* government in the North Korean region is an illegal organization that currently prevents the South Korean government from governing the northern area. A more recent theory, however, opposes the traditional interpretation. It argues that the old theory is not compatible with the policy changes since the Constitution of 1972. Considering the constitutional provisions on peaceful unification, the U.N. membership of two Koreas, and the South and North Korean Agreement of 1991[15], it is reasonable to recognize North Korea as a nation, the theorists argue. The new theory, which is gaining wide supports these days, criticizes the traditional theory as unrealistic, Cold-War minded, and hindering of the unification process[16]. In this regard, the Constitutional Court of South Korea has tried to compromise on the conflicting views. The Court holds a position of "the double characteristic of the North Korean regime," which argues that North Korea is both enemy and friend at the same time. It is an anti-state fraction in view of the territorial clause in the Constitution, while a partner of mutual exchange and cooperation in light of the peaceful unification clause in the supreme law of the land[17].

## III. The Pacifism in the Japanese Constitution

### 1. Historical background of the pacifism

With unprecedented seriousness, the Japanese Constitution embodied the principle of pacifist ideal. There have been a few different explanations of the historical origin of the constitutional provisions. It is no doubt that the Constitution was substantially influenced by the international trend or movement towards illegalization of war after the World War II. The horrible war experience of the Japanese people also made them to support peaceful and anti-war movement as well as the pacific Constitution[18].

Waging the Asia-Pacific War by the Japanese government resulted in atomic bombing in Hiroshima and Nakasaki. The pacifist Constitution of Japan was "a crystallization of the general will"[19] of Japanese people, as the victim of A-bomb. The unique characteristic of the Japanese Constitution is, therefore, a byproduct of atomic bomb era[20].

The demilitarization of Japan, which is stipulated in Article 9 of the Constitution, however, cannot be sufficiently explained by what we described above. It was a direct result of the post-war policy of the Allied Powers, which was manifested in the Potsdam Declaration. It is also argued that Article 9 was necessary to shirk the Emperor's responsibility for the war, and to retain the Emperor system in Japan[21]. There has also been an argument that General MacArthur administration forced Japanese to adopt Article 9, but this is not very convincing[22]. In sum, all we mentioned above consisted of the background of Article 9. The experience and will of Japanese people, the political situation of the post-war Japanese society, and the will of the Allied Powers all together produced the pacifist nature like Article 9. The provision is thus a joint product of the United States and Japan[23].

### 2. The Structure and Interpretation of the Pacifist Norm

(1) The Constitutional Provisions on Pacifism

Section 1 of Article 9 provides that Japan shall not use armed force forever as a means to settle international disputes. The following section goes further by proclaiming that Japan shall not have army, navy and air force, and renounce the right of belligerency. The language of those provisions was so clear that there were few disputes over the meaning of the provisions when they were enacted. It clearly meant that Japan would not retain and use armed force to settle international disputes. Controversies over the interpretation of these provisions have arisen since Japan began to retain *de facto* armed force.

Another interesting point in this regard is the right to live peacefully, which is proclaimed in the Preamble of the Japanese Constitution. The right to live peacefully seems to be a basic ground for all other human rights embodied in the Constitution. By the Preamble, the issue of peace in Japanese society turned into a matter of human rights. It thus should be a top priority of the policy goals in Japan to provide its people with socio-economic environment that guarantees the right to live peacefully[24]. To realize the right, however, Japanese seems to overcome some huddles. Legal theories and judicial rulings have so far failed to reach an agreement on the characteristic of the right to live peacefully. They have also been perplexed at the remedies when the right is violated[25].

(2) The Government's Position on the Pacifist Provisions

When the Constitution was established, the official interpretation of Article 9 by the Japanese government was simple and clear: Japan did not retain armed force, and pursued a policy of thorough pacifism. The only controversy then was the issue of self-defense war. Since international law allows all nations to have a right to self-defense, Article 9 need not be interpreted to prohibit such inherent right. In this regard, the official interpretation was something called "the theory of self-defense without armed force." The theory asserted that Article 9 did not necessary mean to renounce a right of self-defense, but waging any type of war became impossible as a result of demilitarization under Article 9. Public opinion at that time was also favorable for the official position.

The original position and the official interpretation had to face a serious challenge since Japan began to rebuild its armed force in 1950. Despite the suspicious name, it is no doubt that "the Reserved Police Force" was in fact armed forces. In 1952, it was permitted for the Security Guard to engage in overseas military activities to defend Japan. In 1954 when the Self-Defense Forces was established, Japan finally regained military forces, and the conflict with the Constitution became evident. The U.S.-Japan Security Treaty of 1952 also collided with the Preamble of the Constitution.

Under the circumstances, the government and political parties moved to amend the Constitution, but turned out a failure. The next move then was to modify the previous interpretation of the Constitution. While maintaining the position of renouncing military forces, they argued that it is constitutional for Japan to retain armed forces just necessary to defend herself. The new interpretation shows a major shift from "the right of self-defense without armed forces" to "the right of self-defense with armed forces." In line with the new theory, the government also asserted that the scope or limit of self-defense forces might be changed depending on national strength, international politics, and the development of technology. It is therefore obvious that there exist no objective criteria to judge the boundary of self-defense activities under the new interpretation.

When the U.S-Japan Security Treaty was amended in 1960, Japan obtained once again a chance to increase the strength of its self-defense forces. According to the amended treaty, the Japan became able to use armed force jointly with the U.S. forces when the American troops stationed in Japan were attacked. The range of using armed force by Japan was further extended in 1978 when the Guidelines of the U.S.-Japan Defense Cooperation were adopted. The Guidelines allowed Japan to engage in military activities outside the Japanese territory in case that the security of the Far Eastern region was significantly endangered. Under the new security system, Japan has strengthened the capability of its Self-Defense Forces, and the substantial increase of the military power in recent years was quite noticeable[26].

As mentioned earlier, the end of the Cold War has significantly affected the role of the Self-Defense Forces. To cope with the new global order, it has been argued that the Self-Defense Forces need to assist peacekeeping activities of the United Nations. Japan, in line with the trend, accepted an U.S. request and provided 3 billion Dollars financial aid when the Gulf War broke out in 1990. At that time the Self-Defense Forces dispatched a small fleet to the Gulf area. The Law Concerning the Peacekeeping Operation (PKO), which was enacted in 1992, conferred a legal basis for sending troops overseas upon the Self-Defense Forces[27]. Under the law, the Forces were dispatched to Cambodia, Mozambique, and the areas adjacent to Rwanda in 1994. The law of the Self-Defense Forces was amended in 1994 in order for the Forces to provide overseas Japanese with transportation in case of emergency.

The Japanese government in this regard argues that sending the Self-Defense Forces overseas is constitutional. They justify the new interpretation by saying that what the Constitution prohibits is to wage an aggressive war by the Japanese government, but here is a matter of international cooperation as a member state of the United Nations. This new position of the government, as well as the enactment and amendment of the relevant laws and the Guidelines, poses a serious threat to the pacifist nature of the Japanese Constitution[28]. In this respect, it is a quite critical development that the Diet recently established a special committee to inquire into constitutional amendment[29].

(3) Legal Theories and Case Laws on the Issue

The majority of legal scholars in Japan do not agree to the position or interpretation of the government on the issue. They argue that the recent activities of the Self-Defense Forces and the relevant laws are unconstitutional in the context with Article 9. With respect to the meaning of the war prohibited in Article 9 section 1, there are two different theories. One theory argues that the war in the section means all sorts of war, thus Japan cannot conduct any kind of war to settle international disputes. The other theory disagrees: it argues that only a war of aggression is meant by the section, thus a war of self-defense is permissible under the Constitution. Proponents of the latter theory are also split by two fractions with respect to the interpretation of Article 9 section 2. One asserts that what the section requires is to renounce military force only for an aggressive war. The other argues that in order to prevent a war of aggression the section requires to abandon all kinds of military force. The supports of the former theory is a minority among the academics. In sum, the majority of Japanese scholar seems to believe that not only conducting a war, but also the very existence of the Self-Defense Forces is unconstitutional.

Considering the obvious conflict between Article 9 of the Constitution and the relevant treaty and legislation, the author agrees with the majority of Japanese constitutional scholars on the issue. The Supreme Court of Japan, however, has avoided judging on the issue[30]. In Sunagawa case, where the lower court held unconstitutional, the highest court tried to bypass the judgment on constitutionality. Despite the evident unconstitutionality of the practice[31], the Supreme Court did not ruled the issue unconstitutional as referring to the doctrine of political questions. The Court held that since the security treaty in question is of a highly political nature, it is improper for a judicial branch to decide the constitutionality of such treaty unless there exists quite clear evidence of unconstitutionality[32]. This type of passive attitude by the Supreme Court is widely viewed as not only damaging the judicial review system but also hindering the development of constitutionalism in Japan.

## IV. The Assessment of the new Guidelines

### 1. The Legislation on the new Guideline and the Pacifism

Shuhenjitaihou, which is the core of the legislation related to the new Guidelines, has been pointed out as inconsistent with Article 9 of the Constitution by many commentators, including the National Research Association for Constitutional Law[33]. Shuhenjitaihou authorizes Japan to take necessary measures to maintain peace and security of Japan in case of emergency in the surrounding area. Article 1 of the law defines "the Shuhenjitaihou" as situations in the area surrounding Japan, which may seriously affect the security and peace of Japan. The most critical question arises about this law is that it does not provide definitions concerning key terms like "the area surrounding Japan, and "situations which may seriously affect the security and peace of Japan." This deficiency of the Shuhenjitaihou casts a well-founded fear of irrational application and abuse[34].

Since the law requests Japan to assist the military activities of the United States in a situation when Japan was not attacked, Japan now may engage in war-like activities overseas. This kind of involvement runs counter to the original intent of the U.S.-Japan Security Treaty, as well as the purpose of establishing the Self-Defense Forces. It also means a big challenge to the normative power of the Japanese Constitution, which has exercised a significant control against sending the Self-Defense Forces overseas and participating in the collective defense scheme. As a commentator said, it is "the passion-tide" of the pacifism in Japan embodied in Article 9 of the Constitution[35].

Another problem raised by the recent development of the new Guidelines legislation is a potential violation of or threat to the right to live peacefully. The local governments in Japan has developed independent roads toward the right to live peacefully. They have had a strong belief in Article 9, which, they believed, guaranteed such right, thus protecting local residents from the danger of war. The new Guidelines related laws, however, may request local governments to provide necessary assistance in case of emergency. By providing the assistance, the local residents may be exposed to the ravages of war regardless of their intention. This conflict makes it urgent for legal scholars in Japan to reassess about the right to live peacefully in the context of the pacifism in the Japanese Constitution.

## 2. The Real Intention of the New Guidelines Related Laws

Considering the fact that the Japanese government carried out resolutely the legislation in spite of the strong criticism and opposition both from legal academia and the general public, it is quite natural for anyone to investigate the real intention behind such legislation. The official explanation was that such legal changes were inevitable for Japan to be better prepared for the threat to its national security, and to provide a more reliable basis of cooperation with the United States in case of emergency not only in Japan but also in the areas surrounding Japan[36]. This official explanation, however, does not seem quite convincing. As a commentator argued, the recent policy change and legal modification seem to be a joint product of factors of Japan and the U.S. side as well[37]. With respect to the Japan side factors, it is not doubt that the international economic strategy of Japan has substantially influenced such changes. As Japanese corporations became more multinational entities since 1980s, Japan seemed to need a powerful military force to guard their worldwide business interest. The recent development, therefore, is not just a matter of nationalism or pursuing a military super power. It is closely related to the corporate interest in the global market. In this regard, the new policy has may common features with the military strategy of the United States.

In sum, Japan's new movement toward more effective and powerful military power seems to be based on a theory arguing that Japanese business interest needs to be protected from a state of disorder outside its territory, particularly in Asia. The method or approach Japan took so far for this purpose was twofold: Reinforcing the military alliance with the United States under the mutual security treaty was one way, and the other was participating more actively in the peacekeeping operation of the United Nations. Despite the widespread concerns over the new development, the practice of violating or ignoring the principle and provisions of the Constitution in the pretext of protecting economic profits seems very hard to be stopped. The author in this regard agrees with Professor Watanabe, who suggests that Japan reform the economic structure based on multinational enterprises, and rebuild one that does not threaten neighboring nations. He argues that without this kind of reform it is impossible to realize the pacifism of the Japanese Constitution[38].

### 3. The New Guidelines and South Korea's Sunshine Policy

It is widely accepted that the major concern of the New Guidelines and the related laws was directed to North Korea. There have been international disputes over an alleged nuclear facility at Yongbyun, North Korea, launching a long-range missile by North Korea, and an incident of Japanese territorial sea by a North Korean ship. All these incidents offered a good cause for Japan to pass or amend the laws related to the New Guidelines. The external threat caused by North Korea was good enough to suppress the unfavorable public opinion and to justify the extended activity of the Self-Defense Forces.

It was, however, quite odd that there was no severe criticism from South Korean government. Neither the press in South Korea covered the development seriously. It seemed that both the government and Korean people were so obsessed with overcoming the economic crisis after the IMF bailout that they could not afford to assess critically the consequence of the Japanese armament. In addition, there was a viewpoint that related the South Korean silence with the Sunshine Policy of Kim Dae Jung Administration. It argued that the new policy, which pursued embracing the North rather than confronting, needed a more reliable and stronger military alliance with U.S. and Japan to suppress the potential invasion by North Korea. In this regard, a leading South Korean expert in international relations assessed the New Guidelines positively[39].

The author, however, concerns that the recent development related to the New Guidelines may exert a harmful influence upon the peace and security of the Korean peninsula. Since both South and North Korean people had been victimized by aggressive wars led by Japan, strengthening military force by Japan tends to cause anxiety and tension in two Koreas. The new policy and legislation may also give rise to a serious trouble with "the sunshine policy" or engagement policy of South Korea. Under the policy, South Korea takes a great caution not to agitate the North, and tries to build confidence in each other. Both the government and informed public opinion in the South worry that the Japanese policy may hurt the engagement policy and increase the tension between two Koreas. In June 1999, there will be the South-North Korea summit meeting in Pyungyang. The historical top-level talk after 55 years hostility seems to prove that the sunshine policy is a right and effective way to reduce the tension in the Korean peninsula, and to facilitate the peaceful reunification of two Koreas.

Considering all these new developments, Japan need, more than ever, to pay attention to building a regional security system that is well prepared for the reunification of two Koreas[40]. In other words, it would be much better for Japanese constitutionalism not to concentrate on military cooperation with the United States in the supposed contingency by North Korea[41]. Reducing the tension and the peaceful unification in the Korean peninsular is utmost important for the peace and security in the East Asian region. As a leading nation responsible of maintaining not only the regional, but international peace and security, Japan should make every endeavor to facilitate the peaceful reunification of two Koreas[42].

## V. Conclusion

After the end of the Cold War era, the United States, as the sole ultra super power, has been very actively intervene in many regional disputes. Although the U.S. justified its intervention by the cause of humanitarianism or human rights diplomacy, other countries like Russia and China condemned the U.S. military action, especially that of the Kosovo incident. The former enemy states are not only the critics. At home, Dr. Henry Kissinger also criticized the military measures the U.S. took in Kosovo, and argued that the U.S. should reconsider the policy of humanitarian intervention and human rights diplomacy as well[43]. It is therefore unwise for Japan to follow the unpopular diplomatic strategy and military policy of the United States. What Japan should do in this regard is not to strengthen the military cooperation with the United States, but to build a regional security system independently[44].

The Japanese Constitution has provided a leading model of the pacifist principle by Article 9 and the right to live peacefully. It has substantially contributed to regional and international peace. The previous analysis, however, reveals that the New Guidelines and the related laws are clearly inconsistent with the pacifism embodied in the Japanese Constitution. It is more depressing to observe that the conservative majority in the Diet tries to amend the

Constitution in order to eliminate the conflict between the new measures and the constitutional provisions. The correct role designated to the Japanese parliament is not to ignore or nullify the spirit and principles of the Constitution. It is rather to represent fairly the will of its people, and to check the foreign policy of the government in light of the Constitution.

In this regard, the previous action of judiciary in Japan deserves some attention. It is widely accepted that judicial review is pivotal to establish and maintain constitutionalism. Japan has the same judicial system with the United States in this respect, but the Japanese judiciary had been behaved quite differently from American courts. It was the government, not the court, to say the final word on constitutional interpretation in Japan. The Japanese Supreme Court has avoided to judge on the constitutionality of legislation like the U. S.-Japan Security Treaty, the New Guidelines and the related laws. The criticism of such judicial passiveness seems correct, and should be accepted by the judiciary for the rule of law in Japan[45].

1. Guide-Line: Guidelines for Japan-U.S. Defense Cooperation
2. Shuhenjitaihou: The Law Concerning Measures to Ensure Peace and Security of Japan in Situation in Areas Surrounding Japan
3. Jieitaikaiseicouan: The Law for Amending the Self-Defence Forces law (Amendment to Article 100-8 of the Self-Defence Forces law)
4. The Agreement between Japan & USA: the Agreement between the Government of Japan and the Government of the United States of America concerning reciprocal provision of logistic support, supplies and services between the Self Defence Force of Japan and the Armed Forces of the United States of Japan

[1] 山内敏弘・太田一男『憲法と平和主義』(法律文化社, 1998) 50頁。
[2] Despite the appearance and formulation of the joint declaration, the practical effect of the declaration was to amend the existing defense treaty. The declaration should thus have been approved by the Diet according to Article 73 (3) of the Constitution. The announcement of the declaration without the consent of the Diet therefore raises a question of constitutional validity, as well as violating the principle of parliamentary democracy in Japan. See Ibid. p. 46.
[3] The National Research Association of the Japanese Constitution announced on March 16, 1999 a statement on deep concern over Shuhenjitaihou. The statement pointed out that the legislation raised serious questions regarding the pacifism of Article 9, as well as the fundamental principles, of the Constitution. The statement also urged that the Japanese politics should respect the Constitutionalism. For the details, see P. 186.
[4] Weekly Hankuk, May 4, 1999.

[5] The Japanese government used to say that taking collective self-defense measures clashed with Article 9 of the Constitution. The government, however, recently changed the position, and argued that such measures were constitutionally permissible because the self-defense measures both individually and collectively consisted of inherent rights of a nation. In so arguing, the government referred to Article 51 of the Charter of the United Nations, which allowed individual rights of self-defense and the rights of collective self-defense as well. The majority of Japanese scholars oppose the new government position. The scholars argue that although the Constitution recognizes the rights of self-defense, the exercise of the rights by means of armed forces cannot be allowed. It is thus impressible for Japan to engage in military activities to defend other nations, they argue. See 山内, pp. 60-64; It is also widely accepted among international law scholars that those rights of collective self-defense are neither inherent rights of a nation nor evident rights under international law. They view such rights as something new created by the U.N. Charter. See山本草二『国際法（新版）』（有斐閣，1994）736頁；藤田久一『国際法講義2』（東京大学出版会，1994）402頁．
[6] 山内, pp. 51.
[7] Id.
[8] See Carl J. Friedrich, *Inevitable Peace*, 1974.；金哲洙，『現代憲法論』（博英社，1979）96面．
[9] For the details of the collective security scheme, see藤田久一『国連法』（東京大学出版会）1998，314頁．
[10] Cheryl Saunders, "World Peace and Constitutional Law,"『世界憲法研究』第2号（国際憲法学会，1997）p. 71.
[11] 最上敏樹，「冷戦後国債社会における日本国憲法の平和主義」『憲法問題10』（全国憲法研究会，1999）5，38頁．
[12] 山内敏弘，「平和主義の現況と展望」『憲法研究10』（全国憲法研究会，1999）5，76-77頁．
[13] Ibid. p. 47.
[14] 権寧星『憲法学原論』（法文社，1999）169面．
[15] Article 1 of the Agreement provides that the South and North recognize each other's regime and respect it.
[16] 許営『韓国憲法論』（博英社，1999）p. 185.
[17] The Constitutional Court held that North Korea had not yet abandoned its policy of overthrowing the government of South Korea, thus it should be regarded as an anti-state organization although the law concerning mutual exchange and cooperation between the South and North was being implemented.憲裁決⋯⋯⋯。
[18] 山内敏弘・太田一男，*Ibid*. p. 3.
[19] 戸波江二『憲法』（ぎょうせい，1996）p. 87.
[20] 水島朝穂「平和主義」大須賀明（編）『憲法』（青林書院，1996）p. 46.
[21] 大久保史郎「韓半島の統一と日本の役割」『世界憲法研究』第2集（国際憲法学会韓国学会，1997）p. 194.
[22] 山内敏弘・太田一男，p. 5.
[23] 田中英夫，『憲法制定過程覚え書』（有斐閣，1979）p. 90；小林直樹『憲法第9条』（岩波書店，1988）p. 23；芦部信喜『憲法（新版）』（岩波書店，1997）p. 55.
[24] 戸波江二，*Ibid*. p. 90.
[25] For the details, see浦田一郎『現代の平和主義と立憲主義』（日本評論社，1995）p. 108.
[26] The annual expenditure on armament in 1989 was 0.95% of GDP, and consisted of 6.36% of the total expenditure of that year. See日本防衛庁（編）『防衛白書』（1988）p. 375.

[27] The PKO Law has been criticized as legislation against the pacifism in the Japanese Constitution. See 山内敏弘・太田一男, p. 18.
[28] 和田進「安保体制のグローバル化と国民意識・運動」(『法律時報』71巻1号) p. 30.
[29] By way of passing legislation to establish such committee in the Diet on July 26, 1999, the Japanese parliament initiated to deal with constitutional amendment for the first time since the Word War II. (朝日新聞, 1999. 7. 27)
[30] 最（大）判, 昭和34. 12. 16。『刑集』13巻13号p. 3225.
[31] 森英樹, 非軍事平和主義,『現代憲法講義Ⅰ』(法律文化社, 1993) p. 87.
[32] While criticizing the court's ruling, a commentator argues that in order to prevent a treaty from giving an effect of constitutional amendment, the court should engage in the judicial review of treaties. See 水島朝穂P. 317.
[33] See 山内敏弘（編）,『日米新ガイドラインと周辺事態法』(法律文化社, 1999)
[34] 横田耕一『周辺事態の問題性』山内敏弘（編）Ibid. p. 58.
[35] 大須賀明, 全国憲法研究会 憲法記念講演会 (1999. 5. 3) での挨拶文.
[36] 日本防衛庁（編）『防衛白書』, 1998, p. 231.
[37] 渡辺治「安保体制のグローバル化を促するもの」『法律時報』71巻1号 (1999) pp. 7-9.
[38] 渡辺治「日米新ガイドラインの日本側のねらい」『日米新ガイドラインと周辺事態法』p. 36.
[39] 金瓊元, "The New Guidelines of U.S.-Japan Security Cooperation and South Korea," *Chosun Ilbo* [daily newspaper], May 5, 1999.
[40] Professor Okubo criticized the New Guidelines policy in this regard, and argues that Japan has to abide by the pacific principle of the Constitution even for the purpose of helping the Korean reunification. See 大久保p. 167.
[41] 山内敏弘・太田一男, p. 51.
[42] See 金哲洙,「東北アジアの平和と韓半島の統一」『世界憲法研究』第2集 (1997) p. 35.
[43] Henry A. Kissinger, "New World Disorder," *Newsweek*, May 31, 1999, pp. 22-4.
[44] 酒井新二「地域安保こそ日本のめざす道 (論壇)」朝日新聞, 1999. 1. 6. 4面.
[45] 樋口陽一『憲法Ⅰ』(青林書院, 1998) p. 541.

# The Significance of the Constitution of Japan and Japan Association for Studies of Constitutional Law

### Mamiko Ueno
(translation by Mamiko Ueno and Toru Ito)

### Introduction—Constitutionalism of France

'Constitutionalism' makes the students of French public law remember Article 16 of the 1789 French Declaration of Rights. The Declaration states that 'a society in which the observance of the law is not assured, nor the separation of powers defined, has no constitution at all.' From this prescription, it is thought that the guarantee of human rights and the separation of powers are indispensable to the constitutional society in France.

However, the term of constitutionalism did not become established in the French Constitution. It is said that the ideas of Sieyès and Rousseau are intermingled in the Declaration. According to Sieyès, even if the individual has political rights, he/she can only assert through the system of representation of the *nation* within the nation which holds sovereignty and rights as a whole. The *nation* makes laws which represent sovereignty traditionally.... The *nation* makes the normative constitution founded upon the separation of powers and the guarantee of individual rights[1].

After all, the conclusion drawn from the 1789 French Declaration of Rights was that the actualization of the constitution would depend chiefly upon laws, which meant that 'the society would guarantee the individual rights through laws.' On the other hand, the separation of powers meant 'wresting legislative power from the monarch' at that time[2].

*Masanari SAKAMOTO* classifies constitutionalism as two models; the French-type which theoretically pursues the constitutional structure to integrate the will of the people into the ruling process, and the American-type which tries to derive from the tradition the constitutional structure to reflect the plural will of the people pluralistically in the ruling process. At any rate, the starting points of both models are not the same[3].

It was only after establishing the Constitution of the French Fifth Republic in 1958, and more strictly, after allowing Conseil Constitutionel to do judicial review practically in the 1970's, that the meaning of constitutionalism began to be understood in France. But now, for instance, we cannot see terms such as *constitutionnalisme* (constitutionalism) and *supériorité de la constitution* (supremacy of the constitution) in the index to *Droit constitutionnel*, written by seven French constitution professors including Louis FAVOREU[4]. Nor can we find any recent writings titled '*constitutionnalisme*', except *Constitutionnalisme jacoban et constitutionnalisme soviétique* whose '*constitutionnalisme*' means the constitutional system of government[5].

Elisabeth ZOLLER, a constitution professor as well as an American law scholar at the Second University of Paris, indicates two ideas of the constitution in *Droit constitutionnel*. She also makes an explanation of 'general theory of the constitution as a norm', 'structure of powers' and 'guarantee of the rights' based on Article 16 of the 1789 French Declaration of Rights[6].

The first idea of the constitution is that it embodies a political regime of State and cannot be distinguished from the government. The second is that it is the law beyond the government, the whole law-norm with its supremacy over the government. The former, she interprets, as a descriptive constitution and the latter as a normative one. On the latter, she says, "the constitution is the fundamental and supreme law the free people shall enjoy." As far as it is the fundamental law, the constitution is the foundation of political society, and as far as it is the supreme law, the constitution as a norm holds supremacy over all the other laws, which is the fruit of the free people. After distinguishing between 'legality' and 'constitutionality' in her explanation of the creation of the constitution as a norm in America, she insists that considering the view of the constitution at the time of French Revolution, the French established the constitutional state based on laws, not the state on the constitution. It was the idea that sovereign power, genuinely and exclusively, resides with the people that they established in France, just as Sieyès hoped. Article 3 of the 1789 French Declaration of Rights, which still now has validity, states that 'the principle of all sovereignty resides essentially in the nation.' According to Sieyès, "the people will not be located under the constitution, nor can be located, nor should be located." If the people were to be located under the constitution or any other positive law, they would not be supreme rulers any longer. On the other hand, the law is an expression of the general will and it is impossible to distinguish constitutional law and general law[7].

The constitutional tradition in Europe is far from the American tradition. So the idea of controlling the legislative power was not actualized until the end of World War II, though asserted sporadically. However, today the situation has altered dramatically. Not a few nations approve of a normative idea of the constitution. Such concrete developments are seen in the fact that the assembly gradually begins to respect the constitution of State through judicial review. France, accordingly, responds to the streams in Europe[8].

The new idea on the constitution in Europe has been brought by theoretical and political factors. As to theoretical factors, the doctrine of Hans Kelsen has had a great influence. It is based on law-stage theory, a pyramid system whose top is the constitution. He says that the two essentials of law-norm are validity and efficacy, both of which derive from the constitution located at the top in the law-system. Then the first European Constitutional Court based on the idea of Hans Kelsen was established in Austria in 1920, which was different from the American-type. According to FAVOREU, the former is the special court for securing the effect of judicial review, but in the case of the latter, judicial review is in the power of each judge, even if he/she is a judge of the lower court[9].

As to political factors, American constitutionalism has had an influence on the European political thought and ways of the guarantee of rights and freedom. Furthermore, American federalism has had a strong influence on the construction of European Community through American system in large part because America was the winner of World War II. Above all, the role of judicial review in the federal state has been recognized. However, the crucial factor is the necessity of the guarantee of human rights. The assembly is not a bulwark against despotism in Europe as well as in America. The law is now recognized as a mere expression of the government's will supported by a majority, though it was regarded legally as an expression of the general will and seen ideologically as a result of general harmonization. It is surely no accident that the Constitutional Court developed in European countries where a majority dominate the parliament[10].

Representation and political ideology have also changed. Americans have brought Europe their own political culture which is different from Europeans'. When the general will and republicanism do not mean the unanimous consent based on fraternity, a unanimous democracy gives way to a plural democracy. Even the pluralist should respect the rights of the minority, and take precautions against the excessive despotism of the majority. The best way to guarantee civil rights, according to Madison, should be pursued in 'the diversity of interests' which characterizes liberal society. Conseil Constitutionel confirms this new approach, describing the respect for pluralism as 'one of the prerequisites for democracy'[11].

In this way, the developments in the idea of constitutionalism as a norm in Europe have brought on drastic changes. One of them is a change in the character of public law, whose basis has been laid not on the legislation but on the constitution since then. Another is a change in the character of the constitution itself. Constitutional law tends to be regarded not as a political norm but as a trial norm, the law related by a judge. ZOLLER says that these changes have been accomplished according to precedents in Conseil Constitutionel, in spite of a lot of old expectations[12]; the republican tradition in which all sources of law were founded upon the general will, the constitutional tradition in which there was no judicial review except under the political forms such as the First and Second Empires, and the 1958 establishers' intention not to confer on Conseil Constitutionel the status of the defender of rights and freedom.[13] In the France of today, the constitutional law (un droit constitutionnel) is different from the political system that actually exists owing to the right of the Conseil Constitutionel to 'relate the law'. No research on a political system can be carried out without the approach of politics. But the research on the constitution is now beyond the political approach. The constitution has become a main discipline of public law, a foundation of public law, independent of politics. So today, the public law is not based on the principle of legality but on the principle of constitutionality. The French Constitution is divided into two parts; the formal constitution concerning the power system and the guarantee of rights on the one hand, and the practical constitution concerning the civil and political rights on the other hand[14].

ZOLLER, therefore, says that it was not until today that Article 16 of the 1789 French Declaration of Rights is actualized. In the France of today, in fact, the legal state or rule of law is advocated chiefly through the judicial review of the Conseil Constitutionel[15]. We can observe its fusion with American constitutionalism.

## I  The Constitution of Japan

### 1  The Significance of the Constitution of Japan
#### (1)  The Constitution of Japan and Constitutionalism

The Constitution of Japan has been affected by America rather than Europe in its historical roots. The Constitution promulgated in November 1946 and enforced in May 1947, has become worth the name of constitutionalism for the first time in Japan, with the sincere reflections on the political affairs during World War II. As mentioned above, the constitutionalism lies on the guarantee of human rights and the separation of powers, just as stated in Article 16 of the 1789 French Declaration of Rights though it was not understood in such a way at that time. In this sense, the Imperial Japanese Constitution can be called apparent constitutionalism because neither of the above requirements are fulfilled[16]. On the other hand, with the evolution of democracy, it is argued that we need not bother to refer to constitutionalism, for its objective consists in achieving a democratic society as well as the guarantee of popular freedoms and rights. In the Japan of today, however, it is doubtful that the present way of governing is really based upon constitutionalism. The most important thing is the content of democracy.

Constitutionalism also presupposes respect for individuals. It should be founded upon individualism, not totalitarianism[17]. Self-selection by independent individualism and the administration of a community by self-determination, and autonomy must be guaranteed. With this in mind, Article 13 in the Constitution of Japan prescribes respect for individuals and Article 14 deals with equality for all under the law.

The guarantee of human rights, democracy and constitutionalism can take on a great significance in times of peace. The complete guarantee of human rights goes hand in hand with peace, and in order to guarantee these rights, peace is indispensable[18]. Recognizing its importance, the French Constitution of 1791 not only included the Declaration of Rights of Man in its preamble, but also denied the act of war for the purpose of taking over other territories. Even though they had a Constitutional Monarchy, it was the first time such clauses had ever been mentioned worldwide. The Constitution of Japan takes it even further by declaring to renounce the option of war, including not having its own army, as well as aspiring to build and keep the peace without the use of force.

With regards to constitutionalism in Japan, we have to consider the following points: 1. Has constitutionalism as logical thought beyond emotions become established in Japan? 2. Are the Japanese people well grounded in constitutionalism of the West? 3. What prime conditions are necessary to establish constitutionalism firmly in the people[19]? It is often said that Japanese peculiarities make it impossible for us to accept constitutionalism born in the West. But we should keep in mind that the aims of constitutionalism are universal to all mankind and that the need for human rights stems from the age-old struggle, as prescribed in Article 97 in the Constitution of Japan.

### (2) The fundamental principles of the Constitution of Japan

The Constitution of Japan is usually said to uphold three principles: the guarantee of fundamental human rights, permanent pacifism and popular sovereignty. Above all, the guarantee of fundamental human rights is the most significant. For the Constitution gives human rights a character of natural rights as 'eternal and inviolate rights,' and moreover, it confirms the historical universality of human rights as 'fruits of the age-old struggles of man to be free,' while the Imperial Japanese Constitution bestowed an assurance of human rights only within the limits of law. Quantitatively, the human rights prescribed in Chapter 3 (Article 10-40) account for the greater part of the Constitution.

In contrast, permanent pacifism is an important prerequisite for the guarantee of human rights, and popular sovereignty is the best means for it. Of the whole text, it is true that popular sovereignty is suggested merely in Article 1 concerning the Emperor system, but the ideal of permanent pacifism is demonstrated clearly. Structurally, 'rights and duties of the people' (Chapter 3) follows 'renunciation of war' (chapter 2), so it is confirmed that peace is indispensable for the guarantee of human rights. Besides, as mentioned above, a need for pacifism is prescribed very strictly in the Constitution. Naturally, the establishment of these three fundamental principles provokes an argument about the limits to amend the Constitution. In some western countries (e.g. France and Italy), no alteration of a republic system of government is permitted. In Japan too, it is impossible to alter these three main principles[20].

## 2 Problems with the Constitution of Japan

### (1) Continuity and discontinuity of the Emperor system

The Constitution of Japan whose significance is so great bears not a few problems that have to be overcome. First, we have to consider the Emperor system. The old Emperor system under the Imperial Japanese Constitution based upon the sovereignty of the Emperor as a continuum has been changed into the symbolic Emperor system under the Constitution of Japan. This new Emperor system is prescribed in company with the popular sovereignty, and the Emperor's position derives from 'the will of the people with whom resides sovereign power.' While the old Emperor system was also linked to divine right, the Constitution of Japan is founded upon the strict principle of separation of government and religion (Clause 3, Article 20). In the Constitution of Japan, therefore, freedom of religion is guaranteed to individuals. No state religion can be established, and no religious organizations can participate in any matters of the state or local public entities, both directly and indirectly. It is also prohibited for the state or local public entities to take part in any religious ceremonies or activities.

In spite of such fundamental alterations to the system, the same Emperor, *Hirohito*, reigned over the country during and after the war. Though the Emperor declared that he was no longer a living god under the new system, it was hard for the people to recognize the fundamental alterations to the Emperor system. This is the reason why we can observe a state of continuity between the new and the old system[21]. The Emperor, therefore, could escape from his war responsibilities.

Institutionally, it is natural that the Emperor should have only minimal power under the symbolic Emperor system. All acts of the Emperor depend on the advice and approval of the Cabinet regardless of his will. As a matter of fact, however, certain acts can fall into a gray area as they are not prescribed in Articles 6 and 7 as matters of state. This is the result of the Government stretching the meaning, diverting from the original objective.

Moreover, our unsuccessful efforts to dismiss the notion of national structure in wartime made it possible to pass the Flag-anthem bill and to let cabinet ministers (including the prime minister) visit the *Yasukuni* Shrine on matters of state.

To begin with, the Emperor system does not exist as the fundamental principles of the Constitution. As stated Article 1, the position and system of the Emperor depends on the will of the people with whom resides sovereign power[22].

### (2) The state of affairs concerning Article 9

Article 9 is famous for its epoch-making foresight, in particular Clause 2. The clause is well ahead of its time as it prescribes that war potentials will never be maintained and that the right of belligerency of the state will not be recognized. Unfortunately, such foresight makes it difficult for the people to understand its objective. Hence, the reason why the Government can establish *de facto* constitutional revisions in interpretation.

Originally, the renunciation of war as a means of settling international disputes prescribed in Clause 1, Article 9, merely intends to renounce an aggressive war. However, what kind of war can be waged without war potentials nor the right of belligerency prescribed in Clause 2 ? It is therefore interpreted that we cannot wage a self-defensive or an aggressive war. This was how the Government interpreted Article 9 in the early years of the Constitution[23]. However, with the outbreak of the Korean War, the United States began to regard Japan as a military base in the Far East and encouraged the start of the Self-Defense Forces and the conclusion of the U.S.-Japan Security Treaty. Article 9 was interpreted within the limits of the U.S.-Japan cooperation under the Cold War system after that.

Most scholars of the Constitution maintain that we should build and keep the peace without the use of force and that both the Self-Defense Forces and the U.S.-Japan Security Treaty violate the Constitution because they take Clause 2, Article 9 quite literally. In contrast, the Government justifies both the Self-Defense Forces (said to hold the second or fourth place in the world for its capacity) and the U.S.-Japan Security Treaty to support Japan's defense system, arguing that Japan as a state can rightfully maintain minimum forces for self-defense, not war potentials[24]. The differences in opinion between the scholars or activists and the Government over Article 9 are obvious.

### (3) Other problems

With regards to the objectives of the Constitution, the Japanese social structure in itself, causes a lot of problems.

First, Japanese society is controlled by bureaucrats who generally make up future policies. This may be good in terms of achieving social stability, but a daring idea or a policy to meet special needs at that time, has problems being processed. Besides, it is difficult to sever a back-scratching alliance between the big businesses and the bureaucrats. For example, even now, many of the high positions in private companies are held by former bureaucrats.

Secondly, Japan is a business orientated society. According to Article 13, society should be founded upon individualism. However, in reality, Japan is a business or household orientated society. The society is not made up of individuals. The relationship between business and individuals is neither realistic, rational nor based upon the original labor contract. There are many individuals who sacrifice themselves entirely to their companies and some even die from working too hard.

Thirdly, Japan is an unequal society. According to Article 14, the society should offer equal treatment to all. However, this is not the case. It is true that the superficial equality between the sexes is improving thanks to international influences, but we can still observe a lot of discrimination against foreigners on the basis of race or ethnic background. As to the latter, we have to admit that Japan is still a very nationalistic country. Moreover, in the endeavor to promote efficiency, the weak are not well protected socially or financially and most of them suffer from major discriminatory treatment.

Fourthly, the state responsibility as the social state is vague. Japan, as well as other advanced countries, is evolving towards an aging society, therefore it is an urgent necessity to complete a social security and welfare system. However, total equality is not guaranteed, securing finances also promises to cause a lot of problems. Besides, the Government carelessly tends to leave such duties in the hands of the private sector. We have to ask ourselves what part the state should play and what responsibility to the people it should perform.

Most of these problems result from the insufficient knowledge and application of the Constitution. Therefore, it is necessary to have many citizens understand their meanings. It is such a social mission that the constitutional scholars should carry out.

## II  Japan Association for Studies of Constitutional Law (JASCL)

### 1  The organization and activities of the JASCL

#### (1)  The organization and its history

The Japan Association for Studies of Constitutional Law (JASCL), a group made up of a variety of experts on the Constitution, was established by 112 constitutional researchers in April 1965. Their movement tried to cope with the crisis in the Constitution, for the final report had been submitted by the constitutional review panel the year before. The panel, established in 1956, intended to amend the Constitution. As a result, there were both positive and negative opinions in the report on amending the Constitution. Though it did not vociferously claim to amend the Constitution, it proved to be a turning point with revisions to its interpretation. The efforts to amend the Constitution, however, did not die away. Rather, the operations to emasculate the Constitution were carried out steadily with acts such as: the existence of *Mitsuya* Research, the establishment of National Foundation Day, the establishment of *Naganuma* missile base, the celebration of 100 years after the *Meiji* Restoration, etc.[25].

The main activities of the JASCL in its early years were: collecting and analyzing the materials on the Constitution, publishing the results of its research, expressing its opinion, cooperating with other constitution protection movements, giving lectures, etc.. Organized mainly by scholars of middle standing, the JASCL had no special chairman. It elected a few agents to manage the seven blocks throughout the country and became a national organization which delivered its own message and performed other activities only when general meetings were held or when some serious problems arose. The expression of opinion was, in principle, a personal responsibility.

To sum up, the chief aim of the JASCL has been the theoretical research and discussion of topics concerning the Constitution. The JASCL has fundamentally assumed the responsibility of protecting the Constitution and if necessary, all members are willing to make a social or political statement as the organization. Five years after its establishment, organizational and managerial problems were resolved and new rules were laid down in order to revitalize its research activities. Article 1 states that the Association is made up of constitutional researchers and that its main aim is to study the Constitution and promote cooperation among its members in order to protect the Constitution of Japan founded upon peace, democracy and human rights. In other words, the JASCL became a researchers' organization with a firm belief in protecting the Constitution. Article 2 states the following: the Association performs the following activities in order to accomplish the aims of the preceding article—(1) holds regular study meetings, (2) publishes research results, (3) expressies opinions according to events and (4) performs other activities approved by the management committee. Namely, the JASCL expresses opinions and performs suitable activities (e.g. holding lecture meetings on May 3-Constitutional Day) with a view to protecting the Constitution. Surely, the Japan Public Law Association, a group researching public law, already existed before the establishment of the JASCL. But JASCL devoted themselves entirely to the protection of the Constitution.

Here, we would like to confirm the objective of protecting the Constitution. Possible amendments to the Constitution have always lain in Article 9, in particular Clause 2. The need for pacifism is prescribed clearly, deriving from an examination of the facts during World War II and a feeling of remorse. Recently, owing to increasing international influence, such a way of thinking is beginning to shake. So what the future of JASCL should be is in question[26].

(2) **The activities**

At the beginning, the JASCL held sectional study meetings and symposiums, as well as general research meetings twice a year. It also invited lawyers to attend the study meetings concerning the constitutional theory. The meeting to commemorate the Constitution was first called in 1967, and has been held every year on May 3 (the enforcement day of the Constitution) since 1977. The JASCL made frequent statements and appeals for ten years after its establishment. These days, however, it emphasizes holding a constitutional forum for the verification of the Constitution, rather than making statements. In this sense, it can be described more as an academic group.

It has published a journal, *Constitutional Law Review* since 1989, in which the constitutional trends in politics, as well as its activities, are examined.

Now (May 1999), the JASCL consists of more than 420 members, which cannot be called an organization gathering the scholars of middle standing any longer. Every a doctoral student can become a member of the JASCL, provided that he/she has two people to nominate him/her. With the emphasis lying mainly on being a unique group of academic scholars studying the Constitution, its early aim of making necessary statements on the political climate is becoming less and less important.

## 2 Problems of the JASCL
### (1) Changing political environment

A series of political changes in recent years have made the political influence to protect the Constitution weaken. In June 1994, Mr. Murayama from the Social Democratic Party of Japan (SDP) was elected to Prime Minister in the House of Representatives, supported by the SDP, the Liberal-Democratic Party (LDP) and the *Shinto-Sakigake* (Harbinger Party). Surely, admitting the constitutionality of the Self-Defense Forces in the 1993 declaration, the SDP had been posed a question concerning its basic stance as the constitution protection party. But the establishment of the coalition cabinet with the LDP made the stance of the SDP more doubtful. In spite of changing the party's name with the breakup of Mr. Murayama's cabinet in January 1996, not a few members of the SDP went over to the Democratic Party of Japan (DPJ) established in September, and the SDP itself lost many supporters. On the other hand, we cannot call the DPJ a constitution protection party, especially concerning Article 9, for it includes many members transferred from the LDP.

The peace movement had gained ground among the Japanese people as the citizens movement owing to their aspirations for peace, based upon their experiences of assailants of the Japanese Empire during World War II, being victims of the first atomic bombs and suffering many other war casualties. The defection of the constitution protection party connected directly with the movement, however, deprived the movement of its base. The labor movement which sought peace eagerly has no definite party to support. In the meanwhile, the passage of the Guideline bills to enlarge and reinforce the U.S.-Japan Security System was forced[27].

These days, the LDP seeking a new coalition with the Liberal Party (LP) and New *Komeito* got the Flag-anthem bill, the Wiretapping bill and the Numbering bill through both Houses. But we cannot say that they were discussed thoroughly. They were voted upon despite strong opposition from the people.

In the constitutional forum concerning the Guideline bills held in March, more than 400 citizens and students attended to discuss the matter. Moreover, 216 members of the JASCL supported the statement delivered by the constitutional researchers who worried over the bills. All opposition, however, did not bear fruit at the party level.

More and more young people display political apathy. This is the reason why the political groups who intend to amend the Constitution are gaining strength.

The current political climate in Japan loses balance between the citizens movement devoid of its base of self-realization and the conservative parties looking for a chance to amend the Constitution vigilantly.

In July 1999, the Diet Law was amended to set up Research Commissions on the Constitution, whose predecessor had been the Union of the Diet's Members for Establishing Research Panels on the Constitution inaugurated in May 1997. According to the prospectus of the Union, 'this is an excellent chance to consider what our country should be toward the 21st century and to discuss the Constitution of a new era', and moreover, 'it is serious discussion of national ground problems that we statesmen should conduct as our greatest mission'. In fact, the Union had aimed to establish 'Research Panels on the Constitutional System' as ordinary Diet panels for research and investigation on the system and others of the present Constitution, in order to amend it.

Research Commissions on the Constitution will 'conduct broad and comprehensive research on the Constitution of Japan' (Clause 6, Article 102), with its ambiguous purpose, which is agreed that the Panels themselves are not authorized to submit a bill and that each of the Panels will review for some five years[28].

As mentioned above, the activities of the former constitutional review panel gave rise to the establishment of the JASCL established. The situation of today, however, may not be the same as before. For the subtle differences between generations are arising on the meaning and significance of the Constitution.

Having suffered great losses during the war, Japan is currently able to enjoy peace, freedoms, rights and democracy in return, which we have to foster carefully without forgetting their significance.

(2) **The stratified character of the JASCL activities**

Surely, the JASCL is expected to act as a unique academic group for constitutional scholars. Its activities, however, cannot be described as purely academic. It is because the Constitution is intimately related with the political trends. Needless to say, governance should be founded upon the Constitution as supreme law and fundamental norm. It is logical for constitutional scholars to raise the alarm and urge reconsideration when the Government makes a move away from the original objectives of the Constitution.

The constitution should also be studied in terms of law-sociology. Why is it that the ideal stated in the Constitution has not taken root among the people? What kind of form is adequate to make the best use of the Constitution? They are the questions we should investigate. The Constitution is meaningless unless it takes root in people's daily lives. In this point, the JASCL should challenge the problem of different interpretations on the Constitution[29].

The JASCL is expected to act in favor of the citizens in addition to its academic activities.

## Conclusion

After all, one of the most important missions which the JASCL should perform is to raise the people who are literate in the Constitution. It is the important role for the JASCL to inform citizens and politicians of its significance. The Constitution is closely related to politics. For instance, the actual legislation process does not conform with Article 41, which prescribes that 'the Diet shall be the highest organ of state power, and shall be the sole law-making organ of the State.' The discussion of a bill is held mainly in each committee and sometimes a vote is taken without a full discussion. The Diet is nothing but a ceremony to pass the bill[30]. It is important to have a new appreciation of the idea of a parliamentary cabinet system prescribed in the Constitution.

However, it is also important for the JASCL to put forth realistic proposals, through the exchange between the JASCL and practical men, judges and lawyers in order to raise the people who are literate in the Constitution. In the JASCL's general meetings, some reports have been delivered by scholars of other disciplines, but recently, JASCL has had few chances to listen to speeches given by practical men. It has not held small research meetings in accordance with each judicial theme, either. This is partly because the constitutional scholars are too busy on their research, urged to make statements on various subjects at different places.

By the way, when we look at the low turnout figures for every election, the Japanese people, regardless of their high educational level, can hardly be described as a politically aware nation. While the percentage of students who go on to universities, colleges or junior colleges in 1996 was 48.3% for women and 44.2% for men, the turnout for the single-member district system of the House of Representatives in 1996 was 60.23% for women and 59.03% for men. The turnout for the constituency system of the House of Councilors in 1995 was 44.37% for women and 44.67% for men. The figures are becoming lower and lower with the passing of each year. It is not recognized that the political selection and decision of his/her own are important acts to affect the fate of Japan. Though we need elaborate policies with the advent of an aging society like the other advanced countries, public interest in politics is not developing. The illuminating explanation and analysis of the constitutional politics by the constitutional scholars are essential in order to overcome such blocking situations.

In conclusion, the Constitution of Japan was enacted, based upon our self-examination and repentance of World War II. Above all, it expressed the value of peace. The acts to ruin its objectives and ideals can never be allowed. We must not create a crisis, confrontation or bugbear in Asia. We should throw our energies into the establishment of a peaceful and wealthy society in Asia. It is also important to understand other law-cultures and policies through exchanges at international meetings. The JASCL has a lot of things to do for the establishment of peace and the guarantee of human rights. Therefore, it is so significant today to retrospect the history of the JASCL in order to examine its role in the constitutional politics and to reconsider the meaning of the Constitution of Japan[31].

**Notes**

(1) Michel GANZIN translated by Hideo Yoko, "Declaration of the Rights of Man," *The Report of the Institute of Social Sciences*, Chuo University, No. 12, 1993, pp. 449ff.

(2) Ibid., p. 462. See also Tadakazu FUKASE, "The Third Introduction to Declaration of the Rights of Man in 1789," *Hokudai Hogaku*, Vol. 18, No. 3, p. 482.

(3) See Masanari SAKAMOTO, *The Constitution—National Classic*, Yuhikaku,

2000, p. 27, and idem, 'The History of Constitutionalism and its Development," pp. 2ff.

(4) Louis FAVOREU et alii., Droit constitutionnel, 2$^e$éd, Paris, Dallez, 1999.

(5) Achille MESTRE, Constitutionnalisme jacoban et constitutionnalisme sovietique, Paris, P.U.F., 1971.

(6) Elisabeth ZOLLER, Droit constitutionnel, Paris, P.U.F., 1998.

(7) Ibid., pp. 9 et s.

(8) Ibid., pp. 44 et s.

(9) Cf., Louis FAVOREU, Modèle américain et modèle européen de justice constitutionnelle, AIJC., vol. IV.-1988, Paris, Economica, 1990, pp. 51 et s.

(10) Elisabeth ZOLLER, op. cit., p. 48.

(11) Ibid., p. 49. cf. Déc. 93-333 DC, Autorisation démission, 21 janv. 1994, cons. 3, RJC, I, 569.

(12) Elisabeth ZOLLER, op. cit., pp. 49 et 50.

(13) Françcois LUCIAIRE et Gérard CONAC, La constitution de la république française, 2$^e$éd, Economica, 1987, pp. 1085 et s.

(14) Elisabeth ZOLLER, op. cit., p. 50.

(15) Cf., Jean RIVERO, État de droit, état du droit, in L'état de droit; Mélanges en l'honneur de Guy BRAIBANT, Paris, Dallaz, 1996, p. 609. See also Yoichi HIGUCHI, *The Constitution*, Sobunsya, 1992. pp. 9ff.

(16) Toshihiko NONAKA, "The Constitution and Emperor System in Japan," *Jurist*, Special Issue, No. 884, 1987.

(17) Takashi EBASHI, "'The Individual' in the Constitutionalism," *Jurist*, Special Issue, No. 884, 1987, pp. 2ff.

(18) Katsumi UEDA, "The Theory and Problems on the Constitutional Pacifism in Japan," in *The Constitutionalism in the 21st Century History and Problems in the Modern Constitution*, ed. Yasuo SUGIHARA Koki-Kinen Ronbunshu Kanko-iinkai, Keiso-syobo, 2000, pp. 201ff.

(19) Toshihiko NONAKA, op. cit., p. 19.

(20) See also Toshihiro YAMAUCHI, "The Tentative Draft for Constitutional Revision without Respect to Constitutionalism," *Gunshuku Mondai Shiryo*, No. 172, 1995, pp. 64ff.

(21) Yoichi HIGUCHI, "The Constitution of Japan from Comparative Constitutional Law," *Jurist*, Special Issue, No. 638, 1977, pp. 65ff.

(22) Hitoshi SERIZAWA, "Article 1," in *The Commentaries on the Constitution* (4 th edition), eds. Kosuke KOBAYASHI and Hitoshi SERIZAWA, Separate Volume, Hogaku Seminar, No. 149, 1997, pp. 15ff.

(23) Masayasu HASEGAWA, "Article 9," in *The Commentaries on the Constitu-*

*tion* (3rd edition), eds. Ryokichi ARIKURA and Kosuke KOBAYASHI, pp. 33 ff.
(24) See *The Illustrations on the State of the World 1999-2000*, Kokuseisya, 1999, pp. 506ff.
(25) For example, Osamu WATANABE, "The Setting-up of Research Commission on the Constitution," *Jurist*, No. 900, 1988, pp. 100-101.
(26) Osamu WATANABE et al., *Critique of 'Constitutional Revision'*, Rodo-Junposya, 1994, pp. 75ff.
(27) Toshihiro YAMAUCHI, *The New Guideline between Japan and the U.S. and the Law on the Emergency Situations in Areas Surrounding Japan*, Horitsu-bunkasya, 1999.
(28) Kiyotaka MAEHARA et al., "Researching Research Commission on the Constitution," *Hogaku-Seminar*, May 2000, pp. 48 ff.; Hideki MORI et al., "Research Commission on the Constitution—Where will the Discussion go?," *Horitsu-jiho*, Vol. 72, No. 5, 2000, pp. 5ff. and see other special articles.
(29) Mamiko UENO, "On the Interpretation of the Constitution," *Hogaku-seminar*, April 2000, pp. 87ff.
(30) Reiko OYAMA, *Introduction to the Diet*, Sanseido, 1997, p. 94.
(31) Nobuyoshi ASHIBE, "Retrospecting on 50 Years of the Constitutional Law," in *50 Years of the Constitution of Japan and Myself*, eds. Yasuo SUGIHARA and Yoichi HIGUCHI, Iwanami-Syoten, 1997, pp. 134ff.

## References

*The Constitution and the Principles of the Constitution—situations and prospects*, *Jurist*, No. 884, 1987.

*Ten Years of Japan Association for Studies of Constitutional Law—the records of its activities*, Japan Association for Studies of Constitutional Law, 1975.

*Japan Association for Studies of Constitutional Law—the records of its activities 1975-86*, Japan Association for Studies of Constitutional Law, 1987.

*Constitutional Law Review*, Japan Association for Studies of Constitutional Law; Sanseido, Vol. 1-10, 1990-99.

## Additional Remark

In the preliminary research meeting, Prof. *Yasuo SUGIHARA* explained to me about Article 2 of the Law on Science Council of Japan concerning its objectives. It prescribes that the Science Council of Japan acts as the representative organization of Japanese scientists, both domestically and internationally, for the promotion of science, and its aims are the reflection of science in the administration and the public, and the permeation of science into industry and society.

The Science Council of Japan, holding the top-status of all academic societies in Japan, tries 'to reflect and permeate science in the administration, industry and the public' as one of its objectives.

(Special thanks for the advice of Mr. Michael -Dennis BROWN, Prof. of the Chuo University)

# Part IV General Reports

# Asia, Oceania and Constitutionalism

## Cheryl Saunders

In this volume, scholars from different parts of Asia and Oceania offer their perspectives on constitutionalism, now and in the future, by reference to their own constitutional arrangements, in theory and in practice. The diversity and range of the papers demonstrate the advantage to be gained from more systematic and sustained comparative constitutional study across the region, in terms of mutual understanding and collaboration on shared interests and problems. The principal purpose of this paper is to draw together some of the themes that have emerged and to reflect on their implications for the standards and practices of constitutionalism. In doing so, I also provide a perspective on some of the issues for constitutionalism in Australia and other countries in a similar constitutional tradition.

In general, the argument in this paper is as follows. The legal and constitutional systems in Asia and Oceania are extraordinarily diverse for reasons connected with historical experience, contemporary circumstances, culture and tradition. This feature makes the region particularly interesting for constitutional scholars, but also complicates the present exercise. The differences across the region in approaches to government make specific definition of constitutionalism difficult. Too prescriptive a definition also runs a risk of inadvertent cultural bias and unduly narrow focus. For present purposes, therefore, I have chosen to view the concept of constitutionalism more generally, as a combination of two elements, each of which may be satisfied in different ways. The first is limited government in accordance with constitutionally prescribed standards and procedures. The second is government in the public interest, objectively identified, generally through popular consent.

However, defined, constitutionalism never is easy to maintain. Each of its elements is vulnerable. In addition, there often is an uneasy balance between them.

At the end of the twentieth century, a new context for constitutionalism is emerging throughout the world, including in the Asia and Oceania region. Particular influences on this context are the forces of internationalisation, globalisation and international economic competitiveness, which have both negative and positive effects. Many of the constitutional systems in Asia and Oceania have been affected by these forces, with mixed consequences. Overall, there are some signs of a strengthening of constitutionalism, in the sense of a greater commitment to the form and the substance of constitutional law and principle. In addition, there is evidence of increasing innovation in the design of constitutions and governmental arrangements. As a generalisation, this is reflected in an emerging tendency to reject institutions and practices which derive their legitimacy solely from colonial times, to borrow creatively from elsewhere and to reflect local cultures and traditions more closely. In these conditions, it may be possible to hope that a constitutionalism reflecting the circumstances of the Asia and Oceania region has begun to emerge. These are still early days, however, and there are plenty of contra-indications as well. Constitutionalism in the region will need to be nurtured carefully if it is to develop and thrive in the interests of the various peoples.

## 1 FEATURES OF THE REGION

For constitutional as well as for other purposes, the region of Asia and Oceania is one of the most diverse in the world. Geographically, it extends from the Indian sub-continent in the west to Kiribati and other Pacific states in the east and from China and Japan in the north to New Zealand in the south. Within this vast area are some of the most densely populated countries in the world[1], as well as some of the smallest island communities, with relatively few inhabitants[2]. Socially, culturally, politically and economically, the circumstances of the peoples of the region are very different and the demands placed on Constitutions and systems of government differ correspondingly.

More relevant still, for present purposes, is the variety of the historical experience of states across the region. Most countries are the beneficiaries of a long and rich period of cultural development stretching back, in some cases, for thousands of years. In more recent times, however, most were colonised by a European power. Those not colonised nevertheless generally encountered irresistible western influences, at some stage or stages. A range of different western powers was involved in the region at different times. Those with notable influence were Britain, France, The Netherlands, Portugal, Spain, the United States and even, from one perspective, Australia. The colonising powers themselves differed significantly in their approaches to law and government and to colonial policy and practice. With only a few exceptions, in some Pacific Island communities[3], the colonial power has long since gone but its effects linger in constitutional and legal systems as well as in other ways[4].

One consequence is that the region offers a greater mix of constitutional arrangements than Europe itself. Systems with a civilian base are mixed with common law systems in roughly equal proportions. Inevitably, these reflect the essential differences between the common law and civilian principles and method, especially in relation to sources of law and to the role and structure of the judiciary, generally and in constitutional matters. Other important differences may include the way in which international treaties are made and ratified and the status of international in domestic law[5]. In addition, Asia now has a greater concentration of socialist or communist systems of government than any other part of the world[6].

Each system in the region is derivative, in one way or another. In each case, however, the original model has substantially been modified by local history and culture as well as by present social and economic need. Not one is true to the type from which it derived and the admixture of different legal approaches within a single national system is common. This is particularly so where constitutional arrangements are concerned

## 2 COMPARING CONSTITUTIONS

The Asia-Pacific region is a rich resource for the emerging field of the comparative study of Constitutions. The earlier part made the point that, in this region, a wide different constitutional systems, with different legal and theoretical bases, lie in close proximity to each other. Rapidly increasing economic, environmental, social and political interdependence also combine to make the quality of government an issue of shared interest. This alone offers an incentive to develop a reliable understanding of the constitutional arrangements of others. The mix of transplanted constitutional conceptions with each other and with those developed locally also provides an unusual opportunity for close study of the factors that influence the ultimate nature of any Constitution, in form and operation.

Every constitutional scholar understands the close links that exist between Constitutions, their history, the theories that influenced their making and the context in which they operate. In his contribution to this volume, Professor Sugihara Yasuo demonstrates that these influences also affect Constitutions and constitutionalism over time[7]. This contingent aspect of constitutional law dramatically increases the challenge of effective and reliable study of the Constitutions of others and comparisons between them. Clearly, a bare knowledge of the principles, rules and operations of constitutional institutions is not enough. Each system must be understood by reference to its own contextual factors, which may be historical, economic, cultural and social. These factors are likely to be more difficult to identify and to evaluate than the rules of a Constitution itself. The problem is particularly acute for those outside the country concerned, who necessarily lack the innate understanding of the practical operation of a system of government, which comes from lifelong contact with it. This is one reason why collaboration between constitutional scholars from different countries is so important.

These points can be illustrated by reference to the constitutional system of Australia, with which I am most familiar.

First, the Australian Constitution, like most others in the region, is an admixture of different influences. In the case of Australia, the principal influences were Britain and United States, with a small Swiss contribution as well, in the form of the referendum for constitutional change[8]. From the United States, Australia took federalism, a strict, constitutional separation of judicial power[9] and the concept of a written Constitution that represents fundamental law[10]. From Britain it took parliamentary government and a constitutional monarchy, together with an aversion to constitutional protection of rights[11]. Unlike many other countries, Australia adopted its own constitutional arrangements freely, during the colonial phase. And there were relatively few cultural barriers to the successful transplantation of constitutional concepts from the two main anglo-saxon constitutional traditions to predominantly anglo-celtic Australia, although there were some tensions from the mixture of the two[12].

As in all countries, the text of the Australian Constitution conveys only a very partial picture of actual constitutional law and practice. Adaptation and augmentation has taken place through various processes, including judicial interpretation[13], political practice[14] and conventions or common understandings[15]. One dramatic example, which also is topical, illustrates the point.

When the Australian Constitution came into effect in 1901, Australia was still a colony. In some ways, the Constitution reflects this historical fact still. On its face, the Queen seems a powerful figure and Australia still subservient to Britain[16]. Neither is true in fact, however. Even in 1901, the monarch was expected to act in a "constitutional" way, on the advice of the Australian or the British government, in accordance with constitutional convention or unwritten practice[17]. As Australia became independent, more than 50 years ago, any authority of the British government and Parliament in relation to Australia ceased, through a pragmatic process that required no change to the Constitution[18]. This rather casual arrangement was made possible by Australia's own internal stability and its practicelic, almost prosaic, approach to constitutional matters. The limitations of this approach ultimately were revealed in the debate on a republic that culminated in rejection of a referendum proposal in 1999. The issue in the debate was whether a President, chosen in Australia, should replace the Queen and her representatives as Australian Head of State. The practice of the Constitution had departed so far from the text, that it was difficult to explain to the Australian public what the present system was, so as to enable them to evaluate the significance of changes proposed to it[19]. The issue of a republic almost certainly will be raised again. If and when change is approved, the Australian Constitution will reflect the actual practice of this aspect of Australian government more accurately than it does now.

The Australian case also demonstrates the importance of the founding theoretical influences on the form and operation of a national Constitution. An example is the virtual absence of express protection for human rights in the text of the Australian Constitution. Philosophically, this is the continuing legacy of A V Dicey[20], and is one of the points of tension within the Australian Constitution between its British and American sources. The absence of constitutional rights does not mean, however, that rights are unimportant in the Australian constitutional system. Nor, with some important qualifications[21], does it mean that they are unduly at risk. In place of constitutionally protected rights, interpreted and enforced through courts, Australia tends to rely instead on the common law[22], political culture and a set of social and economic circumstances that, so far, have placed relatively little strain on liberal democratic values. If the context in which the Constitution operates were to change, undermining the present easy consensus that rights generally should be respected, a more prescriptive rights regime may well be required.

Finally, Australia also shows how context affects the operation of transplanted constitutional arrangements. An example is the requirement for all changes to the Australian Constitution to be approved by voters in a referendum[23]. In Switzerland, the country from which Australia adopted this aspect of its Constitution, the referendum sits well with the consensus-style politics of a generally educated people, used to direct participation in making public decisions, large and small. It is much less natural in Australia, with its otherwise total reliance on representative government in a highly adversarial Westminster-style political culture. The effective use of the referendum in Australia therefore requires a substantial adaptation of normal practice[24]. Australia's failure to achieve this successfully so far has meant that a large majority of proposals for constitutional change has been defeated[25].

The complexity of contextual understanding of the Australian Constitution is paralleled in every country in the region.

## 3  THE CONCEPT OF CONSTITUTIONALISM

The same variety of the Asia-Oceania region, which makes it so interesting for comparative constitutional study, complicates the analysis of constitutionalism, which is the subject of this volume. The meaning of constitutionalism may vary between different systems of law and government, different ideological perspectives and over time. For present purposes, however, it is necessary to find a degree of common ground. The challenge is to do this in a way that gives substance to the concept of constitutionalism, but which is appropriately neutral rather than culture specific and which is sufficiently inclusive for the purposes of a region as varied as this.

At the very least, constitutionalism implies government in accordance with constitutional procedures and norms. As with its companion, the rule of law, this is a necessary but not sufficient condition, however. The formal shell of a Constitution is empty and meaningless unless some regard is paid to its content. Views about content have changed over time and this potentially is disputed ground. Nevertheless, in the latter half of the 20th century there is wide acceptance of at least two features of a truly constitutional regime. One is that government should be based on and responsive to popular will serving the public interest. Generally this imports the notion that all citizens, or full members of the state, should be treated equally. In most systems it also is taken to require democracy, in the sense of government by elected representatives. The other feature of a constitutional regime is that public power should be limited, that its exercise should not be arbitrary and that it should meet certain normative standards. Increasingly, over the past 50 years, these normative standards have been linked to internationally recognised standards for human rights. The emphases given to different categories of rights and the way in which they can be realised are major issues for contemporary constitutionalism, in Asia and Oceania, as elsewhere[26].

This view of constitutionalism draws broadly on the work of Charles McIlwain who characterised will or "gubernaculum" and law or "jurisdictio" as "the two fundamental correlative elements of constitutionalism for which all lovers of liberty must yet fight"[27]. He devoted his study, *Constitutionalism, Ancient and Modern*, to the potential tensions between them, which still are manifest, despite the passage of time. The logic of his analysis is attractive for present purposes because it recognises the principal purposes of constitutional arrangements while allowing some flexibility in the ways in which they are achieved.

This definition of constitutionalism may go too far for some, but be insufficiently prescriptive for others. Constitutional scholars, working within their own traditions, are likely to be tempted to add further requirements[28]. Within individual traditions, these additions may be appropriate. Each constitutional system is or should be an integrated whole, in which particular features play a particular assigned part. From the perspective of my own tradition, for example, I would add to the requirements for a truly constitutional regime a separation of powers, independent courts, judicial review of legislative and executive action and a high degree of openness and accountability in government. These features would be accepted by many others as well, but often in different forms and with different emphases.

At this early stage of a bold endeavour to work across traditions, however, the temptation to add further features should be resisted, if the bare goals of constitutionalism can be met in other ways. The more prescriptive the definition, the more contested it is likely to be. To make progress in comparative constitutional study, it may be more helpful to begin by accepting that different states approach the goals of constitutionalism differently, within somewhat general limits, on which broad agreement can be reached.

## 4 CHALLENGES TO CONSTITUTIONALISM

Even thus defined, constitutionalism is a notoriously fragile concept. In this part I explore some of the pressures to which it is subject and the consequential problems that arise, by reference to liberal democratic constitutional systems. I do this partly to avoid the risk of cultural bias associated with any attempt at generalisation on a broader scale. In any event, in so far as liberal democracy popularly is equated with constitutionalism, consideration of the tensions within liberal democratic systems may demonstrate the fragility of constitutionalism more forcefully.

Take first the notion that a constitutional system and the government for which it provides are intended to serve the public interest and to that extent at least depend on popular support and consent. The approach of most liberal democracies, through the latter part of the twentieth century, has been to govern through representatives, elected in free and regular elections on the basis of universal adult franchise with more or less explicit acknowledgment of the sovereignty of the people as a whole. One justification for this reliance on representative government has been practicability, given the size of 20th century nation states. Another is the assumption that representatives are more likely to make decisions in the common interest and that they will do so[29].

This model depends on a number of key elements. Elected representatives must be adequately accountable and thus responsive to the people from whom their legitimacy derives. They must act in the public interest rather than in their own. Preferably, they must have the capacity to govern wisely and well.

The traditional mechanisms for these purposes include a representative legislature, as the principal vehicle for public, political accountability and a more neutral and permanent public sector to provide a degree of expertise across the whole range of government activities. Notoriously, the effectiveness of the former is undermined by the sense of self-preservation of organised political parties that are, nevertheless, indispensable to the operation of a representative process. The security enjoyed by the public service, on which its expertise has been thought to depend, also can lead to inefficiency, stagnation or worse. These difficulties vary between different approaches to governance and the different contexts within which Constitutions work. The performance of a legislature, for example, may depend on its size, the electoral system, its tradition of public service in the public interest and the degree of political and social acceptance of public opposition.

Difficulties also arise in connection with the second general feature of constitutionalism, limited government, within the framework of the law and a Constitution. The manner in which this is secured through a constitutional system may vary substantially, in terms of the organisation of public power, the normative rules of the Constitution and the procedures and practices of adjudication. In a liberal democratic regime, however, this feature of constitutionalism presupposes a separation of public power between institutions and, sometimes, levels of government in the interests both of efficiency and the prevention of despotic rule[30]. It presupposes the rule of law at least to the extent that everyone, including the government, is subject to law, which itself satisfies basic norms including human rights norms[31]. And it presupposes a system of impartial adjudication. In many states it is accepted that, through adjudication, constitutional norms may be made binding even on the legislature itself[32].

The reliance of constitutionalism on compliance with law makes a system for impartial adjudication of disputes according to law a sine qua non of a constitutional regime. The principal difficulty here is as it always has been: to secure adequate independence and perceived independence for courts and other adjudicative bodies. Structurally, courts are located within the public sector, from which the most obvious challenge to their independence comes[33]. And in practice also courts are dependent on the executive and legislative branches for the appointment of judges, resources and the enforcement of their decisions. To a greater degree than many other constitutional norms, impartial adjudication relies on self-restraint on the parts of the executive and legislative branches and a willingness to assert themselves on the part of courts. Both the self-restraint of one and the assertiveness of the other are likely to be affected by culture and tradition.

Finally, notoriously, the goals of effective government and limited government, as conceived for the purposes of constitutionalism, are in a degree of tension with each other. Limited government, through law, cannot be secured if popular will is given full rein. But without it, constitutionalism will not exist. On the other hand, the constraints on government must be kept in balance with the positive social benefits that good government can offer. The relations between the two are seldom static. The tension may be beneficial, holding each in check. If the balance tips too far in either direction, however, problems may occur.

There are signs of this at present, in a climate of growing cynicism in many states, about the representative process[34]. This can variously be explained by the greater complexity of government; abuse of power by parties and other holders of power; the failure of entrenched institutions to respond adequately to change; better educated and informed voters; and the loss of respect for authority, as of course. Sometimes the cynicism is justified and abuse of the representative process is itself a threat to constitutionalism[35]. Even where cynicism reflects perception rather than fact, however, it has the potential to undermine support for the system of government on which constitutionalism depends.

Two possible responses have the potential to test the balance within constitutionalism further. One is more frequent use of direct democracy[36]. The difficulties here are twofold: its perceived greater legitimacy, presenting a new challenge to restraint by law and what Professor Pangalangan describes as its "raw, wild power", unmediated by the representative process[37]. The other common response to cynicism about the representative process is to place even greater demands on adjudication, as a constraint on the power of representatives, as in the case of India. If taken to extremes, the potential cost is strain on the frail vulnerable conventions that sustain judicial independence.

## 5 A CHANGING CONTEXT FOR CONSTITUTIONALISM?

At the end of the twentieth century, there has been a new focus on Constitutions and on constitutionalism throughout the world, in consequence of a concurrence of historic events.

Most obviously, the end of the cold war liberated constitutional politics and constitutional imagination. As it happened, this coincided with the growing desire of many former colonies to experiment with constitutional forms that might be more responsive to local needs than largely derivative post-independence Constitutions. For these and other reasons, the 1990s has been a period of constitutional change. Sometimes change has introduced novel principles and practices[38]. More often, it has seen the adaptation of familiar constitutional forms to different circumstances or in new combinations[39]. In general the processes of change have been pragmatic. The Constitutions of the late-twentieth century tend not to have been a response to constitutional theory but an assessment of what is acceptable nationally and, in some cases, internationally and of what is likely to work. The process is far from over and can be expected to continue well into the first part of the 21st century. At the time of writing, the search for constitutional solutions actively is underway in Sri Lanka, Fiji, Papua New Guinea, the Solomon Islands, East Timor and Indonesia, to name only a few. In some of these cases at least, no end is in sight.

The end of the cold war also stimulated globalisation and internationalisation. By globalisation, I refer to the dramatic increase in private transnational activity of all kinds, further augmented by changes in the diversity and speed of means of communication and new forms of information technology. Internationalisation, by contrast, refers to the new range, volume and variety of relations between governments, often conducted through the traditional media of treaties and other forms of agreement but manifested as well in new international institutions and new forms of international collaboration, including regional collaboration.

Internationalisation may be regional rather than global. The most successful regional collaboration so far is the European Union. By the 1990s it is no longer a new phenomenon. For various reasons, however, including changes in geo-political context, the Union has deepened in recent years, producing a hybrid form of association somewhere between a constitutional and international arrangement[40]. The European Union offers a model that other regions may, selectively, follow. The effects of a degree of convergence of the common law and civilian legal systems of its member states inevitably will be felt by states in the same legal traditions elsewhere[41].

Internationalisation and globalisation have been both the cause of and a response to international competitiveness. This last is relevant to the subject of constitutionalism in several ways.

From one perspective it has some potential to reinforce constitutionalism, at least in its application to the economic aspects of national life. A constitutional regime provides a more stable and reliable framework for economic activity. In order to improve its economic performance, a state may itself seek constitutional solutions or be placed under pressure from others to do so. The communications revolution that has accompanied globalisation has relevance for constitutionalism as well. It enables attention to be drawn to constitutional practice that falls dramatically short of world norms. It can be a liberating force for peoples, providing sources of information about the practices of their own and other governments and a means to impose pressure for change.

Constitutionally speaking, however, there is a dark side to these phenomena as well. One, which has been marked in Europe, has been an increase in ethnic conflict, through the collapse of old states or the renewal of the resentment of majorities or minorities in states in which this previously had been suppressed. One of the major challenges for the world today is the development of constitutional solutions for the government of ethnically divided communities, short of the continuing fragmentation that often perpetuates the problem. In some respects this has been a strength of approaches to constitutionalism in heterogeneous societies in Asia. Singapore is an example[42]. Multiculturalism sometimes is achieved at the price of greater authoritarianism, however, giving rise to a question whether authoritarianism is linked to or merely excused by the need to maintain racial harmony in those societies. More homogeneous societies in the region, by contrast have difficulty in accommodating ethnic difference. It seems likely that this will be an increasingly important question, for constitutionalism in all countries, in the world of the 21st century.

Economic competitiveness has forced changes to government practice as well. In some cases this is beneficial, reflecting a process of renewal and innovation that is necessary for all systems. But it can result also in a deterioration of constitutional standards, unless adequate preventative measures are taken. The forms of "economic constitutionalism" may be more narrow and more authoritarian than constitutionalism as traditionally understood[43]. Responses to the pressures of international competition also diminish the capacity of the state to satisfy social and economic needs. The familiar trend towards privatisation demonstrates in a different way the effect of globalisation on the principles and practices of government. The most obvious and immediate consequence of privatisation is that government is smaller. In so far as the state provides services itself, it is likely to do so on a commercial basis, acting in the manner of the private sector. Reductions in the size of the public sector and alterations in the forms of government action affect constitutional and other norms hitherto fashioned on the assumption of the continuation of the traditional division between the public and the private spheres. They also affect the operation of traditional institutions for public accountability and the principles of the rule of law. Both are based on the premise that government will be conducted largely through regulation, in the form of law. Neither is well adapted to the notion of governance through contract or through bargains of other kinds.

## 6 CONSTITUTIONALISM IN ASIA AND OCEANIA

These trends can be illustrated by examples across the world from western Europe, to Africa, to central and eastern Europe, to the Americas. The present concern of this paper, however, is their application in Asia and Oceania.

Most of the phenomena described earlier are present in this region. There have been major exercises in constitutional renewal and experimentation in, for example, Thailand, the Philippines and Taiwan and, more tentatively, Indonesia. There has been innovation in socialist constitutional theory and practice in China and Vietnam, partly in response to the pressures of international economic competition. A fragile new constitutional regime has been put in place in Cambodia. There has been some deliberate regionalism in the deepening of ASEAN and the establishment of APEC.

But the ill effects of globalisation and its associated trends are evident as well. They include the dramatic effects of international economic activity on living conditions in a range of countries and the progressive loss of control of decisions in the public interest to international organisations, international finances and multi-national corporations. The phenomenon and consequences of ethnic strife have been witnessed most tragically in East Timor and continue in other parts of Indonesia still. Ethnic and religious tensions that constitutional solutions have failed to ease have been evident also in other parts of the region, including Fiji, Sri Lanka and Bougainville. There is concern about corruption throughout the region without, so far, signs of major improvement.

More specific insights into developments in constitutionalism in Asia and Oceania can be drawn from the other papers in this volume.

First, as might be expected, most papers place substantial emphasis on human rights, including different categories of rights. The persuasive force of world debate on the significance of social and economic rights particularly, but not exclusively in developing countries is attributable to this region, although others have contributed as well. The emphasis on social and economic rights is an obvious and necessary one in a region in which so many people live in extreme poverty in consequence of exploitation and for whom the notions of civil and political rights are less meaningful. The latter remain an indispensable element in an adequate human rights regime, however, not only from the standpoint of individuals, but also for the role which such rights play in underpinning the accountability and possibly even the competence of government. Where the balance lies between civil and political rights on the one hand and social and economic rights on the other is one of the major issues for constitutionalism in the region.

An associated issue, also relevant in the region, is the legitimacy of and jurisprudential base for group rights, including the rights of indigenous peoples[44]. An issue still to be tackled, of critical importance here and elsewhere in the world, is the nature and scope of environmental rights, including their relationship to other rights. This issue also, notoriously, divides north and south, including the countries in Asia and Oceania[45].

The papers throw some light on the debate about how second and third generation rights might be given effect. Generally, these so-called positive rights are thought not to be enforceable through courts, although the Indian and South African experiences show means by which this can be done[46]. The new Constitution of the Kingdom of Thailand, offers a third way, through the use of the popular initiative. The search for mechanisms for enforcement is one reason for the rise of human rights commissions, a theme to which I return below. There is no doubt that commissions, ombudsmen and other scrutiny institutions of a quasi-independent kind have an important role to play in monitoring compliance with social and economic rights, scrutinising reports to international committees, assisting and developing appropriate national policy responses, and so on. But as several papers remind us, institutions are not an automatic panacea. Their effectiveness depends also on other factors within the domain of constitutionalists including their independence, their composition and the regard in which they are held.

The papers also offer evidence of the pressure to which I referred earlier for a greater direct say by the people themselves in public decision-making. Professor Pangalangan, for example, describes three recent innovations of this kind in The Philippines: the recall of representatives, the legislative referendum and the use of direct initiative for constitutional change. His paper recognises the challenge of this development to constitutionalism, in a final bleak paragraph. And while in a sense he is right, this potentially is a development which can and must be tamed. Properly used, the popular initiative might reinforce popular support for constitutionalism, through improved understanding, force constructive constitutional change and improve the accountability of governments. The challenge is to provide a framework, to accommodate the potentially dangerous commodity of direct democracy within accepted notions of constitutionalism. There been some experimentation with this in Asia. Dr Vishnu Varunyou, for example, describes in his paper the importance of popular participation in the drafting of the Thai Constitution and of the effects of article 170, which enables 50,000 voters to petition the National Assembly to consider a bill implementing constitutional provisions on rights and liberties[47].

Many papers in this volume deal with aspects of judicial review and the rule of law. At least two important themes emerge. The first and most familiar concerns the scope of the role of the judiciary. Experiences reflected in the papers range from the judicial deference of the Japanese Supreme Court[48] to the developing focus on constitutional rights by the Council of Grand Justices in Taiwan[49] to the extraordinary activism of the judiciary in India[50]. The Indian experience also illustrates the limits of the judicial role in the resolution of complex social and economic problems of which the extensive use of child labour is merely one example. To take up an earlier theme, these substantial variations in judicial practice are explicable at least in part by differences in culture and in legal systems.

Several papers also deal with access to justice, in a new theme that may have some links with the emerging phenomenon of people power. Judicial process is often remote. Traditionally, judges have relied on formality, tradition, adherence to established procedures and a degree of aloofness to protect their independence. In a more egalitarian age these features may also, however, affect the regard in which courts are held and, ultimately, their effectiveness in maintaining a constitutional order. Cost and the physical difficulty of approaching some courts also are important factors. Some authors point to the mechanism of the Human Rights Commission and other institutions as a challenge to the role of the judiciary in this regard, or at least a potential supplement[51]. The advantages of such developments are obvious. They have some potential, however, to undermine the independence of the courts, on which the effectiveness of the enforcement of human rights ultimately is likely to depend. One solution is for courts to become more accessible as well. Professor Singh's description of the way in which public interest litigation has revolutionised the adversary system in India is particularly pertinent for this reason[52].

One final issue for constitutionalism that emerges from the papers is more recent. It concerns the international order and has several different facets. The first is the familiar effect of internationalisation on domestic constitutional systems. This may be beneficial, where it leads to wider compliance with appropriate international constitutional norms. But in many states, and particularly those in the common law tradition, it also suggests the need for some adjustment to the internal organisation of power, for the following reason. In most common law systems, the executive alone has the power and responsibility to undertake international commitments. The assumption that international relations are largely the responsibility of the executive government was formed at a time when the sphere of international relations was relatively limited. As international relations expand to encompass matters hitherto principally of domestic concern, questions arise about whether existing systems are adequate to ensure executive accountability for decisions of this kind. In Australia, for example, debate on this issue so far has led to the provision of more systematic public information on treaty proposals and greater involvement of the legislature, at least in a consultative capacity[53].

Finally, there is the question of the constitutionalisation of the international order itself[54]. This may involve more effective ways of controlling international economic activity, on an equitable basis that takes into account the different circumstances and interests of peoples. It also concerns the framework of rules by reference to which the international community itself works. Professor Gong Renren refers to this in his discussion of the concept of international constitutionalism, of which, he says, "peace is the core"[55]. In this connection, Japan's article 9 offers an important international model, which may yet prove to have been ahead of its time.

There are other more mundane ways also, in which constitutionalism has an application to the international order. To the extent that effective decisions now are taken at supranational and international levels, it is relevant to consider how concepts of government in the public interest, relying on consent, the rule of law, and other constitutional norms and procedures might apply in this increasingly important sphere. These issues are beyond the scope of this volume. So far they have been considered to be largely the preserve of international lawyers. As the international order becomes more constitutional in character, however, these are matters on which constitutionalists also have something to say.

[1] India, with an estimated 1,000,848,550 people and China, with 1,246,871,951, both in July 1999.
[2] For example, Tonga with 109,082 people, or Vanuatu with 189,036.
[3] For example, New Caledonia, Guam
[4] Ayesha Jalal *Democracy and Authoritarianism in South Asia*, Cambridge University Press, 1995

[5] For one useful series of case studies see Monroe Leigh and Merritt R. Blakeslee *National Treaty Law and Practice*, Studies in Transnational Legal Policy No. 27, The American Society of International Law, 1995.
[6] People's Republic of China, Vietnam, North Korea, Laos.
[7] Sugihara Yasuo "Asian Constitutionalism and Japan".
[8] Constitution section 128
[9] Cheryl Saunders, "Separation of Powers" in Brian Opeskin and Fiona Wheeler (eds) *The Australian Federal Judicial System*, Melbourne University Press (2000)
[10] Initially, the Constitution was given overriding legal effect as a British Act of Parliament
[11] *McGinty v Western Australia* (1996) 186 CLR 140
[12] C. Saunders "A Constitutional Culture in Transition", forthcoming, (1999).
[13] See, for example, *Commonwealth v Tasmania* (1983) 158 CLR 1, in which the High Court held that the "external affairs" power in Constitution section 51 (29) enabled the Commonwealth to make laws to implement any bona fide international commitment to which Australia was a party.
[14] Examples include the de facto Commonwealth monopoly over the imposition of income taxation and a host of national schemes based on co-operation between governments.
[15] The operation of the Commonwealth executive branch of government and its relations with the Parliament are based almost entirely on convention, rather than constitutional text.
[16] See for example Constitution section 59, which appears to allow the Queen to "disallow" laws made by the Commonwealth Parliament.
[17] J. Quick and R.R. Garran, *Annotated Constitution of the Australian Commonwealth*, Legal Books, 1975, 703.
[18] Described in *Sue v Hill* [1999] HCA 30
[19] Cheryl Saunders "The Head of State - The Australian Experience: Lessons, Pointers and Pitfalls" in Colin James (ed) *Building the Constitution*, Institute of Policy Studies, Wellington, 2000, 276-286
[20] A.V. Dicey *Introduction to the Study of the Law of the Constitution*, 10th ed., 1959, McMillan.
[21] One current controversy concerns the mandatory sentencing laws in the Northern Territory of Australia: Juvenile Justice Act 1983 sections 53AE-AG
[22] *Lange v Australian Broadcasting Corporation* (1997) 189 CLR 520
[23] Section 128.
[24] Cheryl Saunders "The Parliament as Partner: A Century of Constitutional Review"; Information and Research Services Research Paper, Parliament of the Commonwealth of Australia (2000)
[25] Only 8 out of 44 referendum proposals have been approved.
[26] Kishore Mahbubani "An Asian Perspective on Human Rights and Freedom of the Press" in Kishore Mabhubani, *Can Asians Think?*, Times Editions Pte. Ltd., 1998, 57.
[27] Charles McIlwain, *Constitutionalism Ancient and Modern*, Cornell University Press, 1947, 146.
[28] For a recent collection of views of leading anglo-american scholars, see Larry Alexander (ed) *Constitutionalism: Philosophical Foundations*, Cambridge University Press 1998. For an historical survey, see Scott Gordon *Controlling the State*, Harvard

University Press, 1999

[29] Bernard Manin *The Principles of Representative Government*, Cambridge University Press, 1997

[30] M.J.C Vile *Constitutionalism and the Separation of Powers* (2$^{nd}$ ed. 1998) Liberty Fund

[31] For a range of recent perspectives on the rule of law and its meaning see David Dyzenhaus (ed) *Recrafting the Rule of Law: The Limits of Legal Order*, Hart Publishing, 1999.

[32] John H. Garvey and T. Alexander Aleinikoff *Modern Constitutional Theory*, West Publishing, 1994, chapter III.

[33] Martin Shapiro, *Courts: A Comparative and Political Analysis*, University of Chicago Press, 1981.

[34] James N. Rosenau "Changing States in a Changing World" in Commission on Global Governance (ed) *Issues in Global Governance*, Kluwer Law International, 1995, 265; John Uhr, *Deliberative Democracy in Australia*, Cambridge University Press, 1998

[35] Fareed Zakaria "The Rise of Illiberal Democracy" *Foreign Affairs*, November/December 1997, 22.

[36] Markku Suksi, *Bringing in the People*, Martinus Nijhoff Publishers, 1993; Dick Morris, *The New Prince*, Renaissance Books, ch. 47.

[37] Raul Pangalangan, "Why a Philippine Human Rights Commission? Its Place in a Constitutional Order".

[38] Examples include the accommodation of the position of Hong Kong within the People's Republic of China; the attempts to balance the interests of indigenous and indo-fijians in the (now ill-fated) 1997 Constitution of Fiji; and the treatment of social and economic rights in the Constitution of Thailand.

[39] For example, the accommodation of human rights protection with parliamentary sovereignty in the Bill of Rights Act 1990 (NZ).

[40] Dietrich Rometsch and Wolfgang Wessels (eds) *The European Union and Member States* Manchester University Press 1996; J.H.H. Weiler *The Constitution of Europe*, Cambridge University Press, 1999.

[41] B.S. Markesinis (ed) *The Gradual Convergence*, Clarendon Press Oxford 1994; B.S. Markesinis, *The Coming Together of the Common Law and the Civil Law*, Hart Publishing, 2000

[42] Kishore Mahbubani "Singapore: Recipes for a Crowded Planet" in *Can Asians Think?*, Times Editions Pte Ltd., 1998, 183, 187.

[43] Kanisha Jayasuriya "The Rule of Law and Governance in the East Asian State", (1999) 1 *Asian Law Journal*, 107; Kanisha Jayasuriya (ed) *Law, Capitalism and Power in Asia*, Routledge, 1999.

[44] Will Kymlicka (ed) *The Rights of Minority Cultures* Oxford University Press, 1995.

[45] Mahathir Mohamad "Regional Challenges" in Mahathir Mohamad and Shintaro Ishihara *The Voice of Asia*, Kodansha International Limited, 1995, 119, 127.

[46] Constitution of the Republic of South Africa, 1996, chapter 2.

[47] Vishnu Varunyou, "Human Rights and Constitutionalism in Thailand".

[48] Gong Renren "Japan's Constitution and International Law: Focus on the Peace Article".

[49] Jau-Yuan Hwang "Judge-Made Constitutionalism in Democratizing Taiwan - The Role of the Council of Grand Justices and Protection of Individual Rights"

[50] Parmanand Singh, "Protection of Human Rights through Public Interest Litigation in India".

[51] In particular, the papers of Dr Vishnu Varunyou, Professor Pangalangan and Profes-

sor Parmanand Singh

[52] Parmanand Singh, "Protection of Human Rights through Public Interest Litigation in India". See also Mario Gomez *In the Public Interest*, Legal Aid Centre, University of Colombo, 1993.

[53] Mechanisms include the preparation of National Interest Analyses; a parliamentary procedure for tabling treaties; establishment of a Joint Parliamentary Committee on Treaties and the development of an electronic treaties data base: Revised principles and procedures for Commonwealth-State consultation on treaties,

[54] Commission on Global Governance (ed) *Issues in Global Governance*, Kluwer Law International 1995.

[55] Gong Renren "Japan's Constitution and International Law: Focus on the Peace Article".

# Asian Constitutionalism and Japan

### Yasuo Sugihara

## I  Introduction-two concerns

In arguing 'Asian constitutionalism', I bear in mind two theories on Asian uniqueness.

The one is, what is called 'theory of Asian mode of production', 'theory of oriental despotism' and 'theory of Asian stagnation'. These theories may have some relevancy as those which tell us much about politics, economics and culture of some Asian countries in one age. Here I do not intend to argue whether these are scientific or not. However, my concern is that these theories about Asian countries of modern and the present ages worked as a kind of ideology in that these theories maintained and rationalized political, economic and cultural backwardness of Asian countries, which are colonized or semi-colonized through imperialistic policies. In other words, they functioned as a 'doctrine' which legitimates both the mother countries' dominance and progresiveness and the Asian stagnation and backwardness. We should not take for granted the relevancy of these theories when we consider the movement for independence in colonial or semi-colonial periods, the political, economic and cultural development since independence, and the rapid change in recent years of Asian countries in political, economic and cultural terms.

The other is what is called 'the theory on universality of Western constitutionalism' ('the theory on its dominance and on 'Eastward-influencing inevitability) and its counterparts, that is, 'the theory on Asian legal culture' (in particular 'the theory on Confucianism '). Although I also do not intend to argue this point in detail here, I want to indicate the following points, for it is, I think, particularly important to examine the problem from the viewpoint of constitutional science.

First, neither in Western countries does a constitutional theory and a civil (bourgeois) constitution there exist, which have relevancy beyond historical and social dimensions. For example, even in modern ages, there were 'civil constitutions of Scheinkonstitutionalismus' in such countries as didn't experience civil (bourgeois) revolutions while there were 'civil constitutions of modern constitutionalism' in the countries which experienced civil revolutions. The latter have as principles the protection of fundamental human rights, popular sovereignty, and the separation of powers while the former don't. Moreover, in modern ages, there was 'peoples constitutional idea' which also aimed at protecting fundamental human rights although this had other scope and degree than 'civil constitution of modern constitutionalism' had in its concept and its protection of human rights. In addition, Western countries' constitutions have developed its contents considerably from modern ages to the present ages. For example, 'civil constitutions of modern constitutionalism' have changed into 'civil constitutions of the present ages.' The latter contain the prohibition of sexual discrimination, the protection of social rights, the positive restrictions on economic freedom and rights, the introduction of direct election and universal suffrage, judicial review, and the constitutional protection of local autonomy while the former not.

Ultimately, in Western countries the argument on constitutionalism and constitutions themselves are various, depending on what kind of political, economic and social conditions existed. They are not monolithic in historical and social conditions.

Secondly, this is also the case in Asian countries. It is doubtful whether the legal culture of Asian countries can be explained in terms of Confucianism beyond the difference of historical stages or of countries. For example, even if we try to explain Asian legal culture by Confucianism, it has not affected all of Asian countries or has not been understood in a monolithic way. This is all the more so when we take into consideration the drastic change of Asian countries' law and politics.

## II  Asian modern and present ages and constitutionalism

In examining the problems about constitutionalism in Asian countries, I believe that it is important to pay attention to the following points.

First, many Asian countries had been colonized, semi-colonized, and as a result feudal rules had not disappeared in part of those countries. The stagnation in those countries was for the most part caused by the retention of colonial or semi-colonial situation and of feudal rules. The escape from them had been essential to political, economic, cultural development and, needless to say, constitutionalism.

In relation to this point, we should pay attention to the fact that the mother countries couldn't carry through the principle of constitutionalism in political realm simply because they were mother countries. This was 'the double standard; constitutionalism in mother countries and extra-constitutionalism in colonies. Although the constitutions were fundamental rules in mother countries, they were in principle not applied to colonies. Such ideas as inviolate human rights and the guarantee of democracy were not applied to the inhabitants there. The constitutionalism in mother countries had a role in preventing these ideas from being applied in colonies.

This 'double standard' about constitutionalism continues to exist even at present, that is, in the post-WWII era, though in different forms. The examples are a war against national liberation movement (e.g. the Indochina War from 1946 to 1954), an intervention war by which to decide the political regime (e.g. the Vietnam War from 1961 to 1975), and great powers' arms supply which might cause economic stagnation and colonization in developing countries.

Second, the substance of constitutionalism differs remarkably in Asian countries which entered the era of constitutionalism after independence. This difference occurred according to what the political, economic and cultural conditions were, and above all what social strata played a major role in achieving independence, that is, in establishing constitutionalism. Indeed, nothing illustrates this more clearly than the political, economic and cultural variety of the constitutions in Asian countries.

The third point is that the Asian countries have the following problems which are difficult to solve.

1. The problem of how to overcome colonial and feudal remnants. In colonial or semi-colonial era, monoculture was often imposed on the Asian countries while secondary industries were often prevented from developing. These make economic independence difficult even after the political independence. Moreover, these also make public education less established and even make it difficult to train the civilians who overcome colonial and feudal remnants throughout the country.

2. There is always the possibility of being colonized in economic aspects even if political independence has been achieved. Developing countries are likely to seek capital and technology from developed countries in order to

be independent economically. Economic and financial independence is made more difficult when arms import brings about economic debt and 'liberalization without exception' causes economic destruction.

In these situations, Asian countries are entering the era in which to improve legal systems such as constitutionalism. I hope that the wisdom of the people of each country will overcome various difficulties thereby creating constitutionalism which can survive criticisms from historical viewpoints. Furthermore, we should strengthen the academic and cultural exchange which cannot be influenced by national interest and the pursuit of the profit.

## III  Japanese constitutionalism

Since its modernization, Japan have had two constitutions. The first is the Meiji constitution of 1889 (the Constitution of the Empire of Japan) and the second is the current constitution of 1946 (the Constitution of Japan.)

The modernization of Japan was achieved not as a result of a civil revolution but old privileged classes, who were threatened by external pressures, took the initiative of the modernization. This is what is called 'the modernization from above.' That is embodied in the Meiji Constitution which had far more Scheinkonstitutionalismus-character than the Prussian Constitution although Japan learned much from Prussia which also didn't experience a civil revolution. The Scheinkonstitutionalismus-character of the Meiji Constitution can be illustrated by Emperor Sovereignty of Japanese type of divine right of kings, the protection of 'Rights of Subjects' which can be easily restricted according to the provisions of law, and the regime of 'the Emperor combining in himself the rights of sovereignty' which made the separation of powers only apparent. From the viewpoints of comparative study of constitutional law, the Meiji Constitution is quite analogous to La Charte Constitutionelle of 1814 in the French counter-revolutionary era (from 1814 to 1830).

Japanese politics under the Meiji Constitution was partly aimed at 'datsuanyuo (escape from Asia and enter Europe)' and at imperialist policy against Asian countries. In my opinion, the Japanese should recognize more sincerely in what range and to what extent they themselves were assailants. I believe that it is impossible for the Japanese to obtain 'true friends' in Asia without addressing themselves to this task.

The people of Japan enacted the current constitution as a result of the defeat in the WWII. The characteristics of this Constitution are greatly defined by the nature of the WWII. The Constitution of Japan is a civil constitution of the present age which contains as principles 'renunciation of war' thoroughgoing pacifism, protection of fundamental human rights, popular sovereignty and separation of powers. The enactment of this Constitution can be equivalent to Japanese civil revolution of the present ages in legalistic terms because it denied the Meiji Constitution regime whose principles are Emperor sovereignty, 'Rights of Subjects' and 'Emperors concentration of rights of sovereignty.' The current Constitution demands the full modernization on Japanese politics and, furthermore, demilitarization and renunciation of war.

In fact, not a few provisions of the Constitution have been neglected in the actual constitutional politics. Needless to say, constitutional politics permits the existence of the Japanese Army (Self Defense Forces), one of the most powerful forces in the world and the station of foreign armies, and it also strengthens the co-operative relationship between them. However, on the other hand, the Constitution provides that 'land, sea and air forces, as well as other war potential, will be not maintained. The right of belligerency of the state will not be recognized.' These show us clearly how the Constitution has been neglected.

Such kind of constitutional politics was carried out through the abuse and misuse of concepts of key terms in the Constitution, and the neglect of logic and tenor (spirit) in the articles of the Constitution. This is the politics of '*kaishaku kaiken* (interpretative amendment)'. This technique, through which to interpret the wording, logic and tenor (spirit) consciously in a wrong way, aims at deducing a logic too tortured to be allowed unless the provisions of the constitution themselves are amended. This ultimately leads to authorize a policy which is per se unconstitutional. This technique of constitutional politics substantially denies the constitutionalism which requires the constitution interpreted and operated with the respect for the wording, logic, and the spirit of its provision.

1997 was the 50th anniversary of the enforcement of the Constitution of Japan. One of the main subjects of that year was whether the constitutionalism existed in Japan and how to restore the constitutionalism in Japan.

The politics is likely to show contempt for the constitution in the countries where a new constitution was established without revolutionary change of peoples constitutional consciousness. Political leaders often neglect the constitution in the countries where the principles of the constitution dont take root firmly in peoples mind. In order for the Constitution of Japan to do so, the study of the Constitution and the movement to defend the Constitution are essential, which enable the people to acquire constitutional spirit.

The precondition for the study and the defense of the constitution is that the constitution is so adequate that it can satisfy contemporary needs. I believe the Constitution of Japan is worth of them for various reasons.

1. It is the consolidation of human beings long efforts until now in the aspect of the protection of human rights, democracy and the separation of powers. It is no exaggeration to say that the Constitution of Japan is one of the most remarkable constitutions of the present ages. Here I only point out this conclusion and don't argue in detail.

2. Article 9, which provides ' [the Japanese people] will never maintain forces and other war potential. The Japanese will forever renounce war.', is worthy of attention. It is highly valuable in the present ages after the WWII because it represents one example of how to be liable to the war crimes, because it shows the Japanese awareness that war and civilization are now incompatible, because it shows that Japanese security consists in taking initiative of global peace movement, which tries to prevent wars and positively create world peace, and because it shows that the nature of military expenditure is the consumption without reproduction. At the time the Constitution of Japan was established, the Japanese Government also interpreted and explained in this way.

As is pointed out above, the present constitutional politics greatly deviates from the Constitution, especially in relation to Article 9. Peripheral Emergency Act has resulted in bringing about Asian peoples distrust and doubt. I am really sorry for these. It is thoughtless to strengthen this deviation without examining the significance of Article 9 in the aforementioned way. This is not only because this causes a problem in the light of the constitutionalism but also because no examination have been made that is essential to handling serious problems. It should be fully examined, taking into consideration the 50-year-long world history since the end of the WWII, ①whether the compatibility between war and civilization is recognized and strengthened, ②whether the nature of military expenditure as the consumption without reproduction is denied and its reproductivity is proved, ③whether Japan can get 'true friends' in Asia if she goes in this direction.

① Has any war in post-WW II would be able to prove its compatibility with civilization? Has any war been able to prove its effectiveness in protecting human rights?

② Is it not incontestable that the nature of military expenditure as the consumption without reproduction has been proved in the Cold War confrontation and the arms race between USA and USSR? Any country that committed herself to arms race fell into economic and financial crisis . As a result in such a country the protection of human rights under the social (welfare) states constitution has been diminished. The breakdown of socialist regimes in Soviet Union and East Europe was directly triggered by military expansion. It was Paris Commune in 1871 of 'the form of government finally found out (K. Marx, CIVIL WAR IN FRANCE)' which knew the most the nature of military expenditure as the consumption without reproduction. Paris Commune declared the abolishment of a standing army because of its too heavy burden. In this sense, it is irony that socialist regimes in Soviet Union and East Europe broke down although they regarded themselves as descendants of Paris Commune.

The nature of military expenditure as consumption without reproduction is always the case regardless of what kind of regimes they are. It can be a cause of an economic and financial catastrophe either in a capitalist regime or a socialist regime, and either in a developed country or a developing country. According to 'Human Development Report 1996' of UNDP, while economic development still continues in developed countries, many developing countries have experienced economic recession and the economic gap between these countries have strengthened. However, an important question is in what way military expenditure as well as economic debt is related to economic gap. And also, we can never understand the cause of Japan's financial bankruptcy without taking military expenditure into consideration.

③ About the implication which the deviation of Japan's constitutional politics from the Article 9 would have on Asian countries, I would like to hear your honest opinion.

I believe that the Constitution of Japan is a consolidation of long history of mankind. In my opinion, it contains the principles essential to human beings as well as the Japanese. On the one hand, it follows from this that the study and the defense of the Constitution of Japan should be strengthened. Here the problem is that how the researchers of the Constitution of Japan will promote the peoples study of it. The people have sovereign rights and also have full command of politics as the people with all sovereign rights when the people understand their Constitution and makes it their own. Isn't it that 'nothing important will be accomplished without the participation of the people with sovereign rights?

On the other hand, it is necessary to examine in collaboration with Asian researchers the principles of the Constitution of Japan, especially that of renunciation of war. Above all Article 9 will never be complete without renunciation of war, disarmament or denuclearization in Asia. The significance of Article 9 depends, therefore, on how Asian people view Article 9. Im sincerely aspiring to the development of academic-cultural exchange which is not affected by the consideration of national interest and profitability.

# Afterword : Closing Adress

### Kenji Yamashita

The "International Symposium on Constitutionalism in Asia and Oceania" is coming to be closed. It invited constitutional scholars from Australia, China, Philippines, India, Indonesia, South Korea, Thailand, Thaiwan, Vietnam, and has opened an earnest and lively meeting for two days.

As known, Asian and Oceanian constitutional scholars hold a former meeting with reports and discussions on constitutionalism and human rights, here, in Tokyo, four years ago, in 1995, too. The present one is valuable as very much developed from the former. It might well mark a new epoch that such a large number of scholars, if limited participants from the whole region of Asia and Oceania, met together and discussed constitutionalism thoroughly. First of all, I would like to congratulate us on the success.

In Europe and America, negotiations between the East and West had made progress since mid-1970s. In the area of constututional law, it was a symbolic event that the Intenational Association of Constitutional Law (IACL) started in early 1980s. Following the turning point 1989, then, "one constitutional Gemeinschaft (community)" (P. Häberle) was formed and has been developed. On the other hand it is known that various difficulties arise over giving shape to a constitutional democracy where such religious cultures as Christianity, Judism, and Islam both coexist and are opposed to each other, with racial, ethnic and other disputes intensified on additional factors, in the Middle and Near East, in North Africa, and even in the European and American societies themselves.

How about Asia and Oceania? There are problems between east and west, and between advanced and developing countries, which are in different positions. As for religious cul ture, all religions over the world are mixed and or paralleled. Under these circumstances, religional disputes break out constantly. There is a complexity which cannot be made out in the category of Oriental compared with

European and American.

In these situations, for what and how should we make efforts, as constitutional scholars in Asia and Oceania? In abstract and general, it is a working based on the idea of the constitutional democracy, against which few would argue. Againt such as humanrights issues, however, arguments or objections are made out of cultural relativism, criticizing a western model, or other thories. On the whole, those may be made against universalization of the western model. What is called the culture of human societies, to bigin with, has various genres and categories, including art. Based on each of them, each religion, race or ethnic group should be respected for its originality. Similarly, it should also be recognized that each legal culture has its respectable originality. In the present symposium, precious and various efforts were reported, which have given shape to the constitutionalism and the democracy. Stated in the common terms of human rights and democracy, however, uniqueness of each coutry or rgion could not be overemphasized, nor the substance of the constitutional democracy could be quite relativised. Some time ago, professor Cheryl Saunders made a report on the pousuit of commonness of the constitutiona lism, while she point out a plurality of Asia. We need, I think, to have a controversy over this issue, and therby to get a shared recognition of a high-level universality.

As just remarked, Asia and Ocania are plural in various senses vis-a-vis European and Ameican world. It, therefore, is by no means easy, both in theory and practice, that we make efforts to produce the universality of the human rights and the democracy. Those, however, are our inevitable missions, for we live in these resions. Moreover, those are also missions all overthe world, where both of union and disunion appear.

We have deepened our friendship as constitutional scholars whose common goal has been a well established of the constitutional democracy, in the course of the two days discussions. As a Chinese classic reads, "Friends come a long way, that is pleasant"(The Anlects of Confucius). One of our colleagues said once at an international academic conference that " Amicitia, non autorias facit pacem (Amity, not authority makes peace)". Recollecting it, I would like to bring this symposium to a close with such words "Amity, not authority universalizes the constitutional democracy".

Finally, acknowledgements are gratefully made to scholars, who came to participate this meeting all the way from Asia and Ocenia; to all participants; to the staff of the secretariat, who prepared and supported it; and to members of the Nomura Scienc Promotion Foundation, the Japan Federation of the Bar Association and Waseda University, who gave moral amd material assistances to it generously. Thank you so much.

### アジア立憲主義の展望
──── アジア・オセアニア立憲主義シンポジウム ────

| 2003年（平成15年）9月20日　第1版第1刷発行 |
| 3133-0101 |

| 編　　集 | 全国憲法研究会 |
| 編集代表 | 大須賀　明 |
| 発 行 者 | 今井　貴 |
| 発 行 所 | 株式会社 信 山 社 |

〒113-0033　東京都文京区本郷6-2-9-102
電　話 03 (3818) 1019
Ｆ Ａ Ｘ 03 (3818) 0344
henshu@shinzansha.co.jp

Printed in Japan

Ⓒ全国憲法研究会，2003．印刷・製本／東洋印刷・大三製本
ISBN4-7972-3133-5 C3332
3133-0101-01-045-000
NDC分類 323-011

日独憲法学の創造力　上・下
　　　　　栗城壽夫先生古稀記念　　　　予価上下
　　　　　　　　　　　　　　　　　　　各23,000円


憲法答弁集　[1947-1999]
　　監修　浅野一郎・岩崎隆司・杉原泰雄　　予価5,200円
　　編集　浅野義治・植村勝慶・浦田一郎
　　　　　川崎政司・只野雅人


選挙制度と政党
　　信山社叢書国会を考える 2
　　　　　　　　　　　　浅野一郎 編　　　2,800円


憲法学再論
　　　　　　　　　　　　棟居快行 著　　 10,000円


国法体系における憲法と条約
　　　　　　　　　　　　齋藤正彰 著　　 10,500円


憲法第 9 条と自衛権
　　　　　　　　　　　　粕谷　進 著　　　2,427円


信 山 社

保護義務としての基本権
　　　ヨーゼフ・イーゼンゼー著　　12,000円
　　　ドイツ憲法判例研究会編訳


基本的人権論
　　　ハンス・マイアー著　　1,800円
　　　森田　明　編訳


実効的基本権保障論
　　　笹田栄司 著　　8,738円


基本権の理論
　　　田口精一 著　　15,534円


ヨーロッパ人権裁判所の判例
　　　初川　満 著　　3,800円


地球社会の人権論
　　　芹田健太郎 著　　近　刊


信 山 社

| | | |
|---|---|---|
| 議員立法の実証研究 | 谷 勝宏 著 | 15,000円 |
| 選挙法の研究 | 野中俊彦 著 | 10,000円 |
| 議員立法の研究 | 中村睦男 編 | 11,650円 |
| 社会的法治国の構成 | 高田 敏 著 | 14,000円 |
| 自治体エスノグラフィー | 明石照久 著 | 3,500円 |
| 社会制御の行政学 | 原田 久 著 | 5,600円 |

信 山 社

ブリッジブック国際法
　　　　　　　植木俊哉 編　　　2,000円


軍縮国際法
　　　　　　　黒澤 満 著　　　5,000円


国際私法年報 4号
　　　　　　　国際私法学会 編　　3,600円


法の国際化への道
　―日独シンポジウム　　　　　　17,476円
　　石部雅亮・松本博之・児玉寛 編


新しい国際秩序を求めて
　　川島慶雄先生還暦記念論文集　6,311円


ヒギンズ国際法
　　　　　ロザリン・ヒギンズ 著　6,000円
　　　　　初川　満 訳

信 山 社

国家の法的関与と自由
　―アジア・オセアニア法制の比較研究　　　　9,800円
　　　　　　　　　大須賀明　編


フランス憲法判例
　　　　　　フランス憲法判例研究会　編　　4,800円
　　　　　　編集代表　辻村みよ子


ドイツの最新憲法判例
　　　　　　　ドイツ憲法判例研究会　編　　6,000円


19世紀ドイツ憲法理論の研究
　　　　　　　　　　　栗城壽夫　著　　15,000円


韓国憲法裁判所10年史
　　　　　　　　韓国憲法裁判所　編　　13,000円
　　　　　　翻訳者代表　徐　元宇


未来志向の憲法論
　　　　　　　ドイツ憲法判例研究会　編　　7,200円
　　　編集代表　栗城壽夫・戸波江二・青柳幸一


信 山 社